ALSO BY CHRISTOPHER ISHERWOOD

KATHLEEN
AND FRANK

KATHLEEN AND FRANK

THE AUTOBIOGRAPHY

OF A FAMILY

Christopher Isherwood

FARRAR, STRAUS AND GIROUX   NEW YORK

Farrar, Straus and Giroux
18 West 18th Street, New York 10011

Library of Congress Control Number: 2015935185
Paperback ISBN: 978-0-374-18097-3

Designed by Edith Fowler

Farrar, Straus and Giroux books may be purchased for educational, business, or
promotional use. For information on bulk purchases, please contact the Macmillan
Corporate and Premium Sales Department at 1-800-221-7945, extension 5442, or
write to specialmarkets@macmillan.com.

www.fsgbooks.com
www.twitter.com/fsgbooks • www.facebook.com/fsgbooks

1   3   5   7   9   10   8   6   4   2

TO KATHLEEN AND FRANK AND RICHARD

Acknowledgments

Without my brother Richard's constant cooperation and exact memory for detail, this book could hardly have been put together. Don Bachardy, always a much valued critic, has been more than usually helpful; as an American, he was able to read this very English story with the eyes of an outsider and tell me when additional explanations were needed. The late Judge J. A. Reid (referred to as Jack Reid in the text) showed great kindness in answering my questions about Frank's Army life in Ireland and in copying out extracts from military books in his library. He also put me in touch with Major J. H. Mott, who generously lent me a rare copy of Kearsey's history of Frank's regiment during the Boer War. Since Judge Reid's death, his son John Reid has taken a lot of trouble on my behalf. So has Robert Collison, of the Research Library at the University of California, Los Angeles. My best thanks to them both.

Quotations from the following books are gratefully acknowledged:

A. H. C. Kearsey, D.S.O., War Record of the York and Lancaster Regiment, 1900–1902, from Regimental and Private Sources.
C. V. Wedgwood, A Coffin for King Charles (called The Trial of Charles I in the British edition).
Beatrix Potter, The Roly-Poly Pudding.
Max Beerbohm, Around Theatres.
Cyril Scott, My Years of Indiscretion.
Colonel H. C. Wylly, C.B., The York and Lancaster Regiment, 1758–1919.

C. I.

May 1971

KATHLEEN
AND FRANK

1

At the beginning of 1883, Kathleen started her first diary, probably because she had just fallen in love. But she didn't persevere with it. By the end of July, some days are being missed each week; December is a total blank. Then, for seven years, she didn't keep a diary at all—which makes it the more astonishing that she began one again when she was twenty-two and kept it regularly for almost seventy years.

From 1891 through 1895 Kathleen used diary volumes which allowed only two pages to a week. In 1896 she changed permanently to a page-a-day diary, with pages that were about three inches by four and a half. Often she would fill the whole page; sometimes she ran over and had to write less for the next day or two, to catch up with the date. "I'm afraid I'm a slave to my diary," she told Richard, her younger son. Kathleen did have a compulsive conscience—she thought in terms of things-which-had-to-be-done before some deadline day—but her diary wasn't merely another duty. She obviously enjoyed writing it, making time for this among her many occupations, and used it to relieve her feelings in moods of sorrow, indignation or bewilderment. Richard remembers how, when she was an elderly woman, she liked to take out her old diaries and read them to herself, saying that they brought back happier days.

For Kathleen the Past was happier, one might almost say, by definition. Even during her admittedly happy marriage she firmly

9

fixed on one period—the years at Wyberslegh Hall—which was henceforth to be recognized as happier than any which could conceivably follow it. She was intensely obstinate in maintaining this attitude..Like every devotee of the Past she could always find reasons why the Present was inferior to it. Frank's death became her final unanswerable argument.

Kathleen was careful to be exact about names, dates and even times of day, but she did much more than record happenings, she tried to evoke places and atmospheres, she wrote with a strong consciousness of personal and national drama, of herself and the England she was living in. She saw her own life as History and its anniversaries as rites to be celebrated. She could invest minor domestic events with an epic quality. She discovered a mystic and sometimes terrible significance in coincidences. One can almost imagine her prefacing some of the more portentous entries in her diary with the Biblical formula "That it might be fulfilled which was spoken by the prophet . . ."

Christopher, her elder son, revolted early and passionately against the cult of the Past. As an adolescent orphan he was subjected to reminders by schoolmasters and other busybodies of his obligations to the memory of Frank, his Hero-Father. So he learned to hate and fear the Past because it threatened to swallow his future. Later, when this threat had been proved empty and even pathetic, he felt no more than an affectionate exasperation with Kathleen for what seemed to him to be her kind of sulking. He suspected she believed she could actually pressure Fate by it, like a hotel guest who gets better service by refusing ever to admit to the manager that she is satisfied.

Nevertheless, Christopher grew up to become a recorder, too, and so, willy-nilly, a celebrant of the Past; he began to keep a diary and to write autobiographical novels. Today he finds it hard to explain to himself why he never asked Kathleen to let him read her diary while she was alive—perhaps he was still superstitiously afraid of getting entangled in the spider's web of her memories. His failure to express his interest was unkind, in any case, for Kathleen would surely have enjoyed showing it to him, though she never even hinted at this; she had grown so accustomed to hearing Frank's talents praised while hers were disregarded that she now thought little of them herself. The last time they met, she was sincerely surprised that Christopher wanted to take two of her own beautiful watercolors back with him, to hang in his house in California. And there, all the while, in the drawers of her desk, lay the rows of little volumes of her masterpiece. It was only after she was dead that Richard told Christopher how she had once said, "Perhaps someone will be glad of it, some day."

The diary of 1883, scrappy though it is, provides plenty of evidence that Kathleen was already very much Kathleen.

When she began it, she was fourteen years old; she had been born on October the seventh, 1868. She was living at Bury St. Edmunds, Suffolk, with her parents, Frederick and Emily Machell Smith. They often signed themselves "Machell-Smith," with a hyphen—Machell had been the maiden name of Frederick's mother —but they can't have had any legal right to do so, for they had their daughter baptized Kathleen Machell, thus making sure that the too ordinary Smith would never stand alone.

Frederick had a wine business in Bury, which made him a colleague of Emily's brother Walter Greene, who had a brewery. But Walter was far more prosperous and illustrious than Frederick. He went into politics and in due course became Sir Walter Greene, Bart. In 1883 he already owned a large country house with spacious grounds in the neighborhood, called Nether Hall. Nether was the scene of continuous hospitality: dances, shoots, hunt breakfasts, house parties. On January 1 Kathleen writes in her diary, "Back from Paradise to earth, in other words Nether Hall to Bury."

January 11. At six thirty Mum, Puppie and I (in cream dress) start for the Thornhills. Mum wears her velvet. Start home at 12.30 after the most charming time possible. Danced and sat out with A.T. Have turkey and jelly for supper. I wonder if it will be a year before I see A.T. again. I know why I enjoy staying at Nether so much, because of A.T.

• •

(After "I wonder if it will be a year" Kathleen has drawn a line through the rest of the entry, but this isn't really a deletion, since the words are all easily legible; it seems more like a gesture of coyness.)

A few days later, "A. T." (Antony Thornhill) goes back to school at Eton, and Kathleen's life becomes sadly provincial and humdrum. There are few available males and none of any interest; "have Eddie all the afternoon, what a donkey that boy is." She plays cards with a girl cousin and "a new game called religious conversation" with Emily, she trims a hat "for a poor woman," cuts out pictures to paper a wall, looks through back numbers of Punch, *buys an apron with sunflowers on it, reads* Quentin Durward *and finds the ending "not satisfactory," paints a black wood fan and finishes her first chalk drawing, kills 250 snails, goes for long walks to watch the foxhounds meet and short strolls with Emily down the lane, "lovely sunset but awful smells." The only real fun seems to have been taking part in theatricals of various kinds. "A ghost entertainment for the servants. I am dressed as a nun and talk very awfully, the room is quite dark except for one lantern. Lil has a brown sheet and appears. We finish by throwing a sheet over them and run away quick." Another time, Kathleen dresses up as Dolly Varden in* Barnaby Rudge. *This was good casting. Dolly is described by Pierce in his* Dickens Dictionary *as "a bright fresh coquettish girl, the very impersonation of good humour and blooming beauty." When they acted* The Sleeping Beauty, *another girl played the part, however. Kathleen obviously lacked the necessary languor.*

And there were lessons. These included German, taught by a Fräulein. Kathleen hated it and went on hating it for the rest of her life. It was so gross and coarse and ugly, she said. She even disagreed with Frank about this. As for Christopher, he hated French with equal enthusiasm, making fun of its vague weak sounds and declaring that German was beautiful. Actually both of them were rebelling against the "in" language of their generation. German was still "in" when Kathleen was a girl, owing to Victoria's cult of the dead Prince Consort and her kinship with the

German royal houses. But German was soon to be ousted by French. 1883 was, in fact, the very year in which Germany moved into South-West Africa as a colonial power, thus straining Anglo-German relations and beginning to push English public opinion in the direction of the Entente Cordiale.

Antony Thornhill must have spent his Easter holidays else-where, for Kathleen doesn't mention him. In mid-August she reopens her diary after a lapse, to record their next meeting:

August 14. Go to Nether. I wake up to the delightful fact this is the long wished for Tuesday. A thrill of joy runs through me!

August 16. Dull early but clears up nicely before 2 o'clock. Beautiful bright summer's day after 12. Ethel, Antony and I sat together in Thornhills' pew for Freda Jones wedding, 11.30. She appears in a stamped cream coloured velvet dress and worked veil. Bridesmaids rather like toilet tables in spotted muslin over salmon pink. After wedding we three go in boat. Then we walk in garden while E. airs Turk. On Tuesday we go home and I shall be simply miserable.

(Note how Kathleen hastens to prepare to mourn over the soon-to-be-past! Ethel is a cousin, Turk presumably a dog.)

August 17. Spend all afternoon in boat. After tea the dear Turk has to be aired, which Ethel does. As we are standing on the bridge looking in the water, Antony said 'Do you care two pins for me?' I turned hot and cold and sick and giddy, though why I don't know for after all I care two pins for most people, so there was nothing in that. He seemed in earnest *then* but I dare-say we shall both soon change. Papa tries Antony's tricycle and comes to grief but does not hurt himself much.

August 19. Nice day, hot and close. Antony, Ethel and I go to church. After tea we three take a little walk up the harvest fields.

13

After that we walk up to Lodge. Mr Goat the gardener gives us plums and apricots. Somehow we all seem miserable. Grandpapa is much better and walks about. We play Sunday games in evening. Mama to me, 'you will be glad to hear I like Antony immensely, he was so nice about Grandpapa last night, which is a good test'.

August 25. We start for Nether Hall and stay till 6. Have the first happy hours I have spent since last Wed. E and A don't seem to have had much fun since I left, I haven't had one atom. Antony said when he was at Clarke's there was a basket of photographs and Clarke said he could have anyone he liked and he chose one of me sitting on a log of wood with hat and mantle on.

August 30. Kept awake from 3 to 4 by a cow. We arrive at Nether Hall at 2 o'clock for lunch. Antony is still staying there and Mr Thornhill too. After lunch we go in the boat till 3.30 when we come in. Ethel runs to put the umbrellas in the hall, and to my utter astonishment Antony puts a little case in my hand. On opening it I found a little gold ring with three emeralds and two diamonds. The worst part was telling Mum. She said when I was older it was not proper to receive presents from young men, etc. So it was all right.

This is the last reference to Antony in the 1883 diary. They must have met each other often during those seven years which Kathleen doesn't record. Did Antony remain "in earnest"? Did he want to marry her as they grew older? If he did, Kathleen or her parents must have turned him down. On March 18, 1891, she was told by Ethel that Antony had become engaged to a Miss Miller; on September 2, they were married. Kathleen minded this or at least felt that it was romantic to think of herself as jilted, for she kept in her diary a leaf from a quotation calendar with the date of the wedding day: "Who seeks and will not take when once 'tis offered, shall never find it more," Antony and Cleopatra, II, 7.

· ·

Frederick and Emily certainly loved their only child, and Kathleen was eager to return their love, but her relations with them can't have been easy. They were both of them star personalities, demanding complete cooperation from their supporting cast as they played opposite each other, with tremendous power and style, in a real-life melodrama about martyrdom.

Frederick had run away from home at the age of seventeen because his father remarried only a short while after the death of Frederick's mother. He seems to have been something of a Byronic hero, a handsome athletic brooding youth with an ugly disposition, quick to suffer rejection and take vengeance for betrayal. He shipped out to Australia, where he farmed sheep and served in the mounted police. Perhaps he would have been happier if he had stayed there and lived a rough aggressive outdoor life. But he ungraciously forgave his father and returned to England after a few years, surviving a shipwreck on the way—his last Byronic adventure. Back at home, he changed roles, becoming a tamed and chained but still dangerous Victorian Samson, a martyr-moralist, fettered to his duties as son, husband, father, businessman, citizen and Christian. He was also fettered to a hobby, photography. He pursued it with compulsive zeal, to the discomfort of all around him. Everybody was kept waiting while he fussed with his camera. At the beginning of 1883 he was fifty-one years old, still handsome and full of vigor. He often rode to hounds.

Here are some details of a self-portrait:

I am going to try not to scribble so fearfully fast when I write to you as it will get me into bad habits and tend to deteriorate my handwriting for business purposes, besides producing a scrawl which must sometimes tax your eyes and ingenuity to decipher. You must therefore scold me well if I send you any more dreadful scribbles or I may be tempted to relapse into my old ways.

Last Easter Sunday Walter and I received the Sacrament. Though I had you not with me in presence my darling my thoughts were with you and I felt that though separated in the body we were each endeavouring in the spirit to testify our feelings of thankfulness for the great blessing of our risen Saviour. I cannot on looking over the past year feel that I have done much, if anything, in His service. I would feel more earnestness and love but as yet I grieve to say that I have not realized that love for Him as I ought, and knowing that this is the great proof of His abiding in us it makes me feel very anxious to realize more such love as every professing Christian ought to bear in a greater degree according to his advancement on the path of life.

You are a good old dear about your boots. I thought for some reason (which I think must have been told me by someone) that ornamental boots were a weakness with you and I did not like to ask before. But when you assured me that you were willing to wear what I liked, I thought it was a good opportunity to suggest an alteration and it is really (to my mind) a shame to put such wonderful decorations on to neat feet which do not require such arrangements to set them off.

We did not think H.P. spoilt at present, he does not seem inclined to be either fast or slangy and I trust he may never be tempted to either; he is very fond of fun, i.e. dancing, shooting, boating, etc etc, none of them dangerous tastes, and seems chatty without being boisterous or noisy but he has much to go through yet.

Her husband was on the whole very amiable, he was slightly heady one evening but did not arrive at the quarrelsome stage. I hope his son will not follow in his steps either as a gourmand or a squabbler, this last is the result of the former.

Will is very keen about photography which Agnes does not altogether relish and does not seem to support him in his enthusiasm. I hear they have made a sort of compromise, viz that Will is only to take dry plates on his wedding tour, as Agnes thinks a tent etc will take up too much time. I don't know how she wishes to spend it, but I should say, so far as having his society, she would not lose much of that, even if he had a tent.

H.S.'s answer, though ingenious and pretty much what I anticipated, only proves to me what a snake in the grass he must be. Had the accusing letter come from a comparative stranger and a man of his own age, it would have been a widely different thing, but for a man of 50 to enter into a discussion on his conduct with one of 21 is extraordinary under most circumstances and, after all the trouble H.S. has taken, his letter would not bear sifting and analysing piece by piece. Walter's letter is clear enough but is not gentlemanly and he might have stood upon high ground and attacked H.S. without committing himself by the use of such strong language. I can quite understand, knowing Walter as I do, that he was goaded to it and the impetuosity of his feelings got the better of him.

Will has made great progress and, having larger plates, his works make more show than mine, though I honestly think I can beat him yet. I have ordered a new camera to take 12 by 10, 10 by 8 and 9 by 7 views, it will cost three pound ten and the lens and other things will nearly take the sum I told you, twenty pounds. I shall be very particular about the lens. I will execute your commissions as soon as I can. I conclude you want them pour les domestiques.

The above are extracts from letters written by Frederick to Emily shortly before their marriage in 1864. Emily was nine years his junior; she had been born on October the twenty-fourth, 1840. Though Frederick was then only in his thirty-third year, he playfully called himself her uncle and addressed her as his niece. He was capable of playfulness but never of what would nowadays be called humor. Emily was not a humorist, either. She described funny situations as being "droll."

During their engagement, she confessed to him in a letter that she had only just stopped feeling afraid of him. To this he answered:

17

. .

My darling, I will burn your letter and quite quite forgive your doubts and fears, you must not mind if some day when I have you quietly to myself you receive a little punishment from my lips, but it shall be very soft I promise you and when I have you once more in my arms you will perhaps submit.

It is doubtful if Emily did submit, on this or any other occasion. Martyrs are not submitting to you when they let you tie them to the stake. Emily entered upon marriage in this spirit, but there is no reason to suppose that she and Frederick weren't happy together, at least to begin with. Neither understood, but each respected and admired the other. They were playing the game according to the same rules, and for keeps. Their marriage was no laughing matter. That was the whole point of it.

Everybody agreed that Emily was beautiful. She never ceased to be. Her features were of the cast then approvingly called Grecian; her profile was like an engraving of an empress on a coin. Christopher remembers her only when she was past seventy; she lived to be eighty-four. In his memory he sees her either standing or lying down, never sitting. When she walks, it is with a royal air of graciousness and the proud humility of noblesse oblige; she enters a seaside teashop as if she is inspecting a children's hospital. When he thinks of her reclining on a couch in her brocade gown, musky furs and long gold earrings, speaking very softly, with half-closed eyes, he is reminded of Elizabeth Tudor dying, and how she refused to take off her clothes and go to bed.

However, despite appearances, Emily was anything but fragile. If Frederick should perhaps have become an Australian, she should certainly have become an actress. She had the temperament and stamina for it, as well as the restlessness which welcomes constant changes of scene. She was a passionate theatergoer whenever she got the opportunity—the lack of it must have made her hate living in Bury. She dressed somewhat in the style of Sarah Bernhardt, whom she adored.

But Emily was forced, for want of any other outlet, to express

18

her temperament through the medium of illness. Her sudden prostrations and equally sudden recoveries were the bewilderment of her doctors. She was no imaginary invalid, but a great psychosomatic virtuoso who could produce high fevers, large swellings and mysterious rashes within the hour; her ailments were roles into which she threw herself with abandon. And if she hadn't possessed an unusually strong constitution they would have finished her off in her prime.

Emily's one big dramatic scene in Kathleen's 1883 diary is short but in her best manner. It seems that she had set her heart on going to France that summer and that Frederick had vetoed the trip, saying they couldn't afford it. Kathleen describes what followed:

July 13. What a bother money is. Mum can't go to the Ardennes and she was so disappointed, in fact she is getting ill. If she were to go after all it would not be the same. She is calm tonight and I asked her where we should go away to, to make up for the Ardennes, and she said very low (she thought I did not hear) 'to heaven'. Oh, I cried in the night. If only I had money.

July 14. Have headache after last night.

July 15. We three go to church at St Mary's. Poor M. not well, weeps in church.

Kathleen's comment "If she were to go after all it would not be the same" shows how well she already understood her mother. The diary doesn't record if they did go anywhere "to make up for the Ardennes," but no doubt Frederick lived to regret his decision. And less than two years later Emily won the decisive victory of her marriage: Frederick was compelled to leave Bury and take his wife and daughter to live in London, because it had been finally established, after goodness knows how many medical showdowns, that Emily's health couldn't stand the Suffolk cold.

2

Kathleen's new home was a flat in a tall, handsome brick building on Gloucester Road, South Kensington, just north of the Old Brompton Road. South of Brompton Road, Gloucester Road becomes Cranley Gardens. Hence, the building was named Cranley Mansion. It still stands, and its ironwork balconies with their chaste floral designs must please any connoisseur of the period who happens to pass by.

When Kathleen reopens her diary in 1891, she has already "come out" and achieved the status of a marriageable young lady of the upper middle class. At twenty-two it is obvious that she hasn't inherited Emily's Grecian beauty and regal poise; but she is extremely attractive, slender and lively, with a delightful laugh, pretty brown hair, fresh coloring, full red lips and beautiful gray eyes. Her eyes have a hint of sadness in them, and her liveliness has a hint of reserve behind it. She is unexpectedly well-educated and artistically gifted, but she doesn't show off. She tries to be what she will later call "responsive," making a real effort to share in the interests and pleasures of others. But she is temperamental too, and can suddenly turn difficult and ill-humored. Altogether, she is a girl who is destined to be popular but misunderstood. She needs an unusual man—one who will never take her for granted, who will be fascinated by her contradictions, who will patiently and lovingly explore her to the depths.

In January, Kathleen records that a certain Captain C. "says I am very much altered, quite staid and quiet!" No wonder this amused her, for her social life was energetic and often noisy. At the country houses where she stayed, she played bumps and hunt the slipper and threw cushions at the other young guests. She loved dancing and could keep it up all night. If she was quiet, she would probably be gossiping in whispers with the girls or murmuring archly with the men. An elderly hostess was much nearer the mark than Captain C. when she told Kathleen, "Your eyes are not made for your soul's good." And a woman friend of her own age composed a poem about her which contrives to be frank as well as flattering. After speaking of Kathleen's "dainty airiness and wilful grace," it concludes:

> From petulance to stately calm she'll pass
> Before a fly can settle on a glass
> And no madonna could be more serene
> Than can appear at times my dear Kathleen.

And here is Emily's verdict, in a letter written to Kathleen in 1896:

It is stupid of men, that they can't have girls as friends and there let it rest, but it is very rarely possible and I fear, dear, will never be possible between you and any man until you are fifty or more. I dare say you won't believe me, but the truth is you can never be only friends, you naturally flirt and can't be content without personal admiration. Only plain girls or women who are of the angel type (at least men think they are) can have platonic friends. Now you never were and never will be of the angel type, and in this respect you differ from your beloved Mother. I fear you are too fascinating ever for men—

> 'To think of you as a star, far in the heaven above
> Such as one might gaze upon but would not dare to love'.

This I was once—this, dear Lamb, you will never be, nor would you care to be if you could.

Kathleen's reply to these remarks, if any, is not extant; but it can be assumed that they didn't seriously hurt her feelings. Angels and goddesses were on their way out, slowly but surely; woman's fight for equal political rights would render them obsolete. Emily was really offering Kathleen a much more exciting role, that of the mortal modern girl.

What did Kathleen herself expect of life, love and eventual marriage? The only clues in her 1891 diary are these two quotations:

> Man's love is of man's life a thing apart,
> 'Tis woman's whole existence —Don Juan 1. CXCIV

> For every created man there is a created woman who stands to him as the only true wife he can have in this life or any other . . . Those created for each other may not meet or come together in this embodiment, but they assuredly will in another. —Your Forces and How to Use Them.

Neither of these is much use as a guide to conduct. Byron can only advise woman to watch out, for his intentions are dishonorable. The second author seems to advise caution also, and perhaps patience throughout several lifetimes until the true husband appears. Kathleen was certainly cautious, as will be shown later; her flirting must have been essentially defensive, a kind of skirmishing which was designed to keep the Enemy at a distance rather than challenge him to engage.

From April 30 to May 23, Kathleen and Emily went on a tour through France, Switzerland and northern Italy. This is evidently not the first time that Kathleen has been abroad. At Amiens she remarks that they have got the same room in the same hotel as before, and she speaks familiarly of "dear Lucerne."

Kathleen is seldom interesting when she writes about foreign travel; her diary keeps turning into a guidebook. She is an eager,

*intelligent and sensitive sight-seer; she has done her homework
and knows at least something about Savonarola, Dante, Diane de
Poitiers, William Tell; she really appreciates the paintings and the
architecture and the scenery. But there is almost never any personal contact or reaction. "Abroad" is either "beautiful" or
"picturesque," as Baedeker has promised it will be, or else it is
"disappointing," like a restaurant where the food isn't up to
expectations. Only once during this trip—it is on the day of their
return from Calais to England—does Kathleen describe an emotional woman-to-woman contact with one of the aliens:*

Paid our bill, received a Swiss five franc piece in change and
when a little later we gave it to the woman downstairs in payment
for some chicken etc, she refused to take it and declared she had
never given it us. We *were* angry.

May 26. [Back in London.] Took my room to pieces, taking
down no less than a dozen Japanese fans. Their day is over.

*(This is a reminder that the wave of "Japonisme" which
Whistler had helped launch upon England from Paris was now
dying down. As for Whistler himself, Kathleen went to see an
exhibition of his paintings about a year after this and dismissed
them as "horrid impressionist school.")*

*On January 14, 1892, the Duke of Clarence, the Prince of
Wales's eldest son, died in his late twenties. At the time, Kathleen
was staying near Cheadle, Cheshire, with some close family friends
named Sykes whom she often visited. Her first reaction to the
news of the young Duke's death was that it was "fearfully sad, he
was to have been married to Princess Mary of Teck in February."
Then came an order from Frederick that she was to return home,
and Kathleen's loyal grief turned to bitter disappointment. She
had been looking forward to a big ball which was to be held in
the neighborhood on the twenty-seventh. Frederick condemned
it as "dancing on the grave of the dead Prince." When she got
back to London, Frederick made unconvincing attempts to justify*

23

himself. "*Papa says he thought I had been more than three weeks at Cheadle instead of a fortnight, and that I could have stayed. He left it to me to decide, after expressing his opinion* strongly *against it. I don't see how I could have gone against him.*" *On the evening before the Cheshire ball took place, Kathleen was invited to a dance in Kensington and Frederick allowed her to go—thus exposing the hypocrisy of his scruples. The truth was, he didn't like letting Kathleen out of his sight for long, especially when she was amongst eligible young men.*

(On February 6, 1952, Christopher was over from the United States on a visit and staying with Kathleen at a hotel in London. At breakfast time came the news of the death of King George VI. Kathleen was moved to tears. Christopher, as befitted a citizen of a friendly Power, expressed polite sympathy. Then, after a suitable pause, he added, "That means we won't be going to the Noël Coward matinee today—they'll close all the theaters, of course." Kathleen's expression changed immediately. She said with intense conviction, "He would never have wished it!")

February 19. Anniversary of our exodus from Bury seven years ago. The move was in every way an entirely satisfactory one.

(Was it satisfactory for Frederick? He had probably been much happier in the country, hunting and shooting. His income still came from the Bury wine business; in London he kept himself occupied by serving voluntarily on the boards of various companies. He was particularly interested in a chain of dairies and rode around town inspecting them on his tricycle. Didn't he feel humiliated, this rider of the Outback reduced to a milk run and a three-wheeled mount? Wasn't a resentment against Emily and Kathleen expressed by his increasingly tyrannical behavior?)

February 23. We engaged Lizzie Lowes as a cook; I think her manner very disagreeable and independent.

("Independent" is one of Kathleen's favorite adjectives of condemnation; it means that Lizzie didn't know her place. As Kath-

leen grew older and the Past extended its territory in her imagina-
tion, she began to see it as peopled exclusively with retainers of
the feudal type, devoted, loyal, unassuming; while the Present
became the domain of the independent, the ungracious and the
downright rude.)

March 23. Went to service at St Stephen's to hear Shuttleworth
on Parable of Dives and Lazarus. Dives only an ordinarily selfish
and thoughtless man yet look at his punishment. We cannot reap
where we have not sown. Retribution hereafter. Felt as if I was
Dives and . . . Lazarus. Very sorry for Lazarus but could not like
him.

(*Kathleen, like Emily, put preachers and actors in the same*
category. She says of a certain Dr. P., "We thought him an imita-
tion Irving." She enjoyed good sermons as theatrical perform-
ances, without feeling necessarily obliged to accept their ethical
teaching. Why couldn't she like Lazarus? Because he had disgust-
ing sores and sat around helplessly, begging and being content
with crumbs. Her upbringing made her feel guilty for not liking
him; he was one of the deserving poor, he knew his place. Bernard
Shaw—whose plays Kathleen would soon be enjoying without
accepting their political teaching—could have told her she was
right not to like Lazarus, he was indeed disgusting; one of the ugly
phenomena of capitalism which would disappear when socialism
took over.)

May 4. [During another visit to Cheadle.] Hoped desperately
all day something would turn up to enable us to go to the Wor-
thingtons' Fancy Ball. Dressed up in the afternoon out of the
acting box as a milkmaid and wished to go more than ever.

June 10. Mama and I to the English Opera House to see
Sarah Bernhardt in Cleopatra. She was marvellously fascinating
and all the allurement of a Cleopatra. The tones of her voice are
so varied and sweet and though I hardly understood a word I

could watch her and listen to her without once tiring for three hours.

June 16. To Academy in morning with Papa. Don't think English artists can paint flesh colour nearly as well as the French.

August 17. Today is nine years ago since a once important event.

(When Antony asked, "Do you care two pins for me?")
On November 17 Emily wrote to Kathleen, who was staying at Nether Hall:

Mr W, with many apologies, produced a typewritten MS of his poems and asked me to read them, he said he hadn't shown them to anyone. He read me a few and left the precious MS with me. Before he left, he talked about *you* (you horrid little wretch) and said how it had been the dream of his life, since he first knew you, to make a *position* for your sake, that he saw now what a fool's paradise he had been living in, but that I was not to think that *you* had really harmed him, that though a sadder he trusted he was a wiser man, and he hoped you knew how unalterable was his love and affection and *respect* for you. How you had never by word or look lured him on to think you cared for him, that in his folly he had thought that love and friendship must produce love on the woman's side, that he saw how foolish he had been. Poor dear, he leaned against the mantelpiece and wept, a silent weep. At least, dear, you have the comfort of knowing that his love for you has *raised*, not lowered him and given him a wider and a broader sympathy with others. He seemed much older and graver. Life certainly, as far as the love of men and women is concerned, is very strange and a great mystery. . . . He hoped some day to be able to be on the old footing, but for the present he would rather come when we were alone. I felt so glad I had put your photo away.

.   .

26

(Mr. W.–later Sir H. W.–learned to accept Kathleen's un-
availability; ten years later he married a widow and they had a
long and happy life together. Kathleen used to say that she had
never considered him seriously as a suitor, "he wasn't my style";
but they became good friends in their later years, and when he
died he left her a watercolor by John Varley. Richard remembers
him as a "courteous elderly middle-aged man, rather baby-
faced.")

1893. January 16. Mama and I went to a lecture on Plato.
Hoped to have heard of Platonic friendship and philosophy but
was disappointed.

January 26. Wrote out at dictation some of Walk VII in afternoon.

This is Kathleen's first mention of Our Rambles in Old London, *a small guidebook on which she and Emily were working*
together. In its final form it contains descriptions of six recom-
mended walks to be taken in the districts of Smithfield, South-
wark, Clerkenwell, Bishopsgate, the Inns of Court and the Guild-
hall, including visits to various historic churches and houses. The
seventh walk to which Kathleen refers must have been either
omitted or combined with one of the others.
On the title page of the published book Emily appears as sole
author, but "we" and "our" is used throughout the text and there
is one reference to "K. and I." Kathleen contributed three pen-
and-ink drawings and one map; there are twelve drawings and
six maps in all.
Emily probably borrowed many of her historical details and
literary quotations from other writers. She acknowledges that
"we are largely indebted" to Augustus Hare's Walks in London,
which was first published in 1878. But she and Kathleen person-
ally visited all the places described and brought their information
about them up to date. Emily's style may also be borrowed from

27

her predecessors; in any case, it isn't in the least amateur but admirably easy and clear.

Our Rambles makes better reading than Kathleen's travel diaries. Unlike them, it creates a three-dimensional effect by repeatedly contrasting the ancient city with the new. (In the diaries, the places of interest are presented simply as "sights," without any modern setting.) Emily and Kathleen deplore the new, of course, but it is necessary to their enjoyment; it is what turns their rambles into explorations and exhumations. For example, when they visit Crosby Hall—entering it through a cookshop—the thought that Richard of Gloucester and Sir Thomas More once lived there seems romantically heightened for them by the fact that the throne room and the banqueting hall are now dining rooms in a restaurant run by Messrs. Gordon and Company. Their London is full of such ghost-effects.

They had a nickname for their book: "The Prigs' Progress." They can't really have thought of themselves as prigs in the accepted sense—conceited or didactic bluestockings. But they do have an air of being consciously outsiders, even royalty incognito, graciously amused by their encounters with the natives. Here are some glimpses of them on their rambles:

Addressing a young person who was walking into it, we asked her if she could tell us if this was once the home of Charles Lamb. She answered in the affirmative, and kindly invited us in, being herself a daughter of the house. The door opened into a curious old paved passage; on the left was a small quaint sitting-room and at the far end a door leading into a yard, *now* entirely occupied by a soda-water manufactory, though *once* the dear old-fashioned garden of which Charles Lamb wrote. . . .

Going back into Hart Street we found the door of St Olave's open and, entering, encountered a chatty little woman who wondered how we had got in and supposed the tiresome baker's boy must have left the door ajar when he brought the bread which is given to the poor every Sunday. However, as we were there, she seemed quite willing to show us round. She told us that the great *Pepys* used to come to church here and pointed out the position of his seat in the south gallery (now pulled down). The bust of Mrs Pepys was erected nearly opposite his pew, that he might gaze upon her during service. Time has somewhat damaged her nose, although it has in no way impaired the flowing curl which gracefully reposes on her shoulder.

Bearing in mind our previous rebuff, we mentally debated whether we should offer a tip to our present venerable guide; but he, to our great amusement, most kindly relieved us of all doubt on *that* subject by whispering in our ear, as we passed out, in tones the condescension of which baffles description, 'You can give me something if you like'!

Mr W., who said he had been verger there half a century, evidently entertained quite a contempt for the newfangled notion that any danger could possibly be incurred by bad gases proceeding from the coffins, as 'they had never done him no harm', and described the funerals that formerly took place there, when he always lighted up the vaults with a hundred candles or more and strewed sawdust on the ground, to make it 'more cheerful like for the poor mourners'.

On May 15, Kathleen and Emily left for Paris. From Paris they went on to Brittany. At Mont St. Michel they met an Englishman "who knew Mama at 17 when she was Miss Emily Greene. When he first saw us together he thought we were sisters—M. looked so much too young to be my mother." Not surprisingly, he is described as "nice."

From Mont St. Michel they went to St. Malo. Here Kathleen mentions, quite casually, a Mr. T. with whom she goes for walks and has some long talks. There is only one hint of intimacy, on May 28: "Mr. T. and I talked all the evening. Went to bed cross." When Kathleen writes "cross" she often means exasperated, frustrated but intrigued.

However, in Kathleen's diary for *1898* there is an entry on May 23: "Five years by the day of the week since a great event. Is it possible?"

Kathleen sometimes uses this method of reckoning her anniversaries, thus making them into movable feasts like Easter and therefore more sacred, perhaps. In *1898*, May 23 fell on a Monday. Reckoning by the day of the week, the corresponding Monday in *1893* fell on May 22. This was the day Emily and Kathleen arrived at St. Malo; the "great event" must therefore have been their first meeting with Mr. T. Perhaps he just happened to be there as a fellow tourist; perhaps the introduction was made through mutual friends.

Mr. T. was soon thereafter to become very important in Kathleen's life. Emily must have approved of him, for the three of them went on expeditions together. Later, she and Kathleen nicknamed him The Child, presumably because he looked young for his age. The Child worked as a handicapper at race meetings, and this explains why Kathleen, who had never cared much for horses and almost never rode them, developed a keen interest in racing. From *1897* to *1901* her diaries all include lists of racing fixtures.

The Child can't have been living in London in *1893*, for he called on Kathleen only two or three times after her return there. But their intimacy was growing through correspondence; in August he sent her his photograph, and for Christmas "a charming present," which she doesn't describe.

At the beginning of February *1894* Kathleen got the card of admission she had applied for, allowing her to copy paintings in the National Gallery. This became one of her chief activities. The Gallery was, incidentally, an ideally respectable rendezvous for unchaperoned meetings with men.

February 19. Today nine years ago 'Israel came out of Egypt'!!!

(*A characteristically epic metaphor for the move from Bury to London. But, in this case, the Chosen People had brought their Pharaoh along with them!*)

March 1. Down to the National at 1.30. Began a portrait of Mrs Siddons by Lawrence and found it difficult. To the dentist from there. Very disturbing day. The serpent entered Paradise.

(Against this, when she was reading through the diary later, Kathleen wrote "Child." It must have been at the Gallery that they met. "Child" is written against the next day's entry also. His presence—or rather, its emotional impact on Kathleen—is indicated by dots and an exclamation mark, thus: "Down to the Gallery by a little after 10. Worked till 1.30. . . . . ! Miss B and I walked home all the way, at 4." No doubt the long walk was taken by Kathleen in order to compose herself.)

Kathleen and The Child met only twice more in March, once unofficially, once officially; he came to call at the flat. Then, on April 3, Kathleen went up to stay at Cheadle, and there a crisis was reached:

April 11. Grilling hot day ending in a violent thunderstorm which was quite in keeping with my feeling. Met Mr T. Home tired and cross. Completely at cross-purposes. Answered in joke what it appeared he meant in earnest and then could not explain somehow. I never thought till it was too late it was all serious on his part or realized how much *I* care.

She didn't see The Child again until April 22 in London, and then it was at the flat with other people present. Even if they did get a few words together alone, nothing was said to clear up their misunderstanding. On May 7, Kathleen had to go off on another trip abroad with Emily. Two days before leaving she writes, "Sic transit gloria mundi," enclosing it in a black frame like a funeral announcement and adding below it, "Tears and ashes."

This trip also was chiefly to Brittany. They visited many places, but not St. Malo with its painfully romantic memories. Kathleen falls back on sight-seeing as a substitute for enjoyment. Bravely, she finds things as picturesque as she can. But the weather is often rainy and Emily suffers from chills and headaches and Kathleen

31

has nothing to do but read aloud to her in cold hotel bedrooms. Kathleen never complains, but on May 12 at Mont St. Michel she does convey, in spite of herself, the forlornness of being where the Wished-for One is not:

Sat about, went to the post office, wrote, mended and seemed very busy. Mum lay on sofa on terrace and said she was very happy. I sketched and we made ourselves 5 o'clock tea. A number of utterly uninteresting French people arrived.

However, when they return to England on June 5, she writes frankly, "More delighted and thankful to get home than any words can describe."

On July 3, she goes to a dance with The Child and enjoys it immensely, walking home and not getting back till three in the morning, when it is already quite light. On the seventh, he sends her a hamper of sweet peas. On July 13: "The Child came and talked to me, which caused me to think rather seriously." This suggests that he urged Kathleen to make up her mind about her feelings for him; but she evidently didn't. They continued to meet, infrequently, throughout the rest of the year.

1895. January 7. Read 'The Garden I Love' by Alfred Austin, most charmingly and soothingly written.

("Soothing" is another favorite adjective, often applied to books. It used to enrage Christopher when he was a young man. He declared that it betrayed Kathleen's subconscious contempt for all literature.)

February 7. To Gallery. Old German (copying the Raphael) made me quite a pretty speech about bringing sunshine!

February 19. Ten years since Israel came out of Egypt.

March 1. To see 'The Importance of Being Earnest' at the St James's Theatre and laughed much.

. .

(When Kathleen was laughing at his play, Wilde was already a doomed man. Earlier that same day he had applied for a warrant against the Marquis of Queensberry on a charge of criminal libel—with the result that within three months he himself would be tried, sentenced and imprisoned. Kathleen doesn't refer to the case in her diary. And indeed it was many years before she found out why Wilde had been sent to prison. At the time of the trial she was told simply that he had done "something dreadful," and she had inquired no further.)

On March 22, Emily writes to Kathleen, who is staying at Nether Hall with Frederick ("Mr. Puppie"), to announce that Our Rambles *has been accepted for publication by Messrs. Sampson Low, Marston and Company:*

Darling Kath, I feel so full of chat and rather *elated* that I must send you a line tonight. I think too that Mr Puppie will be interested to hear of my visit to St Dunstan's House this morning. I found G. was just in the act of writing to me, and pulling a little note out of his pocket he said 'I am going to do a very unusual thing, I will show you what the Reader has said of your book. "I can most unhesitatingly recommend this little work. It is very interesting, full of information and written in good literary style." ' Now I hope you and Mr Puppie will feel more *admiration* and respect for my literary powers than you have hitherto done. I am swelling with pride and taking sips of chamomilla to soothe myself. G. is going to talk to Mr Marston. He expects I shall have to guarantee twenty pounds, but if it only sells of course I shall never have to pay it, and if I had to pay it at end of year and it went on selling, I should get it back. Goodbye, dear Lamb, much love to dear old Pup and all at Nether from your swollen Frog of a Mother, who will try not to burst with vanity and pride before your return.

March 23. Papa and I send off a telegram of congratulation to M. The Walks are accepted!!!

. .

(*A draft of their telegram is scribbled by Frederick across Emily's letter: "Thousand congratulations with intense admiration keep the swelling down."*)

April 4. Agreement of The Prigs' Progress arrives to be signed.

April 10. Help M. correct the most obvious mistakes in the proofs.

May 3. We go to Sampson Low and Co in Fetter Lane to see how the cover is progressing.

May 4. Down to Fetter Lane about preface. Find specimens of the book cover ready.

June 7. *Book out.*

June 14. Nice little notice in *The Times* about 'Our Rambles', also in a paper called *London*.

(The Times, *June 14:* "*Mrs Machell Smith's* Our Rambles in Old London *is a small volume which at least will serve to remind average Londoners of the little they know of their City and the pleasure they may derive from knowing a little more."*
The Speaker, *June 29:* "*There is much pleasant gossip in the book, a few facts not generally known, and illustrations which sometimes make us sigh for ancient glories which have had notice to quit in recent years in deference to stern utilitarian demands."*
The notice in London *cannot be found.*)

Maud, a member of the Sykes family at Cheadle, had got married the previous year to a Colonel Greenway. Colonel Greenway's regiment was stationed at Colchester, Essex. Maud had already become a leader in the social life of the garrison. She was high-spirited and attractive, enjoyed entertaining and had a talent for singing, dancing and acting; she took part in all the local theatricals.

On July 15, Kathleen went down to Colchester to stay with the Greenways. Many officers came to the house to lunch and dine. There was a cricket match on July 16 and a picnic the day after.

July 18. Maud and I to lunch with Mr A. in camp. After lunch, Maud to the General's to practise songs with Mr Isherwood. Mr A. and I wait outside.

Against this entry—evidently many years later, for her hand-writing has changed—Kathleen has written, "Was introduced to Frank!"

3

When Frank first met Kathleen he was just twenty-six, having been born on July the first, 1869. His full name was Francis Edward Bradshaw Isherwood. (The Isherwoods often called themselves Bradshaw-Isherwood, but with somewhat doubtful right to do so; Frank's baptismal name Bradshaw was a precaution, like Kathleen's Machell.) His parents lived at Marple, a village in Cheshire not far from Cheadle. He was the second of five children, three boys and two girls. He had joined the York and Lancaster Regiment in 1892 and was now a lieutenant.

Frank was a nice-looking, well-built young man of medium height, with a strong straight nose, fairish hair already receding a bit at the temples, a small shaggy moustache, pale-blue eyes which were innocent but humorous. He looked younger than his age. He could dance and ride adequately, was a fine long-distance runner and an energetic player of most outdoor games. He painted and drew, not yet well. His chief enthusiasm was for music. He was an excellent amateur pianist. Also, he could sing music-hall songs with funny grimaces and clown broadly as a character actor; he often played comic female roles. Maud was rehearsing songs with him because they appeared together in plays and concerts.

Although Frank was bold enough to perform in front of an audience, he seems to have been shy in private conversation, especially with girls. He had learned, no doubt, not to talk much about his deeper interests; when he did so, an older woman would be his preferred confidante. With his brother officers he was most at ease when they were taking part in some sport or violent horseplay. Altogether, he wasn't the kind of man one would expect to make a career of soldiering; yet he was efficient at his job and quite content with it.

Most of this Kathleen could have seen for herself or guessed or found out from Maud—that is, if she was sufficiently interested to make the effort. Was she interested? Not much, it seems. This definitely wasn't a case of love at first sight. Indeed, there are indications in Kathleen's diary that she was carrying on a mild flirtation with the officer referred to as "Mr A.," the one she waited with while Frank and Maud rehearsed.

And then, of course, there was The Child. In the 1895 diary, more than twenty dates are marked with parallel dashes, slanting upward from left to right; these denote meetings with him. His name isn't always mentioned, but when it isn't one finds that Kathleen spent part of that day working at the National Gallery. On September 3, when she was staying in Surrey and he was somewhere in the neighborhood, she writes, "So near and yet so far!"

While staying at Nether Hall, Kathleen went to a children's dance on New Year's Eve disguised as "Miss L. Abney":

'Miss L. Abney' greatly enjoyed herself, dressed in a short white muslin frock, high at the neck, blue sash and hair hanging down, tied on the top with blue ribbon. I.P. identified her; others only thought what an extraordinary likeness to Miss Machell-Smith!!

1896. January 1. B.L. and A. drove out to Nether in afternoon, latter very full of the girl who was so wonderfully like me at the dance last night, only she was 'darker than me' and 'not so pretty'!!! I did not appear, in case the likeness might be too striking.

(Frederick took a photograph of Kathleen in her disguise and wrote on the back of it, "K. M-S as 'a girl of 16.' " It is hard to say if the twenty-seven-year-old Kathleen does or doesn't make a convincing teen-ager; teen-age girls often look much older, anyway. But Kathleen did continue to look relatively young throughout her life. Her complexion remained fresh, and at eighty she could have passed for sixty.)

January 28. To Goethe lecture. He seems to have got himself into an endless tangle of love affairs & then stupid idiot never married the one he admired most—*'the* idyll of his life'. I have *no* sympathy or admiration for Goethe.

January 30. To Gallery. Finished sketch of man in scarlet cloak out of a group picture by Velasquez—also scored off Miss I. who came up and said she could see by the way I had improved I had been having drawing lessons. Told her with glee I hadn't had any for more than a year! She was always so keen for me to take lessons. Mama and I to see The Prisoner of Zenda. Enjoyed it immensely. Most touching ending. Sentiment of the best.

January 31. Read Sims' Life of Goethe in evening, could shake him he annoys me so intensely, even his plays are simply an outlet for his miserable and everlasting love-affairs. Such a mockery to call it *love*, and then not to care enough to give up a little worldly ambition in order to marry the 'adored' object of his affections.

February 4. Joined Miss B. at the Queens Club. Found there was not an instructor disengaged, so, she having hired a machine, we took it in turns trying to wobble about. She helped me and to my great satisfaction I managed to go all round the ground by myself and it is a quarter of a mile round. Of course asphalt is delightful for riding on.

. .

February 18. Papa and I to dine at the House of Commons and after to listen to debate. Was much struck by the untidy appearance of members and the rude way they talked if anyone dull was speaking.

February 22. I was interested to hear that Effra Road takes its name from the river which once flowed where the road now is, & down which Queen Elizabeth used to come in a stately barge when she visited Sir Walter Raleigh at Raleigh Hall near by. So even prosaic Brixton has its romance.

February 23. Mrs. B. to supper. They discussed the *new photography*. It seems an extraordinary thing, you can see the bones inside a person, the money in a purse etc. [*Roentgen had discovered X rays the previous year.*]

February 26. [At Colchester.] Mr Isherwood of the York and Lancaster came to dine and sang after. Liked him very much, he is so fond of pictures and architecture, and actually declared he enjoyed an afternoon at Westminster Abbey far more than Westminster Aquarium!!

February 28. We went to a sergeants' dance in Drill Hall in evening. Room gaily decorated. It was very bright and amusing and enjoyed it much. Danced with Mr Isherwood, Mr C., Mr N., and Major S., all of the York and Lancaster.

(*According to Kathleen's program, she had only one dance with Frank; it was the quadrille from* Utopia Limited. *But these two dates mark the beginning of a realization that they had something, perhaps a great deal, in common.*)

March 3. [Ely Cathedral.] Such a view, miles and miles of flat fen country as far as the eye could see. There was a dear old-world desolate windy many-centuries-old feeling about it all.

· ·

March 10. Went to Goethe lecture. Miss J.H. did not attend it but careened up and down outside on her bicycle. Why? Consider a bicycle most unseemly for a woman with grey hair.

April 9. [At Brighton.] After lunch to Devil's Dyke on the Downs. Celebrated gipsy in scarlet with orange scarf told me money wasn't everything, that I had been talking lately of a voyage, had a roving disposition, liked travelling, drawing and pictures, that I had a happy hand and the happiest time of my life was coming. My troubles were over, as if that were likely!!

April 11. Mama felt very poorly, the air being so strong tries her head and she slept badly.

April 12. Poor M's head very bad and she decides we must leave tomorrow. We sat in the Gardens round the corner and pretended it was 'great fun'.

April 15. By the day of the week it is only two years ago today since I did what I have never ceased to regret. If *only* I had the chance again.

(*According to Kathleen's way of reckoning, Wednesday, April 15, 1896, corresponds to Wednesday, April 11, 1894, the day on which Kathleen failed to understand that The Child was in earnest.*)

April 18. To Colchester. *The Burlesque* began at 3. Maud as Fatima acted extremely well and looked charming. Mr Isherwood was splendid as Sister Anne. We went behind the scenes after and had tea with company. I sat by Mr Isherwood who amused me much.

May 10. Mama with me to Kennington, St John the Divine's, to hear Canon Knox Little. He has a marvellous way of lifting one up from the cares of this world. Nothing seems to matter as long as one is good and true and self-sacrificing.

May 13. Very warm. To Park. All the nice people watch the riders, although the bicyclists have no lack of audience.

May 14. Down to see poor Miss R. who haven't seen since her sister's death. She was sitting all by herself alone in the dark. What a very sad place the world does seem sometimes.

On May 19, Kathleen and Emily started on a trip to France, to see the castles of Touraine. "Travelled to Paris with a pretty young Frenchwoman and her adorer who was so demonstrative I got quite a crick in my neck looking the other way." *In Paris they visited the new Salon in the Champ de Mars.*

The picture of the year is Dagnan-Bouveret's *Last Supper*. It is full of feeling and expression and most striking and solemn. *On dit* there has been nothing to equal it since the one by Leonardo da Vinci. Crowds were gathered round it. An extraordinarily clever portrait of a young man by J. Sargent.

Kathleen also took another look at Notre Dame and was "scandalized to think I ever thought it could compare *with Chartres." They returned home on June 6.*

July 18. To Hurlingham in afternoon. Polo and exhibition of motor cars. I drove in one. They are ugly and clumsy, heavy and smell horribly of paraffin.

July 20. To Limehouse to lunch with Jennie and spend afternoon at the Dalgleish St schools receiving money from parents for 'the country holiday fund' and adding up dirty cards. I do hope I did them all right and made the entries correctly! Jennie gave out tickets and labels to those who had collected enough to go and a woman examined the heads of some of the children who, if it was a question of cutting off their hair, preferred to forfeit their country outing. The heat and smells of fried fish most trying. After all, I don't think I could work in the East End, at least not live in such a depressing atmosphere. Jennie is wonderful. Home with a very bad headache and a sad conviction that I am a very useless incapable person.

July 25. To Victoria for Gatwick. Had lunch and met The Child, who pointed out all sorts of celebrities in the racing world.

August 13. Chaperoned Hilda and Bobbie at tea and felt quite fifty and fat and important. Took them to the Imperial Institute in evening where they had a tiff, told them how absurd they were, and they made it up and Bobbie said I looked like an angel in heaven, such was the state of exhilaration to which he was raised again, and we all drank small brandies and sodas and I think they are very nasty.

August 22 [at Colchester]. Mr Isherwood to lunch. Bicycle in afternoon, the longest distance I have been (six miles each way). Had our tea by the river near the mill and sketched. Enjoyed it immensely. Mr I. and self about equally bad!!

August 26. Ride to camp to have tea with Mr Isherwood. He has such a funny little tiny room blocked up by a big piano and the walls hung with sketches. 'Scorched' some of the way back.

October 17. Saw the coach returning from Alexandra Park, full of men. Picked out The Child at once.

November 4. L. told me some *very* distressing news, not generally made public yet. Oh ye moral young men, when it comes to it, you behave as cruelly heartlessly and dishonourably as the worst. I am simply *disgusted*.

(*There is no clue to the identity of the moral young man. But Kathleen's outburst is in itself interesting because it betrays an attitude toward men in general which will become even more evident later.*)

November 5. To lecture at the Arts and Crafts Exhibition by Cobden-Sanderson, very dreamy, unpractical and poetic. Most amusing audience of collar-less men with bright ties and women in floppy dress.

November 12. Heard Mr Lethaby on *Beautiful Cities*, which was very charming and fantastical and romantic and utterly impracticable and received with immense applause. London without telegraph wires, which were after all put up for men's amusement! With no buses in the chief thoroughfares, which should be lined with trees and grouped with fountains and statues. That a girdle should bound the limits of London in the form of a lovely park, etc.

November 14. *Trial trip of the motor cars to Brighton.* On and after today horseless carriages are allowed to be used. There was a meet of them by the Metropole at one end of Northumberland Avenue, but no one seems to have calculated on the dense crowds of people there would be to see them. We went down to Westminster Bridge over which they passed, but instead of one long procession they came in twos and threes and very ugly and clumsy they look and so unfinished without a horse.

At the beginning of her 1897 diary, Kathleen has copied from The Romance of Isabel Lady Burton *a series of rules for a good wife. Here are some of them: "Allow smoking. If you don't someone else will." "Never permit anyone to speak disrespectfully of him before you, if so leave the room." "Never answer when he finds fault, never reproach him when he is wrong." "Do not bother him with religious talk. Pray for him, do all you can for him without his knowing it." "Keep everything going and let nothing be at a standstill. Nothing wearies like stagnation." Thus speaks an ideal martyr-wife of Emily's generation. Kathleen must surely be repelled by such precepts. But, if so, why does she quote them?*

43

There are also instructions and a list of tools required for book-binding. Kathleen often bound books, including many volumes in the Tauchnitz Edition of British Authors which she had bought on her travels in Europe. She did this work with skill and taste.

There is also a list of "Things I Want": "Tiny diamond crescent for hair, long-shaped old silver box for hairpins, silver-topped scent bottle, old shoe buckles (large.)"

1897. February 15. [Colchester.] Maud practising her cat and mouse dance with Mr J. Mr Isherwood playing accompaniment.

February 16. Awful blow in the evening. Nathan sent the wrong cat's head for Maud to wear, so we determined to make one ourselves.

February 17. Drove into town first thing to get eyes and material to make a cat's head. We bicycled to Lexdon and Mr Isherwood and I did a little sketch of a farm house. Cat's head finished, made of all white fur, glass eyes and padded nose and cheeks and big black whiskers, quite a success.

February 18. The play very well received, good house. Mr Isherwood as Sarah a general servant was simply killing. There were roars of laughter.

February 20. It is so amusing behind scenes where there is a good deal of love-making being practised among the ladies and gentlemen of the chorus.

February 27. Mama and I to National Gallery where met Mr Isherwood and we went round the pictures together and compared notes on our own favourites, enjoyed seeing them with him very much as he pointed out several new things about them I had not noticed before, and we liked very much the same ones.

. .

March 17. All the way up Piccadilly we walked behind The Child, who looked very down in his luck. We passed him and he saw us and spoke.

March 19. Was seized with the wildest and now hopeless desire of going up to Southport again for the Grand National. Dreamt about it all night. After all it would have been much more amusing than getting a new summer dress, and cost about the same. Oh dear, oh dear.

March 30. To Dante lecture in afternoon. I don't see the least good or satisfaction in doing right here, if one is only ultimately to reach a circle where none of one's friends are. It seems according to Dante there are degrees or circles of blessedness even in Heaven and in each circle everyone is content, feeling the fitness of being there and just there. I suppose they have forgotten the past altogether.

(One can hear the pitying, faintly contemptuous tone in which Kathleen would say this. What's the use of being in heaven if you've forgotten the Past?)

On May 10, Frank writes his first letter to Kathleen. He is painfully self-conscious, and this makes him facetious. "Dear Miss Machell-Smith," he begins, "if it does not savour of impropriety to accept such a handsome present from a young gentleman, I hope you will keep the Pall Mall *as long as you want to . . ." He mentions some exhibitions of pictures he has seen, says that he has been taking lessons in watercolor painting, hopes to have the pleasure of meeting her again before long. He signs himself "believe me, yours sincerely, F. Bradshaw Isherwood."*

June 12. [During a horse show in Richmond Park.] The Child very absent, evidently looking for someone.

June 14. Expected The Child but he did not come. Blessed is he that expecteth nothing!!

June 21. I began our Jubilee decorations with flags and coloured twill, one balcony all red and blue and another yellow and red, looked very effective. After dinner we strolled out to criticize other people's decorations and admire our own.

(Queen Victoria's Diamond Jubilee was held the next day. Kathleen went to watch the procession, which was two miles long. Unfortunately she was overcome by the heat and fainted, so she missed seeing the Queen drive by.)

June 26. [Kempton.] Victor Wild made his last appearance (in the Coronation Stakes) when the winner became possessed of a huge and rather vulgar gold cup. I never saw anything so human and pathetic as the old horse. He came up the course with Morny Cannon on his back (and carrying long way top weight of 9.13) and looked first to right and then to left as if he were expecting the applause which greeted him, then he bowed in the most natural way just as if he were Royalty. Public opinion was divided between him and Sandria who I am glad to say came in only 3rd and Victor Wild came home victorious amid bursts of applause.

July 3. Down to Hurst Park by Members' train. Child and brother travelled with us. I was very rude.

August 9. [While staying in Scotland, near Kelso.] A dinner at the Poor House which we attended at 1 o'clock. Much struck by the cheerfulness and great cleanliness of the place. The Master took us round. Those who do a little work have broth, 4 ounces of meat and 8 ounces of bread for dinner. Tea and bread for breakfast, and porridge. The non-workers don't get so much meat.

On August 16, Kathleen and Emily went to stay at Oxford, which they both loved. This was the time of year at which the public could attend extension lectures. They invited Frank to join them for the weekend. He and Kathleen were both keeping

*architectural notebooks in which they drew plans of the churches
at Yarnton and Iffley and sketched various details. They also attended a lecture on the French Peasant Painters and were told
(by Miss Rose Kingsley) that, to be a realist, one must (1) paint
with absolute sincerity and (2) be in sympathy with the subject
chosen.*

*After this, they didn't see each other for the rest of the year.
They didn't even correspond, until Frank wrote to her on December 20:*

I executed the other day a work of such embarrassing excel-
lence that I couldn't resist having it framed to send to you, hoping
that you will hang it up somewhere. I have had such a very dull
autumn here, it seems quite endless to look back upon. I haven't
done any churches lately and I want someone to revive my enthusiasm badly. I find it very difficult to keep up 'the sacred fire'
all by oneself . . .

And again on December 22:

I have accepted the Sykes invitation, so if you don't scrape up
enough money to go I shall be properly sold. If I might be allowed
to travel in the same train, we might find ourselves in Lichfield
Cathedral en route, measuring tape and all, though I'm afraid 50
feet wouldn't go far . . .

*On January 11, 1898, Kathleen and Frank did travel up to
Cheshire together as he had suggested, stopping off at Lichfield
and visiting the cathedral, though without trying to take its mea-
surements. Kathleen in her diary gives it a lukewarm notice:*

First view very picturesque with three spires. Dull rather damp
town. Chapter House too stumpy. Cathedral as a whole beautiful
but rather too much broken up into parts. Good stained glass in
Lady Chapel and fine geometrical windows. No Norman work.

· ·

While staying at the Sykeses' they attended the Stockport In-firmary Ball and went into Manchester to see the pantomime, which was Puss in Boots. *Next day they were out together again, to visit the Whitworth Gallery. It was closed and they missed the bus and returned late. Kathleen writes, "When we got in, pre-tended we were very bored with each other!" (No doubt to prevent their hostess from suspecting that the outing had been romantic.)*

Then, on January 15, Frank took her over to see the family home at Marple. Kathleen evidently didn't meet his parents. She mentions only a sister of his (this was probably Esther) whom she thought very pretty. These are her first impressions of Marple Hall:

It is an awfully picturesque approach and a most fascinating old place, I like the drawing room so much with the bow window looking over the terrace and hills beyond, and the room itself full of old china, pictures, tapestry and old furniture. The whole house is very rambling and fascinating.

On January 18, Kathleen returned to London. About the same time, Frank left with his sister Moey for a trip to France and Italy. His letters to Kathleen suggest no great advance in their intimacy; they are still addressed to a young lady rather than a human being:

Dear Miss Machell-Smith, it was very nice of you *indeed* to write me such a delightfully long letter and I waved it well in the air at the breakfast table so that everyone should see how popular I was! There was only one other man there and my Sister took a violent dislike to him. She told him that Florence quite came up to our ideals and he said in the most superior voice, 'ah, you hadn't such a high one as I had' . . . San Marco is the least disappointing place I have ever seen. And the Ducal Palace! I can't resist saying it's like lace, though it is dreadfully obvious. I shall keep this letter and read it over tomorrow, and see if it doesn't look too gush-ing. . . .

February 23. Zola after 15 days trial sentenced to a year's imprisonment and fined for trying to find out the truth about the Dreyfus case.

February 24. Lecture on Japan delivered by Mrs Bishop who has lived there a good deal. Said they were adaptive people but not imitative as generally supposed. Their army splendidly organized. Only needed Christianity to make them the greatest nation in the east.

March 7. To Free Library Reference Room, Chelsea, to read Bacon's essay on Building with a view to drawing plan and elevation of Bacon's ideal palace, but the description baffled me completely.

March 10. To the Writers Club to meet Mr Isherwood and his Sister just back from abroad and had lunch there (shockingly served and cooked) and much talk about Italy etc.

March 20. Mama read to me 'Christ in Hades' by Stephen Phillips, the supposed rising poet who some say should be poet laureate. Did *not* like it but thought little passages in 'Marpessa' also by him exceedingly pretty.

March 24. Mama in bed with internal chill.

March 28. Dr in afternoon, thought Mama a little better, don't myself and she is so depressed. It is a form of this horrid influenza.

March 29. Wrote for Mama who moved into drawing room after lunch on sofa. Had scalloped oysters for lunch and was able to eat them. She can hardly fancy anything.

April 8. Mama keeps very weak and hardly seems to make any progress.

．　．

April 15. Mr Isherwood called for me and we went to the
South Kensington Museum and spent some while there. To lunch
at the Hotel d'Italie in Old Compton St. Then we went to the
Institute of Watercolours. Struck me suddenly that of course I
oughtn't to have gone to lunch at a restaurant like that!

*(This late-Victorian code of propriety is baffling, because some
of the earlier rules have been relaxed while others haven't. If
Kathleen could ride in a train with Frank and be all alone with
him in Lichfield, why couldn't they have lunch together in a
public restaurant? Did Soho restaurants have such a bad reputation? Or was the objection to this one that it was also a hotel, with
bedrooms available upstairs?)*

April 22. Miss E. and E.W. called. Did not see them. Am keeping myself out to everyone, as Mama does so hate my being called
away when with her.

April 25. Dr came and thought Mama decidedly better, but she
collapsed dreadfully in evening and was so weak she could hardly
speak above a whisper. Slept with her.

April 28. Dr spoke of Mama going away in ten days which
cheered her immensely. She is not to go for even a drive first but
to save up for the journey. I wonder if he realizes how *awfully*
weak she is, besides hardly eating anything, and out of London
there are no dainties or things to tempt her appetite.

April 30. Mama very poorly with pain in back of head and
nervous that a whitlow was coming on her finger. I don't see that
her appetite is a bit better. She could hardly *touch* the new peas.

May 2. Slept in Mama's room last night and had a rather bad
night. Felt tired and headachey all day. It is six weeks today since
Mama began to be ill. She is fearfully weak.

．　．

May 3.   *'Slept* and dreamt that Life was beauty
          Woke to find that Life was Duty'

(It was a very enjoyable dream even though it lasted so short a time!) Felt very headachey and tired. Out early to do household shopping. Rested after, as head felt too bad to go for an omnibus airing.

May 4. Mama took quite a turn, determined to throw off the influenza, declared she was quite well, didn't want a maid and would go to the Extension lectures in June.

May 6. Mama full of plan to go to Switzerland in August and stay two months. Said she was quite well now, nothing whatever the matter with her, and only took her medicine to please Papa and me. All the evening kept rolling and unrolling the ribbons on her dress and did not seem at all herself.

May 7. Mama not at all herself, fancied the influenza had been only a dream and that she was quite well. Ate hardly any breakfast and took beef tea under pressure at 11, but had oysters scalloped, champagne and liquid jelly for lunch and quail for late dinner.

May 8. Mama seemed quite drowsy and half asleep and would not take the least notice of Papa or me. Dr C. said at once she must have a nurse. Mama did not like it at all and refused at first to have her nightgown and things changed. Nurse thought very seriously of her. I feel so distressed I can't manage by myself as I know how she hates nurses.

May 9. Dr C. at 10. We got my darling comfortable first and the Nurse went home after to rest. The Nurse returned at 9. Mama said to me, 'send her away', if only I could manage all by myself I gladly would.

·   ·

May 10. Fed Mama every two hours but she was not at all herself and lay quite rigid. I did not know what to do, felt I could not manage alone if this went on, as could not change her by myself and the sheets were all wet. Glad when Nurse got back at 10. We made her comfortable and she did not resist *much*.

May 11. Drs B. and C. came at 10. The former thought seriously of her but said this was a form it often took with highly bred people.

May 16. Dr B. saw decided improvement but said it was an exceptional case and an anxious one. Irritation of the spine where it joins the brain, requires careful watching. Very tired by evening!

May 17. Poor darling Mama *very* irritable when we washed her and put her in clean things. Nurse and I felt quite disheartened. However when Nurse had gone and I gave her some cream with brandy she took a turn and talked more or less all day. Got out for three quarters of an hour at 6.30. Went down to Embankment Gardens and read Carlyle's French Revolution under the shadow of his effigy and within a stone's throw of his home. It added greatly to the interest and charm of the book!!

May 19. Notes to answer of enquiry. Washing, drying, changing, feeding filled up the day! Dr B. came at 6.30 to meet Dr C. Dear cheery old thing, thought Mama decidedly better, patted me on the back and said he should give me a medal. She asked for champagne in evening and ate double quantities of jelly. *Death of Mr Gladstone.*

May 21. Mama a better night and quite chatty and herself, longing to get up and go and see things and asking to have the window open that she might hear 'the nice noise' and very tired of the quiet and dullness of bed.

.   .

May 26. Dr B. said that many far stronger people than she had sunk under this abdominal influenza and without great care she would not have pulled through at all, he felt very doubtful at one time.

May 29. Mama's window open all day and she seemed so nicely. I told her she would soon be sitting in a chair. A minute or two later I went on to her balcony to watch the people coming from church, when suddenly turning round saw the bed empty and darling M. reposing on the sofa! She did it to give me a surprise. I was startled and helped her back to bed, she was rather exhausted after such an excursion!

May 30. Darling Mama a better night and continued to give us delightful surprises throughout the day. First she was helped on to her sofa while the bed was properly made for the first time. Then after retiring to it for a time she got up and sat in a chair with the window open for a good half hour!!!! Then during the afternoon she got up and walked round the room to try her powers, and 'the little red gentleman' was forsaken for the more usual modes.

(*"The little red gentleman"* = *a bedpan?*)

June 2. Mr Isherwood called for me. We looked at his sketches.

June 7. Mabel called. She was very sweet and amusing and after the hateful modern sort of way Mr A. announced his engagement this morning, it was most refreshing to hear her talk after seven or eight years of matrimony, how she grudged each day away from Jim.

June 8. Went for a walk. On return horrified to find Mama sitting on balcony and a damp drizzle falling. Expected Papa would have been there or would never have gone out. Very annoyed.

· ·

June 12. Mama came in drawing room for tea. Wore a blue bow at throat of her tea gown to mark its being Sunday!

June 18. Mama and I in a victoria for an hour round Battersea Park. The first time she had been out since March 24.

June 22. Miss E. to see me. Thought me looking very worn and ill, she said! However mercifully it doesn't matter now.

On June 28, Kathleen and Emily went down to stay in Sussex, at East Grinstead, for Emily's convalescence. They were there for a month. They both needed the change; and here, at least, Kathleen could get out in the fresh air after her long confinement to Emily's sickroom. But she also needed company of her own age and the opposite sex. This led to complications.

The complications began to develop on July 8, when Kathleen went to the races at Lingfield and met The Child. He came back with her to the hotel where she and Emily were staying and sat with her out in the garden till dinner. Sometime that evening a friend of The Child, a Mr. L., appeared at the hotel. He was probably drunk. Anyhow, he made a nuisance of himself which was somehow connected with a perambulator.

July 9. Mama had better night, in spite of certain upsets in the hotel which however did not occur in *our* passage. Bobbie *very* annoyed and the baby disturbed. To races after lunch, walked back with The Child, met Mr L, with some conversation re last night's doings. Owned to the perambulator and suggested apologizing to Hilda. Hilda did not welcome the idea and went to bed early, so Bobbie received it instead, with result that he was very cross with me!

(Bobbie and Hilda are the same pair referred to on August 13, 1896, when Bobbie told Kathleen she was "like an angel in heaven." Was Bobbie cross because he suspected Kathleen of

54

having encouraged Mr. L. to come to the hotel by flirting with him at the races?)

July 10. The Child came in after we had done dinner. Said he had commissioned Mr L to take me out bicycling. Very kind I'm sure!

(Kathleen's sarcastic comment may be understood in two ways: she is hurt because The Child passes her off onto someone else instead of offering to take her bicycling himself; she is indignant that he can be so inconsiderate as to try to involve her with a man who has caused a public scandal and offended her friends. Nevertheless, she wants to go bicycling with someone—the only alternatives are Bobbie and Hilda—and she does like Mr. L., despite his behavior or perhaps even because of it.)

July 11. Mr L asked if he might show me the way if I wanted to take some bicycle rides. Certainly it is no fun going alone, but Mama seemed rather shocked.

July 12. Mr L wired to Penshurst to know what days we could see it. Very disappointed that Mama disapproved of my going today. Bicycled with Hilda to the station. Very tired of perambulator fuss etc, it's getting so out of date and tiring. It's so stupid too when I wanted to go bicycling. If only he hadn't gone and got into a row just now!

Kathleen must have pleaded or sulked or otherwise moved Emily to relent, however. For, only two days later, she and Mr. L. rode over to the village of Penshurst; they got tickets at the post office which enabled them to visit Penshurst Place, the ancient home of the Sidney family and the birthplace of the Elizabethan poet. They admired the Vandykes and the Lelys in the gallery— at least, Kathleen did; Mr. L. probably regarded the sight-seeing as one of those things you had to endure if you were in sufficiently attractive company. Then they had tea at the inn. Kath-

leen's account of the day ends enigmatically: "Enjoyed it very much, most invigorating in more senses than one!! Horribly shocked to hear I was supposed to have been on the stage." Is the outing described as "invigorating" partly because of Mr. L.'s behavior? And was his behavior prompted by the belief that Kathleen had been an actress—someone you didn't have to treat with the respect due to a starchy young lady? All that can be said with certainty is that Mr. L. didn't displease her by word or by deed, for they went out together again on July 20 after a separation caused by Frederick, who came down from London to stay at the hotel for four days and photographed every picturesque spot for miles around. And there were three more rides after this one. On July 27 they rode twenty miles. Kathleen writes, "Last expedition, alas!" Next day, she and Emily returned home.

A curious sequel to these events took place on August 1, when Kathleen and Hilda went down to the races at Hurst Park:

The Child there and of course lectured me severely on the bicycle rides which, as I reminded him, were all brought about through him. Pretended all sorts of things which I knew were not true but made me feel a little uneasy, all the same. As to my companion being a 'fit' companion or not, he should have thought of that sooner! He promised to get the photos if they are there, which he says they are not. Of course they are.

The first "of course" seems to mean that Kathleen now regards The Child as a typical male hypocrite with a double standard. He quite admits that Mr. L. is "fast" and an unfit companion for Kathleen. But Mr. L. is his friend and a member of his own sex, so if Mr. L. wants to get to know Kathleen better The Child will arrange it; Kathleen is, after all, merely a girl. "Pretended all sorts of things I knew were not true" suggests that Mr. L. has been boasting to The Child about the things that went on during the bicycle outings. The Child says he is shocked, but Kathleen suspects he is just teasing her. She wishes she could believe that he is really shocked, however, because that might mean he is jealous; which is what she would like to make him, but can't.

*As for the photos, there is a clue in Kathleen's diary, July 21:
"Conversation re photograph at Old Mill House with Mr L.
Hilda agreed with me." Whatever it was that Kathleen and Hilda
agreed about, this can be taken to mean that Kathleen had been
photographed with Mr. L. in a pose which was mildly compromising; maybe he was standing too close to her. Kathleen, having
now been made to feel uneasy about Mr. L.'s character by The
Child, wants to get the photos back. The second "of course" implies that The Child knows the photos still exist and that he is
lying to oblige Mr. L., who wants to keep them.*

*Despite all of this, Kathleen's attitude toward the two of them
remained indulgent and amused, rather than hostile. When she
and Emily returned to stay at East Grinstead late in September,
she resumed her expeditions with Mr. L., apparently without any
objection by Emily. On October 1, she complains that Mr. L.
"was faithless and did not come to take me for a ride." On
October 9, the last day of their visit:*

Was sitting at tea when The Child appeared, come to see what
I was up to! We sat out on the verandah when it got too damp
and dark in the garden and talked till 7 in the dusk. He was returning to town that night and had brought his young brother
with him, but they missed their train. Mrs D was awfully excited
by the appearance of The Child and asked Mama if it would be a
thing she approved of! How we laughed. Mrs D tried me a good
deal. Asked my age and was very annoying and impertinent, considering The Child is my friend.

*Here Kathleen takes sides, for once, against her own sex, as
represented by Mrs. D., a nosy fellow guest at the hotel. If Mrs. D.
was asking Emily whether or not she would approve of The
Child as a possible husband for Kathleen, then "How we laughed"
means that such an idea is so utterly out of the question as to seem
absurd. But why?*

*The last half of the last entry in the 1898 diary, December 31,
is written in pencil, perhaps so that it could be erased later if
Kathleen wanted to forget about it:*

When did they first say he had spoilt the girl's life? Did he really confide in Mr F? Was he married time of G.N. 96? Did he ever suggest the girl was desperately in love, and what did he say about her? How meet the girl's successor and when first?

"G.N. 96" must surely refer to the Grand National. In 1896 it was run on March 27 and Kathleen was there to watch it, wearing a "black and white shepherds plaid and scarlet toque." She writes that she "did not see The Child till at the station on our return. Report not true, I mean it was not him but someone else."

One more piece can be added to this jigsaw puzzle; its date is July 23, 1898, during Kathleen's first visit to East Grinstead:

The following gave me subject for thought. W.B. a singer, sister understudy Savoy. Marriage not announced on account of money expected. Information from two women who knew the wife, both separate sources. Also one woman, Mrs C, who knows the brother?

And now, since this is anyhow only a guessing game, here is a guess, perhaps utterly wrong, at an explanation:

It was The Child who was secretly married to W.B.'s sister. They were seen together by someone at the Grand National in 1896, and this someone told Kathleen. She asked The Child about it when she met him at the station afterward; he denied the whole thing and convinced her, temporarily, that the someone had been mistaken.

However, during the first visit to East Grinstead, Kathleen found out the truth; it was vouched for by two or three witnesses. She also found out, later than this, that she was being gossiped about by The Child's male friends; they were saying that he had allowed her to fall "desperately in love" with him without knowing that he was married or about to be, and had thus "spoilt her life." Probably Kathleen was no longer in love with The Child but still felt a strong friendly regard for him and hated the thought that he could have bragged about her in this heartless, shameless way. She preferred to blame his friends.

Who was Mr. F.? This remains unanswered. How much did Emily know of what was going on? She may well have known about the marriage but not about the gossip; she was very careful of Kathleen's reputation and, if she had known, would never have allowed Kathleen to see any of these men again. Who told Kathleen? Mr. L., probably—which would make him even more of a cad than he appears already. Why did Mr. L. think Kathleen had been on the stage? Could he have somehow got her confused with The Child's wife, who had been an understudy at the Savoy Theatre?

In any case, if this explanation is even partially correct, Kathleen seems to have behaved with great generosity throughout this humiliating affair.

4

*October the seventh, 1898, was Kathleen's thirtieth birthday.
She gives no hint that this anniversary depresses her, beyond
noting that the weather is gray. Still, thirty is thirty, even nowadays; and in the nineteenth century it made you into* la femme de
trente ans. *Certain men might confess to a preference for you, but
it was a connoisseur's preference, backed up by the claim that you
were now more mature, more capable of emotional intensity,
more experienced in the arts of love.*

*Poor Kathleen! As the Woman of Thirty she can't be taken
seriously for a moment. Still inexperienced and immature, her
charms are the charms of her early twenties. Her behavior is
appropriate to her youthful looks and therefore in danger of becoming increasingly artificial.*

*Most of her friends would probably admit that they no longer
expect to see her married. If The Child hasn't "spoilt her life" he
has undoubtedly disillusioned her. She still likes some men as individuals, but she is building up a hostility toward the sex which
she will never lose. ("All men are selfish," Richard remembers her
often saying.) Also, in self-defense, against the probable future in
store for her, she is cultivating a disdain of marriage. She speaks
of a woman she meets at a party as an "irresponsible sort of
grownup child to whom it is absolutely essential to have a man
and children." Hearing of the unexpected engagement of a cousin,
she comments, with evident dismay, "Thought she meant* never

to marry." The majority of her female contemporaries are, of course, married already.

Indeed, Kathleen may be thought of, at this point, as one of those unfortunate girls who somehow get themselves caught in a generation gap. On one side of her is the generation of the Martyr-Wife; on the other, the generation of the New Woman. Across the gap, Lady Burton confronts the heroines of Bernard Shaw. Kathleen's temperament is quite alien to the grimness of Lady Burton's marriage rules, yet in her heart she does unwillingly believe that "life is duty." She can admire Shaw's Vivie Warren for boycotting men and their double standard, yet her conservatism and her strong sense of womanliness are outraged by Vivie's mannish business ambitions.

Kathleen does sometimes dream of making an independent life for herself; two years ago she was talking half seriously to a friend about the possibility of their becoming missionaries in South Africa. But one can't imagine her doing this, or even settling down to slum work with Jennie in Limehouse; she may have the necessary courage, but she lacks the conviction.

So, if she is to become an old maid, it will have to be on other people's terms, not her own. This very year, Emily has given her a frightening demonstration of what it would be like to spend the rest of her youth as a daughter-nurse. Yet life with Emily would offer consolations as well as austerities; it would be a path of duty but also a nest of safety; it would be toilsome and tame but also snug and full of shared interests and tenderness. Kathleen's uneasy conscience would find rest in it, for how can you ever feel guilty when you are looking after your own mother? Emily is now only forty-eight; she could be counted on to provide Kathleen with an occupation for at least twenty years, and to relieve her from making any more decisions; in sickness or in health, Emily would always be decisive and capricious and selfish enough for both of them.

Emily has listened sympathetically to Kathleen's romantic confidences and smiled indulgently at her flirtations; yet, by her own example, she has been teaching Kathleen to despise men. Year by year, she has been withdrawing herself from Frederick and thus drawing Kathleen also away from him. Emily and Frederick have now only one thing in common, their attitude to the question of Kathleen's marriage: in principle, they will agree that Kathleen should certainly have a husband, if the right one can be found; in practice, one or the other or both of them will be able to produce perfectly reasonable and fatal objections to any suitor whatsoever.

Frederick at his most suspicious could not have feared Frank as a prospective suitor in 1898; indeed, he seemed to be making little effort to keep himself in the running even as a friend. During the second half of the year Kathleen didn't see him at all and he wrote her only two letters, both of them in answer to letters from her. The first of these is almost entirely about himself. For the past year he has been stationed in Yorkshire, at Pontefract, which he hates:

I did not answer your letter as I was in negotiation for an exchange and wanted to tell you the result. I heard this morning that I had got it, so I shall leave this—may I say 'accursed'?—place next week. I hope for ever. I shall go back to Colchester—how delightful it is to write it—and on the 14th August we shall go to Dorchester for the manoeuvres. I am quite silly with delight. The idea of being busy and no more a gilded flutterer! But I must spare you any more raptures, or you will think me a fool or worse a nuisance.

The second letter congratulates Kathleen on her good fortune: she was about to leave for Italy with Jennie. Jennie was a most desirable traveling companion, because she knew the country well and spoke Italian fluently. They started on October 13.

October 15. [At Menaggio, Lake Como.] So restful, so Italian, so perfect. Sat for ever so long on the wall looking down at Menaggio. Groups of peasants constantly passing with great baskets of fruit or vegetables, a constant procession which seemed to be making a series of pictures just for us. It seems a horrid simile, but except at the theatre one never sees anything so grouped or natural out of Italy.

October 20. There is something indescribable about the charm of Italy, but Ouida gives one more the idea of its atmosphere than anyone.

October 26. [On the way to Assisi.] Train crowded, travelled with three odious Italians, more odious far than Germans, middle-class shop-people. The man made the most filthy noises and spat incessantly for 6 hours, one woman was sick and the other had such an awful squint I could hardly enjoy the view.

On October 30, while at Perugia, Kathleen got a letter from Emily, telling her that a friend who was in the War Office had been dining with them and had said he feared England might go to war with France at any minute, because of the Franco–British confrontation in the Sudan. (Marchand and his troops had hoisted the French flag at Fashoda, whereupon Kitchener had hoisted the British and Egyptian flags and had "invited Marchand to withdraw.") The War Office friend had added that in the event of war he would send a gunboat to bring Kathleen and Jennie home. This amused Kathleen and rather thrilled her, but she and Jennie can't have been seriously alarmed, for they continued their tour as planned and even returned through potential enemy territory.

November 17. Got into Paris an hour late. Paris looked so huge after Rome and felt cold. Some odious Frenchmen in carriage most rude and made one feel that the French and English just now are anything but friendly! Made insulting remarks about the English and pointed us out at the station as the 'two English there'. We had a very smooth lonely crossing. So few people travelling, owing to war scare.

．　．

The crisis continued until December, when the French, being uncertain of Russia's support in an international showdown, had to accept the humiliation of recalling Marchand.

The beginning of 1899 found Kathleen and Emily staying on the Isle of Wight, at Ventnor. The list of wants in her new diary shows that she now has the silver box for hairpins and the scent bottle, but needs an antique silver mirror and a silver stove for curling irons. The diamond crescent has been dropped from the list; perhaps such an ornament is no longer in vogue. There are nine pages of racing fixtures and results. There is also a long list of foods "Mama fancied when ill." Emily was in good health now, however; she even walked to the top of St. Boniface Down, the highest point on the island. They came back to London on January 14.

Meanwhile, Frank and Moey had gone to Italy. In a letter from Rome he says that he likes the Sistine Chapel and that the pension where they are staying "is the most skittish place. . . . They have concerts twice a week, dance on Thursdays, and on other nights play puss in the corner etc. We have held ourselves severely aloof from these frivolities so far, but there is no knowing what we may not be forced to do before we leave."

February 8. R has been staying at Calcutta with the Curzons and attended the first drawing-room of the new Viceroy. Says Lady Curzon is charming, so natural and quite as to the position born, how marvellously adaptable these Americans are. They say her father is a quite rough unpresentable old person. To be an American is a pedigree in itself.

(What Kathleen seems to imply is that any American would be accepted by English society. What she strangely neglects to mention—she must surely know it—is that Lady Curzon's father is a millionaire!)

. .

March 10. A large field for the National Hunt Steeplechase, nineteen, and some bad tumbles. Met The Child, who travelled back with me.

March 27. Sent for Dr for Mama was very poorly. A sort of eruption round her eye with very bad neuralgia. He said it was herpes, a form of shingles which comes on the face and is most painful. Mama very wretched and unable to bear light.

March 30. Mama slept better and pain not so bad, but all the right side of face is swollen and looks very bad, she can hardly open her eye and feels so sick poor dear. Dr brought lotion and gave her ipec. and rus. to take alternately every hour.

(This refers to homeopathic treatment. Emily had been converted to the theories of homeopathy, and most of her doctors were homeopaths. Like the representatives of other small and ridiculed minorities, they were apt to become fanatical. Christopher remembers one of them, an otherwise mild-mannered gentleman, who had written a book called Knaves or Fools? *against the allopaths, the orthodox medical majority.)*

April 3. Down to Kempton. Sloan the American jockey was riding, his first appearance this year. He looks just like a little monkey on a horse and rides all of a heap, right over the horse's shoulders. Saw but did not see.

(This last sentence may mean that Kathleen saw The Child with someone whom she did not choose to recognize, perhaps his wife.)

April 14. To Cecily Roche, 4 Hanover St, to be fitted. These new tight-fitting skirts are very unbecoming to stout people, and very trying to thin ones like me!

• •

On April 26, Frank wrote to Kathleen from the infantry bar-racks, York. (If he did get sent to Colchester from Pontefract, he can only have stayed there a few months.) From his letter it appears that Kathleen has written to tell him that she can't come up to visit him at York, because of Emily's illness. He continues:

I do wish there was any chance of my being in town. It seems such a long time since we met but I am so terribly impecunious! And I always have to be careful not to blast all hopes of going abroad next leave. It's so dreadful in the service, one spends most of one's money on other people's pleasures—a dinner to the Bays (though I don't know that there is much pleasure in that for any-one) a race lunch, and, heaven help us, a ball. I am reading very slowly with the aid of a dictionary Goethe's Dichtung und Wahrheit. I hope you will write and tell me how Mrs Machell-Smith is. I want to say something very sympathetic but I don't know how to.

(The Bays were the Second Regiment of Dragoon Guards, known as the Queen's Bays. Frank made a tactless slip when he wrote that he couldn't come down to London to see Kathleen because he had to save his money for his next trip abroad. Kath-leen must have thought him a bit ungallant.)

On May 4, Kathleen, Emily and Frederick left for a trip to France, Switzerland and the Italian lakes. Emily's eye was still inflamed, but she seems to have been in good spirits. Kathleen writes that she took quite long walks in the mountains; "Mama goes about in smoked glasses and is very frisky." Frederick photo-graphed a great deal; "the camera as usual played all its most fiendish tricks." He had to leave them and return to England before the end of their trip, so Kathleen was free to make a new friend:

Had a long conversation with Mr G.B. outside under the trees by the lake and we exchanged addresses. It is a mushroom friendship with a vengeance! But so much zest added by the fact that the Sister evidently was not keen for me to stay on.

(*Mr. G.B. was sufficiently interested to visit Kathleen later in England, unaccompanied by his possessive sister. But they didn't continue to see each other.*)

June 2. [In Paris.] Sarah as Hamlet *simply genius personified*, never enjoyed a Hamlet to compare to it.

(*It was about this performance that Max Beerbohm wrote, "Her friends ought to have restrained her."*)

June 9. [Cranley Mansion.] People do look so smart and London looks very full. Am not at all pleased to be back and wish we had been spending the summer away!

June 10. Papa and I bicycled down to Richmond Horse Show. A great deal of traffic and really felt more nervous than I ever have done. Papa will ride in front too so that practically one might almost as well be riding alone. Of all the people I ever rode with, Mr L was far the most considerate and suited me the best.

The somewhat defiant tone of Kathleen's tribute to Mr. L., the unfit companion but considerate fellow cyclist, makes a suitable ending to this chapter of her life. But Kathleen doesn't seem to have had the least suspicion that a new one was just about to begin.

On July 12, she traveled up to Scotland to stay with some friends. The train made a stop at York, where Frank met her at the station. "Mr Isherwood got me coffee and strawberries, twenty minutes, a rush and a chat." This was their first meeting for more than a year, so each was in a position to form entirely fresh impressions of the other.

Kathleen came back to London on July 26. The next day she and Emily went to stay at Oxford.

67

July 29. Very close and hot. Sat in garden till lunch. Mr Isherwood arrived about 1. We went on the Cherwell and took tea basket with us.

July 30. Very hot bright day. All drove to Port Meadows, taking lunch and tea with us. Landed in meadow up backwater near Cassington. Mama went to afternoon service there. Mr Isherwood and I sketched in churchyard.

July 31. Mr Isherwood and I went to the Botanical Gardens to look at Magdalen Tower and subjects to sketch. The sundial and corner with Matthew Arnold's rooms at Corpus seemed attractive, and then we went on to the Cathedral. Poor Mr Isherwood upset boiling water on his leg, making cocoa after dinner.

August 1. Mr Isherwood and I out to Corpus to draw the sundial and Matthew Arnold's rooms in the first quad. I did not even succeed in drawing mine! Returned to fetch Mama and together to hear lecture on Matthew Arnold. In afternoon sat in garden with Mr I who read Cyrano, Mama rested. To Iffley and sketched mill. It puts me to shame how *immensely* he has improved in the last two years while I am worse than before.

August 2. Hot and bright. Mr Isherwood and I to see the lovely tapestry at Exeter, then into Jesus and saw a very good portrait of Queen Elizabeth by Zucchero, also a watercolour portrait of Holman Hunt. After that we sat in the gardens of New College till lunch, and out under the apple trees in our own little shady garden till nearly 4. Mr Isherwood left soon after for Marple.

Nearly two years after this, in a letter from South Africa, Frank writes: "It was at Oxford that I first discovered . . . You didn't discover anything until later." Certainly there is nothing in Kathleen's diary to suggest that she has fallen in love; but her behavior toward Frank must have been at least encouraging, or he would never have written to her as he did on August 13 from York:

I went yesterday to an open air performance of 'As You Like It'. There was quite an ideal Silvius who said his beautiful lines, the best in the piece, to my mind, in a way which sent a thrill through one and created for me quite a new set of illusions—at least, not illusions I hope. Yours *very very* sincerely, Frank B. Isherwood.

(In Act Five, scene two, Silvius is asked to describe "what 'tis to love" and answers:

> *It is to be all made of sighs and tears; . . .*
> *It is to be all made of faith and service; . . .*
> *It is to be all made of fantasy,*
> *All made of passion, and all made of wishes,*
> *All adoration, duty, and observance,*
> *All humbleness, all patience, and impatience,*
> *All purity, all trial, all obeisance . . .)*

Kathleen and Emily had left Oxford on August 8. When Kathleen got Frank's letter, she was in Cheshire, staying with the Sykeses. On August 18, Kathleen and Emily drove over to Marple Hall. Frank was there, on leave from York, and showed them some of his sketches of Italy.

August 19. Mr Isherwood drove over and he and I drove to Chorley Hall. Had a great surprise. He asked me something so utterly unexpected. We picnicked in a barn full of hay and afterwards sketched. Chorley is inhabited now by farmers, it is partly gabled and stone mullioned windows and partly black and white timbered. Mr I drove me back.

August 20. Spent a very reflective day.

. .

(The "something so utterly unexpected" was obviously Frank's proposal of marriage, but it seems probable that Kathleen didn't give him a definite answer until about three weeks later, while they were staying with the Greenways, who now lived at Hexham in Northumberland. Years afterward, when Kathleen was sorting Frank's letters into packets, she wrote on the first packet, "From May 1897 to August 1899, before our visit to Hexham," implying that it was at Hexham, not in Cheshire, that their new relationship began. There are no letters from Frank during their short separation from August 20 to September 7. Kathleen may have asked him not to write to her while she was making up her mind.)

September 7. [At Hexham.] Mr Isherwood arrived about tea-time. We all went in evening to see a touring company perform 'The Sign of the Cross' about Nero and the early Christians. It was wonderfully done all things considered, but bordered too much on the profane where it did not verge on the ridiculous.

September 8. Maud, Mr Isherwood and I joined a picnic party (given by Mr A.) at Hexham station. Mr I. sketched after, and Mr A. told us if we missed our first train back there was another soon after and it wouldn't matter. I don't know if this was his idea of humour but the second train never stopped and we were stranded till 6.45. Had tea at gamekeeper cottage by roadside. Home 8. Coolness.

(This suggests that Kathleen and Frank were already being talked about as a pair of sweethearts, and that Mr. A. therefore thought it would be a good joke to strand them out in the country, alone together. The coolness must have been in Maud Greenway's behavior when they arrived back, late for dinner.)

September 11. To Hallington, where there are some reservoirs in a wild open sort of country. Here Maud and C. fished after a picnic lunch and left Mr Isherwood and I to sketch. We found a long low ivy-covered house with a terrace and a very gay little garden. We asked the old man if we might sketch it. The old man gave me a large bunch of flowers. The sketches were never finished.

September 12. Mr Isherwood left, returning to York via Durham. To meet Mama at 11.23 from Carlisle. She arrived so done up after her awful journey from Scotland that she decided to stay the night.

Next day, Kathleen left with Emily for Bamburgh, where she found this letter from Frank waiting for her:

I got your wire on getting back here, my dear one, and will do as you wish about writing to your Mother. I hope she will be all right tomorrow and able to travel. Perhaps you would have time to write to me when you get to Bamburgh, just a line. I have thought out such a diplomatic letter, not 'dragging you in' at all, and have tried to remember all day that you have still got to see what I look like when you get back home. I travelled with a bride and bridegroom tonight. Isn't that a good omen? I wonder where . . . we shall go. Ever your Frank.

From Frank, September 14, York:

I have just sealed up the momentous letter, to your Mother. I kept it three days and thought it read rather well, I hope she will think so too, I am sure. It seems so absurd to feel frightened of her, of all people. I am so glad you are coming to York. I want to have a talk with you so badly. I have done nothing but scheme and devise things since I saw you but none of my schemes seem to amount to very much or bring any promise of great wealth.

September 15. [At Bamburgh.] Read out loud to Mama till tea. After, it cleared a little and there was a marvellous stormy sky and the most glorious red and purple sunset. This is wonderfully fascinating country and the quaintest seaside I ever saw, with its mighty 'rock-based castle', the village street with its queer little houses and bushes of fuschia, the forest of trees at the top of street with rookery and the grey deserted-looking church and the raised monument to Grace Darling in the graveyard that the sailors can see from the water. Mama and I very happy here. She wrote today to ———, in answer to his letter.

(This last sentence is one of Kathleen's many mysterious reticences. Why can't she say straight out whom Emily is writing to? Can this be simply caution? Emily is in the secret already, so Kathleen can only be afraid that her diary may be read by Frederick, which seems most improbable. And then, if Kathleen is really so cautious, how can one explain all her indiscreet references to The Child? Is it caution or a kind of coyness which makes her go on referring to Frank as Mr. Isherwood or F.B.I., although they are practically engaged?

Quite aside from caution or coyness, Kathleen always enjoyed veiled allusions and elaborate circumlocutions for their own sake, and sometimes she employed them with brilliant irony. For example, during the Second World War, when the government warned citizens to be tight-lipped for security reasons, Kathleen responded hyperobediently; in her letters to Christopher in America she stopped using the word war *altogether. On one occasion, after telling him that she had been to a wedding, she added, "Owing to the political situation, there was a large hole in the roof of the church." This delighted Christopher so much that he repeated it to Auden, thereby inspiring the opening lines of "Advent: Two" in* For the Time Being:

> *If, on account of the political situation,*
> *There are quite a number of homes without roofs . . .)*

September 19. The day was pronounced fit for the drive to Holy Isle. At 10.15 we were all ready but it seems only a dog-cart can go across the sands, at sight of which conveyance Mama flatly refused to go! Read the paper after lunch. It looks as if now there

must be war in South Africa and troops are being despatched.
Kruger won't give in.

(*This is Kathleen's first reference to the South African crisis,
though it had existed for several months already. Kruger wanted
a completely independent Boer republic, with the British and
other resident nationals as second-class citizens. He meant to
dominate South Africa. So did the British. Both sides were in a
mood to fight. The Boers despised the British Army and felt sure
they could drive it into the sea; at worst, they were confident
that the European powers would never permit their defeat. The
British despised the Boers as a lot of thick-witted farmers who
would never be able to transform themselves into organized
soldiers. Furthermore, Joseph Chamberlain negotiated with Kruger on the assumption that he was bluffing and would back down
at the last moment, while Kruger was in fact merely postponing
the clash until he was absolutely ready for it.*)*

September 25. Started for York, which reached about 4. Mr
Isherwood to meet us. Left our things at the Station Hotel and
then to tea at Terry's, after to St Martin church. Past All Saints
On The Pavement, pretty openwork steeple designed by Sir
Christopher Wren. Holy Trinity, saddleback tower, old high
pews and 'three deckers', very musty. Through The Shambles,
odd little narrow street. Mr Isherwood to dine. Sat in hall after.
Talk in long corridor with orange and blue carpet. Fire in room
in evening and to bed depressed.

September 26. Down at 10 and found Mr Isherwood waiting for
us. To Minster. To Guildhall. Smugglers Passage down to river,
very old, very cold, had 'sensible' conversation in it. Mr Isherwood
saw us off by the 4.50, reached London about 8.45.

*The sensible conversation and Kathleen's depression must have
been about Frank's lack of money and the consequently dim
prospects of their getting married soon. All this doesn't seem to*

have upset Kathleen very much, however, for next day she writes:
"Put away and rearranged some of my things and felt extremely
pleased with my room, and with London, and contented gen-
erally!" No doubt she was content to enjoy the status quo of her
relationship with Frank for a while—its relative secrecy, its ro-
mantic vagueness, its freedom from obligations and definite com-
mitments. She had no cause, yet, to worry about his safety. As his
letters show, he still wasn't expecting to be sent to South Africa:

The war is the great topic here; we have all got little schemes
in connection with it. Mine is to do the Army Service Corps work
in their absence in the Transvaal at five shillings a day. Five
shillings a day is seven pounds ten a month, with which I shall
pay all sorts of bills etc and generally hasten the millennium. Is
that sensible?

Kathleen evidently found it a little too sensible. She doesn't
want Frank to get hurt, but she does want to be able to think of
him as heroic; after all, he is a soldier. She must have betrayed
this feeling in a letter, for Frank replies, "I didn't altogether like
your assuming that I chose to go into an office instead of going to
the 'Seat of War'. I never had a chance of the latter and there was
no alternative to the five shillings for bill-paying."
Meanwhile, they exchanged photographs. Frank writes:

I have got a gold frame with a sort of curly pattern round it
for the fancy dress one. *Very good* and *very expensive;* and for
the small ones a real leather dark green one—your colour, dark
glossy green like the leaves of a jasmine. . . . Your photograph is
looking so good-tempered that I begin to think you couldn't be
annoyed about anything. But I know you can. Don't I? Of course
I am delighted to send you my photograph, and I had one waiting
for you to ask for it. (I am rather like a woman in many ways,
you know.)

October 10. *Boer Ultimatum* requesting us to withdraw troops
and not allow those on the high seas to land, etc, within 24 hours.

74

In event of no satisfactory reply being received within that interval the Transvaal will regard the action of Her Majesty's Government as a formal declaration of war.

October 11. The Boer Ultimatum is of course a declaration of war and the 24 hours ends at 5 p.m. today, when war may begin any time. The whole country seems in favour of it and the Boer partisans and those who have tried to hold meetings in favour of peace have been simply unable to get the public to listen to them.

The next day, Kathleen got a note from Frank's Mother, who was then staying in Suffolk and would be returning to Marple by way of London on October 18. Elizabeth Isherwood was a gentle anxious little woman, shy in manner and capable of strong affection. When one considers that she is writing as a prospective mother-in-law to a girl whom she hasn't yet set eyes on, the simplicity and friendliness of her tone seem beautiful:

Dear Miss Machell-Smith, my son Frank tells me that you kindly say you will meet me in Town on my way home? It is so good of you and I shall like very much to see you. I hope my plans may not be inconvenient to you but I am afraid a drive from Liverpool Street to St Pancras will not be the least attractive and I feel rather ashamed to propose meeting you in that way. Would you like to meet me St Pancras at 1 o'clock as I should get there about that time and we could lunch together? If the day I mention is inconvenient, which I am afraid it *may* be to you, I shall hope for the pleasure of meeting you another time.

The meeting took place and was a success. Kathleen wisely went out of her way to secure this inconspicuous but important ally; she met Elizabeth at Liverpool Street, crossed London with her, lunched with her and saw her off from St. Pancras. A few days later Frank reported:

My Mother has been telling me how kind you were and how nice and how handsome etc and you've made quite a conquest of her and I think she thoroughly sympathizes with me. I never can realize that you need sympathy too. Or do you?

Frank keeps probing like this, and at the same time trying to reveal himself to Kathleen:

One gets a tired feeling, is it worth going on at all—when one has no one to tell one that it is. I suppose I'm dreadfully wanting in self-reliance. But if one has an alter ego to tell one that it is, what a joy and a help that must be!

Kathleen seems to have been a bit suspicious of this alter-ego role. She refused to be a mere uncritical reassurer. In fact, she must have reproved him for conceit, for he protests:

I think you might know me a little better than you do. My high opinion of myself is so very skin-deep and not always even that. But I suppose when all is said and done we do know very little of one another. Letter-writing is *the* way, I feel certain. A thing seems to go for so much when one writes it and one can write things which one couldn't—with that extraordinary shyness about one's feelings which one has even with one's nearest—say. Is there anybody in the world you could say just anything to? I am so used to having my own private thoughts and interests and feelings that I really can't realize the bliss of having an alter ego to share all one's feelings and tastes. I suppose though I should never find a woman to share all my feelings about everything. The war for instance: will you be very angry? I couldn't help roaring over your little bit of . . . ? about it. I don't think of the horrors at all. We have a small detachment of mounted infantry out there. Altogether there are five, all of them pushing officers who have managed to scheme their way out there. I don't suppose any more of us will manage it. Personally I am not going to try. I should like very much to go with my regiment, all the fellows I know best, but couldn't face a lot of strangers. I haven't got a good enough opinion of myself, you see! This letter's all about myself,

I'm afraid. My 'late correspondent' used to say it was the most interesting topic to write about. I wonder if you think so. This isn't self-conceit because I don't mean myself but oneself—but of course you'll understand.

This passage gives us a glimpse of Frank in his feline aspect. Badly as he needs an alter ego, he won't let Kathleen criticize him and get away with it. So, after a touchingly boyish confession of loneliness, which must surely soften her up, he administers a sudden sharp smack of his paw, reminding her that she is a woman and therefore incapable of understanding War. What he calls Kathleen's "little bit of . . . ?" must refer to some emotional phrase in her letter which strikes him as laughably insincere or an echo of newspaper heroics. (If he had been writing eighty years later, in our own forthright epoch, he would probably have called it "your little bit of shit.") There is a second, softer paw-smack in the last sentence, it seems. Isn't "but of course you'll understand" said sarcastically? Kathleen's assumption that he prefers five shillings a day to fighting in the Transvaal still rankles, for he finds it necessary to explain his attitude again—and this time he gives a different explanation.

Frank's "late correspondent" was an Irish authoress who was soon to become a distinguished figure in the London literary world. He had met her while he was stationed in Ireland, shortly after joining the Regiment, in the early eighteen-nineties. She was a few years older than he was. Frank had nicknamed her "Venus" for reasons unknown. Certainly she wasn't beautiful in the manner of a love goddess, but she could well be described as fascinating, with her cat face, her round luminous naughty eyes and her soft melodious mocking voice. Her conversation sounded like Henry James dialogue and contained many French words; her wit was Irish and sometimes surprisingly coarse. When Kathleen finally met Venus, years later, she was repelled by her cigarette smoking and said that it seemed to make her drunk. Christopher, as a small boy, was fascinated by it. Venus smoked as the women of that period smoked, with an exquisitely sophisticated inter-

77

weaving of sinuous gestures, never allowing you to forget for an instant the presence of the cigarette, the emblem of this daring delicious vice.

On October 22 Frank writes:

I had a letter yesterday from 'the late correspondent' saying that she found that everything was a mistake and that she was wrong in feeling that Platonic friendship was impossible. I feel that it's very possible with her and was very glad to write and tell her so.

Kathleen's comment on this in her diary is: "Heard that the 'Late Correspondent' thinks she was wrong and that Platonics are possible, etc. So of course know that will end."

On the surface, the meaning of all this seems obvious: Venus and Frank have found their correspondence becoming increasingly less Platonic and more romantic; so Venus has told him that, since they can't be lovers and can't be Platonic friends, they had better stop writing to each other. There has been a break in their letter-writing, which is why Frank calls her "the late." Now, however, Venus has decided that Platonic letters are better than no letters; probably her ultimatum was just a bluff, anyway, to see if she couldn't make Frank declare that he is in love with her. Kathleen, with feminine cynicism, refuses to believe that Venus will be able to keep up the Platonics; she'll start getting romantic again.

What Frank writes about Venus in his next letter contradicts this view, however. And Venus herself, when she talked about Frank to Christopher twenty-five years later, would always insist that they had never been more than friends (though she did archly call Christopher their spiritual son). So it seems probable that Frank was just playing up Venus a little as a romantic threat in order to make Kathleen jealous and therefore more interested in him. But Frank lacks the kind of boldness shown by The Child or Mr. L. He is now afraid he may have gone too far and hastens to reassure Kathleen:

. .

I don't think you need mind about the other Correspondent. She is so totally a correspondent, a person (almost unknown as a person) who writes letters and books which appeal to me. Her views of everyday life I don't like a bit. I wouldn't say this to anyone but you, my alter ego. As she has influenced me so much I shall always have a deep feeling for her, just as I have for Walt Whitman or George Eliot or Wagner.

Venus' views of everyday life were indeed not such as would appeal to Frank or to Kathleen. It is doubtful if Frank ever knew how drastically she condemned the British for fighting the Boers. She once shocked and delighted Christopher by remarking nonchalantly, "At least you can be thankful Frank wasn't killed in that war—as bad as having your father shot while he was robbing a house."

November 1. Very bad war news. Disaster to a column of troops sent by Sir G. White from Ladysmith.

November 2. It seems from papers today that the mules with ammunition took fright and made away, leaving our men with only their bayonets and so more or less helpless. It is thought the Boers managed to scare the mules in some way to bring about this result.

Under the influence of the British press, which was already reporting atrocities (such as Boer soldiers advancing under a flag of truce and then opening fire) Kathleen has accepted the suggestion that all the enemy's military moves are treacherous, unfair, diabolical, etc. She obviously feels that the scaring of the mules was not quite cricket. Another day, she writes that "our men haven't a chance against these Boers who are all entrenched and fire out upon them"!

November 10. Heard that the Bury and Ampton Balls are put off on account of the War but that they are going to give a little dance at Nether instead on the 16th. Heard also Mr Isherwood will *not* be able to go there for it. They are to be mobilized on

Saturday and all leave stopped. It is *simply sickening* and I hope every Boer in the country will be killed.

On November 12, Frank wrote to Kathleen:

We don't know when we shall go but we shall begin to mobilize tomorrow. My Mother is going to ask you if you could join her at the Station Hotel here on Saturday next for a night or two. Do come if you possibly can. Otherwise I don't see when I can see you.

November 14. Discussion as to York. Mama very unhappy over it and Papa most disapproving. So had to give it up, though can see *no* reason for not going, myself. Felt cross and virtuous.

On hearing of this decision, Frank writes: "I don't like your Father at all, so there."
Kathleen left for Nether Hall the next day. While there, she got this letter from Emily:

Darling Kath, I do indeed feel *most strongly* that I am right about York, or you may be very sure I should *never* have gone against your wishes—for to do this costs me almost as much as your disappointment does you; indeed I have thought of little else and didn't get to sleep till 5 a.m. this morning. It is, I know, very *hard* for you, dear, still going appears to me so very compromising—no mother would think of asking a girl to come unless she felt quite sure that girl was engaged to and in love with her son, not a great friend only. It isn't as if you had been asked to Marple, but to an hotel. My own dear love, do do believe that I am acting entirely for what I believe to be the best for my own one darling Lamb. If you were really deeply in love for the first time, it would be quite different, but you are not and you might regret, oh so deeply, compromising and binding yourself in the hurry of the moment, stirred up to do so because he was going away. I must end or I shall miss the post, so with boundless love but *unshaken* conviction, rightly or wrongly, that I am *right*, always your loving Mum.

Emily's pathos, endearments and italics give her away; she knows her position is false and she is frightened.

Since Frank visited them at Oxford in August, Emily has shown him every mark of favor and has tacitly encouraged the romance. How can she write this nonsense about Kathleen compromising herself by going to York and staying with Elizabeth Isherwood at a hotel? Emily knows perfectly well that Kathleen is compromised already, even if she doesn't love Frank, for she has made Frank and Elizabeth think that she does. Emily must also know that Frank is not the sort of young man who would try to hold a girl to a promise she didn't want to keep.

When Emily and Kathleen returned to London at the end of September, Emily evidently felt she was obliged to tell Frederick about Frank. Why? Obviously because there was some kind of understanding between Frank and Kathleen. Perhaps also because Kathleen insisted on his being told; which in itself would prove that her intentions were serious. Nevertheless, in breaking the news to Frederick, Emily must have minimized it; otherwise Frederick would have made far more fuss than he did.

Now, at the moment of crisis, Emily is simply playing for time. She declares as emphatically as she can that Kathleen doesn't love Frank, hoping that Kathleen will come to believe her and gradually forget Frank while he is away. Caught between Frederick and Kathleen, Emily has lost her nerve and made the wrong choice; instead of defecting to Frederick she should have remained loyal to the lovers. This would have been not only more courageous but more prudent. Frederick, in the last resort, can only rage and roar. But suppose that Kathleen and Frank are prevented from seeing each other before he leaves, and that he goes to South Africa and is killed? May not Kathleen then blame Emily and hate her for the rest of her life? Emily must see this possibility already. That is why she is frightened.

But Emily is lucky. Frank puts all the blame on Frederick and writes generously about Emily to Kathleen, thus encouraging Kathleen to forgive her: "I wouldn't on any account be a cause of any unpleasant feeling between you and your Mother, to

*whom I feel so deeply grateful. I know she wants to do her best
for me as well as for you." Then, on November 25, Frank manages to get one night's leave and comes down to London. Kathleen
writes about this with her usual reticence and one has to remind
oneself that, under the proper circumstances, togetherness in a
teashop or on top of a bus can be just as exciting and memorable,
if not as satisfying, as in a forest or a bed.*

November 25. Mama and I to Haymarket where we met Mr
Isherwood, lunched and he and I to see 'The Royal Family' in
afternoon, very pretty piece. Tea at the South Kensington Museum and home to dinner.

November 26. Frightfully muggy. Mr Isherwood and self on
bus to St Paul's. After, he and I to lunch at Hotel d'Italie and
walked across St James's Park to Tate Gallery. Found it closed
but said to open at 4, so on bus to Peckham to pass the time. Alas
on our return discovered board stating that only till October was
it open on Sunday. Home to tea and to see Miss Robins after.
Mr Isherwood left at 10.30, arriving York 3 a.m.

*It is to be noted that Frank and Kathleen had their farewell
lunch at the supposedly unsuitable Hotel d'Italie (see April 15,
1898). Was this a last little gesture of defiance? Miss Robins was
an elderly lady who had one of the other flats in Cranley Mansion.
She had shown great interest in their love affair and was therefore
regarded by Frank as being a favorable influence on Emily, whom
she often visited.*

*Although Kathleen's diary doesn't mention Frederick, he was
certainly present when Frank came to the flat, for Frank writes,
just after his return to York:*

I am at last sending you the eight shillings I owe you for the
theatre tickets. I hadn't an opportunity of settling up on Sunday
under your Father's eagle eye! I was not quite sure whether he
meant to snub me heavily when I left, or not, by saying 'good-
night' instead of 'goodbye'.

There was more to the situation than a snub, however. Frederick and Frank must have had a serious private conversation that day. In a letter written sometime in January 1901, Frederick claims that Frank assured him, before leaving England, that there was no engagement and that nothing would be done without informing him. Even if Frank did say this, he was prevaricating rather than lying, since the engagement wasn't a formal one according to the conventions of that period. But Frederick's letter and its implications must be discussed later, in its proper place.

Frank to Kathleen, December 2:

This is *the* most unsettling week we have had and almost impossible to write in. Today we have been inspected by the General and to lead up to that there was a week of hard work, getting the men into their clothes, etc. Mrs H is very amusing. She implored me not to go near any wounded Boers—it was so dangerous —and was quite plaintive because her Son's coat was made of a different stuff to ours. She seemed to think the Boers would spot the difference at once and shoot him for it.

December 7:

I have been playing the piano hard today, laying in a stock of memories. I think you realize the advantages of art and culture (horrid word) more than usual when you are left to your own devices.

December 12:

I haven't had time to write you a word, and now I've written ten bills and cheques, after having inspected everything in my Company and packed all my things and seen my piano downstairs. My piano nearly turned turtle over the bannisters, imagine my feelings. I turned away. I really could not look. After two minutes of absolute agony I heard the pound of castors on the level floor and I breathed again. I hope you will write to me *very* often. And when you do write, please put a thin paper and envelope into your letter, and at any rate I shall have something to write *on*. I expect we shall go now to Port Elizabeth and go up country from there.   Goodbye, F.B.I.

December 13. The last of the Fifth Division embarked today. The York and Lancaster on the big White Star Line *Majestic* from Liverpool. It is expected to do a record passage and arrive about the 28th.

Frank appears with four other officers in a photograph taken earlier that year. They are in dress uniform, with white gloves, spiked helmets, tasseled sashes and swords, and they are standing on the entrance steps of a building. Only the colonel wears medals and has spurs on his boots. He has been posed in profile, gazing off scene and ignoring everybody, with his hand on his sword; he looks like an antique waxwork, put there to show why the Boers think the British Army is a joke. The captain is a waxwork figure, too, but a more up-to-date one; he holds a cigarette between his fingers. (This is Captain Cobbold, who will reappear as a colonel near the end of Frank's story.) In the background are two second lieutenants, clean-shaven youths with quite human modern faces; one has flap ears, the other is beefy but handsome, both hold themselves erect and square-shouldered, very conscious of their military status. By contrast, Frank's attitude as he leans against a pillar is relaxed and casual, disrespectfully so, considering that he is in the presence of two senior officers. His fancy uniform and absurd helmet seem to amuse him; he may actually be grinning, underneath his thick moustache.

This picture—together with others which show the men doing physical drill, being medically inspected or parading for church—was later published to illustrate an article on the York and Lancaster Regiment in the Illustrated Sporting and Dramatic News *of May 5, 1900. Its editor comments: "Since the photographs were taken, too many of the brave fellows pictured have fallen."*

5

Frank embarked in the middle of what was soon to be called "Black Week." Between December 10 and 16, 1899, three British generals in three separate combat areas met spectacular defeat with heavy casualties: Gatacre at Stormberg, Methuen at Magersfontein, Buller at Colenso. In each case, the defeat was due to gross military mistakes, not bad luck; and this disaster was made even more humiliating by the fact that other British forces had already been trapped by the Boers in three towns, Mafeking, Kimberley and Ladysmith, where they were now under siege without any immediate hope of rescue.

In most European countries, the Anglophobe majority greeted the news with virtuous vicious glee; in the United States, certain senators expressed righteous wrath and demanded intervention against the British. (All these were secure in the knowledge that their governments would do nothing dangerous to help the Boers.) In England, newspapers attacked the Enemy for dirty fighting, the Government for incompetence and the antiwar Opposition for treason. It was one of those crises in which every political attitude seems ultimately dishonest, and Kathleen, like nearly all her fellow newspaper readers, was tossed about in a storm of conflicting reactions.

December 16. More depressing news. Buller, on whom we had been depending, *has failed* with severe losses on the banks of the

Tugela. The War Office and the Generals are being tremendously censured. They say the Generals have no tactics, do not know the country and have rushed into needless danger with great sacrifice of life. Our men have fought splendidly.

December 17. My patriotism wavers sadly and the loss of all these men seems an awful price to pay for England's glory. They say defeat means the downfall of the Empire. Even that does not seem to be so terrible as this slaughter. I feel as if those who have gone never would come back, and is it worth it?

December 18. Felt horribly depressed, but the news this morning of Lord Roberts and Kitchener's appointment is very cheering and most popular. Poor Lord Roberts, the death of his only son is announced at Colenso on Friday. Lunched with Hilda, who takes my view of the war. Mama is very down on me for such sentiments!

(Lord Roberts was now being made commander in chief in South Africa, with Kitchener as his chief of staff. For the public it was a magic mating of power-figures: the tiny legendary hero of the Indian campaigns with the big modern administrator of the Sudan. Roberts deeply moved the crowds who came to watch him sail from Southampton, by wearing civilian black, instead of uniform, in mourning for his son Fred. Fred was posthumously decorated for his bravery at Colenso. He won the Victoria Cross; as his father had, forty years earlier.)

On December 21, Kathleen and Emily went down to the Isle of Wight again, to stay at Ventnor. Kathleen's diary notes that Emily's first concern, on arriving at their lodgings, was to have all the furniture rearranged, "as usual!"

December 26. Damp depressing day, cold and drizzle later. Those poor things at the Convalescent Home were sitting out in their little wooden sheds all today, and when I ran out to post letters just before dinner there they still were, each with a dismal little light in the cold night air.

On December 28, Kathleen got a letter from Frank, written on board the Majestic *and mailed to her from St Vincent in the Cape Verde Islands:*

This boat is quite beautifully got up, oak everywhere and lovely friezes and dadoes in beautiful designs. I sit and revel in them because my artistic instincts are rather likely to starve in the next few months. I am feeling dreadfully unsociable though. The amount of talk that goes on about nothing at all is perfectly astonishing. I have done a lot of reading. Oh, bye the bye, didn't your Mother tell me that I was like the man in The Egoist (I am wading through that as I know she said I ought to read it) but I do hope I don't strike her like that. I feel much more like the man in Frederic's 'Gloria Mundi' and there is something in the girl which seems like you. Perhaps because they had lunch at a restaurant together. The weather makes it impossible to picture England and Christmas and all that sort of thing. The sea a lovely dark blue and the sky a lovely light one. Last night there was a beautiful sunset which I tried to paint without much success, and tonight there are little clouds all round the horizon with a mysterious pinkish dusky background.

(Christian Tower, the hero of Harold Frederic's novel, belongs to an aristocratic English family but feels himself a stranger in England because he has spent his early life abroad. He is slender, boyish and sensitive but capable of unexpectedly courageous actions. Frederic writes of him that he had "the terrible boldness of the timid person . . . innocent and complicated, full of confidence in a stranger but his doubts about his own values were distressing." Christian is looking for an "ideal relationship" with a woman. Maybe Frank's feeling of identification with him was strengthened by the fact that the heroine of Gloria Mundi *is called Frances!)*

December 31. And so ends 1899, with much trouble and bloodshed in front of us, I fear. The *Majestic* reached Cape Town
yesterday after a passage of 17 days and left for Durban.

*(During the Boer War, the existence of the telegraph and the
nonexistence of the airplane created a huge gap between public
and private communication which must have made the anxiety of
lovers and relatives acutely painful. You could read about a
battle in your London newspaper the day after it was fought,
thanks to the telegraph, but letters from South Africa had to
travel by train and boat. Frank's letters will be quoted from on
the dates when they were written, but it must be remembered
that they didn't reach Kathleen until nearly a month later.)*

1900. January 3. Windy and Rain. Review in *Fortnightly* for
November of *The Letters of Mary Sibylla Holland*, delightful
extracts. Description of the primroses and lambs which to her
old Aunts were not real but 'only reminded them of the real
lambs of fifty or sixty or seventy years ago'!

*Letter from Frank, written on January 6, from camp at Est-
court, Natal:*

We have got up here within twenty miles of Colenso, which
can be seen from the hill in front of the camp and from which we
can hear the guns firing, and yet it's quite ridiculous how do-
mesticated one feels. As to realizing that we really are on active
service and within twenty miles of the enemy, it's absolutely impossible. The rumour is that we are to make a flank march and
get round the Boers' right. Probably by the time you get this you
will have seen all about it in the paper. I expect it means some
hard marching and a bit of a fight. There is such a lot to do settling into a camp, to get things in train. What I have seen of
South Africa has been rather fascinating, much better than I
expected. Cape Town I didn't land at, but Table Bay with the

great flat-topped mountain towering above is very fine. Durban is rather pretty from the sea. There is a long low hill covered with bungalows and trees along the harbour. We had lunch at a hotel where we were waited upon by the most delightful dignified Hindoos in white clothes and jewelled pink sashes. The Blacks are most amusing, always in fits of laughter and enjoying everything so tremendously. Our journey up here was like a royal progress. Everyone within sight of the railway waving flags and pocket handkerchiefs and all the stations crowded with people anxious to give us tea, pineapples, bananas and everything they had. Imagine, some of the men ate four or five pineapples! As you get to Pietermaritzburg you pass through some very fine rocks and get on to open country like the Sussex Downs; that indeed is the sort of thing we have got here, and one feels exactly as if one was on manoeuvers there. In case we are moved off suddenly and I haven't time to write more, goodbye.

(*Frank was now with the forces commanded by Buller. Their first major objective was to raise the siege of Ladysmith, which is less than forty miles from Estcourt, to the north. But the British were still on the south side of the Tugela River; their recent attempt to cross it had resulted in the defeat at Colenso.*)

January 7. [Shanklin, Isle of Wight.] Sat out on the verandah all the morning in the sun reading Adam Bede and the Psalms. Neither at the Old Church or the New did they have special intercessions or war offertories, which by command of the Queen should have been in all churches today throughout the kingdom. But really in this island I doubt if they realize there is a war. There was a war litany but rather a mawkish one.

January 8. Sir George White reported from Ladysmith the enemy attacked early on Saturday morning, they were beaten off but continued and the last telegram announced that he was *very hard pressed*. No more news after.

• •

January 9. Sir George White seems to have been able to hold Ladysmith on Saturday and repulsed Boer attacks, with however considerable losses on his side and heavy ones on the part of the Boers.

January 10. York and Lancaster Regiment said to be at Estcourt. Out with Mama in town and along esplanade.

January 11. Lords Roberts and Kitchener have arrived at the Cape, and *The Standard* says it is expected now that 'order will be gradually evolved out of chaos and the campaign conducted on prudent, intelligent and scientific lines'.

January 13. Very cold. Mama however quite wished to leave and I am delighted to get home again. Bright in London, flat looking nice and Papa had got a lot of flowers for the drawing-room and me a surprise, a *new carpet* for my room.

Letter from Frank, written on January 13, from Springfield (to which Buller was moving his troops in preparation for another attempt to cross the Tugela River):

Your letter brought an atmosphere of England and 'send-offs' and what one might call an 'absent-minded beggar' sort of feeling. You know I never realized that one would be quite out of that here, and it is so supporting to be thought a hero and keeps you up on the hottest day. The heat is the worst enemy we've met so far, but today we are moving up to the Tugela and tomorrow or the day after there will be a fight at Potgieter's, I expect. We are very glad now that we are on this, the Natal side. Originally we were to have been sent to Methuen but the Colenso reverse made them want more troops here. We were very disappointed at first, but there are no flies, no dust and lots of water here, so we are much better off. I am so glad you talk so much about the Army. I'm sure when I get back from here I shall never be able to talk about it. 'Ah, if you'd been in South Africa, etc'.

One always finds people have been somewhere that you haven't and insist upon talking about that.

(Kipling's poem "The Absent-minded Beggar," set to music by Sir Arthur Sullivan, had become one of the theme songs of the war. The "beggars" were the men who had "absent-mindedly" left their families and jobs to join the Army. There was already an Absent-minded Beggar Fund, and Kipling himself came out to South Africa about this time to supervise the distribution to the troops of tobacco, pajamas and other comforts which it had provided. "Potgieter's" is Potgieter's Drift, one of the fords on that part of the Tugela; "Drift" means a river crossing or ford in Afrikaans.)

January 15. Began reading 'Gloria Mundi' by Frederic.

January 17. Mama and E. to see *Midsummer Night's Dream* at Her Majesty's, which they say was simply lovely. Tree most attractive in his white ass's head!

January 19. News last night that the Tugela *has* been crossed in two places, at last.

January 20. To see if there were any fresh telegrams at the War Office. (There is a specially reserved entrance and room for ladies, and telegrams are pinned along the walls inside.) But there was nothing special. To see *A Message from Mars*, a pretty little piece you might take any child to.

January 21. Papa and I walked to the Camera Club. Wonderful exhibition of photos of animals; cats, dogs and poultry etc. News of the fighting yesterday. One man severely wounded of the York and Lancaster, first intimation of where they were, and not a pleasant one. It was over the Tugela, near Acton Homes, at Venter's Spruit.

.   .

January 22. Heard from Mr I, posted at the Cape. Mama and I to Kensington Palace. The part built by Kent not nearly so nice as Wren's building. Saw the Queen's bedroom and the antechamber where she received the ministers in the early morning and was told she was queen. Her toys and nursery also shown.

Letter from Frank, written on January 22, from Venter's Spruit (Afrikaans for stream), Tugela River:

A letter *quite* from the front, in fact written actually under fire. We have fought out first battle, the day before yesterday; at least, we were under very heavy fire for several hours and deployed and careered about without much effect. We had a terribly long morning of waiting, from 3.30 a.m. to about 2 o'clock, under a burning sun—imagine it in January—and then we moved forward under fire and got it pretty hot, 77 killed and wounded. You will of course want to know, was one frightened. Personally as long as I was moving and under the excitement of getting the men together and all that sort of thing, I wasn't in the very least. One had a most 'supporting feeling', as you say, of heroism, but since then we moved on to this valley where we have sat for two days doing nothing and every now and then having shells pitched into us. You can't imagine anything so demoralizing. The awful sinking at one's stomach pit when you hear that nasty buzz, followed by a plomp and a burst. Then there are nasty pieces of shell which wander about and are quite capable of taking one's head off. 'I feel dreadfully sorry for the men, having to lie out doing nothing under fire' is the polite and proper way of putting it, but one's sorrow is mostly for oneself, *really*. Don't be annoyed at the dirtiness of this letter. I am in person exactly like an Italian monk, and when you realize what that means! I wish you could see us cooking such nasty messes as we make on our little fires, and then we all lie down together as close as we can to keep warm and forget our sorrows and discomforts and the fact that we haven't had our boots and puttees off for a week. You see, I'm piling it on to give you that comfortable feeling you like so much. The views of the mountains we have had here and at Springfield have been lovely. Extraordinary great precipices and pointed peaks all tumbled together, and the most varied lights. Sometimes they are a filmy blue, sometimes a dark mysterious purplish colour, just like the 'old master' mountain in fact, both in shape and colour. Saint Jerome would be quite in his proper background against them. This morning just at daybreak there was a rich orange ring in the sky just above them, fading away to primrose, to dark blue and then, far up above one, the southern cross shining faintly. I think the stars at daybreak are so comforting. As the day begins again and the fusillade starts and everything seems so unpleasant, they seem to say 'God's in his heaven, all's right with the world'. I hope this will be decipherable when you get it. I have only had one letter from you so far but we hear that there is a large mail bag down at Frere. I wish we could get it. Frank.

We don't know what's happening, even at Colenso and Pot-gieter's, or where Methuen or Gatacre or Roberts are. I hope the absent beggar's not forgotten. I assure you we are anything but absent-minded.

January 23. Fighting continues, and they are slowly and steadily advancing towards Ladysmith. Discussion as to whether Ruskin, who died on Saturday, should be buried in Westminster Abbey or Coniston as he wished.

January 24. I walked back through Pall Mall, looking in at War Office to see if there was any news. 'No news from South Africa today' the only notice on the board. So whether they have stormed Spion Kop or not is still uncertain. Notice of two more wounded officers in York and Lancasters in Sunday's fight. Ruskin is to be buried at Coniston.

January 25. Great excitement. Spion Kop is taken by Sir C. Warren.

•   •

January 26. Spion Kop abandoned. Why?

Letter from Frank, written from Springfield, January 27:

When we got back to civilization (represented by a clean shirt and one's tooth-powder) again yesterday, I got your two letters, the last from Ventnor. 'We think of you so much' you said, and I can't tell you what a difference it makes to think that you do. I only hope that we shall meet again in this New Year, in that delightful time when I get back and everything is going to be quite different 'somehow'. At any rate, I'm quite 'grown up' now. That week in the valley from where I last wrote to you would have aged anyone—and my beard! I'm not sure whether I should like you to see my beard or not. People say that it improves my appearance, but to my own mind I look like a bush-ranger. You will have seen about our battle in the papers. (This is the way that I always evade military detail.) We had a terrible time in that valley, with every now and then a boom and a rush and a bang and a shell among us. It's absolutely astonishing, though, what very little harm they do. I saw one burst absolutely among a party of men, and no one was touched. On Wednesday there was an attack by our brigade on the hill on the right (we were not in it as we were sent to General Hart for the first show on Saturday) which we watched through our glasses. We could see our people drive the Boers back from their trenches, and then began a terrific fire of shells which literally decimated them. The General and Staff were all wounded or killed and the Twentieth who were in front have only seven officers left, two of whom were slightly wounded. At night they evacuated the hill and the night before last we recrossed the Tugela and came back here, having lost upwards of a thousand men for as far as I can see absolutely nothing. We are exactly as we were a fortnight ago, but they say Buller's pleased so I suppose there's more in it than meets the eye. To my mind, the only thing to do is to hold the Tugela by a comparatively small force and send everyone else round to push on up to Blomfontein and Pretoria. Ladysmith might have to go, but we don't seem to be going to relieve it this way. We move so slowly and the enemy move so quickly that a hundred of them seem to be in two places at once, to hold them against us. Besides which, I am sure we waste time unnecessarily. If we had only attacked the first day we crossed the Tugela, hardly any men and only one gun at most were there. By all which I hope you're not bored to tears.

You can't think how delightful the idea of your lodgings and visit to Ventnor and indeed the whole of your lady's life seems to one, knocking about out here. Not that I am unhappy in the least or feeling anything but glad (at least, glad isn't the right word) to be out here; but when you're wet through and bivouacing, or sitting down to a tin of bully beef for dinner, having already had the same for breakfast and tea, it's rather refreshing to think of Miss Robins (for instance) and imagine her atmosphere of Beethoven and refinement. I am always surprising myself thinking tenderly of all sorts of extraordinary people in their comfortable home lives. An old Aunt of mine, who used to give us tea when we were schoolboys at Cheltenham, almost made me cry the other day!

I'm afraid, you know, I'm not really built for a warrior, it's all very well, this knocking about and of course has a great many compensations, but these are not really the things which lie on my 'soul side'. Poor Bradshaw, who was killed the other day, was quite different; it was his meat and drink. His letters were full of his skirmishes and fightings and everything appealed to his sense of humour, and his idea of bliss was active service. That's the style of man that appeals to most people, I think—even to the other sort of man himself. Do you remember in *Trilby* that little Billee, 'young Greek that he was', couldn't understand Trilby being in love with him and not with the other sort of man, Taffy or The Laird.

Pictures . . . I wish I could see some. To go to a gallery with one's mind quite fresh from 'outside things', what a chance of rare impressions. I think generally when one goes one feels it's just the moment when one *can't* appreciate. Mrs D. shall have my khaki coat to paint on. I'm sure it's been saturated enough with everything, water from the heavens and tea, coffee, jam and everything imaginable from earth have gone over it.

(Captain William Bradshaw had been killed in mid-December. He was one of Frank's few close Army friends; indeed, it was in memory of him that Christopher was baptized with the second name of William. Captain Bradshaw wasn't related to Frank's family, however.

Frank's forecast of "some hard marching and a bit of a fight," in his letter of January 6, was no doubt deliberately understated, but he can't have been expecting anything much worse than what actually happened. The march from Estcourt to Springfield (January 9–10) was made wretched by torrential rains and swollen streams, and, since much of it was during the hours of darkness, the men kept stumbling over chuck holes and slithering into gullies. They had to toil continually to drag their cumbersome ox-drawn supply wagons out of the mud. When a halt was ordered, they were so exhausted that they threw themselves on the sodden ground and fell asleep in the downpour.

Writing on January 13, Frank says that they will be moving up from Springfield to the Tugela River next day; actually they didn't leave until January 16. Buller had good reasons for this delay, but it was to cost many casualties, since it gave the Boers much-needed extra time to prepare for the British attack.

All along the northern side of this section of the Tugela there is a range of hills. Here the Boers had taken up their positions. Behind them was the open plain which extends without further natural obstacles almost to Ladysmith. The hills opposite Potgieter's Drift were particularly easy to defend, because of their horseshoe formation, so it was decided by Buller to demonstrate in front of this ford with some guns and troops and meanwhile send the main attacking force to Trichardt's Drift, a few miles upstream to the west, where they would try to turn the enemy's right wing. Two more days were wasted there, however, because the guns and wagons could not use the ferry as the troops did and had to have two bridges built for them. The troops began to cross the river on the morning of January 17, but the York and Lancaster Regiment was in the rear, so it didn't bivouac north of the Tugela until the night of January 19. This was below the heights called Venter's Spruit Hills.

On January 20 they were ordered to advance. Frank's company, Company B, was among those in the first line of attack. They had to work their way upward along rocky ridges under a blazing sun. The enemy fire was so heavy that they could move ahead only in short rushes. The British guns, firing shrapnel to support them, set the grass of the hillside alight, filling the air with thick smoke. After fighting for hours, they reached what they had thought were their objectives, only to find that the Boers were now strongly entrenched beyond them. They were eager to charge these trenches, but permission to do so was refused by their commanding general; frustrated and angry, they had to stay where they were and shoot at the skyline "in hopes," as a regimental historian says sarcastically, "of annoying the Boers behind the hill." Meanwhile, reinforcements were moved up to join them, until their positions were uncomfortably crowded and became bigger and better targets. Some of the troops actually found themselves in a crossfire between the two sides. And now the fierce sunshine was followed by heavy showers and a bitterly cold night, throughout which they had nothing to drink but an issue of rum and nothing to eat at all.

The Regiment's casualties for that day were ten killed and seventy-three wounded. (It will be noted that these, the official figures, are higher than those given in Frank's letter.) During the next four days, thirty-two more were wounded and two died of their wounds. Yet the Regiment was comparatively lucky: it was not involved in the disastrous attempt to occupy Spion Kop. The British attacked the hill on the night of January 23–24 and were forced to evacuate it twenty-four hours later after twelve hundred men had been killed or wounded. On January 25, the troops in other parts of the battleground received the news, incredulously at first, that they were defeated and ordered to withdraw. By the morning of January 27 they were all south of the Tugela once again; the sole success Buller could claim was that they had re-crossed it without losing anybody or anything else.)

January 28. The evening paper states (official) that Spion Kop is abandoned and Sir C. Warren has retreated to the south side of Tugela without further loss of men. But it means that the five days fighting has practically been in vain, more lives lost for nothing and we no nearer Ladysmith.

January 30. Lists of killed and wounded at Spion Kop, a greater number of officers killed there than at either Magersfontein or at Colenso, 29 in all. Mama and I to lecture on Italian Painters, the pupils and followers of Giotto in the Fourteenth Century. Interesting.

January 31. No official news, but one of the special correspondents of the *Daily Mail* reports Buller addressed his men saying they would be in Ladysmith *within a week*—and this after that awful reverse too. He must be mad or drunk, probably the latter, from all accounts of him.

(Buller certainly was apt to make rash statements and he did have a reputation for hard drinking, perhaps exaggerated. Kathleen hated him simply because she saw him as an incompetent commander who held Frank's life in his hands. Buller's poor judgment may have lost many lives, but it was his determination not to lose more which made him withdraw from the Spion Kop battle when he might well have fought on to a costly victory. It has never been denied that he was a brave man who shared the hardships of the campaign with his troops and was extraordinarily popular with them, despite his tactical errors.)

February 7. We went to Albert Hall, box. A large patriotic concert. Chorus of 800 voices and Madame Albani, Edward Lloyd etc. Mrs Pat Campbell recited *The Women of Britain*. Songs nearly all patriotic.

February 8. The Irish seem to have been making themselves ridiculous in the House over the War and suggesting it was time it came to an end and we made peace! Horrible as it all is, I don't think even I desire that. Buller has made his third effort and is across the Tugela again (on Monday 5th). Oh for better luck. The first list of casualties out in the afternoon paper but one hardly dares read them.

February 10. Buller has had to retire across the Tugela again.

Letter from Frank, written February 10, Spearman's Hill: (From this position, south of the Tugela, the British could see the ridge of Spion Kop across the river.)

Have you ever longed to be a gypsy? I've read George Borrow and sympathized with his vagrancy and love of knocking about— and do you know, now that I am a wanderer and go to sleep under the sky, I long for it sometimes more than ever, to have a little cart and a little tent beside it and wander about from countryside to countryside at your own sweet will, not with a train of soldiers. Don't you think it would be heavenly or does your love of "things" come in your way?

It's wonderful what a lot of things you can do without when you are put to it. I have three stages: the utterly destitute, when you have nothing but what you carry on your back (and very little in my case, my back's such a weak one), the well-to-do, when you have a bundle weighing twenty pounds, consisting of a blanket and a coat and a change and a tin of cocoa, and the affluent, when you have thirtyfive pounds with all your goods, Shakespeare, books to read. Even at my worst, I always carry my knitting! It's such a resource. We sat out the other day in a horrible wood, destitute of shade. Everyone else tried to sleep and were devoured by ants, but I knitted knitted on a pair of socks to march into Ladysmith! The irony of it—the very next day we retired and are again behind the Tugela. We were not the front in this last expedition so did not lose heavily. We were under fire for about four hours one day and were very pleased with the way our new men behaved. We had just got a draft from the 3rd Battalion out.

Since writing I have got your letter. I am afraid your love of "things" makes the cart out of the question for you. Or would a "Mrs Jarley" sort of home content you?

If a Boer patrol appears on the hills ten miles away, we fall in and stand for hours. The Boers seem to know when it's just meal-time and always manage to appear.

(Mrs Jarley is a Dickens character in The Old Curiosity Shop. *She lives in a caravan, but a very neat one, with curtains in the windows.)*

Letter from Frank: (Kathleen has sent him the paper on which it is written. To encourage him to date it, she herself has written: "Date . . . 1900" and, underneath, "One of my very annoying ways!" Frank is referring to this at the beginning of his letter. He has filled in the dotted line with "Feb. 17?"; the question mark is maybe merely to tease her.)

It is in the worst possible taste certainly but not *in the least* annoying!! In fact I don't think anything from you *could* annoy me at present. There's a pretty speech! I have just got your letter with the pen and ink sketch of Ventnor in it. I am not quite sure whether the mails are an unmitigated blessing. They *do* upset one's equanimity. Yesterday I had made up my mind that I was contented with South Africa.

Last time I wrote 1 quite forgot to say how thankful I should be for artistic papers. My people said they were going to send *The Artist* and *The Studio* and all sorts of delightful unlikely things, but I have never seen them.

I know your starved feeling all among new things so well.

Never come to the Colonies if you don't want a bad attack of it. I can't sketch here a bit. For a painter of old houses, South Africa is as naught. I have tried some of the hills, which *we* are making historic, but the candid remarks of my brother officers about them are thoroughly well deserved. 'Them' here means my sketches, though I own the grammar is bad and the hills get and deserve some candid remarks too.

February 21. The official news this morning states that Buller occupies Colenso and the Tugela has been crossed for the fourth time.

February 25. With Miss Robins at 9.30 to War Office. We wanted to hear about Major B, where he died. He died at Wynberg Hospital, no further information till the mail, 3 weeks hence. Frightfully sad, he started so full of hope, the same day Mr Isherwood did. Felt very unhappy and depressed.

February 26. Mama and I to see 'She Stoops to Conquer', very amusing. Miss Emery and Mr Maude in it. Enjoyed going with Mama but do not feel at all in a theatre spirit. More casualties from Buller in afternoon. Why doesn't he reach Ladysmith???

February 27. *Capitulation of Cronje,* an unconditional surrender. From Lord Roberts to Secretary of War: 'Paardeberg 27th Feb, 7.45 a.m. General Cronje and all his force capitulated unconditionally at daylight this morning and is now a prisoner in my camp. I hope Her Majesty's Government will consider this event satisfactory, occurring as it does on the Anniversary of Majuba.' Revenge at last. London wildly delighted.

The capitulation was one of the first of many successes which Roberts would now achieve on his drive eastward into the Orange Free State and northward into the Transvaal. This flank attack on the Boers was the main operation of the War. Ladysmith—"the terrible old lady," as the soldiers called it—was an unimportant objective strategically speaking, but the British press had made it a national prestige-symbol, so Buller had to keep trying to relieve it. The men of the York and Lancasters were involved in two more of his attempts.

After the regiment had recrossed the Tugela on January 27, it was joined by a draft of men from the Third Battalion, just arrived from England. Frank refers to them in his letter of February 10, but he does not mention a more remarkable addition to the ranks, a liver-and-white pointer dog which was later named Pompom. Pom-pom joined them at Venter's Spruit, during the battle of Spion Kop; probably he had strayed from some farmhouse in the neighborhood which the owners had abandoned. When under fire, he barked at the shells and darted and snapped at the bullets as they struck the ground; his absurd fearlessness delighted the men. Thereafter he became the regimental mascot.

Buller's next plan of attack was to break through to Ladysmith by way of Vaalkrantz, a ridge to the east of Spion Kop, after crossing the Tugela at a ford called Munger's Drift. At the same time, a smaller force was to cross at Potgieter's and make the Boers reveal the positions of their guns by drawing their fire. The York and Lancasters were to be part of this feint.

They crossed according to plan on February 3 and occupied three kopjes, on which they remained throughout the rest of that day and the next, enduring great heat and the discomfort of being crowded together. An eyewitness comments that the time was passed "very irksomely."

Early on February 5 they began to advance toward the supposed positions of the Boer guns on Brakfontein Ridge. They were covered by a brisk fire from their own artillery. But the Boers didn't reply, and the ridge ahead showed no sign of life. When the British troops had come within fifteen hundred yards of it, they were ordered to lie down in the grass and on no account to shoot unless a really good target presented itself. None did. The British artillery continued to bombard the ridge.

About noon, the Boers suddenly opened fire, doing great damage to the exposed British batteries. Their own guns were so well hidden that the British were even now unable to locate and silence them. A furious artillery duel went on for two and a half hours. The York and Lancasters were then told to retire to the kopjes. They did so in good order, keeping well extended—with the result that their casualties were light, three dead and twenty wounded.

From the kopjes, on February 6, the York and Lancasters watched the main British attack, which succeeded in capturing one end of the Vaalkrantz Ridge. They themselves were only intermittently under fire. This must have been the day which Frank spent knitting.

On February 7 the Boers brought up reinforcements, and their guns began to make the British positions on Vaalkrantz untenable. So Buller decided to withdraw. On February 8 the British again recrossed the Tugela. The York and Lancasters were attached to a force which was moved back into reserve at Springfield. They remained behind the front lines for the next eighteen days.

Meanwhile, on February 17, Buller attacked a hill called Hlangwane, south of the Tugela near Colenso, driving the Boers off it and back across the river. If Buller had followed up this success it seems probable that he could have broken through to Ladysmith then and there; but again he hesitated. He did not cross the Tugela until February 21, by which time the Boers had put five thousand men into the hills opposite. One of these, Pieter's Hill, gave its name to the battle which followed. The British failed to capture the hills. After three days of bloody fighting, an armistice was agreed on, so that both sides could remove their wounded and bury their dead. The British and Boer soldiers mingled, exchanged tobacco and boasted to each other of their readiness to continue the war indefinitely. It was the British who withdrew from the battlefield, however. They recrossed the Tugela while the armistice was still in effect.

But Buller's tenacity was more than equal to his indecision. On February 27 he was ready to try again. The pontoon bridge which had been used in the previous attack was moved farther downstream and a sign was attached to it: "To Ladysmith." Across this bridge his troops advanced into battle, the York and Lancasters among them. Frank can hardly have been feeling at his best, for the regiment had moved up from Chieveley, a march of five and a half hours, that same morning. But their spirits were raised, before going into action, by the announcement of Cronje's surrender. And for them too this was to be a day of victory:

Going in single file, along the edge of the river, under cover of a heavy artillery fire from our guns, a gradual ascent was made until the railway was nearly reached. Then came about 500 yards of almost open ground between us and the Boers, who were strongly entrenched on a small kopje, and here the first company came in for a very warm fire; but in face of that the kopje was carried with the bayonet. They were now almost opposite Pieter's Hill, and immediately began to climb the heights. The shells directed at the West Yorks burst all around, and they were also raked by a sharp fire from a gully on their right. Still on they went, and in spite of a stubborn and gallant defence, the Boer position on Pieter's Hill was successfully stormed. Ten men of our regiment were wounded, two seriously.
—A.H.C. Kearsey, D.S.O., War Record of the York and Lancaster Regiment, 1900–1902, from Regimental and Private Sources.

Next day, some of the British cavalry, scouting ahead, found that the Boers had practically abandoned their positions around Ladysmith. This was, in fact, a general and disorderly retreat northward. The Boers were so disheartened that they would have surrendered in masses if Buller had sent troops to pursue them, but he didn't realize this until it was too late.

The York and Lancasters were not among the first of the British to reach Ladysmith. They remained encamped in the neighborhood until March 3, when they took part in the formal entry of the town. This is how Lieutenant Kearsey's book describes it:

*It seemed hard for the rescuers to realize that this was
indeed the town they had so long and so desperately
tried to relieve, but the reality of it was brought home to
them only too vividly on looking at the thin white faces
of the worn-out defenders who lined the streets. Was it
likely the rescuers could cheer in the face of so much
misery; was it likely the rescued had strength left to give
vent to their enthusiasm, however much they might feel?*

*And so, on through those woebegone ranks the reliev-
ing force marched at a quick pace; on past the Town
Hall, where Sir George White and his staff were stationed, past Tin Camp and Rifleman's Post, out and
beyond to their camp north of Ladysmith, where for
three days the York and Lancaster rested.*

March 1. Relief of Ladysmith. News reached us about 11 a.m.
and *the excitement was intense.* In the City, all round Mansion
House, traffic was stopped, men shouted and cheered, sang God
Save the Queen, waved flags, cheered Buller and Sir George
White. Processions and shouting all day and until a late hour of
the night. Flags decorated the shops and windows and the rejoicing was very great.

March 3. The poor things in Ladysmith seem to have had to
live on very low rations, half a pound meal daily and horseflesh
and of course no vegetables. They have had much disease among
them and Buller reports they will want a little nursing before fit
for the field.

March 8. Mama and I to London Street through which the
Queen drove on her way from Paddington to Buckingham Palace.
She is come up for a few days on purpose to drive about among
the people and there certainly in all the world can never have
been anyone so universally beloved as she. Her sympathy and
love for her people have been most touching, all these sad days.
She drove by in an open landau with about a dozen of the Life
Guards in attendance, no one else to guard her, and it was the

same all day, immense enthusiastic crowds everywhere, and at night they assembled in thousands outside Buckingham Palace.

March.9. Mrs W. thought me most unchristian, wishing Kruger to be killed, and took a very different view of the War to mine, so we did not agree! Got two letters from Mr I in evening.

(There was a family legend, often repeated by Emily to Christopher, that a gentleman calling at the flat during this period had been imprudent enough to express some mild sympathy for the Boers and that Kathleen had terrified him by blazing out, "Well, all I can say is, if you were a Boer and I had a gun, I'd shoot you dead!"

Even if this isn't true, it is obvious from Kathleen's diary that she has now resolved whatever doubts she has had about the War by concentrating on simple personal loyalty: the War is her war as long as Frank is in it.

But Frank was no longer in the War. The letters Kathleen refers to above were the last she would get from him as a combatant. A few days after the relief of Ladysmith—certainly before March 9 —Frank contracted typhoid, then usually referred to as enteric fever, and was taken to a hospital at Chieveley. Typhoid and cholera, caused mainly by drinking polluted water, were becoming an increasing danger to the troops. By the end of the war the British had lost almost twice as many men from disease as from death in battle.

It seems that cases of sickness were not as a rule reported in the English newspapers, unless the patients died or were about to be invalided home. Kathleen had to wait more than five weeks for any news of Frank, and her anxiety mounted as the succeeding mails brought no letter. Then at last, on April 15, Elizabeth Isherwood wrote, enclosing a note she had just received from an Army nurse at the Chieveley hospital; it was dated March 15 and assured Elizabeth that Frank was now quite out of danger, though still too weak to write.)

.   .

Letter from Frank, written April 3, from the Chieveley hospital:

I must write you a line to tell you I'm in bed recovering from enteric. I didn't have it very badly but the recovery is an awful long job. I don't seem to get any forrader. I get nothing but milk and long for something more to eat. When I come in a book to a meal it nearly kills me. I was in all the fighting to Ladysmith and then collapsed and came down here to Chieveley. Peaceful Miss Robins—I'd give anything to go to lunch with her. Sometimes I lie and think of all the things I should like to eat. I think a lemon ice, some very nice plum cake, and roast beef are what I particularly long for. My regiment are up two miles north of Ladysmith in a horrible place. I don't think there will be much more fighting on this side. Even Buller won't run his head against their positions unnecessarily. Don't repeat my 'even Buller' as I don't think one ought to run down one's commanders. Last week when your letter came, in which you said I was often in your thoughts, I was so weak that I burst into tears and had to be mopped up by the nurse.

Letter from Frank, written April 18, from the Chieveley hospital:

Venus has a new book ready but is waiting till the war fever has abated. She annoyed me intensely by telling me one of her characters, of whom she quoted some horridly affected speeches, was me; and, to crown all, his friend, who was rather worse than himself, called him 'Cis'. I boil with rage when I think of it, even now. The worst of it was that what he said was something I had written about one of Schumann's pieces, which looked immensely affected afterwards and which, in any case, I wouldn't have *said*. It's so different to *write*, nicht wahr? I forgot, though, you hate German. My fellow invalid, who was brought up at Frankfurt, has infected me with a longing for a winter there. You wouldn't approve? He is a nice chap and talks about pictures and books. However he has that failing, which I think is more a man's than a woman's, of nearly always making his talk personal. It's rather annoying, when you want to discuss Dickens's points, zum Beispiel, for the conversation to go off into a recital of the edition of Dickens and the books he has got. Don't leave such big blank pages in your letters. It's making me feel that you have got tired of writing to me.

Letter from Frank, written April 23, from the Chieveley hospital:

I heard a good story of a man in hospital who asked one of the lady nurses to wipe his face and she said, 'oh yes, certainly, and I shall be the fourteenth lady who has wiped your face this morning.' The nurses are such 'bricks', to use an almost obsolete word. Always cheerful and good tempered. We have now got four volunteers in the tent. They are so awfully military. Even in bed they lie at attention. My original companion and I have the most tremendous discussions about everything and anything. Last night we discussed a sort of glorified Rowton House for young men with about two hundred pounds a year. They were to have two rooms and there was to be a salle à manger where they could have breakfast and dinner. The charge was to be about six shillings a day. I made out the builder would make six or eight per cent and I think the idea a magnificent one, don't you? It arose from advertisements of restaurants in the Sunday Times. My beard came off when I got here. This may leave you under the impression that I am bald. Under the barber's hands, I mean.

(In this letter Frank also asks Kathleen to get him a number of books and send the bill to his Father. His list includes Bacon's Essays, Reynolds' *Discourses on Art,* Captain Cook's *Voyages,* Montaigne's *Essays, A Sentimental Journey, Tristram Shandy, Robinson Crusoe, anything by Washington Irving, Paul et Virginie and Manon Lescaut—both of these in the original French.)*

. .

Letter from Frank, written May 7, from a hospital for convalescents on the Mooi River (this was on the railway line running south to Durban):

I have moved at last. On Monday I tore myself away from Chieveley and the nurses, of whom I had got quite fond, and came down here. At Estcourt, we had lunch and I dared to face green peas and apple tart. They tasted absolutely delicious after two months of slops but I have had dreadful indigestion ever since. The country after Estcourt got barrener and barrener, and when we got to the top of a hill and saw an enormous camp in a sort of yellow brown wilderness and I had an instinctive feeling that it was Mooi River, my heart sank. While we tore down the hill (railway travelling is most exciting here) I tried to pretend it wasn't going to be, but it was no use. I think it's almost the nicest of my castles in the air, the cottage on St Ives terra firma from which I should learn painting. I should like to have someone with me who painted (not as well as myself) and we could go in the caravan together afterwards—from Plymouth to one of the southern French ports, and then through the Basque country in autumn. 'Ah, ces longues jours d'automne!'

Letter from Frank, written May 20, from the hospital ship Simla:

You may have seen in the paper that I am being invalided home. I am very glad to be so, as I feel that, as far as I am concerned, the War is over and that I should see no more. Do you think we might be asked to Hexham again? I can't quite make up my mind which, of all the delightful things I can think of, I shall do during the summer. You know what a schemer I am, so often the reality turns out better than anything one has planned. For instance, I never dreamt of coming home so soon. 'Invalided' sounds so awful, but as a matter of fact I am fairly hearty. I have to be careful what I eat—no Italian restaurants—and I am not very muscular yet. We are rather a lugubrious crew. Everybody tells you his symptoms and the details of his illness but doesn't listen a moment to yours. An awful parson sits opposite me at meals who looks out of the corner of his eyes with the air of a hunted criminal. I hope he will be arrested at Cape Town. He is so depressing.

May 24. Note from Mrs Isherwood. They have received wire: 'Meet Simla . . .'!

May 29. Felt in so happy a mood. It is a pity the Fates always discover it and never allow it to last long!

May 30. Prince of Wales won the Derby with Diamond Jubilee. At any rate, if realization falls short, nothing can take away the content of anticipation!! Mama still suffering from her enlarged gland, poor darling, but it is not painful.

Letter from Frank, June 15, from 23 Clarges Street, London:

I arrived today and am staying here with my brother till Monday afternoon. Could we have a day together on Sunday? Would you arrange anything you can and tell me. I am abominably healthy! F.B.I.

June 17. At 11.30 Mr Isherwood came, looking brown after the voyage. We all three went up to the Gardens and he came back to lunch. In afternoon he and I went to the Tate Gallery in hansom.

6

Both from the little that Kathleen says in her diary and the much that she doesn't say, it becomes obvious almost at once that something is wrong.

It is possible that Kathleen was disappointed when she saw Frank again, that "realization" did indeed fall short; but this seems unlikely. And if she was disappointed she would hardly have admitted it even to herself; too much emotion had been invested in Frank during the months he was in South Africa, it couldn't be written off as a dead loss. A much more probable explanation is that she had been expecting that Frank's return would somehow magically remove the obstacles to their getting married or at least becoming officially engaged. She should have known her Father better. Frederick was still Frederick; the fact that Frank was now the next best thing to a wounded hero made absolutely no difference to Frederick's attitude toward him. Kathleen must have been quickly forced to recognize this.

Her diary contains no direct comment on their meeting, but her feeling of discouragement is evident. On June 18 Frank went home to Marple Hall and then set off with his Mother for a holiday in Devon and Cornwall. Kathleen remained in London. On June 19 she complains of the great heat, on June 21 she is depressed by a rainstorm. By the end of the week her spirits have sunk even lower:

. .

Very heavy rain about 4 a.m. which woke me and kept me awake a long while. Got up and studied the A.B.C. map and tried to amuse myself thinking of a tour!! Am so tired of the noise and dust and people and so awfully depressed, nothing nice seems possible and all sorts of depressing thoughts keep coming. Wonder if Dr Williams's little pink pills for pale people upset my liver!!

On June 26, Jennie does manage to make her laugh by taking her to see Maeterlinck's tragedy Pelléas and Mélisande; *but even Kathleen's amusement seems related to her negative mood: it is very unlike her usual good manners to show disapproval so aggressively in a public place:*

Pelléas Mr Martin Harvey and Mélisande Mrs Patrick Campbell. A series of pretty mediaeval sort of Burne-Jones pictures. The conversation of the most obvious and uninteresting, everything repeated over two or three times, weird, half poetical and often bordering on the ridiculous. For instance, when Mélisande lets her hair down from the turret window and her lover rapturously exclaims 'it seems all alive'! Jennie and I laughed so, we quite shocked our neighbours!

(One of these might well have been Max Beerbohm. He took the play most seriously and complains in his review of "these asinine titterers.")

Kathleen left on June 30 to stay with some friends in Scotland. On July 3 she refers to a friend who is going out to Mendoza in the Argentine to marry a man she has been engaged to for five years. Kathleen's comment, "Some people have *pluck," suggests an admiring envy. Does she wish that she too had the pluck to take action and break the deadlock in her own life?*

It is Frank who now seems oddly lacking in impatience and quite content with the status quo; perhaps this is the apathy of the convalescent. Kathleen got three letters from him while she was in Scotland, all of them gossipy and all written without the least hint of emotional strain. In the first he describes Exeter Cathedral and apologizes for using the word "delightful" so many times. In the second he tells her that he has settled down with his Mother for a month at St. Ives in order to take lessons in watercolor painting. In the third he says that he doesn't "feel in the least drawn towards acting now, somehow—I am getting old, I suppose. Two odious people, one an Austrian painter here, have asked me my age lately and when I refused to tell them, because I thought it was great impudence in both cases, they both guessed I was twentyfour. Such a horrible priggish age! Do you remember my indignation at being called 'Cis'? I should think 'Cis' was just twentyfour." As for the future, Frank doesn't appear to be worrying about it much; the aim of his planning is merely that Kathleen and he shall be invited at the same time to visit the Sykeses and the Greenways.

Kathleen was also getting letters from Emily in London:

Darling K, to see Dr B this morning. Dr B declares it is all *gout* in the throat and that I am going on beautifully and that there is nothing to be frightened about, tho very uncomfortable. He hopes it will gather and burst and so get rid of the gout, I can't say I do, it is painful enough as it is!! Goodbye my own love, from your poor little Baby Mama.

Darling Kath, it is awfully hot and I feel *thankful* you are out of town, although I miss you dreadfully. Everything seems against me. I simply can't *bear* the sight of the porter, it has quite got on my nerves—which I know is most silly. I always walk both up and down which is very exhausting, but I simply can't face going with the porter yet. I don't feel depressed now about my gland itself, but it is the never-ceasing pain day and night that wears me out and makes me tearful. Of course when I am out of doors or amused it seems better, but the least thing makes me 'wag my head', so it is a good thing you are out of it and some day no doubt my spirits will return.

. .

As shown in the last chapter, the swelling of Emily's gland had followed promptly on the news of Frank's impending return from South Africa—a psychosomatic warning that "Baby Mama" would defend her prior claim to Kathleen's time and attention against all comers. But the warning was unnecessary, for Frank was making no counterclaim, and Kathleen, who wasn't having much fun in Scotland anyhow, at once wrote that she would return to London a day earlier. Emily, feeling perhaps a little ashamed of "Baby Mama" now that she had got her way, replied:

I expect you will think me a fraud when you arrive, as I shall be so cheered by the sight of my Mama as to appear quite jovial! I believe at the bottom of my heart I have been pining for you, tho thankful you were out of the heat. Last night beside my throat a violent pain came on in my left side, going right through to my back and hurting me when I breathed, but as it has nearly gone after covering it with pinewool, I conclude it is only rheumatism. I feel better today at the mere prospect of soon seeing your cheering little face and *chatting* to you. Goodbye darling Lamb, I remain always your own loving Baby and Mama. What news of Mr I? But you will tell me when you come.

When Kathleen got back to Cranley Mansion, she found that the lump on Emily's neck had indeed grown much bigger since she last saw it. That was Emily's power; she could always produce evidence which Kathleen was forced to accept, however unwillingly. But, just because of her experience with Emily, Kathleen grew to be highly suspicious of the sicknesses of others. Once, in 1937, her skeptical attitude so enraged Christopher that he nearly died of blood poisoning in an effort to convince her that he was really ill.

Within four days of Kathleen's return, she and Emily are settled into lodgings at Oxford. They walk in the town, visit some of the college buildings, sit in the gardens and then dine cozily in their sitting room by "nice sociable lamplight." To all appearances, Emily has recovered completely.

· ·

On August 4 Kathleen went down to the Isle of Wight to stay on board Uncle Walter Greene's yacht during the Cowes Regatta. It was said to be "a bad Cowes" this year because the Duke of Saxe-Coburg, one of Queen Victoria's sons, had died and there was an order for general mourning. King Umberto of Italy had also died, shot by an anarchist, and it rained throughout most of the regatta; but Kathleen managed to enjoy herself nevertheless. While visiting one of the other yachts she met a major theatrical celebrity:

I like his face and he makes beautiful melancholy bows, but finds it rather difficult to forget, I think, that he *is* Mr Forbes-Robertson the actor. He is studying his part in *The Devil's Disciple* and also learning Othello.

On August 13, Kathleen and Emily went to stay with the Sykeses. While they were there, Kathleen visited Marple Hall again and was visited at Cheadle by Frank's younger brother, Jack, his younger sister Esther and her fiancé, whose name was Joseph Toogood. (The younger generation of Isherwoods consisted of Henry, b. 1868; Frank, b. 1869; Moey, b. 1871; Jack, b. 1876; and Esther, b. 1878. Kathleen had now met all of them.)

Frank himself bicycled over to see her several times and they picnicked together. Meanwhile, Emily's swelling burst open and began to discharge pus, causing her great pain when the dressing had to be changed and making Kathleen feel obliged to stay and look after her, instead of leaving with Frank for Hexham. However, by the end of the month "Baby Mama" had relented: Emily went south with her swelling much reduced while Kathleen and Frank went north, to spend a happy but seemingly uneventful week with the Greenways.

On September 13, after returning to London for a few days, Kathleen was off again, accompanying the ever restless Emily to a hotel at Forest Row in Sussex. Emily's doctor had told her that "the country was as good as the sea and that sea for glands was all moonshine!"

• •

September 21. Mama read out loud as usual in the evening, till the invalid lady upstairs sent down word she could bear it no longer and compared it to listening to groaning, which tickled us immensely!

September 22. A morning of extreme agitation, as from Papa's letter he left it uncertain whether he was coming or not, and the hotel was full up, bar one room, and Mr Isherwood coming too. A wire which didn't reach till after 10.30 announced Papa arriving in the afternoon! Hurried to wire to Mr I, wondered where everyone was going to sleep and then awaited events. Went to meet the 1.35 by which Mr I arrived, not having received my wire before leaving!!! Miss M promised to do her best with a room over the way. In the afternoon we walked to a view of Forest Row and after tea up to the golf links, sitting in the garden sitting room in the evening. Papa arrived by the 3 train.

September 23. Fine and sunny. All four to church, after which Mr I and Mama sat in the garden and Papa and I walked to Brambletye ruins, which he photographed. All up to the golf links about 4, had tea at the hotel, Mama and Papa walking home after and Mr I and I exploring into the Forest, the bracken turning colour among the pines was lovely, and then out on the open, walking towards a dark line of trees gleamed through the most gorgeous coppery crimson.

September 24. Mr I left by the 10.14.

On September 26, Kathleen made what she describes as a "pilgrimage" to East Grinstead, where she and Emily had tea at the hotel which was the scene of her encounters with The Child and Mr. L. in 1898:

It felt empty, wicked and as mysterious and lovely as ever and I felt I might at last loathe the place and never wish to see it again. Glad to get back to dear cheerful ordinary little Forest Row.

That same day Frank wrote:

In case there is any difficulty about Saturday I should prefer to come to you on Monday or Tuesday. On Friday Venus and I meet for the first time in five years. I like the idea of the haystacks and church but I don't really want any other attraction than that, as *you* described it, amiable literary-invalid air which enwraps your Mother and yourself when you are alone together. In the presence of the IGNORER the amiability disappears. As you won't be in town I can't ask you to meet Venus.

The nickname for Frederick must have been newly invented; it sounds like a description of his behavior during the previous tense weekend at Forest Row. Frank's next meeting with Kathleen, in London on September 30, was a delightful contrast: Frederick and Emily had gone to stay with Walter at Nether Hall, so they were able to spend the whole day alone together. They took a train to Maidenhead, then hired a canoe and paddled along the Thames to the village of Bray, where they attended the harvest thanksgiving service and had lunch. The reference to "the haystacks and church" in Frank's letter suggests that their trip had been planned by Kathleen in advance.

In the course of this day another nickname must have been invented, for when Frank next writes to Kathleen he calls her "Elizabeth." Why was this particular name chosen? Frank definitely wasn't identifying Kathleen with Elizabeth Isherwood; his relationship with his Mother had no such hidden depths and Kathleen must have known this, or she would have protested violently against the nickname. A clue is given by Frank's remark about the "amiable literary-invalid air which enwraps your Mother and yourself." Victorian literature's best-loved invalid was named Elizabeth. Robert Browning was one of Frank's favorite poets. Frederick, though not crazy enough, would do for Mr. Barrett. Kathleen would surely be delighted to play such a romantic role; she had an exceptionally strong constitution but rather liked think-

ing of herself as fragile, at this time in her life. And Frank may well have felt that Fate had cast him for Robert, for he must have realized (though he couldn't say so to Kathleen for fear of offense) that he would one day have to rescue her, as Robert did Elizabeth, from illness—not her own, in this case, but Emily's.

After September 30, Kathleen and Frank did not see each other for nearly three months, because Frank rejoined the Regiment and was sent over to Ireland. So a period of correspondence follows. Fortunately, Kathleen kept rough drafts of the letters she wrote; the final versions, like nearly all the rest of her letters to Frank, have been lost or destroyed. The forced lightness of their tone doesn't hide an underlying tension. The very fact that Kathleen made these drafts may mean that she felt she was playing a game of skill which demanded careful consideration before each move; her deletions are revealing. This is a phase of frustration, mistrust and sexual hostility between the two of them. Neither is content any longer with the status quo; it is beginning to exasperate them both. How long will the war in South Africa drag on? How long will the Ignorer continue to ignore their relationship? How long will Emily's health make Kathleen feel guilty about leaving her? How long will Frank remain too poor to get married? The answer seems to be: indefinitely—which for lovers is as bad as forever. It is a dangerous situation, of a kind which many young couples are unable to endure and finally escape from by breaking with each other.

Letter from Frank, October 12, Marple Hall:

My dear Elizabeth, my Brother came back from staying at Lyme in a very lordly mood and rather snubbed me when I mentioned the Sykeses. Just at the present moment he is rather in my bad books. He was so very lordly and grand when he was at home, so I don't feel that I take much interest in his affairs. However tell me exactly what happens. Remember I shall not be in England for long and if I go back to Africa and you haven't been kind to me while I've been at home and the climate killed me or anything, your remorse would be terrible.

Draft letter from Kathleen, October 14, while staying in the country (her meetings with the Sykeses were in London, before she left):

Dear Friend, coming down here has rather put the Sykes element out of the foreground and I'm afraid I may not give them their proper value in the picture. However, to begin at the beginning . . . Marjorie arrived, looking very pretty and reminding one of a fascinating little kitten. I heard all about the tea for the second time, details given with an air of pleasurable excitement, blushes, she evidently flattered but not unduly elated. My suggestion of likeness to Forbes-Robertson well received. It appears too that the ROMANTIC element is not lacking either—had I heard?—curse on every eldest son—on reaching his twenty-first birthday he dies—averted in this case by a vision telling him to go into a monastery—wasn't it too romantic for words? (I said I had never heard anything to equal it.) Next day, the Sister (Isabel) came to lunch. Story of tea for the third time (rather vaguely); the two Mr Isherwoods had been over. They had been before. Evidently amused and taken by Marjorie and had written to know if they might come again. Pouring wet afternoon. Came in spite of it. But of course I knew the youngest, didn't I? We had stayed at Maud's. He was the one with the moustache. The other was clean shaven and an R.C. Hoped there wouldn't be another R.C. in the family. Next day, Mrs Sykes (the Mother) came to stay. Account of tea for the fourth time. The Pope had been over a good deal lately, and written (apparently for no reason in particular). It was most amusing. All this said with that 'good-natured-detachment-from-her-surroundings air' which so exactly describes her. Mama innocently remarked he must be very taken (she knowing your absurd views of the family). 'Oh, she didn't know', rather deprecatingly, but evidently of that opinion too. At any rate, one Roman Catholic in the family was quite enough. She was not so surprised at his coming as I expected, but then from a Mother's point of view it naturally wouldn't be the least surprising. I must say, I wonder rather if it would be a good thing for the child—she really is too young at present. And I can imagine your Brother being most unpleasant in an anti-purple-of-commerce mood. Matrimony is such a frightful step for a woman.

(*Kathleen has struck through this last sentence, evidently meaning not to include it in the final version of her letter.*)

However, now I've told you what happened in a more or less solid fashion—which is more than you deserve after your mean attempt to work on my feelings by alluding to South Africa and the climate. You know how that sort of thing always takes me in. [*This sentence also has been struck through.*] Just like Mama reducing me to submission by saying Papa is nearly seventy.

I feel distinctly cool to 'our Maud' and don't think I shall ever go and stay there again. I only saw her in a hansom on my way to the station.

Have you heard yet when you go to Ireland? And Venus, what does she think of you after the meeting? Has she sent you an analysis of your character? I have a slight cough, one of Mama's sisters died in a decline. You would be sorry if you refused me anything after it was too late. It is most ungrateful not to like the way I begin. Venus would tell you the thing to say to a charming woman would have been, you would rather be her *friend* than anything more to anyone else. Elizabeth.

The chief subject of these letters is Henry, Frank's elder brother. Henry, then thirty-two, was the best-looking of the three Isherwood sons. He had blue eyes, curly hair and the sort of features which are often described as aristocratic but in fact usually belong to leading actors. (Kathleen is being both satirical and accurate when she likens him to Forbes-Robertson.) The Henry whom Christopher remembers was still handsome, but advancing age and confirmed vanity had given his face an expression of rather endear-

ing silliness. He lisped slightly and dropped his final g's, as in huntin', shootin'; otherwise his enunciation was so precise that it seemed affected. He spoke with distinguished gestures and a loud harsh laugh like a parrot's, making one continually aware of his white teeth and his gold rings.

Henry, as the eldest son, would in due course inherit the Marple estates and money from his father, John Isherwood. The rest of the children were thus left to make their own way in life, with little or no assistance. This was the customary arrangement and it had the advantage of keeping a property in one piece. No doubt most younger brothers and sisters recognized the good sense of it in theory, but it inevitably created a psychological barrier between them and the heir. This didn't worry Henry, however. He took his privileged position for granted and already behaved with the grandeur of the head of a family. John Isherwood, who lazily hated disputes, abetted him in this attitude by agreeing to whatever he demanded.

One expression of Henry's grandeur was his use of the hyphen. He always called himself Bradshaw-Isherwood. Later, when he married Miss Muriel Bagshawe, he legally enlarged his name to Bradshaw-Isherwood-Bagshawe and seemed to find nothing ridiculous in signing himself "Henry B-I-B." (Christopher, from his schooldays on, groaned under the weight of his huge name, and got an aggressive satisfaction from officially dropping the William and the Bradshaw when he became an American citizen, in 1946.)

It was entirely natural to Henry to love the peerage; its members were the pillars of his world. At Marple, the nearest peer was Lord Newton; he lived just outside the neighboring village of Disley in the great mansion called Lyme which is referred to in Frank's letter. From Lyme to Cheadle was a deep social step downward for Henry; the Sykeses could be classified, at best, as upper middle. They had plenty of money, but they had made it in business.

It is plain that neither Frank nor Kathleen seriously expects Henry's flirtation with the young Sykes girl to come to anything. Indeed, they are actually using it here as an excuse for an oblique discussion of their own relationship and its difficulties. (Kathleen's letter proves that a previous pair of letters existed and has been lost—she must already have addressed Frank as "Dear Friend" and he must have objected to the word, which she now defiantly repeats; also, Frank must already have described his visit to the Sykeses with Henry, since Kathleen speaks of having been told about it by Marjorie "for the second time.")

The "curse on every eldest son" may have been a family superstition, or Henry may have invented it on the spur of the moment to impress Marjorie. Anyhow, it had this much basis in fact: certain Isherwoods of earlier generations had experienced a strong and even morbid feeling of guilt on behalf of their ancestor John Bradshaw, who was Lord President of the High Court that sentenced Charles I to death in 1649. One of them had actually made Charles a sort of shrine (which will be described later), and no doubt she prayed to him to intercede with God that the Family might be pardoned for Bradshaw's sin. So why shouldn't Henry make a more drastic expiation by becoming a monk? As a very young man, he had been converted to Catholicism by no less a person than Cardinal Vaughan, the builder of Westminster Cathedral. Henry had even brought him to stay at Marple. (John Isherwood's comment was, "A pretty state of affairs—Henry worshiping the Virgin Mary!") Not long after this, Henry did enter a monastery but left it again within a year, because of an attack of rheumatic fever. The rest of the Family regarded this episode as merely funny.

"The Pope" is a nickname for Henry, of course. Kathleen fully shared the Sykes prejudice against Roman Catholics. She regarded them as unscrupulous liars and agents of a foreign power. Worst of all, in her opinion, were Catholic converts; she called them "perverts."

"Your absurd views of the family" seems to mean that Kathleen is accusing Frank of sharing Henry's snobbish attitude toward the Sykeses: Henry must be "very taken" with the Sykes girl, for otherwise he would never stoop to pay court to such a low-caste person. "Purple of commerce" is a phrase which Wilde puts into the mouth of Lady Bracknell in The Importance of Being Earnest.

Henry loved to adorn his talk with quotations. It seems that he has been using this one as a metaphor for the pretensions of wealthy merchants like the Sykeses to a place in society. What must sting Kathleen is that such a sneer at the Sykeses is equally a sneer at the Smiths. Frederick is just a retired wine merchant, and even Uncle Walter, seen from Henry's viewpoint, is merely a brewer with a baronetcy. And, speaking of pretensions, Kathleen may also feel a bit guilty if she remembers how condescendingly she wrote in her diary about Lady Curzon's "quite rough unpresentable" father!

If Henry were asked why he considers the Bradshaw-Isherwoods socially superior to these merchants, he would reply without hesitation that the Isherwoods are "landed gentry." Which simply means they are farmers who made their money so long ago that their origins can be decently forgotten and that they have lived in the same house for three hundred years, on unearned income from rents and investments. Kathleen is aware of this, but she can't dismiss Henry's snobbery as a harmless joke until she is quite sure that Frank isn't infected with it. Her implied challenge to him is, Do you choose me or Marple Hall?

Letter from Frank, October 16, Marple Hall:

My dear Elizabeth, What *did* 'Our Maud' say about us at Cheadle? I don't think it could annoy me so much as Isabel explaining to you that I was the one with the moustache. I think her whole behaviour was most impudent. She can't have thought for a moment that I went to Cheadle from anything but good nature to my Brother. I had such a charming feeling of detachment and of pulling the strings all the time that it's particularly tiresome to be taken for one of the marionettes.

Venus wrote me a very nice letter thanking me for what I had done to give her a good time in town. I don't know that I wasn't rather a cad about her. But then I comfort myself with the thought that you are my other self, so it doesn't matter telling you—or aren't you, and does it matter? Frank.

Draft letter from Kathleen, October 25, Cranley Mansion:

I'm afraid you won't be properly sympathetic, the grievance about Our Maud is only the old one. I do think she might let it rest. When she went to Cheadle she must needs hold forth about our being left behind at that picnic again. Now I acknowledged, didn't I, that it was annoying for her, missing her bicycle ride home and having to wait dinner, but, having said how sorry we were, surely she might have buried it? However, Marjorie says she was talking about how disgraceful it was, how we got left behind *on purpose*, how the whole neighbourhood was talking of it, how she quite dreaded our coming again, or something to that effect. And it is so obviously ridiculous that we *should* want to get left behind when we were staying in the same house. I must say, it does annoy me unspeakably. If we had had either of us even a ghost of an intention or desire to lose the train, I wouldn't mind so much. Will you *please* oblige me by being a little angry?

Maud Greenway's remarks refer to the afternoon of September 8, 1899. Allowing for the fact that she is an actress and that her provincial existence probably needs drama to enliven it, Maud's indignation would be unconvincing but understandable if she had voiced it immediately. But when it is remembered that all this has happened more than a year previously and that Frank and Kathleen have meanwhile paid a second visit to Hexham and been welcomed with apparent friendliness, Maud's outburst to her family at Cheadle seems hysterical and indeed scarcely sane. The obvious explanation would be that Maud is in love with Frank and therefore madly jealous of his romance with Kathleen; but there isn't any evidence that this is so.

Kathleen, on the other hand, may well be jealous of Maud—not as a sexual rival but because Maud has a special relationship with Frank, based on their acting and making music together, in which Kathleen can't share. This jealousy could cause her to exaggerate the bitterness of Maud's remarks without being fully aware that she was doing it. Having written that Maud said "she quite dreaded our coming again," Kathleen does seem to have qualms about the accuracy of her reporting, for she adds, "or something to that effect." It is Kathleen who is now trying to create drama out of this ridiculously unimportant episode. When she writes, "If we had had either of us even a ghost of an intention or desire to lose the train . . ." it is she who sounds slightly hysterical, she is protesting far too violently. Why in the world shouldn't she and Frank, a newly declared pair of lovers, have wanted to lose the train? Could anything be more natural? To say that they didn't need an opportunity like this of being alone together, since they were staying in the same house, is merely disingenuous; they can't have had any real privacy if Maud was watching their conduct so closely. Kathleen is actually challenging Frank to show some romantic feeling and confess that he had wanted to lose the train and be alone with her that afternoon. Her reason for asking him to be angry with Maud is that this would be a proof of his loyalty.

Letter from Frank, October 28, Marple Hall:

My dear Elizabeth, I have always said that 'Our Maud' was a bounder. I really don't think we need be very much annoyed, as we have got such fun out of her tricks.

I am going to get to Ireland on Wednesday morning. Of course I shall be in dreadfully low spirits, so a letter awaiting me to cheer me would be a kind and friendly act. Besides, one looks so much more important with plenty of letters waiting for one.

My Brother had lunch with the Sykeses at Chester. When you think that the hotel was full of 'the proper Cheshire people' you'll realize what this means. Don't be anything but a 'dear loyal fellow' about this affair. I am dreadfully afraid you'll end by giving us away.

Draft letter from Kathleen, October 29, Cranley Mansion: (Note how she maliciously hyphenates Frank's names, thus equating him with Henry!)

Dear Mr Bradshaw-Isherwood, your letter tried my patience sorely. I absolutely refuse to make any more protestations. I said I wouldn't give the show away and if, after that, you feel you can't trust me, we had better drop the subject of the marionettes altogether. I'm getting rather tired of them. I think my marionette is able to take care of herself. I wish you would remember that I have absolutely no sympathy about 'the best people' and that sort of thing. At this minute I feel nothing would induce me to go to Hexham again and I hate to think I am under any obligation to Maud. You asked me to write and I've written, rather crossly it is true, but that is your own fault and you'll be able to wave it about just the same. [*This sentence has been struck through.*] Welcome to Ireland. Let me hear how you get on and if it is to be Peace or War. Seriously, I *am* rather hurt. K.M.S.

"My dear loyal fellows" was a phrase used by the headmaster of Frank's public school to refer to his favorite pupils and ex-pupils, the ones on whom he knew he could rely. Frank had told Kathleen he had never belonged to this select band.

When Frank urges Kathleen to be discreet, he seems to be referring to Henry and Marjorie, their "marionettes"; but this doesn't make sense. Frank and Kathleen have been merely making believe that they are pulling the strings of the affair; there is nothing Kathleen could give away but a harmless private joke. What Frank does fear (but daren't admit to) is that Kathleen in a reckless fit of temper will break off relations with Maud permanently for both of them.

Kathleen guesses this and resents it. But she daren't say so—an open quarrel with him over Maud might become really serious. Instead, she pretends that she is angry with Frank only because he doesn't trust her to keep her mouth shut.

Frank has refused to show his loyalty by condemning Maud. He has failed to be romantic about the lost train. His request to be written to in Ireland couldn't be more tactlessly worded. (Kathleen shows that she feels this when she echoes a phrase from his

126

Venice letter of 1898, "I waved it well in the air so that everyone should see how popular I was!") In less than half a dozen sentences, Frank has managed to disgrace himself thoroughly.

Letter from Frank, October 31, The Barracks, Newry, County Down:

My dear Elizabeth, I am so sorry. I am a fool . . . and an ass . . . and anything you like, and of course I didn't mean a word of it. *I know you're as silent as the grave.* I have just arrived here. I do enjoy a journey so very much and I had a particularly nice one last night with a beautifully calm sea, a good boat. The loch up from Greenore to Newry is very fine scenery. Big mountains quite down to the water's edge and all the autumn colouring very brilliant, I got quite excited over it. The guard insisted upon giving me his arm across the rails so as to save my going over the bridge. Irish people take a tremendous refreshing interest in one. My own quarters are horrible and look into a blank wall. I have hired a piano and I daresay shall manage to be very happy for a short time. PLEASE FORGIVE. F.B.I.

The draft of Kathleen's reply to this is missing. On November 3 Kathleen notes in her diary: "Went all alone to the South Kensington Museum, spending a pleasant and quite elderly afternoon." This must have inspired her to write to Frank about "the pleasures of advancing age" on which he comments in his next letter.

Letter from Frank, November 6, Newry:

My dear Miss Machell-Smith, when you are still on the wrong side of thirty I call it mere affectation to speak of the pleasures of advancing age. Now I, who am on the right side of the stile—it's a sign of grace on your part to know which is the right side, though —have a right to speak; as long (this is my theory) as you have anything to learn, you can be happy. I am feeling in a particularly serene 'Miss Robins' frame of mind. The wet day on the river is in full force, but I am smiling, oh so sweetly. For those who can read it there is a look deep within the middle of my eyes which tells of crosses nobly borne, etc etc, etc—but you're not properly impressed, though, and I don't think it's quite nice of you.

The Mess is chiefly composed of subalterns of twenty or so, and the way they rather modify their conversation to suit my maturer mind and the delightful look they give to see how I am taking their jokes, makes me feel most superiorly grownup. Isn't it nice to be able to give one's opinion quite finally and recklessly without feeling that there may be somebody in the room who knows what a fool you are? (I can't help thinking that your marionette may have given you a chance of experiencing this.) The Colonel and Adjutant come and ask *my* advice on *military* questions!! And you think it foolish of me to want to go out to South Africa again. You don't really, if you think of it. I should be a very poor sort of creature if I didn't.

Write me a *nice* letter soon, please. I didn't like your last so much as usual. I had one from Venus by the same post, much nicer—but I suppose this is the sort of thing one doesn't say to a charming woman.

Despite Frank's recent apologies, he seems to be deliberately provoking another quarrel in the last paragraph of this letter. Perhaps he feels that quarreling is the only mode of intimacy open to them at present. Here is the draft (undated) of Kathleen's reply:

I thought I told you how very old I am, but you never listen properly to what I say. . . .

(In those days it was still thought slightly improper that a woman should be even the least bit older than her man. Kathleen was Frank's senior by less than nine months, but she was probably sensitive about this—especially as John Isherwood continued to remark on the difference in their ages even after they were married. John was really fond of Kathleen and meant no malice; it was simply that he found difficulty in getting rid of an idea once it had entered his head.)

. .

. . . It has often struck me how wonderfully conscientious you are in trying to prevent my getting conceited, if you notice even a little innocent gratification on my part you immediately explain away any reason for it. But my greater and growing grievance is your really extraordinary lack of appreciation of my letters. We can't all be Venuses, and of course if you compare them with hers —and comparisons are odious, and I shouldn't *think* of saying to you how much more charmingly and appreciatively and cleverly another person wrote to *me*. And I maintain my letters in their way are most delightful. *I certainly will not be dictated to* how I write; be thankful for what the gods give you lest they get angry and take away such things as ye have—for I shall cease to write at all if this goes on.

Kathleen's threat doesn't seem to have made much impression upon Frank. When next he writes (November 13) he continues for three pages about William Morris, George Eliot, Walt Whitman and Carlingford Castle, which he has been sketching, before he finally touches on anything that concerns both of them: "This is the third letter I've written—charming woman—two of them are in the fire. What awe you have inspired in your humble and devoted F.B.I."

On November 14 Kathleen drafts her answer:

Was my last letter so *very* irritable and perverse, I wonder? At any rate you manage to put *me* quite in the wrong, with a tact and cleverness which both amuse and crush me!! But of course it is you who are *really* in the wrong. . . .

Kathleen prints this last sentence very carefully in tiny block capitals, seemingly to indicate that it is a theatrical "aside," spoken under her breath, which he is not to hear. But then she crosses out the whole passage. Does she suddenly suspect that Frank is making fun of her and decide not to risk falling into his trap by taking him seriously?

The letter she actually sent him must have begun with the

description of her visit to the military camp at Aldershot on November 10, while she was staying with friends in the neighborhood. The occasion was the ceremonial return of General Buller to resume the Aldershot command, which he had held before the outbreak of war. A short while earlier, Buller had been politely relieved of his duties in South Africa, created a Knight Grand Cross of St. Michael and St. George, recalled to England and received with public honor. He was extremely lucky to have Victoria for his sovereign, not Kathleen:

We saw Buller's homecoming. I felt really it was rather against my principles to have gone at all, but curiosity was too much. Lady Audrey seemed to be enjoying it all immensely. They say she has kept the whole thing together and worked up the reception. But he looked so much thinner than in the pictures that I couldn't detest him quite as cordially as I hoped; besides, he had such a stupid heavy dummy air that I felt myself becoming even a little sorry for anyone so foolish. But as for the brilliant reception the papers wrote of, that was all a fable, we thought it a *very* lukewarm welcome and no real enthusiasm at all, except perhaps when the poor wounded soldiers went by.

Kathleen then announces, with an air of casualness, that "Maud is in town again and I'm going to see her and rather hope she may be amusing . . ." This sounds as if Kathleen is making peace with Maud for Frank's sake—which would be a graceful and clever move, forcing Frank to join her in resenting any future slanders. But Kathleen spoils everything by adding, ". . . and perhaps give me news of you!," thus betraying her continued hostility and jealous dislike of the fact that Frank and Maud are writing to each other. How clumsy and vulnerable she seems in moments like this, and how little a match for Frank's mockery and feline slyness!

Letter from Frank, November 16, Newry:

My dear Elizabeth, I opened your letter in a great hurry and was delighted to find that it was not addressed to Mr Isherwood, which I hope means that I am quite restored to favour again. Rather mean of you, I think, to go and see 'Our Maud' without giving me due notice. May I give up being offended with her now? Write and tell me what she says but remember that there is nothing which annoys a charming man so much as to be told that he hasn't been mentioned.

I am very much amused at the spectacle of Miss Robins being put through a course of problem and vocal plays. Why did you sympathize with Buller because he looked stupid? It seems to me that's just what is so infuriating about him.

In Kathleen's letters and her diary there are references to Miss Robins' theatrical initiation. On October 9 Kathleen writes:

Miss Robins up to discuss whether we *really should* dine at a restaurant; her Elder Sister didn't approve at all of public restaurants without a gentleman. She pretended she was going entirely to please me and resigned herself to it with a delightful little air of excitement. We went to The Comedy Restaurant, quite a success, and she had taken seats for The Gaiety after! She was rather pained and perplexed by *The Messenger Boy*. I said but surely you knew the Gaiety pieces are always music and songs and dancing. She replied with great dignity she knew of course it was 'a vocal play, but not like that'. The drop-scene upset her dreadfully. However we went home in a bus, which she seemed to think would whitewash the evening by ending it respectably—indeed she especially stipulated for the bus before we started because of its respectability, although she consented to be fast and go there in a hansom.

Kathleen also notes that Miss Robins was taken by Frederick and Emily on November 15 to see the Kendals in what was evidently a "problem" play and that "poor Miss Robins was made very solemn" by it. There may have been other attempts to turn her into a regular theatergoer, but they were doomed to failure; she simply didn't have the temperament. Her idea of a thrilling evening was very different:

November 14. To see Miss Robins. She asked me to come and watch tonight 'to win the treasures of the skies', but meteors are such uncertain things and I went to bed.)

Draft letter from Kathleen, November 21, Cranley Mansion:

Maud said she hadn't heard from you lately, but Marjorie had told her you had had some new photographs taken and she wondered how it was you hadn't sent her one—which of course is very astonishing. She is under a new doctor now who wants her to come to London very frequently and says she must go about and enjoy herself! (This is to cure asthma.)

When do you go before the doctors again? I shall think them worse than idiotic if they say you are fit to go back to South Africa again.

With regard to the beginning of letters I shall make some remarks about that another day.

This time, Kathleen managed to strike the right note; her cattiness about Maud amused Frank, and his next letter to her (November 23) shows his approval—at Venus' expense, however:

A person who takes one quite naturally is such a relief. This is of course aimed at Venus, who is just now terribly out of favour. She wrote me a most irritating letter, reading all sorts of 'cursed subtleties' into my little remarks and saying my actions were 'indignes'. I think this made me more angry than anything, as why on earth she couldn't use English, I don't know.

One of the young subalterns is a lover of Omar. I had him to tea and we each sat up with our copy of the Rubaiyat and quoted it at one another. His way of getting out of the fact that Omar was a pessimist was to say that Omar was speaking ironically whenever I quoted anything especially pessimistic. I revenged myself by making him read some Walt Whitman and Browning's 'Apparent Failure' to show him what true optimism is.

Draft letter from Kathleen, November 25, Cranley Mansion:

It seems to me you two spend your life in scenes and making it up—or to be accurate, Venus in making scenes and you in making them up! However, I suppose you like it!! On the whole I feel very kindly disposed towards her, for I am inclined to think that indirectly it is to her I am indebted for a sable tie and an old lace scarf, etc! Papa has never forgotten how you went to London to meet a girl!! It cheered him wonderfully.

Kathleen also mentions Frederick's gift of the sable tie in her diary. She seems still fond enough of him to be able to find his obstinate stupidity amusing rather than infuriating. Not only does Frederick flatter himself that Frank is about to jilt Kathleen, but he believes he can console her with consolation prizes!
Nevertheless, Kathleen is certainly hitting at Frederick (as well as at Frank) when she goes on to discuss the character of Isopel Berners in Borrow's Lavengro *and* The Romany Rye, *which she has just been reading:*

I was glad when she went away and left him and told him how truly selfish he was—his attitude as to what effect *her life* would have upon *his* (a sort of adjunct to his happiness) *annoyed me intensely*, he never considered the least the effect of *his* life upon hers, or if it would add to *her* happiness to marry him and carry out his exceedingly selfish programme. It *was* so like a man, at least like a great many.

Letter from Frank, November 27, Newry:

I laughed so much at the idea of your old lace and fur tippet. I am sure if Venus had an idea that you had got anything out of her even indirectly she would write straight to the IGNORER and undeceive him. I wish he had a kinder heart, God forgive him

—you see I am getting so dreadfully Irish from going out into the country and talking to the delightful peasantry.

We went to lunch with some people on Sunday—the host and hostess were particularly manly fellows but they had a most extraordinary son of twenty whose great idea of pleasure seemed to be to dress up as a woman and act (not a comic woman). His walking-out dress was most startling, a white squash hat very much on one side and an astrakhan coat with an enormous chain covered with seals hanging down from his neck, and his hands covered with lady's rings. The poor old Colonel and I were quite flabbergasted at such an Aubrey-Beardsleyish-looking creature.

We have got a tremendous event on tomorrow. The 'Omar' subaltern has bet that he will run to Rostrevor (8 miles), we giving him five minutes start, and that we won't catch him. I think it's very sporting of a 'poor ould crayture' like me to start, don't you?

(*Frank's next letter reports that the 'Omar' subaltern 'beat our heads off' and won his bet.*)

Letter from Frank, December 12, Newry:

Your letter, dear Elizabeth, chilled me considerably. I suppose, with people like ourselves of varying moods, we can't hope to be at the same point in our orbits very often. I was thinking so kindly and so frequently of you last evening, and indeed I usually am. And then by the next post I am called 'dear Mr Isherwood' (this subject is *not* dropped).

If one goes about advertising one's inner soulside to all the world, what will be left for the supreme moment of which Browning speaks? But I am being rather unfair. You don't want me to expose my second soulside to anyone—do you? It's only my habit of viewing myself theatrically—sentimentally—that you don't like. I must confess that I detest it in other people . . . but where I differ from you is that one can or cannot help it. It's all a matter of temperament, my dear Elizabeth. 'The world of Nature for every man is the phantasy of himself', as Carlyle says in the book I am just reading.

I am going to Yorkshire for Christmas for a few days. I had an idea of paying a flying visit to Town, but you will be in the Isle of Wight?

(The draft of Kathleen's letter, to which the above is a reply, is no doubt the one in which she stated her views about the way letters should begin. It is missing, however, so there is no clue to Kathleen's reasons for addressing Frank as "Dear Mr Isherwood." Another question remains unanswered: Since she can't have disapproved of nicknames—having allowed Frank to give her one— why didn't she give him a nickname and call him by that?)

Kathleen answered Frank (December 16) by drafting a letter which started without any form of address, and calling this to his attention:

You notice my beautiful submission? So may the subject please be dropped *now?!* All the same, I can't resist the last word, which is that before long I think you will come to take my view of beginnings.

When do you contemplate taking your flying visit to London? Having got so far you might just as well run over to Ventnor, you really ought to see it. Some people say it reminds them of a foreign place—the little houses in terraces one above the other overlooking the sea—the downs at the top—all sorts of green thing growing out of doors, lovely views facing south. Our rooms are up very high, not giddy heights, but near the downs—and sunsets and sea views—Browning conversations with Mama—do think of it.

Telegram from Frank, December 18, Newry:

THANK YOU VERY MUCH.

• •

135

(In a note written the same day, Frank explains, "I didn't sign the wire as I thought the IGNORER might open it in your absence.")

December 18. Home to tea and had on toque which I had entirely retrimmed last night, new satin crown, rosettes, clean new wings. Was bending over a book when the whole erection caught fire in the candles and was ruined. So vexed!

December 21. Papa left for Nether and we left for Ventnor. Cheerful rooms. Mama's room and the drawing-room facing south and mine the downs at the back. Rearranged room.

Meanwhile, Frank had written that he would be arriving to visit them at Ventnor four days after Christmas:

I am so looking forward to it. In fact I have been so cheerful since I decided that the other fellows here have taken it into their heads that I am going to be married and have done nothing but chaff me ever since. I said to one of the sergeants the other day that he was a lucky chap to be able to, and that being a poor man I was unable to follow his example, and he said 'I suppose all expenses are relative, and when you get into the upper classes it must cost such a lot to dress them!' Please thank your Mother very much for having me at Ventnor. I have put three Brownings into my bag and your Morris books. F.B.I.

December 27. Rather rainy. Went down to the town before lunch and to 'Montrose' where Mr Isherwood is going to sleep. To the station to meet him by the 3.36 train and we walked back here. After tea we went into the town together.

December 28. It rained all day and blew as well. He and I went to the town and along the cliff back through Bonchurch.

December 29. We walked up to Carisbrooke and saw the castle and the donkey turning the wheel to draw up the water from the well. Then we went to have tea with Edward W. at Valetta on Castle Road. We found it all spread out and a message we were to begin but he mightn't be able to get back, and he didn't and we sat talking till five and nearly missed our train, 5.17, and had a memorable journey back.

December 30. After tea he and I walked down to the Post Office and found it was shut for telegraphing, except by paying extra fee. After that we walked back slowly in the rain along the road at the foot of the down till supper time.

December 31. He left by the 10.25 and we travelled together as far as Shanklin, where I crossed over and got a train to bring me back almost at once. He goes back to Ireland tonight. It turned colder and there was a strange lurid sky, as if the dying Year and the New Century meant doing mysterious things.

Letter from Frank, December 31, Golfers' Club, Whitehall Court, London:

My Elizabeth, I have done *all* my shopping but no wire from you! The man at the goldsmith's shop quite entered into the spirit of the thing. I suppose I'm after all not the only man who has bought a ring there, though one feels quite as if it was the first time it ever happened to anybody. I shall produce the result at Cheadle, *if* we get alone together at all. There never was any-one like your Mother to be with, and of course we can't hope to have such a happy time again. Most people don't seem to re-member that they were young once. . . . I have taken a vow that I will never go into a railway carriage and disturb a tête-à-tête *as long as I live.* I got your Mother a Walt Whitman. Do read the poem on page 115:

'Low hanging moon, what is that dusky spot in your
    brown yellow?
Oh it is the shape of my love,
Oh moon, do not keep her from me any longer'

• •

137

There is a 'nachtstueck' by Schumann which always reminds
me of it. A murmuring rushing accompaniment with every now
and then a passionate rush of the wind, and by and by a slow
intense melody.

> 'Oh rising stars,
> Perhaps the one I want so much will rise,
> Will rise with some of you. . . .
>
> But soft! Sink low!
> Soft! Let me just murmur,
> And do you wait a moment you husky-noised sea,
> For somewhere I believe I hear my mate responding to
>   me'

I am afraid 'the one I want' will not rise for me for many a
long day after this. But (your wire has just come) *we shall meet
next week*, no, this week. I have got almost a new kit and you
in your green! I *wish* we could give out that we were just engaged! I want to tell everybody. *The man at the goldsmith's shop
knows!* YOUR Frank.

7

Something tremendous has happened. But what, exactly?

It can't be said that Frank and Kathleen have become engaged; they have been engaged for eighteen months already. Or that their engagement has become official; it won't, in fact, be announced in the press until September 1902. The ring which Frank now buys Kathleen is a symbol of private understanding and mutual reassurance; it isn't for public display. What has happened can best be described as an emotional breakthrough.

How was this breakthrough achieved?

If Frank had come to Ventnor determined to bring matters to a head with Kathleen, the tone of his December 12 letter would have been more demanding. Instead of mildly hinting and waiting for her to invite him, he would have told her that he positively must see her while he was over in England. What seems more likely is that these two strongly inhibited people obeyed an impulse which neither would consciously recognize. Once they met again, something decisive was almost certain to happen; they would come much closer or draw much further apart. All that was then required was the opportunity: Edward W.'s (deliberate?) non-appearance at tea and the empty compartment on the train back from Carisbrooke.

Frank's great handicap was that he was so well qualified to be Kathleen's friend. Their shared interest in art and literature was actually an emotional barrier between them; when two people have so much to talk about to each other it is harder for them to find the all-important intimate silences. Kathleen used to call The Child her friend, but he certainly never forgot for an instant that she was an attractive girl, to be treated accordingly. This may have frightened her sometimes, but at least she knew just what it was that he wanted.

If one tries to imagine the scene of Frank's proposal to Kathleen in 1898, one can only do it in terms of their inhibitions: Frank covering up his awkward boyishness with poetical quotations and cynical jokes; Kathleen flirting to conceal her terror of the enemy, Man. Whatever Frank actually said to her on that occasion must have sounded painfully prim. (As soon as he was at a safe distance and could write letters, he regained his fluency but lost some of his sincerity.) He must have kissed her, of course, but this was surely done in a most delicate, respectful, unsatisfactory way, and Kathleen wasn't capable of encouraging him by making a passionate response. Their so-called engagement was actually a kind of literary charade: they were playing a Mr. Browning and a Miss Barrett who talked poetically of elopement but would probably never elope.

So a breakthrough was their only way out. Frank had to take Kathleen in his arms and kiss her as The Child would have kissed her if she had let him. Kathleen can't have changed very much since the day of Frank's proposal. But Frank himself had changed —he evidently wasn't just boasting when he wrote that the War had made him "quite grown up"—and that was what counted.

Once Frank had forced Kathleen to admit that he was not only a "dear friend" but a live human animal of the opposite sex, he could quote all the poetry he wanted to without turning back into a charade character. Their engagement was now a real engagement, and neither the War nor the Ignorer nor Frank's lack of money was any longer a reason for despair; these had become mere material obstacles which could keep the lovers apart for a while but could never cause them to leave each other.

After prolonged scientific deliberations and much letter-writing to the newspapers, it had been announced by the Astronomer Royal that 1901, not 1900, would be reckoned as the first year of *the twentieth century. This is what Kathleen means by her reference to "the dying Year and the New Century" in her diary.*

In the 1901 diary, Kathleen's list of wants includes an old-fashioned green and paste brooch, a strong revolving bookcase, a really good small atlas, a traveling flask and a traveling clock. There is only one list of racing fixtures, clipped from a newspaper. The bookbinding instructions and notes on invalid cookery are repeated. So is a quotation which she must have admired greatly, for she kept copying it into her diaries over a period of thirteen years: "Look not mournfully on the past, it will not come again; wisely improve the present, it is thine; go forth to meet the shadowy future without fear and with a Christian heart."

After such sternly noble sentiments, it is all the more surprising to come upon the verses which follow:

> *Mary had cake and Mary had jelly*
> *Mary went home with a pain in her ——*
> *Pray don't blush and look so red,*
> *Mary went home with a pain in her head.*

> *Little Miss Muffet sat on a tuffet*
> *Eating curds and jam*
> *There came a big spider and sat down beside her*
> *Which made Miss Muffet say—*
> *'Go away naughty spider'.*

Obviously, Kathleen thought them funny—that is to say, slightly daring. Did she ever repeat them to Frank? If she did, he must have been amused and charmed by this proof that "Miss L. Abney" was still alive and coexisting with the cultured and sophisticated "Elizabeth."

Letter from Frank, January 1, Station Hotel, Belfast:

My Elizabeth, you were the first person I thought of this century. I wore the ring, our ring, on my little finger. I told it that next week it would be with you and that it must be good.

I have just been before the board. I was properly tapped and listened to down tubes and things, and was pronounced to be no longer a sickly soldier. I hurl defiance in the IGNORER's face. An old porter at Stranraer was the first person to wish me happy new year. So I told him to drink to my girl's health. He's the second person who knows about it. If the two should chance to meet and put two and two together . . . and tell the IGNORER!!! We shall have a lot to talk about at Cheadle. I hope there will be a great many dances. God bless you, Elizabeth.

Your Frank.

Kathleen returned from Ventnor to London on January 2. Frank must have left Ireland again very soon after being examined by the medical board, for he was able to join her at the Sykeses' in Cheshire next day.

January 3. Had B. to do my hair. Started soon after eleven for Euston and it was fortunate I did, as the cab had to go right round by Westminster, the traffic being stopped for Lord Roberts who arrived today from South Africa. Travelled up the 12.15 train. F.B.I. arrived to stay at dinner time. We had a sort of tea-dinner at seven. The dance began at nine and was most delightful, and built-out room and the conservatories all lighted—quite a fairy land, and more than fairy ring. [*Against this, Kathleen has written later:* "My engagement ring."]

January 5. F.B.I. drove home at midday.

Letter from Frank, January 5, Marple Post Office:

I have walked up here with my Mother to send you a wire. I felt a little shy when I had to face the People. My Mother and I haven't talked of you. In fact I don't want to talk about you. I want to keep you all to myself.

Letter from Frank, January 5, Marple Hall:

• •

My Kit, we were very lucky at Cheadle, and now that I haven't got you to turn to the rooms seem rather empty—but we've got some delightful things to look back on. May I take it for granted that you think so? Your Mother wrote to me—and I have written to her and asked her if she thinks that all this is for your happiness, which is after all what I want most—*no empty words, I mean it*—and to try and influence the IGNORER to look more favorably upon me. I said that I didn't mean to write to him until just before going abroad. You say in your letter you don't like my going abroad. My darling—you may be sure that the memory of these past days will keep us together and be a blessed something to keep me straight and fit to come back to you. A girl like you can do a lot for a man when she chooses, and you have chosen, haven't you? I do miss you so. There is something frightening almost in being alone again, indeed the whole of the last few days inspire me with a sort of awe. 'The terrible god Love'. Your lover Frank.

Letter from Frank, January 6, Marple Hall:

My darling, I am writing you this in case I don't really see you tomorrow—and even if I do I shall give it you. There are so many things that we can't say to one another yet. Perhaps someday the 'scar'—you remember Browning's fireside—will disappear . . . and at present I love your reticence, that power of yours of just not expressing yourself. You are 'the one I want' and more, you are the type of the one I have always wanted.

About yesterday morning, it seems a little as if I had desecrated you, as if that scene in the wooden passage—I mean, I couldn't bear anything vulgar or outside to touch our feeling for one another. It's such a sacred terrible thing that you have given yourself to me—nobody must laugh or peep or pry at it. Yesterday evening I played all the beautiful love pieces I know—a musical festival in your honour—for you the unmusical. Your lover, Frank.

(The lines by Browning to which Frank refers are from "By the Fireside," one of Frank's favorite poems:

If you join two lives, there is oft a scar,
They are one and one, with a shadowy third;
One near one is too far.)

January 7. Left Stockport by the 12.10, F.B.I. meeting me at station. We travelled together as far as Macclesfield, he bicycling home from there. Further south, snow on the ground. Reached London about 4.20 and home at 5. A wire to welcome me. Sat over the fire and thought. It has been a most happy time.

(*The telegram which welcomed Kathleen said,* "THINKING OF YOU HARD." *Frank signed it, knowing no doubt that Frederick and Emily were both away from home.*)

Letter from Frank, January 7, Marple Hall:

My Sweetheart, I have just got back. I tore back on my bicycle —mad and feeling so strong. I never have felt such a man as I do now, since I have had you to make me one. Everything of today is imprinted on my memory. Your coming up the steps—I saw you first today! Your green coat and blue dress. The violets gave just the right note to it. Your voice—your eyes. I made the most extraordinary schemes, riding home. My own Kit, I am always your lover, Frank.

On January 8, Kathleen notes in her diary that she has had a "most kind" letter from Elizabeth Isherwood. This is the draft of her reply:

My dear Mrs Isherwood, thank you so very much for writing to me so kindly. It is so nice to feel that we have *your* sympathy and that you are glad too. Thank you too for asking me to stay which I should like to do some day very much. It would be a great pleasure to meet you again and we have such a great bond in common now that I think, as you say, we must be friends. I hope it will draw us together and that you will like me for his

144

sake. I only trust that I shall be able to make him happy. I will do my best. With love and thanks.

Letter from Frank, January 8, from the train on his way to York:

My sweetheart, I got you letter just before I started. You have made me feel most thoroughly unsociable and tiresome. I hated the sight of my relations because, poor things, they were not you.

I don't want you to tire yourself too much on Friday and spoil the dance. It will be delightful if we get a corner to sit in by our-selves and I think I should like to see you again in the green dress. It was your coming-out dress *for me*.

Don't suppose that I have developed any bad traits in my character. My writing's slanting because of the train. It does seem a long time since yesterday morning, but by the time that you get this it will be the day after tomorrow that we are meeting. Your Frank.

(Emily practiced character-reading from handwriting and firmly believed in graphology as an exact science. Frederick had come, through experience, to rely on her methods or at any rate on her intuition; whenever he got a business letter from a stranger he would bring it to her to decide whether or not the writer should be trusted. (Whether he really trusted anyone anyway is another question.) It was from Emily that Christopher would later learn never to betray his vanity by making a penstroke under his signature or his defeatism by letting his lines slope downward.

Frank's humorously skeptical reference to his character must be prompted by a character analysis of himself which Kathleen has just sent him; it is in her handwriting but obviously composed by Emily:

F.B.I.

Will: very determined, masterful
Disposition: self-willed, headstrong, courageous

145

Affection: sincere, loyal, rather exacting

Temper: not good

Capabilities: enthusiastic, an excellent ruler and commander but likely to be rather domineering and dictatorial; vigorous, forceful, persevering and level-headed, self-contained and self-controlled; unselfish, individual; cultivated and refined; determined and patient in gaining a given desire; energetic, quick in thought and decision; critical, cautious; very self-reliant, sound in judgement; frank and possessing very strong abilities, courageous, manly, difficult to depress or discourage; a very strong personality.)

January 11. Had some talk with Papa re F.B.I., then down to Gallery to meet him. Lunched at the Gourmet in Lisle Street. Dined at Miss Robins. Frank and I on to a dance at the Bolton Garden Rooms. We sat and talked a good deal and left about 12.30.

January 12. Very foggy and dark as night, but not thick. Mama and I drove down to the Haymarket to meet F.B.I., lunched and afterwards to the Lyceum to see Lewis Waller in *Henry V*, he was splendid and we all three enjoyed it much. Had tea after and F. had to catch the 6.40 home.

Letter from Frank, January 13, Marple Hall:

My Sweetheart, the letter to your Father is written. I must say I think it looked very well on paper and fairly unpremeditated. If he saw the numerous scraps of paper covered with rehearsals for it, he would not, I'm afraid, be impressed.

I have just been talking to my Father. He fell in with all my ideas in such an astonishingly easy way that I began to think there must be more in it than met the eye. *Marriage* however wasn't mentioned and we only spoke of my going in for the adjutancy and the probability of its leading to another appointment and my having one of the small farms, the house of which he offered to do up for me.

I do so long to show you all my haunts here and apparently you are never going to come. There was quite a hunted look came into your eyes at the thought of it. Darling, I love your eyes. I don't want them to have a hunted look, but that look of kindness —of love—which seems to me to sweep everything before it and make nothing else in the world worth anything beside it. Can it be possible that I am anything to you? I can't realize it—except sometimes when you are in my arms.

Letter from Frank to Frederick, January 13, Marple Hall:

Dear Mr Machell Smith, I have for some time been wishing to write to you on the subject of my relations with your Daughter, and as she tells me that you have spoken to her on the subject I feel that I ought to lay my position before you. With your consent it is my intention to put my name down for the Stockport Volunteer adjutancy which falls vacant in May 1903 and which I think I should have no difficulty in getting. The pay and allowances for this are about three hundred pounds. My Father allows me a hundred and fifty. I could of course apply for any other adjutancy but I think it would be a great help to us in many ways to live near my People, and that any Volunteer connection which I formed would be useful in augmenting the interest which I already have in the County, in the event of my wishing to get a constabulary or other appointment at the expiration of this one. I should be very glad if, before leaving for Africa, which the War Office tell me I shall not do until the end of the month, I could have the opportunity of speaking to you on the subject. Believe me, yours sincerely, Frank Bradshaw Isherwood.

Letter from Frank, January 14, Marple Hall:

My darling Kit, I wish you hadn't been depressed by the sermon about inconstancy. I don't like that even as a joke. You said the other night that you had always believed in me, and made me feel a better man straight off. Perhaps you hadn't much reason for believing in me about other things but as far as this one matter goes I am *really* perfectly trustworthy. *Do* let me make you believe so. Your Father, I shall never call him anything else if your Mother doesn't like it, needn't base the least hopes on Venus. I am writing to her to announce our engagement as you said that you thought I had better. Sometimes I feel as if I had been a little caddish about her, and I rather thought once or twice that you looked as if you thought so too. Perhaps this is the weakest point about friendship between a man and woman that one must be rather given away by the other when his or her time comes to fall in love. Your lover, Frank.

Letter from Frank, January 15, Marple Hall:

My own darling Kitty, I am thinking of you all the time wondering how you will get on tonight down at Worcester. I am feeling too a little bit jealous of your partners. There will be a great many of them I hope, not more than one dance apiece! I hope I haven't got a nasty jealous temper but I don't altogether like to see you with another fellow. Perhaps you'd like me though to be a little bit that way. I remember in a play the heroine saying, I love you because you are so jealous, because you are so strong and so ugly. I am afraid I'm not particularly strong and I don't know that I'm ugly(?) So shall I be the other?

(*On January 15 Kathleen went to stay with friends near Worcester and attended the ball to which Frank refers. She describes it as follows: "A large ball, over four hundred, room hung with bright pink which though cheerful was not good with all the scarlet coats. Home at 4. Danced everything."*)

Letter from Frederick to Frank, apparently a draft; it is undated, but Frank's next letter shows that it arrived on January 17:

It is about eighteen months since you proposed to my Daughter and I think it is now rather late in time to begin to talk of ways and means. Had you considered these beforehand you might possibly have considered yr position not sufficiently promising to think of marriage. You must remember that until now, except from hearsay of others, the amount of yr income has not been mentioned to me, and when I spoke to you before you left England I expressed plainly to you my opinion that under yr circumstances you ought not to have proposed. You then told me there was no engagement between you and that nothing further would take place without informing me. I know you have not acted up to this promise as I find you have given my Daughter a ring which is generally considered to indicate an understanding of an engagement. You have taken frequent opportunities of meeting and you write as if everything was arranged except what to live on.

You ask me to meet you and talk matters over. I fail to see what there is to discuss, as I certainly do not at all approve of the prospects you offer. My Daughter is old enough to decide for herself and consequently I cannot prevent her actions, altho I do disapprove most strongly of the whole proceeding. You have both been accustomed to live in comfort of most kinds and altho my Daughter has mentioned the idea of starting on a small income I consider that six hundred a year is the least sum possible to commence with, and even then where would you be in case of a bad illness or a family? Unfortunately you seem to me to think that what you are to live on is quite a secondary consideration. I have seen so much of life as to know the folly of such ideas and I don't think it was at all fair to my Daughter to endeavour to gain her affection without having some reasonable income to offer.

(*Note how Frederick contradicts himself. Having clearly stated that he has only now, for the first time, learned the amount of Frank's income, he goes on to say, in the very same sentence, that he told Frank—on November 26, 1899—"under yr circumstances you ought not to have proposed." This means Frank must already have told Frederick at that meeting what his circumstances were. The fact that Frederick isn't writing what he truly feels— that he is a peevishly jealous parent pretending to be an objective reasonable worldly-wise man—makes his arguments muddled and unconvincing.*

It must have amused Frank to be told that he was accustomed to live in comfort; yet, from Frederick's viewpoint, this land-owner's son did no doubt seem to have led a relatively sheltered life. From college Frank had gone to Sandhurst and from Sandhurst straight into the Army; he had never been obliged to rely entirely on himself and his own judgment. Even in South Africa, all that was expected of him was to obey orders and bravely endure the heat and the cold, the rain, the insects and the bullets. If he had made any serious mistakes, his superior officers or his men would have had to cover up for him somehow. Frank had never known the torments which any stay-at-home merchant must feel when he faces, all alone, a decision which could make him bankrupt.)

Letter from Frank, January 17, Marple Hall:

My dearest Kitty, your Father's letter saying that he could not approve of any of my proposals came this morning. In it he said that he saw no good in giving me an interview but I have written again to ask him to do so on Monday. If he still refuses I shall write and ask your Mother if she would let me have a talk with her. I cannot see that my position is so unreasonable or that I acted dishonourably, as he appears to think.

You must make up your mind, if your Father refuses to consent to our marrying, what you will do. I should be very loath indeed to persuade you to anything which would be a trouble to your Mother and which could bring any discord between you and her or between her and your Father, but I do think his position is not reasonable. We should of course not be well off and have to live very carefully, but both my People and, I believe, yours started on the same amount and what your Mother told me of her settlements provides for you in the future.

I want you though to think very seriously what marrying me would mean. I should be obliged to be away a good deal—at night sometimes—and should not be able to go away very much from home. I don't think our income would run to much travelling about. Do please realize it all you possibly can because you have to make up your mind *finally* on Monday. I care for you too much my Kitty to want to marry you if it wouldn't make your life happier in every possible way. I can't bear anybody to think that I have acted without due regard to your happiness, which I promise shall always be my chiefest consideration. Your devoted Frank.

Draft letter from Kathleen, January 18:

I found your letter, dear, when I got home tonight and I will try and realize it all I can, as you wish, but there is so much to say and it is so hard to write. And I wonder if you realize it either? That frightens me too. You are just as fond of travelling as I am. Are you *sure*—really truly realizingly sure—it would all make up and you would *like* living in one place, and the work? Of course the income doesn't sound to *me* so frightfully little but then I'm afraid I haven't had much experience how far money *does* go.

Then you see I'm not robust and strong like some people who could really do a lot of household work and things themselves. Please consider it well, too, because my happiness would depend also on *yours*.

I *don't think* I should find it dull living in the country, and Mama could come and see us? And you said you shouldn't the least mind my going away to see her, didn't you?

I gather from your letter you rather wished it settled one way or another when you come, and ask me, supposing Papa refuses our marrying on the adjutancy, what is to be done? I don't see that there is anything to be done in that case but give it up altogether or wait, and I am ready to wait if you are. I am too tired to write or think any more tonight, dear, and so I haven't touched on what makes it all seem worthwhile to me, or thanked you for your thoughtfulness for me, dearest, your Elizabeth.

. .

My dearest Kitty, I want to write to you an absolutely level-headed letter, even at the risk of annoying you a little, to impress upon you that there is something in what your Father says. The life I can offer you *is* truly a poor one and there are all sorts of unpleasant contingencies of the sort which stern parents rake up, which might leave you very badly off indeed. You'll have to put up with pigs and lots of other things you don't like!!!!!

The weather here is lovely. The sun seems to want to show me that Marple is a perfectly possible place to live in in the winter. I do wonder so much if you will like it. It has a great many drawbacks!!!!

I don't feel as if I was worth all this trouble. Be sure that I really am before you take me!! I am rather an extraordinary lover I'm afraid but you'll realize that it is all a wish to make your happiness a certainty which forces me into this unloverlike attitude. Your Frank.

Draft letter from Kathleen, January 19, Cranley Mansion:

You talk so frighteningly of the things to be faced that I tremble—and should like to know exactly *what* the things are, and the consequences, and all the depressing side? I am a horrible coward I know, and the realities of Life and the dark side of existence never seem to have come my way—but, as for giving up, there are a lot of things I shouldn't mind in the least, which of course would be essential to some people. You may be right and I don't know what it is to be poor. I always thought *we* were poor and I've never wanted to be any richer than that. Then, as for the married people I've known, it is true, now I think of it, I was always rather sorry for them, they often seemed so worn out and worried and made me go home most glad and thankful to be myself, but it wasn't because they were poor (as a matter of fact none of them were) and I can't think of *myself* as unhappy and discontented and worn out at the farm—with *you*. (Cows and pigs I do hate!!!!! but I think I could get over that!)

January 19. Very bad report of the dear Queen, nervous prostration and other symptoms. The Prince and Princess and other members of the family have hastened off to Osborne. It would be such a terrible thing for the country if anything happened to her, and last year she had so much to break her down; the War, which she took so much to heart, and the death of a son and a grandson.

Letter from Frank, January 19, Marple Hall:

My darling Kitty, In accordance with your dear wise Mother's advice I told my Father about you. He pretended that he knew all about it all along! Oh these fathers! But rose nobly to the occasion and consented to give us two hundred pounds allowance and Wybbersley Hall to live in. This is the place from which the Bradshaws originally came before they lived here and is a large farm house; the front part, where we should live, being let off to 'gentlefolks'. It is up on the hills between Disley and Marple, about one mile from Disley station and two and a half to Marple. There are most beautiful views all along into Derbyshire. The only drawback to it is that it's a long way from Stockport. I should have to give up my pigs and fowls!! for which I believe you, horrid little thing, would be rather glad.

There were also suggestions about the settlement which he has written to my brother Henry who is in Rome. I do hope he'll rise to the occasion. I was in such low spirits before but everything seems all right again. My darling, I feel almost as if you were my wife.

Venus wrote me a very nice letter wishing me good luck but at the same time goodbye as she said she knew I didn't want to write to her any more. I am rather sorry but in a way I didn't, so it's all right.

Of course I shall be happy when we are married. I wanted to marry you first! When I first mentioned it you had never even thought of it, so it's quite absurd to pretend that I shan't. Work is not a thing I mind on the whole, and if you don't go away too often . . .'

I saw three magpies this afternoon which is always supposed to mean a wedding. I hope it referred to ours! Not to the Toogood one, which is next Tuesday week. Till Monday, adieu. I do hope that your Father will see me. Your Mother will tell him what I can now offer. Your lover, Frank.

(The name Wyberslegh has always been spelled in a variety of ways. A local guidebook, published in 1903, preferred "Wibbersley," which is closest to its correct pronunciation.

Henry, as the eldest son and heir, had to approve any settlement of money made by his father on any other member of the family.

As has already been said, Esther was engaged to marry Joseph Toogood. He was a clergyman. John and Elizabeth, Henry, Frank and Jack all strongly disapproved of this match. They seem to have felt that Esther, the baby of the family and a strikingly beautiful girl, was throwing herself away, in a mood of defiance or caprice, on a nearly penniless nobody with a funny lower-class accent. But time was to prove Esther's choice a most lucky one. Joe was a good-natured young man, unfailingly cheerful, blessed with considerable sex appeal, a fine talent for wood-carving (with which he decorated his church) and a first-rate mathematical brain—he had been a senior wrangler at Cambridge. Their long and happy marriage produced a daughter and a son; it ended with Esther's death in 1944. Jack later changed his opinion of Joe and used to say that he had "a superiority complex in the very best way," which was meant as a compliment. Kathleen liked him from the beginning.)

January 20. Mama and I to Holy Trinity. Special prayer for our dear Queen and at some churches 'God Save the Queen' was also sung, kneeling.

. .

January 21. Discussion at breakfast re F.B.I. More discussion after, I suppose inevitable but depressing. I took Mama to the New Gallery where they [*Emily and Frank*] had a long talk in the afternoon and joined me at Harrods for tea. After, we went to the South Kensington Museum and returned home at dinner time quite limp and worried! Though really the possibilities do seem more possible. The Queen's condition showed a slight improvement.

Letter from Frank to Frederick, January 21, Golfers' Club, Whitehall Court, London, S.W.:

Dear Mr Machell Smith, as I shall not have the opportunity of speaking to you, I am writing to express my regret that I allowed myself to propose to your Daughter without first consulting you, thus breaking the terms of my promise. And I trust that you will accept this apology. Believe me, yours truly, F. Bradshaw Isherwood.

Draft letter from Frederick to Frank, January 22, Cranley Mansion:

Dear Mr Isherwood, in reply to yr letter, you expressly urged me twice over to meet you and I fixed this morning at 10.30 (altho I did not see any use in our meeting at present) therefore *I gave you the opportunity of speaking*. Had you taken the proper course you wd have consulted yr Father and considered what you could offer in the way of income etc before you proposed. You could then have come to me in the first instance with something really tangible and all unpleasantness might have been avoided, altho I should have felt that my Daughter's prospects were not as good as I could have wished. Yr position now is that you first propose without considering the future, you then promise on yr word of honour that nothing further shall take place without consulting me, and you break that promise. *A man's word is his bond.* Put yourself in my place and what wd you think of anyone who treated you in such a way. I accept yr apology, which is somewhat tardy, but to my mind that does not cancel the Bond. Yrs truly, Fred. Machell Smith.

(There is a puzzle here. Frank writes on the twenty-first to Frederick, "I shall not have the opportunity of speaking to you," although he must already know that Frederick has offered to meet him next morning; Emily would have told Frank this when she came to talk to him at the New Gallery in the afternoon of the twenty-first. If Frank had merely found the proposed time inconvenient he could have suggested another, since he was remaining in London until the evening of the twenty-third. So it must be supposed he decided that a meeting would be useless, though he is unwilling to say so for fear of weakening his own case. Emily may well have been instructed by Frederick (who obviously didn't want to see Frank under any circumstances) to talk Frank out of keeping the appointment, with the excuse that they had no new grounds for discussion. This would explain Frederick's ambiguous phrase "I gave you the opportunity of speaking" and the fact that it is underlined; Frederick is congratulating himself that he has made the gesture of granting Frank a hearing and at the same time put him in the wrong by maneuvering him into refusing it.

Both letters seem insincere. If Frederick has such a low opinion of Frank why does he waste time lecturing him about honor and the Bond, as though Frank were his own son? Frederick pretends that if Frank had come to him "with something really tangible" there would have been "no unpleasantness"; but of course he would have created objections to the engagement anyway, and he knows that Frank knows this. As for Frank, his apology sounds empty; it costs him nothing to make, because he isn't really in the least ashamed of himself. This too is only a gesture, cynically intended to please Kathleen and put Frederick in the wrong.)

January 22. [*Kathleen has drawn a black border around this page of the diary.*] Met F.B.I. at the Haymarket at 1. We went and lunched together at a foreign restaurant opposite Lisle Street and agreed to discuss nothing unpleasant, being both quite tired out! To two of the Bond St galleries. Took the twopenny tube from Oxford Circus to the Bank (the first time we had been in). A crowd outside the Mansion House looking at the latest telegrams which alas said, 'My painful duty obliges me to inform you that the life of our beloved Queen is in the greatest danger. Albert Edward.' We had tea and returned to Gloucester Road by Underground Railway, walking back through Hereford Square. It seems quite wrong somehow to be so happy with this awful sorrow to the whole Nation. Later the news came, *Death of the Queen*, a peaceful end, surrounded by children and grandchildren. She was such a great good and noble queen and no king can ever take her place. It is an *awful* loss to England. The Queen passed away at Osborne at 6.30 pm.

January 23. The 'King' returned to London, and at the Privy Council took the title of Edward VII. Got a note from F.B.I. suggesting a day in the country. To Chingford where it was sunny and crisp and no wind. We lunched at a dear little restaurant where the woman in a check bodice looked quite Italian! Had it in a little room upstairs looking on to green—the name was Poli, quite foreign. Walked into forest and sat on a log among what we think must have been the hornbeams that Morris loved.

January 24. The Court go into mourning for a year, that is till Friday Jan 24, 1902. Black trimmed with crape at first. To Debenham and Freebody, Marshall and Snelgroves—black, black, black . . . Bumpus had his windows with crape scarves across and the upstairs ones filled in with purple. Every window has a single black shutter up, and all theatres are closed till Feb 4th. The German Emperor remains on for the funeral. It seems to me so horrible, the way the moment the Queen is dead everyone talks of the King.

(*What Kathleen really mourns is the ending of a gynarchy; England's women are now once more subjected to a man!*)

January 25. 'It is expected that all persons upon the occasion of the death of Her late Majesty of blessed and glorious memory do put themselves into the deepest mourning. Norfolk, Earl Marshall.' They told us yesterday people were buying black with white in, which are all being returned as fast as possible to be made all black. Crape bows are tied on all the whips of the cabs, bows and scarves of black float from many windows, and a touch of colour seems extraordinarily out of place and seldom seen anywhere. We went to Harvey and Nichols, where they were sold out of black skirts. Invitation from Mrs Isherwood to stay at Marple, a very kind note. Put black revers on to jacket.

Letter from Frank, January 25, Marple Hall (this and his next few letters are written on black-edged notepaper):

Darling Kitty, I got a War Office letter this morning ordering me to embark on the *Roslin Castle* about the 4th, so I shall be here all right for next week. Henry wrote this morning saying that he fully approved of our marriage and would do everything he could for us. What he said came to this—for his part he wondered at my caring to marry on so small an income but he supposed that I knew my lady and that she would not mind settling down with me on it; that he didn't look upon our marriage and the Toogood one in the same light and that he would do everything to forward the former, etc. He always has rather imperial ideas about things.

Just returning from interview with Cavington, the Volunteer colonel, at lunch in Manchester. He seems rather a nice chap. He wants very much to get a local man as he says he has known so many adjutants who came not knowing what Stockport was like and were disgusted and would do nothing. I really see no reason why I shouldn't like the job; indeed I have just been balancing up in my mind what my life would be unmarried and married, and the advantage is all on the one side: Life abroad in different places (or life in garrison towns at home which I am sick of), fellows I like very much to associate with, who however are coming and going continually and who, after all, don't share any of my tastes. *On the other:* Life in a home in England and association with *the* person who shares *everything* (nearly) with me. (It was the scoffer in me, what Venus used to call Frankenstein, that put in that 'nearly'—I was thinking of the pianoforte!!!) And a settled object in life. God bless you, my Elizabeth, and make your life all the happier for your lover Frank's presence in it.

January 27. Mama went to Holy Trinity where they seem to have had a most touching service. At some places they sang God Save the King, but I don't like that.

Letter from Frank, January 28, Marple Hall:

My dearest Elizabeth, the day after tomorrow you'll be here. You must think of us at 10.30 tomorrow. It seems so dreadfully sad now that the time approaches. Esther is in the highest spirits, going to what we all think is certain unhappiness. It must be an awfully difficult miserable thing for a girl to marry without the approval of her family—and the thought of all this makes me (in a most modern spirit) feel for and sympathize with your Father, who after all I suppose is only doing what we have done in his own way—what he thinks is the best for you. You will perceive that I am in a very humble conciliatory mood, but I don't promise you that it will last. Indeed I am quite certain that it will not.

Letter from Frank, January 29, Marple Hall:

My darling Kitty, everything has been so unpleasant today. The wedding is over and the bride and our new brother Joseph departed. It was very quiet, no entertainment at all, and I have rather come round to your way of thinking that a very quiet wedding is the best and what I should like when our turn comes. There is such a lot to think about and to make me feel very solemn. I had heard the marriage service before, of course, but today I thought more about it and about you, for the first time, in it. 'To have and

to hold till death us do part'. I shall always think it so good of
your Mother not to hate me for wanting to take her Daughter
from her. Please give her my love and continued thanks. Till
tomorrow, addio my Kitty. Frank.

*(The Queen's death gave the Family a perfect excuse to con-
duct this much disapproved-of wedding as gloomily and cheaply as
possible. If poor Esther minded, she couldn't say so; any com-
plaint would have been an outrage against patriotism, religion and
public decency. But perhaps her show of high spirits, to which
Frank refers, was partly an indirect protest.)*

January 30. Mama drove with me to St Pancras and saw me off
by the 12 o'clock for Marple via Leicester. Frank met me and we
found Mr and Mrs Isherwood in, and his youngest brother Jack
appeared at tea. Music in the evening.

January 31. We painted in the ante-room till twelve and then
went down into the valley at the back of the house and up the
opposite hill all clothed in snow. Directly after lunch we started
driving with his Mother through Marple, which is quite a large
place, up past the church the Grandmother built and along the
Ridge, a wonderful expanse of snow hills and all very wide and
open, about two and a half miles to Wybbersley. Entered from
farm courtyard at back. Mrs Cooper, farmer's wife, showed us
dairy, cheese parlour etc and got permission from their tenant, a
widow lady who has been there nine years, to go over the front of
the house. This has a drive up, a little lawn in front and garden to
one side, all a good deal out of repair but quite possible to make
nice. Wybbersley is where the Bradshaws came from. The widow
lady took us all over. Mr Isherwood said he was prepared to put
it in thorough order. We sat in the library and wrote to Mama
after tea.

February 1. We painted in the ante-room together till twelve
and then went with Mrs Isherwood and the dogs in the park,

round. After lunch she and he and I went to see a Mrs Leach who paints very well, and she showed us her sketches. There was an old house in Kent down to the water and a very pretty grey one that we thought we should much like at Wybbersley!

February 2. Rather raw and damp. We drove to the memorial service at three o'clock. All the blinds were drawn in all the houses and everyone of course in black. The crowds in London will they say be greater than on any other occasion and it will be immensely impressive. Mama and Papa are going to see it from London St. I can't feel *the least patriotic* about the King, or think he can be *half* as beloved.

Letter from Emily, February 3, Cranley Mansion:

Called at 7.30 yesterday morning, started 8.40. Horse horribly frisky, kept me quite warm with terror!! Reached hotel in safety by a side route—a comfortable sitting room with balcony, guests only numbered sixteen in all, so everyone could see well. I alone of all the guests had a chair on balcony to watch procession, as I couldn't stand. At 11 all had hot coffee, tea and sandwiches, whiskey for those who liked. At 12.15 the first arrivals began. We had the most perfectly splendid view, all down London St, and the procession passed us quite close going into Paddington Station. It was all most solemn simple and touching. I just took it in as a whole till dear Lord Roberts came on a black horse, then I used my opera glass. Also when She arrived, it was so awfully pathetic seeing Her drawn on a gun carriage by the eight cream coloured horses of Jubilee renown—but I never at any funeral felt so strongly before, that She Herself was not on the bier but watching it all from somewhere and rejoicing in Her people's loyalty. It took much of one's sorrow away. Then came the King looking so marvellously majestic tho white and tired; on his right the German Emperor looking sad but full of observation. I saw him splendidly. As the King rode into the station he reined his horse back and let him go first. The Queen and Princesses were quite invisible in their splendid carriages drawn by four horses. From our balcony with opera glasses we could even see all the Royalties entering the railway carriages, and the Bier, which was placed in the middle saloon. Those who didn't go to Windsor came back, Lord Roberts and the King's horse led by grooms. So we saw everything that was to be seen, including the mob. Eight women were carried away fainting before the procession arrived, but no one whilst it passed.

I most certainly think Wybbersley sounds much nicer than a villa in Marple and full of possibilities. There would always be the village and station to walk to, and the hills. It all sounds to me at present like a dream. It is impossible for me to imagine your really living there, away from me, but I shall try to be strong and of a good courage. Goodbye, darling and love to Frank always, from your Mama.

February 4. Snow nearly all day. Frank and I painted in the dining-room in the morning, he a snow scene from the window and I tried a bit of the tapestry. In afternoon I sat with Frank while he packed and it snowed steadily.

February 5. Frank and I painted in the dining-room. It was very bright and sunny. Then we walked to the station to make enquiries about the trains to catch the 'Roslin Castle'. In afternoon he went out with his Mother and the dogs and I continued to paint till 4. After tea and his boxes had been fastened down we went and sat in the firelight up in the drawing-room until dinner time. I went in with him as it was the last night. After dinner Mrs Isherwood and I played patience and he knitted, and then she went down and put the dogs out and later, after he had changed, we went down to the smoking-room and had sandwiches and things and waited round the fire for the brougham to come and take him away. . . . He left soon after 12. Just as I was getting into bed, Dobson came back at a great pace for his helmet which had been left behind.

(*The phrases "to take in" and "to go in with," used in the sense of escorting or being escorted by someone into a room for dinner, no longer even appear in most modern dictionaries. According to protocol, Kathleen would normally have "gone in with" John Isherwood and Frank would have "taken in" his mother, leaving Jack, as the younger brother, without a partner. Kathleen, who loved all rituals—except those of the Catholic Church—must have fully appreciated the beautiful significance of this change of partners on the last evening; it was a sort of betrothal ceremony.)*

February 6. Mrs Isherwood and I had a tete a tete breakfast, both feeling very depressed. His brother Jack showed me his Japanese prints and then I painted while Mrs Isherwood did the flowers and then we went out and took the dogs, who also seemed depressed. Met Mr Isherwood on his return from his daily visit to the village. Said I must tell Papa he would do all he could about Wybbersley etc. Mrs Isherwood came to see me off by the 1.55 and I reached St Pancras a few minutes before six very tired and neuralgic. To bed directly after dinner. The German Emperor left for home amid a good deal of public enthusiasm.

Letter from Frank, February 6, on board the Roslin Castle *an hour or two before sailing:*

My darling Kitty, Am now safe on board. Not a particularly nice looking ship and very poky little cabins, two in them. I got into mine before the other man and strewed it with my baggage. Where he'll put his I don't know.

I am thinking of you at Marple. Are you painting or is my Brother amusing you? The ship is crammed with hordes of women seeing their men off. I am glad you think this is a mistake. You heard of course how I discovered that my helmet was left behind and how Dobson galloped back and got it for me.

I am just beginning to realize, darling, something has been in my life for the last few weeks, a different taste in my mouth, a new hunger, and now I shall have nothing but that last left and some pleasant, very very pleasant memories. I am so glad that you came to Marple. It tied us tighter together and now I think nothing can prevent our becoming someday even nearer than we have ever been, and husband and wife. My darling, I'd give a lot to 'squeeze' you, as you used to say, 'in two'.

This is going to be a thoroughly uninteresting hanging-about day. They say that we shall not start till four o'clock. I rather begin to envy the people with women seeing them off! Goodbye, my darling. Don't you get into any mischief till I come back to share it with you. Your lover, Frank.

8

Letter from Frank, written on the Roslin Castle, *February 7–10:*

My darling, I am going to write to you a little every day. The Needles looked awfully pretty in the sunset. I tried to do a little picture of them. Two sergeants who were standing near took the greatest interest. One begged me to put in two little clouds which 'looked as if they were going to dissolve over the rocks'—which I did. This pleased him enormously and he said in a most self-satisfied voice 'it isn't everyone as would have noticed them clouds'.

The domestic everyday virtues are so much more difficult than to be what Miss Robins calls a hero. As you've only seen me at the domestic times I can't imagine why you care for me at all. Perhaps it is for my failings. It is quite dreadful when one realizes the amount one thinks of oneself. Believe me, Dearest, I will try to attain to your frame of mind when you say: I hope you will be happy because that will make my happiness. That's one of the things you have got to teach me.

At St Helena I am alternating between hoping that we shall and shall not land. The only way, I believe, up from the beach is by hundreds and hundreds of steps. I've always heard people speak of it as the giddiest place known and I tremble at the thought of finding myself half way up there.

• •

(Throughout his life, Frank suffered from vertigo—a weakness which Christopher inherited. Frank's fears about the six hundred steps up from the beach at St. Helena—Jacob's Ladder—proved baseless, however; he later told Kathleen that he had found them "not in the least giddy.")

February 14. To see the state procession for opening of Parliament today. The state coaches of the peers and peeresses came first, the fat pompous coachmen in powder and velvet, and footmen hanging on behind. It was so picturesque but so unusual, it felt more like Drury Lane. The Royal State Coach, all gold and crystal, hasn't been used for forty years and was a magnificent affair. We saw the King and Queen beautifully and the Queen looked lovely, marvellously young and so pale and sweet.

February 20. Took ring to be made smaller.

February 21. Ring came back, and fancied they had put on a new and thinner gold band. Made myself quite unhappy about it!

February 22. Out early to the goldsmiths who assured me that the central stone was perfectly firm and that the gold band looked smaller because of the bit taken out.

Letter from Frank, mailed after arriving at Cape Town, February 27:

(Feb 11) The sun set most magnificently scarlet and gold, there were long streaks of reflection on the water. It was like the stage direction in Tannhauser when Venus is going to appear. Even the men stopped shouting songs about their mothers, which is how they generally spend the evening—

> 'And give the news to Mother
> And say how dear I love her
> And tell her not to wait for me
> For I'm not coming home'

is a great favourite—and looked at it. Doesn't Browning speak somewhere of things at sunset looking as if they must speak and unburden themselves?

Don't let us degenerate into mere friends or mere lovers at any time. We must be both, and both to their fullest extent.

(Feb 16; on the Line.) I do hope you will share with me my passion for out of doors; out of doors physical, mental and spiritual. We do live so very much too much indoors in every way at home. It will be your job to keep the windows open when we are living together in a house! 'The world is too much with us, late and soon'. I remember your saying rather plaintively 'what a lot of poetry you know'!! I hope though you've noticed that I never quote it *except on paper*.

(Feb 19) Two years hence, shall we be sitting in the Cheese Parlour? Or probably, as it's afternoon, in the west drawing-room. The white room with its red cushions and its pink mistress—my missus!!

(Feb 27) We got to Cape Town yesterday and instead of being allowed to go quietly to a hotel for a day or two they made us come here (Officers Mess, Green Point). A tea party and a band were going on in the Mess. We all felt awful sweeps coming in among the young and beautiful ladies. There was a very good piano and a lady came forward and sang and we had a great conversation. Colonial ladies are such an extraordinary mixture of free-and-easiness and extraordinary propriety. She asked me where I came from, etc etc, but all this time almost talked about '*Mr Shakespeare*'. *You* were the last woman I spoke to—and I felt inclined to tell her what an honour it was to be the next!

Letter from Frank, March 1, Officers' Mess, Green Point, Cape Town:

I remember feeling quite annoyed with you because you didn't agree with my ideas of decoration for Wybersley. Now I feel that you can paint the house sky-blue or any colour you like if you'll only come and live in it.

I wonder how the Toogoods are getting on. I can't help feeling rather sorry that I went away without any sort of letter or message from or to her and I have almost made up my mind to write to her by this mail. I think you would advise me to, if you were here.

Your People are, I know, very kind to you, at least of course your Mother is angelic and I am beginning to feel that F. Senior isn't so bad after all. If I were to meet him out here I should rush at him and be delighted to see him.

Letter from Frank, March 13, Marine Hotel, Durban:

Here I am! Going up country tonight IF all goes well. There are all sorts of rumours here that there are negotiations going on and that the war is virtually over, and people seem to think that we shall be among the first for home, so I hope that Wybersley is not very far off now.

I wish you would tell me what you do as a rule on an ordinary day. I want to be able to think of it and get into your habits! With best and warmest love, your future husband Frank.

(While Frank was in England, the War had changed its charac-
ter. During the summer of 1900, the Orange Free State and the
Transvaal were formally annexed to the Queen's dominions; that
autumn, the aged Kruger fled to Europe because his countrymen
did not want him to fall into the hands of the British. It had be-
come evident that no foreign power would now intervene to save
the South African Republic. Roberts returned to England, and
the British public was given to understand that the War was as
good as won and that all that was still needed was police action
against a handful of diehards who fanatically refused to surrender.
However, by the beginning of 1901 it was obvious to the whole
world that the Boers were far from defeated. Their territory had
been annexed in name only; it remained unconquered. Their gov-
ernment had no fixed seat, but it still functioned and had a strong
will to resist. Their mobile units kept in constant touch with each

other, and their military movements were coordinated. They were making raids into Cape Colony, harassing troop concentrations everywhere and cutting railways.

Kitchener, now supreme commander, was fighting a largely invisible enemy in a war without geographical objectives, hunting him back and forth across a vast terrain in the hope of trapping him or at least gradually reducing his strength. It was a doubtful hope. The Boer commandos were perfectly familiar with this terrain and natively accustomed to its hardships; most of its inhabitants were their secret helpers, and they themselves could easily pass for noncombatant farmers when in danger of being caught. One couldn't even enjoy the minor triumph of capturing their artillery; they no longer had any and didn't need it.

The British, in their frustration, had resorted to measures which troubled their own consciences. They seized the Boers' livestock, burned their farms and then interned the women and children who had lived on them, lest they should starve. The places of internment were ominously referred to as concentration camps; nobody starved in them, nobody was mistreated, but many thousands died, mostly children, of measles and other diseases spread by overcrowding and lack of sanitation.

The hopes for peace which Frank mentions in his letter were based on negotiations between Kitchener and Botha, begun on February 28. Kitchener, who knew that this guerilla warfare could continue almost indefinitely, was eager for a settlement; his terms were the best he had the authority to offer. But Botha still demanded independence, and this the British Government would not grant. For a while it seemed that a compromise might nevertheless be reached. Then Botha got the news of a temporary success from his fellow leaders, De Wet and Steyn, which moved him to decide that the Boers should fight on. On March 16 he broke off negotiations.

On March 22 Kathleen comments in her diary:

The terms of peace published that were offered to Botha, as Lord Kitchener drew them up, far too lenient, which seems astonishing in a man like him, but even as they were finally sent, revised by Milner and Chamberlain, they were far easier than those beastly cowards, liars, humbugs and scum of the earth deserve. *However they were. refused.* Gen Botha's brother got killed a day or two ago, would that we could kill Botha himself and De Wet.)

Letter from Frank, March 15, Ingogo, Natal:

My darling Kitty, I got your letter this afternoon. I was so pleased as I was feeling a little homesick. I had got to my journey's end and found myself in a tin hut, by myself, where I am going to live for the next I don't know how long; the men living through a thin tin wall. I am very determined at present not to be annoyed by their conversation but I don't know how long that will last. Everyone seems rather down on their luck, and though by way of being very pleased to see me and telling me repeatedly that I was a sportsman to come back, as no one else had attempted to do so, they didn't seem to take much interest in my doings or my affairs —with the bright exception though of my particular friend Michael Halford. I couldn't resist telling him about you and he insisted on talking about you as Miss Rachel Smith!

The arrangements at Durban for landing the baggage were simply shocking. All one's baggage had to be weighed by a man who didn't understand English! A shouting screaming mass of subalterns, you can imagine the state of chaos. In my excitement I believe I knocked a man down who hit my porter in the face, as I found him prostrate at my feet. I finally started without my bed valise containing all my boots and blankets etc and without the arsenal of guns which I so kindly brought out for my brother officers!

(*Ingogo is north of Newcastle on the Natal railway. Two companies of the Regiment had been stationed at various posts in that area since December, guarding the stretch of line between Newcastle and Charlestown, which is up near the Transvaal border.*)

• •

Letter from Frank, March 19, Ingogo:

My darling, it seems so amusing to get your letter about wall-papers and brown curtains, here in my wigwam. The walls are tin and the floor of dirt, made 'sad' (solid or compact—you'll get to know this word when you live up North) by water thrown on it.

You will like to know what my day is like. We get up at 3.30 and stand to arms until 5. I tramp round the sentries and generally get tied up in the barbed wire which surrounds the post. Then we go to bed again and get up about 7.30. Breakfast, and then I ride or walk round my posts, which extend up the line for ten miles, but I haven't succeeded in seeing the farthest one yet. In the after-noon I ride out to call on another post. Dinner and then another round of sentries and bed about 9.

I don't feel very sorry that you didn't get into the Queen's Hall on Ash Wednesday. I don't approve at all of what the great British Public looks upon as a sacred concert. Most of the pieces are chosen because they are in slow time.

We came out with a lady who was going to join her husband. She had had consumption in England and was supposed to be dying and he was dangerously wounded and made prisoner at Spion Kop. I rather envied him. It's almost worth being parted for a meeting like that!

Letter from Frank, March 25, Ingogo:

I have done you a little picture of my wigwam. I live on the farthest side from the guard tent. The men live in the middle. This morning at breakfast they took quite three quarters of an hour to explain to one of them the riddle: 'King Charles laughed and talked half an hour after his head was cut off'. I nearly had the man in and explained it to him myself in desperation.

Letter from Frank, April 4, Ingogo:

My dear Kitty, I am sending you a panorama of Ingogo. Would you mind sending it on to my Mother? I know she will like to have it. You see, I am somehow not quite so sure of your interest as of hers. When I'm not with you I can't help feeling you're with F. Senior, and I know he wouldn't be the least interested and it must damp you *a little* sometimes.

I saw a most beautiful effect last night at a large circular pond. All over the pond was a grass green weed with slashes of silver water showing through here and there, behind it was the pinky yellow grass, behind that the bright blue hills and a rosy yellow sky behind it all. I am falling deeply in love with this country. My brother officers sarcastically remark wait for a month or two and see what you say then!

We had a bit of a railway smash yesterday at my farthest post about 10 miles from here. Lukas Meyer and his commando descended on the railway and blew up a train. By an extraordinary piece of luck a train full of troops was standing in the station at the time and they were able to reinforce my eighteen men and drive the Boers back, not giving them time to carry away much loot and provisions which they came down for. I spent a most boring day up there in the pouring rain yesterday, all talking as hard as ever we could, but there was nothing to be done as the enemy had long before we got there retired into the mountains. They were caught by another post retiring and we know of two killed and one wounded and a prisoner and think there were others, so I hope they got a lesson and won't bother us again. I comfort myself by the thought that very soon we shall be settled down comfortably at home and I shall look upon this as an affair of my youth and years ago.

April 4. Heard this morning that Dr Burnett died quite suddenly two days ago. Papa and I most awfully shocked and grieved, we owe him so much and whatever Mama will do without him I can't think. He was so bright and strong and reassuring, one felt better for seeing him even, and she has been under him fifteen years.

In the paper after lunch, I saw The Child's death, only 36. That seemed to cast a further gloom, a final break with much that was happy.

April 5. Poor Mama very low and depressed. In afternoon to the Queen's Hall especially to hear the Symphony Pathétique by the Russian Tchaikovsky but liked much better some out of Lohengrin by Wagner. Should like to hear that Symphony again, I believe we were too near. *J. kos-kay.*

April 6. Mama and I both felt very low and neither of us could think of anything to do. Dr Burnett buried today and The Child's funeral also today.

Letter from Frank, April 12, Ingogo:

My dear, I have just got a delightful letter from you. I am feeling so happy at your saying that I am woven up in all you do. I am glad that your Father still talks about us and that you wear THE ring and speak of me to him, but I wish you could make him think that I am not at all unreasonable and would not for worlds make a pauper of you.

I have just heard that the Store and Hotel about three miles off has been burnt down and a man with whom we were having tea yesterday got wounded as he refused to turn out of his house. I feel very sorry for his wife who is living there too. You needn't —and I hope you don't—feel the least alarm on my account. They don't wish at all to come into contact with soldiers—these ruffians. Women and children and unarmed men are about their form. I wonder so much how you would take it, if Wybersley were surrounded by the enemy and I were wounded. Would you be a heroine or would you scream? There are so many incentives to make a man brave, principally because he is expected to be so, but a woman has her choice and nobody thinks much the worse of her if she is a funk.

Did I ever tell you about my Grandmother who, when the Chartists marched down to Marple with the intention, I suppose, of sacking it—she being alone at the time—went to the gate with my Father in her arms (he was a baby at the time) and told them they ought to be ashamed of themselves and were to go home to their wives at once. One man said 'the Missus speaks correct' and by degrees they slunk off home. Ours was the only house untouched in the neighbourhood. She was a most tiresome meddling woman in many ways but in that way I'm sure you would resemble her and rise to the occasion. I think a great danger is worth going through for this—that one knows afterwards whether one can stand fire or not. I suppose this is the reason why active service is so popular.

I like your idea of beginning all over again when I get back. We shall have the curious Ventnor feeling again, as if we were almost afraid of one another. I have taken out your portraits to see how they take this remark. I don't think the one in the large hat quite understands what I mean. The two evening dress ones are not thinking of me at all. The portrait which hasn't yet been taken, the portrait of my Elizabeth, knows though, doesn't she?

I am very much struck with this sentence in one of Bacon's Essays which I have been reading: 'A man's nature runs either to herbs or to weeds; therefore let him seasonably water the one and destroy the other'. I must keep before myself all I can that you wouldn't like a weed for a husband.

(*Henry, who welcomed any opportunity of adding glamour to the family history, used to claim that the encounter between his grandmother and the Chartists had been alluded to by Disraeli in his novel* Sybil. *Disraeli does indeed state that he knows personally of an instance in which the strikers from a manufacturing town in Lancashire entered the grounds of a neighboring squire in search of food.* "The lord of the domain was absent . . . His wife, who had a spirit equal to the occasion, notwithstanding the presence of her young children . . . received the deputation herself." *But this was a quite different kind of encounter. The strikers were* "mild and respectful," *the lady most hospitable. Having fed all two thousand of them, she let them walk through her gardens.* "Not a border was trampled on, not a grape plucked; and, when they quitted the domain, they gave three cheers for the fair castellan." *There is, however, a much more dramatic, apparently fictitious*

174

scene in Sybil; *its heroine confronts a raging mob known as the Hell-Cats who have just drunk the wine cellar dry and set fire to the house. All that Sybil can hope for is a bodyguard to help her and the other women escape. She recognizes some of the men and boldly harangues them in a style not unlike that of Mrs. Isherwood: "Bamford, if you be my father's friend, aid us now; and Samuel Carr, I was with your mother this morning: did she think I should meet her son thus? Oh men, men! What is this? Are you led away by strangers to such deeds? Why, I know you all!")*

April 16. Lady M. said how fond all his family had been of The Child, what a comfort he had been with his younger brother and sister and how sad it all was.

Letter from Frank, April 18, Ingogo:

A propos of your remarks about one feeling more religious in an old and beautiful building etc, I never can see why one should snub one's intellect and all one's best feelings in thinking about religion. It seems to me that all that is part of *our* religion, of ours who can understand and feel that. I think if you should ever be put to it, though, you would find how extraordinarily little one is affected by one's surroundings. I could live quite comfortably with a beaded mat, always provided that the window was open so that I could pitch it out if the worst came to the worst.

Two letters from Frank, both mailed from Ingogo on April 26 but written during the previous three or four days:

My dear, I was so pleased with your letter. This week it finds me in all the throes of moving. My Company are being scattered like a rocket to all the distant hills and I am going to squat on the railway about four miles off. (It sounds like a person in the Nonsense Book.) I have made lots of wishes over the new moon about us both, and this country is a perfect mine of horseshoes which I always pick up and wish in the same way.

•   •

(April 24; Three Bridges.) My move is over and I am seated under a mimosa bush at the side of the railway at a round table which came out of O'Neill's farm. The people in the mail which has just passed envied me very much as I was just enjoying my lunch and a whiskey and soda, which was very acceptable after a six o'clock breakfast and a ride over the hills. It's all quite idyllic and I am sure I shall be quite attached to it after a day or two. I am a very catlike person and tremendously fond of home, but I am not sure I shouldn't like to be a cat on a ship or a train or something that moved. A cat in a caravan! That would be nice.

I liked what you said of burial so much. A grassy daisy-strewn mound does seem much better than an urn, but I am dreadfully uncertain really about the personal rising again. It seems so impossible that we shall not and yet so impossible that we shall, in other ways. It will be your business to reconcile me to all the conventional usual beliefs. One wants to believe them all if one can, I think. And now, Cattarina mia, addio. Sempre tuo, Frank.

(April 25) I woke up quite cheerfully here though the trains make an awful noise in the night. They go within twenty yards of my head and then curl backwards and forwards up the hill, so that they make all the noise that they possibly can. I imagined you smiling at me when I woke up. I can see that nice smile so clearly sometimes. Another little way of yours that I think of very often is when you hum—it's not exactly humming, though—and you put your arms on the table and look up and argue. It's generally at breakfast that you do this. However, as in our menage we are not to have breakfast (wasn't that settled?) you must learn to do it at other times. I shan't dispense with any of your little ways.

I want to tell you about my new little home. The walls are made of old sleepers off the line with a bank of earth below them, and we are planning to get maidenhair fern from the banks of the Buffalo to plant in it. On the table are two large bowls (really chocolate tins but no matter) of roses which I have got from O'Neill's farm. My servant, who has an extremely genteel manner and ideas, said that the place began to look quite like home. So I said that I didn't think it could be much like his home. (He lives in Sheffield.) He replied with conscious pride No, it couldn't be like a house with seven rooms, as his was.

Last night I went out on patrol on the railway and crouched about and hid and fancied I heard people coming to blow up the line, but nothing at all happened. It was beautiful coming back, though. We were in a very high piece of railway and could see the first flush of the rosepink sunrise and the deep gloomy blue of the Berg stretching away into the distance, and in the foreground the railway curve, the metals gleaming brighter than anything. What a difficult blue the upper sky is at that hour, really blue, not purple nor grey. I wonder if you have ever felt the curious feeling of fear that a high fall of water gives me? Last night I had to absolutely force myself up to the bottom of some water which comes over a dam near the reversing station, on which I have a post.

In a way I am afraid I am not manly (or manlike?) and that is— I know it's not what I ought to say—I like to be wooed, and you did woo me a little bit in that letter. Someday it will be every day of my life that I shall hear and see you, and it seems too good to be true. Though my shifting casual sort of life makes me realize that things aren't at all solid.

I am so sorry about your Mother's trouble and about yours too. I don't feel in any way that I dislike your feeling an old friend's loss and I know that with your sweet nature you naturally must feel anything of that kind. But I also know from the same reason of your nature that the more we are together the more you will become, as you once expressed it, 'dependent' on me, and I can only hope that I shall be worthy of such dependence and not a broken reed.

I am afraid we of the younger generation are sometimes dreadfully callous. You're not, my dear, I know that, and I am so sick of people who are.

On April 27, Kathleen, Emily and Frederick started on a trip through France, Switzerland and Italy; they returned to England on *May 25. Only a few of Kathleen's diary entries are worth quoting:*

April 27. It felt so good to be abroad again. The red roofs, the flatness, the poplars fresh and green and the peasants in their blue blouses. It seemed just as if we had been looking through dirty glass for ever so long and now at last the atmosphere was clear.

April 28. [At Rheims.] Papa and I went and sat in the cathedral. It interested Papa very much seeing the priests 'tinkling about and changing their dress'.

April 30. [At Lucerne.] Switzerland makes me feel brisk and managing, even though it is so damp and nasty.

May 2. [At Milan.] Mama and Papa to see Leonardo's Last Supper. I waited for them outside. Didn't think it worth paying a franc to see it again. They never had.

To the Simonetta Palace. We heard 'the wonder' for which we had come—one of the men talked through a trumpet out of the window and a whole series of the most marvellous echoes was the result, from the wing opposite right away into the far distance. The final treat was to fire a gun off and hear the echo of that, which was supposed to be something tremendous, but I utterly refused to have this part of the entertainment for which, by the way, you paid 25 centimes a shot!

(*Kathleen maintained a hatred of loud bangs throughout her life. Christopher got the impression that they made her indignant as well as nervous—that she took them as a personal affront. At the theater, whenever she suspected that a firearm was going to be discharged, she would stop her ears with her fingers long in advance and keep them closed long after the shot, lest it should be repeated. Thus she prevented herself from enjoying some of the greatest scenes in dramatic literature—and occasionally even from knowing what the play was about!*)

178

May 5. [At Venice.] The good people went to church but I got no letters and did not feel the least good. Lovely day, but news of fighting on the 29th. Simply did nothing but sit about all the morning. The sunshine and the brightness and the glamour of Venice made me feel I didn't want to do anything else.

Letter from Frank, May 6, mailed from Ingogo:

Dearest Kitty, I am just off again—to Volksrust this time. I had, as I told you, settled down and made myself most comfortable. It's most dreadfully annoying. Volksrust is in the Transvaal—the coldest place in the Colony they say—so it will give me another bar to my medal. I think I shall have four—Cape Colony, Tugela Heights, Relief of Ladysmith and Transvaal. Perhaps I may go on a little expedition into the Orange River Colony, in which case I should get that.

I had a most delightful letter from your Mother this week, kind and good. I like feeling that a person whose life is such a success as hers is, such a success I mean in fulfilling its métier, can speak of herself as struggling and trying to do right. Last night I was patrolling on the line and I took your Mother with me, at least spiritually. I thought of her and the noble ideal of life which is hers, and of living up to her counsel. It was the most lovely brilliant moonlight night with some of the stars low down on the horizon twinkling like jewels. It is all so associated in my mind with you both, as this place altogether is.

May 7. This morning we saw the great Duse walking in the Piazza with two cavaliers and quite a mob of admiring Venetians following her. She is acting here tomorrow night.

May 20. [Traveling from Lugano to Basle.] At Lucerne we were turned out and joined the first part of the train, but there was only enough dinner for the first lot and so there we had to sit, hungry. I felt so hot and cross when I got in and, seeing only two sleepy-looking priests, said rather loudly that one could do very well without foreign languages till one wanted to swear. We heard a great chuckle and discovered they were as English as ourselves, Bishop Lucy and Father Gordon, going back to England.

Letter from Frank, mailed from Volksrust on May 15, written during the three previous days:

(May 12) You said that you tried to make your letters reflect your various moods but I am afraid if this one is to reflect mine it will be one long grumble. You must pity me very much as long as you see Volksrust at the top of my paper, for of all the poisonous places that I have ever seen . . . ! Everything is covered with dust, one's eyes are full of it and one's nose and one's temper, and altogether it is most odious. Some of our fellows say that it is a delightful station and when I say 'why, in the name of goodness?' they say 'because there is polo three times a week'! This is not unfortunately my idea of bliss, and when you get into a place that is as flat as your hand (and as dirty as mine is at present) I think you grumble too (?) I can't imagine you at Venice now in the least, though I have been trying to manage it by reading an Italian paper Henry sent me. However I was called away at intervals of two minutes to go and look after the beer barrel we were getting into the Mess, and the cook came to say that he had no pie dish of the right size and then we had to go to church parade and stand with the dust swirling round us and altogether my attempts at an Italian atmosphere have been quite a failure. Still it's nice to know there is such a place and that you are enjoying it. 'And Langness has its heather still—thank God!' Do you know those lines of T. E. Brown's? That sort of optimism unfortunately rather deserts me when there is any need for it.

(In the poem referred to, Brown is consoling himself amidst the humdrum circumstances of his life as a schoolmaster at Clifton College by thinking of the distant romantic places he knows:

Alert, I seek exactitude of rule,
I step, and square my shoulders with the squad;
But there are blaeberries on old Barrule,
And Langness has its heather still—thank God!)

(May 14) Since writing the last I have had a bad go of tooth-ache which has bowled me out completely. All the others have gone off on a little expedition for 4 or 5 days and I am left alone in the mess-house, very cheap and swollen about the face. I am afraid that they have gone down into the Orange River Colony, which will be awfully annoying for me as I haven't got that bar to my medal.

I am afraid that you will not all be going up to Marple this summer and I so particularly wanted your Mother to see Wyb-bersley and F. Senior to see my People. I am quite beginning to like him. That little scene in which he began by calling you Piggins and ended by calling me Frank tickled me immensely.

Letter from Frank, May 22, Volksrust:

This is a land of effects. Not always pretty ones, but still effects. The sun has such a great canvas of bare hill to paint on. Last night there was a large grass fire towards the sunset, as if Hell were just the other side of the hill. There is a strange blueness about an African town at midday, from there being so much corrugated iron about. The shade on it in some lights is brilliant azure, the colour of a dark sky. Indeed I am not sure that corrugated iron is such a very ugly thing as it is generally supposed to be.

I have had rather a longing for snow and frost and blue mist this morning when I was reading Jane Eyre. I pictured Wyb-bersley and throwing up a window in the morning to find a little heap of freshly fallen snow crouching in the corner of the sill, as if it was trying to keep in the shade and not be melted.

I looked at your photographs. The one I like much the best is the smiling one in pink, with the star in your hair. When you smile at one, that's just what you are like—a star—and you are going to be my star, aren't you? Something for me to steer a straight course by.

Letter from Frank, May 30, Volksrust:

There are constant expeditions down to Ladysmith with Boer prisoners. It's a most unpleasant duty as you travel in a goods train and are shunted at every station to let everything pass you, and when you are coming back after delivering your prisoners you are probably seized upon to do escort to some other convoy or something. It's a most unwise thing to leave your regiment's protecting wing out here as you get ordered about by everyone and bossed by staff officers who are probably junior to yourself.

Your Rheims letter has just arrived. It made me very happy, my dearest, that I was so associated in your happiness in being abroad. I liked F. Senior for thinking your Mother nicer than you. It's just what he ought to think, but it seems so funny to think of comparing you to anyone else, you are quite apart from everyone else as far as I am concerned. Dearest, I think sometimes that we are more lovers than we have ever imagined, and that we really know more what love means than a great many people who talk more about it.

Letter from Frank to Emily, June 14, Volksrust:

Dear Mrs Machell Smith, I am writing to thank you for your little note written from Venice. Letters like yours are a great stimulant to one to make one wish and try to be as worthy of them as possible. I hope that you will not mind my having sent this one on to my Mother. I felt that it would be a very great pleasure to her to see it and to know what kindness and goodness you are showing me, and I hope you will not feel that you dislike her seeing it. I hope that you enjoyed your Italian time and have not felt the travelling too fatiguing. Believe me, yours affectionately, Frank B. Isherwood.

. .

(*On this letter, Emily, who is evidently forwarding it to Kathleen, has written, "I don't quite like his Mother having seen it but I do like his honesty in telling me."*)

Letter from Frank, June 15, begun at the Salisbury Hotel, Newcastle, Natal, but mailed after his return to Volksrust:

The place is full of officers' wives who have come up to be near their husbands. Why fellows marry such people I cannot think and I kept on saying to myself, my girl is not the least like that. I can quite understand people thinking it is not a good thing for a girl to marry a soldier when they see soldiers' wives as a class.

I came down here to see a dentist as I have had such constant toothache. He didn't do very much for me but promised me I shouldn't have any more. However, he told me that he always got away to train a horse at 3.30, and as it was 3.15 when I got to him I felt that he didn't take much interest in me. Life would be so much more bearable out here if it wasn't for horses. If you don't talk about them you feel that you are looked upon as quite an outsider.

I always feel rather bitter about soldiers in general when I get away from my own regiment. They are so delightful and I think different to almost any other fellows that one meets. I always think that if I had gone into any other regiment in the service my life as a soldier would have been a miserable failure, but they are so good to me and like me in spite of my numerous shortcomings —numerous, I mean, from their point of view. I am not going to pretend that I think I have very many from any other.

I came past my old habitation at Three Bridges. It looked thoroughly deserted and degraded, and a lot of men were sitting about my own little wigwam.

(Next morning, in the train going back to Volksrust) I have been thinking so much, after last night, of the position of a soldier's wife. I hope so much that you will never have to feel that you are one. The living about uncomfortably and being

183

rather at the neighbourhood's mercy is what I should very much dislike for you.

F. Senior seems to be very skittish, dancing about on the balcony, saying 'Bo' from behind curtains and snatching your letters. I hope the balcony isn't so high as your own at home. It makes me quite sick to think of anyone jumping about on that.

(Frederick's skittishness was probably exhibited while they were at the hotel in Venice, a month earlier; a letter from Kathleen describing it could have reached Frank about this time. It isn't mentioned in her diary—perhaps because she only found it strange and therefore noteworthy when she imagined how it would appear to Frank.)

As for what you say about my Mother, I think if I may say so that you don't understand her. She is a difficult person to understand sometimes, very quiet, very undemonstrative and apparently not taking very much interest in anything. That's one great reason why it would be so nice for you to go to Marple when I am not there, you really would get to know her much better. She is so very self-sacrificing that, if I am there, she hardly likes to speak to you for fear of being in the way.

Letter from Frank, date uncertain, Volksrust:

'The dearest Mama'—I am glad that she thought it nice for me to call her that, and I can't think of any better name for her, as you suggest I should. I always think names should arise naturally.

This Sunday I went up to Majuba. It is a most extraordinarily built mountain. Huge mounds, on top of them an immense rock only climbable in two places and those very steep. I thought of 'Childe Roland to the Dark Tower came'. Indeed Africa reminds me always of that poem as one rides along the veldt—wretched thin grass on it, where there is anything, with black patches, the traces of veldt fires; and the whole country strewn with sheep and cattle, dead and dying with starvation. One might have got into the path which was pointed out by the 'hateful cripple'. It's both a hideous and a beautiful country—hideous per se, but the lights and colouring are most beautiful. Of course a lot of it, I suppose, lies in the eye of the beholder, as the others think it a great joke when I point out these things in a moment of expansion and I have to pretend afterwards that I meant to be funny.

On June 22 Kathleen paid a visit to Marple on the way up to Scotland. Joe and Esther Toogood, Moey Isherwood and her friend Miss Lander were already staying at the house. Kathleen knew this in advance; evidently she had decided that she ought to meet them and make herself agreeable to them for Frank's sake. Frank himself, when he heard of the coming confrontation, was alarmed on her behalf and wrote to her admitting that Esther was "not much inclined to like you," that she and Moey were "always rather like two cats together" and that Miss Lander was "such a dreadful person to have to talk to, I can never think of anything to say to her."

Nevertheless, Kathleen's brief visit—she arrived just before supper on the Saturday and left after breakfast on Monday—can't have been such an ordeal as Frank feared. Esther may have shown the resentment she had every reason to feel—her Joe had been disapproved of by Frank while his Kathleen had been warmly received—but Kathleen must surely have understood this and made allowances. (Later in life, the two women were able to become quite fond of each other.) Elizabeth Isherwood was kind and welcoming as always; she met Kathleen at the station and spent much time with her, walking in the garden and showing photographs of Frank when he was a child. As for Moey, she wrote enthusiastically to Frank, who reported back to Kathleen, "You seem to have thoroughly bewitched her and poor Miss Lander." Kathleen genuinely liked Moey; she spent a day alone with her at Ipswich a few weeks later.

Why, then, does Kathleen note in her diary (on June 27, while still in Scotland): "Feeling absurdly nervous and depressed; refreshing my memory was a great mistake!"? The draft of a letter to Frank, dated June 30, shows that Kathleen's visit to Marple has disturbed her profoundly but not in a way which has anything to do with the Isherwoods as individuals; somehow it has aroused her latent dread of marriage and of the responsibilities and duties of a daughter-in-law. She writes that she sometimes fears "I should never get absorbed in the things that model wives are supposed to —and might turn out a failure altogether!" Frank had to keep reassuring her on this point, as will be seen.

While Kathleen and Moey were together at Marple Hall, Kathleen may not have realized what a very sick woman Moey was. Ten days later, she got a letter from Frank telling her, "Poor Moey is in a very bad way; the doctor told her that one of her lungs was quite hopeless and that the other was a good deal affected. I had hoped so much that she would get quite well again, which I am afraid is now hopeless. I am afraid she feels it a great deal, though she is not a person who says very much."

Moey (Mary) Isherwood, the elder of Frank's sisters, was born on October 3, 1871. She was generally regarded as the only plain member of the family; she had a sallow skin, an unremarkable nose and rather heavy cheeks. However, with her large serious gray eyes and interesting, temperamental mouth, she would have made an attractive young man; she looked like one in the starched masculine collars she often wore. The heroine of one of her books wishes she had been born a boy and pleases her brothers by taking part in their games; they call her "no end of a good fellow." Moey herself played golf in all weathers until she got rheumatic fever. The doctor then told her she should live in a dry climate, so she had moved from wet Cheshire to the East Coast.

Moey's stories were for children—A Credit to the Colours, The Little Lady, Me, Nos and the Others*—and the view of life which they expressed was perfectly suited to their publisher, the Society for Promoting Christian Knowledge. Moey seems to be speaking much more as her natural self in an article she wrote about a visit to the Brontës' home at Haworth: "To realize happiness is the saddest of all joy, for the truly happy are those whose happiness is a matter of course." Her temperament was melancholy, no* doubt because of her chronic ill health, and also difficult and complex. The servants at Marple Hall complained that she gave herself airs and that she ordered them about imperiously. Yet she held socialistic views and tended to make friends with people of the working class, mill girls and others. She never showed any inclination to marry.

Miss Lander was a trained nurse; she first came to Marple to nurse Esther through an attack of scarlet fever. Thus she and Moey met. The two of them opened a curiosity shop together in Essex, but their relationship was not harmonious; Miss Lander was a domineering character. Richard remembers Kathleen telling him, "Miss Lander laughed too loud and Moey was getting afraid of her." So they parted.

Early in the nineteen-twenties, Moey became a Catholic. This must be one reason why her middle age was much happier than her youth had been. Another was the discovery, some time before this, of an almost ideal companion named Myrtle. Kathleen met her in 1915 and was favorably impressed: "She is the smallest thing in maids I have ever seen, only twentyfive but a monument of wisdom. Mr and Mrs Myrtle occupy the attic. 'Mr Myrtle' is only a recent addition." Myrtle and her husband looked after Moey devotedly for the rest of her life. Despite her damaged lungs, she lived to the age of sixty-three. She died in the cottage at Colchester where she had spent many quiet years, on July 5, 1935.

Letter from Emily to Kathleen in Scotland, July 1, Cranley Mansion:

Darling K, I am *really* very well, thank you darling and Miss M said yesterday how very well I was looking. Don't darling worry about me or the future. Let us enjoy each other, and of 'the griefs unborn rest secure, *knowing* that mercy ever will endure'. I *know* it is *very* trying for you, Frank being so far away, but as you can't marry yet it really is better so. You would get so worn out if you were constantly meeting and writing. You remember what

187

a wreck Edith became. Try and get into a torpid state and say to yourself Nothing, Nothing. Or fit your mind on a teacup or the knob of a bed, and don't get worrying ideas about Frank, and leaving me, all will come right and things will fall in their natural places, and as long as we are both in the world together, nothing matters much. Daughters always do seem to be able to see a lot of their mothers after marriage if they wish to, and to come to them if ill, but I hope I shall not be ill. Dear Dr Burnett seemed to think I shouldn't be.

I suppose you can't feel you are just great friends and not engaged? I am sure dear that you are very fond of him, fond of us both only in different ways. Believe me, all will be well, and he is so nice to me, nicer than anyone who ever cared for you.

Letter from Frank, July 2, Volksrust:

I am feeling rather amused at the idea I had when I was at home, of augmenting our income by keeping hens. We've got some here and I feel so hopelessly vague and ignorant when I have to go and see which are fit for killing etc etc, and they seem to me thoroughly uninteresting, partly because the authority on the subject is one of our militiamen to whom I have taken a dislike. I don't think anyone likes him much and V described him as being like a woman who had taken to drink, which exactly hit him off. It's just a little bit annoying to be bossed by these young militia captains who *of course* are in everything—age, experience and service—*immeasurably* one's inferiors!!

(Frank was still a lieutenant when he wrote this; hence his bitterness. He was promoted captain later in the year.)

Have you told anyone about—us? I am afraid that by degrees I have told all the fellows in the Regiment, at least all the ones who would be interested. The ones who remembered you were properly impressed and quite took the proper point of view, that they wished you were going to join the Regiment, as it were, but that you weren't at all the sort of woman that would like it, or that one could expect it of.

(*This last sentence refers to Frank's plan to get himself appointed adjutant of the Volunteers at Stockport after the war—which would mean leaving the Regiment, at least temporarily. Frank seems to be probing to find out just how strongly Kathleen would object to becoming a Regular Army wife sometime in the distant future.*)

I'm not particularly fond of female society, unless I can get *the* particular female society I want, which is of course superior to the best male society.

I am a mass of bruises today with a black eye. We had a most violent game of hockey yesterday against the North Staffords, who are very good, and everyone in their team at some period of the game fell upon me.

Letter from Frank, July 15, Volkshurst:

I have just been attacked by Michael Halford. You say that I am not properly grown up; I think if you saw him you would call him perfectly babyish. He is always pulling someone's hair or making a noise of some kind. I don't know why I am so fond of him, but I really like him much better than any other man I know, a sort of instinctive fondness more than liking. The sort of feeling one is supposed to have for one's brothers, and—as a rule—hasn't.

Kathleen returned to London on July 15. On July 20 she went with Emily to the races at Sandown, but without much enjoyment; the reason is obvious, though her diary does not mention The Child. "My first day's racing this year and there seemed a sad blank about it all, and not at all the same as it used to be."

.   .

189

I was thinking how amusing it would be if one could piece the various utterly unlike bits of one's life together—if Miss Robins could suddenly pass the gate or if John Wood the blacksmith at Marple and all his family could be translated into Africa and walk in to see 'Mr Frank'. It would be something more than amusing if I could get a wire 'shall be on the mail today, K.M.S.' We should have lunch at the station (rather an Italian-looking restaurant) and then I should take you what I call your walk. It is a path which leads along the ravine which runs up to the town. There are high cliffs with the Boer refugee camp perched up on one side of them and at one end a tiny reservoir with a little white house which, about half past four, catches the sun and makes a brilliant reflection in the water. After that we should shop. They never have anything that you ask for. You just buy what they have got in case you should want it. After that, we would have tea, with condensed milk in it so that you might feel you really had been on active service.

My dearest, I don't want anything in marriage but you—and a happy you. I have always envied the married people who were comrades, people who shared all their happiness and their work. We unfortunately are not artists, at least not professionally, but we can live in a great many ways as if we were. The last thing I want is to make a hausfrau of you.

You need not be afraid of me in any way, in fact I am the most manageable person in the world. Of course if you have any doubt about marriage from the other point of view and feel that you don't really like me well enough to spend your life and give up a good deal for me, you *must* say so. We *shall* be quite different to most married couples, and I can't think why you should now suddenly think otherwise.

On July 25 Frederick left London for Wales, where he joined Walter Greene on board his yacht; they were to cruise north to Scotland and visit the Glasgow Exhibition.

July 30. Uncle Walter wrote word that poor dear Papa had been very bad but was better; he had been in dreadful pain from 11 pm on Sunday till 2 pm yesterday. Fortunately they were anchored at Gourock and able to have doctor and surgeon from Glasgow and now he is moved to nursing home. Wired to Uncle Walter if we should come and he wired back he had taken rooms and we had both better come.

July 31. Arrived Glasgow about 9 am. Found dear Papa in such pain. Sat with him all the afternoon, he kept asking when the doctors were coming and longed for relief. The operation was 4.30, four doctors, quite satisfactory, but a mercy it was done today. To bed very tired but Mama has borne it all wonderfully.

(*Frederick must have been suffering from a stoppage of the bladder. The surgical "wound" so often referred to later must be a suprapubic incision. In those days before antibiotics, this would be apt to become reinfected and keep breaking open. Kathleen used to say vaguely that the original trouble was due to Frederick's not having been circumcised when he was a child. A friend of the family once assured Christopher that the surgeons not only removed Frederick's prostate gland but also castrated him! When Christopher was going through a phase of Freudian myth-making, he loved to believe this and interpret it as the vengeance of the Female on the Tyrant Male, a ritual act subconsciously willed by Emily and Kathleen.*)

Letter from Frank, August 14, Volksrust:

I am wanting your letter badly and hoping that you will have got over your anti-matrimonial fit and be thinking of Wybersley in the same sort of way as I am, as a heaven on earth. I think one of the rooms would be pretty done in the different shades of colour that one sees here, slate grey-blue (of the tin roofs) blue (of the sky) and dark purply blue (of the mountains) and just a touch of veldty velvety brown-gold. How would that do for the drawing-room, or would it be too cold?

I am so very glad that you and Moey met again. It has been such a great pleasure to her, poor girl, to make friends with you. She enjoys making plans and managing you, so you mustn't mind for once. You can manage her brother as much as you like, to make up for it.

August 14. Both felt much depressed by hearing the doctors want to do something more to poor Papa. When shall we get out of this dreadful atmosphere of homes, nurses and doctors? He was naturally very low at the prospect, not so much the operation as feeling it meant staying on longer.

August 26. Everything at a standstill, poor Papa very low.

August 27. Found Papa had had a very good night. Today, after more than four weeks, he got up into an armchair, managing to struggle there with the assistance of the nurses.

Letter from Frank, August 27, Volksrust:

My Dearest One, my thoughts are full of you and the anxiety you and the Dearest Mama have had—I hope *have* had. It must have been a terrible shock to you both.

My dearest, I had been fancying—I can tell you now it is over—that you were feeling that perhaps, after all, you got on very well without me and matrimony was a toss-up rather, etc etc, but somehow your letter has reassured me immensely. It rather amused me to find that, when I brought my thoughts up to the point and I had faced it and gone on through life alone, I always found that you were perched up somewhere aloft in a corner of my mind, watching my career with the greatest interest. If I tried the other alternative and went on not alone—all the other possible young women seemed such a comedown and so utterly different.

I have been doing up my birthday present to you. I don't know if it will reach you quite on your birthday as it has to go to Moey first, to get a binding. I hope it will be a nice one. I asked for glossy green and jasmine flowers which I always look upon as your emblem. I think I told you this once before and you received it rather coolly.

I have been so interrupted by the other fellows, though, this morning. Longden rushed in to take my photograph, painting. I can't imagine why. Then Morton arrived to ask me if I had a sparklet bottle. When I said 'yes, why?' he said 'oh, I've got one too' and walked out. Then the sergeant major came to ask me to act 'The Blind Beggars' with one of the men. He read me extracts from it and could hardly speak for laughing. He kept on saying it was so very laughable. I must say, I couldn't see it, but anyhow I'm in for it on Saturday next. To crown all, my servant then insisted upon talking about the money his wife has come into and whether I advised him to go out to Australia, where it appears his treasure is. When I said that I thought he would be unwise to leave his good situation in Sheffield, he said in the most superior way that he shouldn't require another situation as he would 'have an independence'. I wish you could see him, he is so very genteel and amusing.

Letter from Frank, September 3, Charlestown, Natal:

I am in hospital with a sprained ankle. I was trying to get on my pony with a gun in my hand and I think I caught my big shooting boot in the stirrup and wrenched it when the pony began to jump about. I hope it will be only a matter of a day or two, as they seem to have come to the conclusion that there are no bones broken.

I always used to think that when I was properly grown up I should know for certain what my beliefs about the fundamental things were—but I don't think I know any better than I did ten years ago, except insofar that I care a great deal more, which is perhaps a step in the right direction. I suppose we people who are so occupied with feelings do have more difficulty in making up our minds than the people who pin their faith on facts—the doers as opposed to the dreamers—and they are so superior, those doers, and the poor dreamer, borne down by the weight of mere numbers, feels that they must be right and that facts, solid solid facts, must be the beginning and end of all things. But they'll find out some day they're wrong, every one of them. Hurrah!

I think it is queer how very much I am comforted and affected by quotations. Whenever things are annoying me very badly and this life out here is seemingly particularly bald and uninteresting, I think of *Thyrsis*—its last lines: 'Why faintest thou? I wander'd till I died . . .' and it somehow puts one on one's feet again.

September 11. ORDER OF RELEASE CAME. Dr D. said to me, when are you going to take your Father away? And added he might go to the Hotel any day now. Almost too dazed to grasp it and when Mama came she couldn't realize it either—in fact we all three felt like people who have seen the light after much darkness.

September 12. Went up to the Home. We found Papa looking quite himself, all dressed and the same as he used to be. We simply could hardly believe our eyes. Frank's name mentioned in Lord Roberts's dispatch. So pleased.

(*The dispatch was officially dated September 4, but perhaps made public later. It contained a list of officers and men "who have rendered special and meritorious service."*)

September 23. LEFT GLASGOW!!! Almost wept with joy to see 'London–Euston' on our train! Papa very tired and to bed as soon as he arrived.

Letter from Frank, September 26, Charlestown:

I can't realize that I am grown up, that I am going to have a wife and an establishment of my own and all the rest of it. It's come upon me as a particular shock this morning as I looked at the medical sheets, which are hung up above everyone's bed in hospital. There are three fellows here who are what I call regular grownup men, great big—it's rather a nasty expression but forgive me—hairy men; well, I found that I was four years older than any of them, I who am not grown up at all. I wonder if I have the secret of eternal youth, or shall we say perpetual childishness. I believe you have got this 'gift' (?) too, so we shall be just as childish as we like.

Letter from Frank, October 3, Ingogo:

I am out of hospital at last.

I can realize perfectly that you can be tiresome and aggravating in the extreme, indeed I have seen you! And very glad I should be to see you again, even in your crossest mood!

I have now got a man named Stansfield who was Bradshaw's servant and was with him when he was killed, whom I think I shall like. To begin with, I feel in a sort of way as if I were doing Bradshaw a kindness and that he will be pleased (I never can realize that he is dead, in fact I feel that I am going to write and tell him about his old servant. I wonder if it's possible that he knows all about it.) Then the man himself is a nice good-tempered boy who smiles to himself over his work. He comes from Mexborough which is the next place to Conisbrough Castle, which Sir Walter Scott in the early morning saw off the top of the coach and which gave him the idea for Ivanhoe. It is a most picturesque ruin but surrounded by coalpits. This is rather irrelevant but it somehow interests me. The flies are beginning to be awful.

On October 7 Kathleen received Frank's birthday present to her. It was the volume of favorite extracts from books which he had copied out and sent to Moey to be bound. The envelope of an accompanying note was sealed with wax enclosing a "Kruger ticky," a threepenny bit with Kruger's head on it. Frank wrote that "they are rather scarce."

. .

October 16. All disheartened and depressed by Papa's wound bursting out after it appeared to be healing.

Letter from Frank, October 17, Ingogo:

Last night I went on a walk by the river. There are birds down there twittering and flying round their nests and there is a certain amount of green and a stillness, all very pleasant for the soldier who is walking out, even though it is only in spirit, with his young woman. The thought came to me as I was doing this: what a curious idea that is—that a great, what is called a too great, affection for anyone can be a means of drawing one away from God. I always think that it is just in these things that God reveals himself to one. Of course it involves some day a great sorrow for one, when one has to leave or be left by the object of one's affection. But if one is unwilling to leave this world because of one's best and highest feelings binding one to it, one can't be so unfit for the next. This looks dreadfully trite on paper, but as it came to me by the river, in the stillness of the gorgeous evening, it seemed almost inspired.

October 18. Went in the morning to the Polytechnic housewifery class on home linen and cleaning glass. Next time we do the cleaning ourselves. A very giggly set of girls, one newly married, two or three engaged. These giggled especially and were very conscious of their rings. In fact the only stolid ones were a child of fifteen and myself!

Letter from Frank, October 23, Ingogo:

In the article 'Magic' by Yeats, he seems to have the idea that the barriers of time and space are to a great extent of our own erection and that, the nearer we get to nature, the less we feel them. I have often felt this myself, in a cathedral or an old monastery or at Marple. The dead people who have lived there before one seem to make the atmosphere heavy with their personalities. This idea of an all-pervading intelligence has the drawback that it involves a loss of personality, a thing one couldn't face; but it also has the advantage to me of making us sometimes very near one another.

My Mother told me that she hoped she should meet your Father, which amused me very much. She is quite prepared apparently to take the warpath on behalf of her son. I should love to see her armed to the teeth. I have bought a lot of Kaffir things —beads, knobkerries, assegais and shields. I hope you will approve of them to have in the hall.

October 23. Papa went off to consult Sir Buxton Brown, the specialist. It was a *great blow* to learn that he thought he ought to go to a home and undergo treatment for *three weeks* to get rid of the present discomfort and heal the wound.

October 25. We went with Papa to 49 Beaumont Street to settle him in. Poor dear, it felt rather like taking him to prison.

October 26. Papa had chloroform this morning, the edges of the wound cut where they had hardened, so that they may heal up better. The sitting room still felt heavy with chloroform.

Letter from Frank, November 14, Ingogo:

I agree with you, only more so, in disliking art furniture. There is nothing, to my mind, so inartistic. I think a room should grow—in one corner a Boer chair, in another a basketwork one. Isn't a basket chair companionable when one is sitting alone at night? The other night it lightened incessantly, as light as day when the flashes came and then pitch dark. It was most dazzling and made one feel like a person in a cinematograph. The colouring, dark purple sky and bright green hill, which one saw for a moment by the lightning, was most extraordinary.

I'm afraid it [*referring to one of his paintings*] doesn't suggest all that I feel at sunrise—the aloofness of it, and there is a feeling of dread too, a sense of all that's going to happen. I have often tried to discover if sunrise and sunset actually look the same—if the lights and the shadows fall in the same way. They certainly feel quite different. What one feels at sunset is the best advertisement that life can have. After all the pinpricks of the day one feels very peaceful and that after all it was worth getting up and starting the day, which one sometimes doubts at sunrise.

I wonder if one will feel like that when one has to set altogether and finish with everything in this world. I never feel that we need worry about what's going to happen in the next. It probably won't be at all like anything we can imagine, or even like anything that we can desire at present, but I am sure that it will be all right. Discussions about it seem just as profitable as those interminable ones about when the war is going to end, which bore one so dreadfully out here.

Letter from Frank, November 21, Ingogo:

My going home and Wybersley etc, looked at from quite a sober absolutely grownup sensible point of view, seems so hopeless that I can't help thinking that I shall find myself transported there quite unexpectedly on a magic carpet of some sort or other. When we have discussions in the Mess as to what is likely to happen and if we shall stay here for ever, the Colonel, who is always most optimistic, ends up by saying 'well, they must do something soon, they can't carry on like this much longer'.

I shall always be glad that I came out here, though, as I think the fellows who haven't done so and have taken billets at home haven't played the game at all and everyone out here is very down on them. I was very much pleased with a sentence in a letter of Lousada's to the Colonel, as I think the former is quite the wisest man and the best judge of character we have got. It was: 'I am sorry that Isherwood didn't get anything in the Honours. He is always keen and shows that it is quite possible for a fellow to get back (from England) if he wants to'. I think you will be pleased with this. It's made me feel very virtuous ever since, and yesterday morning I tried to take a proper interest in the ration returns even, which I must confess really bore me to death!

(*Major—later promoted to Lieutenant Colonel—F. P. Lousada was second in command of the Regiment when it sailed for South Africa on the* Majestic *in December 1899. In the list of honors referred to, he was made a Companion of the Order of the Bath.*)

I think a little praise from the right person makes one realize that no part of one's life is wasted if one is trying to do one's work. It must be particularly pleasant for you to feel how absolutely necessary you have made yourself in your world. Three people that one knows of, whose lives would be spoilt if you weren't there! There aren't many people who can say that of themselves. I think you and your influence have altered me completely, or at any rate my ideal self. One knows too what you are to the dearest Mama and I suspect to your Father as well. If I had never heard anything else of you I should be most strongly drawn by that close intimacy between you and your People.

Most people seem to me to neglect their parents shamefully. Even my beloved Stevenson, whose new life Moey sent me the other day, behaved I think badly to his. How I wish we had had the chance of knowing him. Wouldn't a stay in Samoa with him and 'Fanny' have been delightful?

I am giving up the quartermastership, as the Quartermaster Sergeant has got it. It is rather trying for him, becoming an officer suddenly after twenty odd years of the ranks. He struggles hard not to call one Sir, all the time looking as if he thought himself very impertinent.

November 22. Papa out in all this damp to his two meetings and did not return till teatime. Do hope he won't take a chill, but he is so delighted to get about that one cannot stop him.

November 23. Begin *Kim* by Rudyard Kipling, delightfully glamourous vague pictures of India. Papa to see the doctor who was pleased with him.

Letter from Frank, November 28, Ingogo: (The final packet of Frank's South African letters has been lost, so this one is the last which can be quoted from here.)

I wonder if you have got anybody who you fancy yourself rather like and to whom you are enormously drawn. (I am describing my Robert Louis Stevenson feelings.) Moey sent me a number of The Bookman full of R.L.S. portraits. I rather wish she hadn't. He was very unattractive looking. I have always tried to take refuge in imagining Mrs Stevenson as better looking, but there are pictures of her too, and she looked—I am sure she wasn't—quite impossible. However, that's one of Stevenson's great attractions—on paper, bien entendu—that he cared nothing for appearances, although that is a respect in which I don't fancy myself like him at all.

It is quite one of the sine qua non of my future life that I am to be launched into the most intimate relations with them all. I wonder though whether his bohemianism and his radicalism might not put one off a bit. One is so innately aristocratic, at least I am. You won't misunderstand what I mean and will see that I refer to my instinctive attitudes and not to any qualities in myself. I feel this Tory in myself so much out here. I cannot hobnob as so many fellows do with advantage with Jack, Tom and Harry, and there is nothing which the colonial resents so much as that want. I was very much struck when I went to Newcastle with Swanston the other day, at the way in which he talked to the guard and the people in the shops, and at the good results. We got waited upon and talked to in a way in which I never get treated.

I think *our* portraits would come out in print much better than the Stevensons'. What a pity your husband's life is never likely to be written!

9

Kathleen's chief concerns during the next months were the state of Frederick's health and Emily's reactions to its ups and downs. On November 30, the doctor told Frederick he might certainly go to stay at Nether Hall for Christmas and even join in the shooting parties. But, the very next day, Frederick's wound broke open and he was ordered to bed with a nurse in attendance. On December 9, the doctor was again "in one of his hopeful moods" and predicted that Frederick would be able to go to Nether after all. Kathleen was irritated by his optimism, it made her superstitiously afraid. And she was proved right:

December 16. The wound hasn't begun to heal yet. Mr B. probed it today and it was only a surface healing. Poor Papa very depressed in the evening, what with the discomfort and weariness of it all.

On the morning of Christmas Day, Kathleen was kept running backward and forward between Frederick and Emily, who had taken to her bed, too. Emily got up for lunch, but later some visitors came, causing her to collapse "quite exhausted and unable to speak, hardly"; in the evening she revived sufficiently to enjoy the turkey, plum pudding and champagne. Frederick grumbled all day long because they were not at Nether. Kathleen, healthily selfish for once, admits that she spent a very pleasant Christmas, *pleased with her presents and by the news, which must have just then arrived, of Frank's promotion to captain.*

Next day, feeling perhaps that she wasn't getting Kathleen's full sympathy, Baby Mama became "very poorly and not up to seeing anyone." Kathleen, realizing that she meant business, at once wrote to Ventnor to reserve rooms for them both.

By the end of 1901, the pubic had forgotten its earlier jingoism and had grown peevishly bored with the war. Even Kitchener was temporarily out of favor, for not having won it yet. As for Buller, he had destroyed what was left of his reputation by making an indiscreet and absurdly muddled public reply to criticisms of his generalship. For this he lost the Aldershot command and had to retire into civilian life.

The Liberal leader Campbell-Bannerman (referred to as "the beast" in Kathleen's diary) had made a speech denouncing the British use of concentration camps as "methods of barbarism"; King Edward felt that this was going too far and giving encouragement to the enemy. But Lloyd George went much further, in his fearless campaign against the war. On December 18 he actually dared to hold a rally in Birmingham, which was Chamberlain's political home town. A mob forced its way into the hall, yelling, "Pro-Boer! Traitor! Kill him!" Lloyd George would almost certainly have been lynched if the police hadn't smuggled him out of the building, disguised in a constable's uniform. Four years later, the Beast had become Prime Minister, and the Traitor was a member of his Cabinet!

According to Kathleen's 1902 diary, she still wants the traveling flask, the revolving bookcase and the small atlas. Additions to the list are Hutchinson's Extinct Monsters, *Ruskin's* Stones of Venice *and "a scent thing that squirts out." For the first time since 1896, there are no lists of racing fixtures.*

On January 1, Kathleen left with Emily for Ventnor. "I hope it speaks well for the fortunes of the New Year that actually for the first time for months we were able to do the thing we had planned, without something disappointing happening to put us off!!" How-ever, on January 19, Frederick's wound burst open again. "His one idea seemed to be that Mama must not come home because of it." But—

January 21. Mama perfectly wretched all day and it is really no use thinking she can remain on here till the nurse has left. She fretted and cried and made herself so absolutely miserable that I simply couldn't stand it, and wrote to know if the doctor doesn't think we might return by Saturday. There is nothing at Ventnor to distract her.

So they returned to London two days later—to find Frederick unexpectedly, almost disappointingly, better and "wonderfully himself." On January 25, Kathleen went to see a musical comedy called The Country Girl, *in which she describes the leading actress, Evie Green, as looking "recklessly handsome." Early in February she started copying again at the National Gallery, which she found delightful, although she was "disgusted to find I couldn't draw a bit, the charcoal simply wobbled anyhow."*

February 25. Heard from Mrs Isherwood that Frank has been selected for the Stockport adjutancy. In afternoon took Papa out for just a quarter of an hour's walk—his first.

March 3. Heard that Aunt Kelly had passed away, she just sank to rest, quite herself and the old dignity to the last. They had in a nurse to help make her more comfortable, and after arranging her said, 'there, dear, that's nice' and Aunt Kelly at once flew at her and said 'don't call me dear, say Ma'am', a characteristic little touch I admire immensely.

April 8. Nurse packing up to go. Papa in a nervous state, very natural I suppose after being dependent on a nurse for eleven weeks. She came to see me before leaving in a most odd excited state, said that when the doctor saw him she expected he might order him back to bed, much trouble ahead and I need not delude myself it was his nerves now, it was far worse. Felt dreadfully worried. Mama took him to see the doctor and he said that everything was extremely satisfactory! Papa did not seem the least cheered and sat all the evening sighing and hardly speaking.

April 9. Wind due east and had dreadfully bad head, aching all over and felt sick. Tried to get up but had to go back to bed, felt so tiresome and useless, but think it was partly being so worried by nurse yesterday. Nurse amongst other things has set Papa against me and one can't help feeling rather bitter against such women when one sees the influence they get over the minds of their patients. I conclude she didn't like my thinking and intimating that I hoped Papa would get free from his old invalid ways and be more himself.

April 10. Papa came back from his meetings in the most abject state of depression. The doctor saw him again today and practically dismissed him for the present, said he simply must rouse himself and go to places and theatres and distract his mind. All the same, I blame B. for putting in his head that the doctors made a mistake in Glasgow, as he harps on that and wishes he had died there. He looks, eats and sleeps well. His cure is worse than his disease, poor dear.

April 12. Placards large with rumours of peace negotiations. The Boer leaders are at Klerksdorp discussing it. Meeting of the Cabinet today especially summoned. I do hope there will be no concessions. We have gone through far too much to give in an inch, and must win ultimately. They say the King is set on the war being over before the coronation.

(*Already in January the Queen of the Netherlands had offered to mediate between the British and the Boers. The British Government declined but said that it was always ready to consider peace proposals from the Boers themselves. It did not seem possible that they could go on fighting much longer; so many of them were being taken prisoner in the big drives which Kitchener kept making across the Transvaal and the Orange Free State. Some Boers, including the younger brother of Christian De Wet, had actually volunteered to fight on the side of the British, because they hoped to bring the war to a quicker end by doing so.*

Nevertheless, De Wet, De La Rey, Smuts, Steyn and others were still at large with their commandos and were even still sometimes defeating the British; near Tweebosch, on March 7, Methuen himself had been wounded and captured with the entire column under his command. In Cape Colony, Smuts was besieging a British garrison at Ookiep.

The negotiations Kathleen mentions above were inconclusive for the time being; though the Boer leaders had probably given up all hope of getting independence, they continued to use it as a bargaining point. But Kitchener's position was stronger than in the previous year; at one of the meetings he was able to announce an impressive British victory in the western Transvaal, and this decided the Boers to discuss his terms with delegates from their own commandos and abide by their vote. Even so, negotiations dragged on until the end of May and might easily have broken down if Kitchener had not been such a persuasive diplomatist. During a deadlock he had told Smuts, "My opinion is that in two years a Liberal Government will be in power, and it will grant you a constitution." The Liberals did sponsor a constitution for South Africa, though it didn't go into effect until 1910.)

April 24. As I was dressing for dinner received the long-looked-for wire. Returning by the *Orient*, which starts on 29th. Joy!

The Orient *reached Southampton on May 22; Kathleen went to Waterloo that afternoon to meet Frank when he arrived on the boat train. Half an hour later they took another train down to Bookham in Surrey, where Kathleen and Emily had been staying for the past week. Frederick had visited them there but had sulkily taken himself off before Frank's arrival.*

May 23. Very steamy close day, dull and heavy and a sort of hothouse dampness falling. Frank and I started in the donkey cart to go to Leatherhead but after we had got to Bookham village it refused to budge an inch and we had to leave it at the Anchor and walk to Leatherhead from there! We picked it up coming home and it consented to return. In afternoon Mama and F and I went by train to Horsley and had tea in rather little inn near the station and then walked on to the Common after our return. We sat in the hall and billiard room in evening.

Frank left next morning. He wrote to Kathleen that afternoon, from London, before traveling on to Marple:

My dear, I got up in good time and did all my business most satisfactorily. I found I had a further balance of two hundred pounds, one hundred of which I arranged should be further invested in Consols. So I have now three hundred in them. The man at Coxes seemed to think I was doing a very sensible thing, as he thought if I kept them in for about a year I should make fourteen pounds on each share. Our batta won't be paid us for some time, but he thought that there was an idea afloat of raising officers' pay! A good point to tell F. Senior! I am just going to write a rough draft of THE letter.

I thought about you all the way up and the people in the carriage wondered why I kept on smiling to myself. If they had seen you and the dearest Mama they would have known. I don't think even I had quite remembered when I was away how nice you both were—and you know you haven't altered in the very least, as you threatened to. I wonder if you thought *I* had!

I see that fellow Green that I came home with was received in triumph and there was an account of it in The Daily Telegraph, which rather annoys me. I only got into the North Cheshire!!

My dear, I am so glad that I have got you to come back to. Ever your Frank.

"Batta" is a word of Anglo-Indian origin and formerly meant the extra pay given to officers who were serving in India or in a military campaign elsewhere. "THE letter" is the one which Frank is about to write Frederick, asking for an interview to discuss his financial prospects. Frank isn't merely joking when he says he is annoyed by the reception given to "that fellow Green." Evidently he is hoping to get at least a small public welcome when he arrives at Marple station. His next letter betrays his disappointment—"I got back all right and was met by the family only."

Here is Frederick's altogether predictable reply to Frank:

Dear Sir, I am in receipt of your letter of the 25th and I shall be obliged if you will send a written statement of anything that you wish to say about your case, as at present I know next to nothing, and it is useless for me to see you until I have a plain statement of facts to consider. I am obliged for your enquiries about my health, which is slowly improving. Yrs truly, Fred. Machell Smith.

Have you ever explained to your Father my reasons for objecting to your proposal for my Daughter? I will write to him after I have heard from you.

Frank answers this by telling Frederick that his father will lend him Wyberslegh, "which is at present being put in a thorough state of repair." He mentions his appointment to the adjutancy and describes his financial prospects:

My affairs stand thus: two hundred a year, to be settled in the marriage settlement on my Wife and children; three hundred a year pay and allowances. I have now saved four hundred, three hundred of which is invested in the funds. Sixtyfive pounds is owed me by the Public (batta).

This last sentence must surely be an intentional paw-smack in Frank's best feline style. Isn't he, in effect, telling Frederick: "That sixty-five pounds is what you owe me for going out there and fighting your war for you—and don't you forget it"?

Frederick's next letter is a presentation of three separate arguments against Frank's suit. What Frederick seems not fully aware of is that his arguments really cancel each other out. They are:

1. That Frank's offer must be rejected because it doesn't provide enough money for him and Kathleen to live on.

2. That Frank's offer must be rejected because it is far less than the amount of the settlement which Frederick and Emily are prepared to make on Kathleen; Frederick apparently realizes how dangerous this admission is, as soon as he has written it, for he hastens to add: "although the income arising from it is contingent upon our lives. . . . We may however live for some years longer and meanwhile your means will be very limited, as expenses in married life generally increase."

3. That Frank's offer must be rejected because it is irrelevant; no matter how little or how much money Frank has, he is anyhow morally unworthy to marry Kathleen—Frederick here repeats almost word for word what he wrote in January 1901:

You tell me that you spoke of my objection to your marriage on pecuniary grounds only, and you don't know of any other. This statement I do not understand. When I first wrote to you I did say that I thought you had no right to propose unless you had some prospects of being able to keep a wife. You then said there was no engagement and gave me your word of honour as an *officer and a gentleman* that nothing further should take place without first informing me. *You did not keep that promise* and wrote me an apology. I told you I thought that a man's word was his bond and I did not consider your bond cancelled by the apology. I believe my Daughter was aware that this was *my strongest reason* for objecting to your proposal, and I wish you clearly to understand this.

Argument number three is, of course, unanswerable. Since apologies are useless, Frank can never redeem his honor; he will remain a liar and unworthy of Kathleen throughout eternity. But

Frederick isn't about to let his moral indignation get the better of him, for that would put an end to the gloomy fun of heckling Frank. So, after delivering this seemingly final judgment, he returns to argument number one and ends his letter in cross-examination:

How is the two hundred a year you propose to settle secured? The house you are to live in rent free should also be secured to you as long as you occupy it, or, on leaving, a sum equivalent to the rent it would let for. I presume you propose to furnish from what you have saved? Have you any further expectancies at the death of any relatives? I am yrs truly . . .

Letter from Frank to Kathleen, May 30, Marple Hall:

Your Father and I are deep in correspondence; on my side very polite, on his—! *My* Father seems to think it very amusing!

I have been twice over to Wybersley to see about things. The builder is an awful old dodderer and wants very firm handling.

June 1. About supper time L. spied out that Bailey's Hotel had run up their flag and one or two houses in Gloucester Road had suddenly put out flags, and we could only conclude it meant *peace was proclaimed*. Before bedtime newspaper men were shouting it. It was stuck up outside the War Office at 5 pm.

June 2. Mama, E. and I went out before 10.30 and took a bus down to the Mansion House and on to Liverpool Street to see how London was receiving the news of *Peace*. Flags appeared leisurely during the morning but there was not the frantic excitement that filled the air over the Relief of Ladysmith and Mafeking. Bands of students went about shouting and there was a big rather aimless crowd in front of the Mansion House and a few roughs blowing tin trumpets. But we were so disappointed that the proclamation *Peace is Proclaimed*, which the papers said stretched across the Mansion House yesterday, was taken down and all was grey and silent. The bells of St Paul's were ringing, but it was rather amusing to read the exaggerated accounts in the newspaper after having been in the City and seen for ourselves.

Letter from Frank, June 2, Marple Hall:

I gathered that you didn't like my saying that my Father was amused at F. Senior's letter. I am afraid we are rather happy-go-lucky people and perhaps it seemed to us needlessly mysterious and grand. What for instance could he mean by saying in a post-script 'have you explained to your Father my reasons for objecting to your proposal'? My Father took it into his head that it was because of my Grandfather; but I don't think your Father knows anything about him.

(Frank is referring to Thomas Isherwood, husband of the redoubtable Mary Ellen Isherwood who dismissed the Chartist mob. Thomas had a stroke, not long after his marriage, which left him unable to speak. John Isherwood had also had a stroke, a less serious one, when young, so he may have regarded this as an hereditary affliction and therefore as an excuse Frederick might use to reject Frank. None of John's children did have strokes, however.)

Letter from Frank, June 9, Marple Hall:

My Father has written to your 'Papa', not very satisfactorily, I am afraid. However I came to the conclusion it really was no use his suggesting anything until he could really settle it with Henry. He is inclined to do all he can but he has an expensive family and of course you can't get blood out of a stone. However, you've got to marry me now—whatever he gives. It would be abominable if you threw me over after engaging my affections as you have somehow managed to. I am sure I don't quite know how you've done it, either, but I *won't* marry anyone else, as you are so fond of suggesting.

• •

Letter from Frank, June 14, Marple Hall:

My dear Kitty, I didn't mean to say anything rude! Only to be rather playful and amusing. My gambollings seem though to have been in 'excessively bad taste' and I am sorry.

We won't talk again about the 'Dearest Papa'!!

Moey has an idea that I might be able to get a sale for some of my African sketches, so I am busily engaged in copying and turning out fresh ones. It would be very nice to discover a fresh source of revenue wouldn't it? She is a wonderful person for selling and buying and always makes things pay and is going to hawk them round to the different picture shops and curio dealers in her part of the world. I rather think too of sending something to the Manchester summer exhibition. Majuba or Spion Kop or something might take.

Letter from Frank, June 15 (?), Marple Hall:

I have just had such a delightful *African* letter from you. I wish you would go on writing to me like that, in the way that you used, before the D.P. came between us. He really would be very much pleased if he realized how completely he spoiled a good deal of our last meeting! We won't think and talk of him again next time at all. I think that's the best plan.

June 23. Bus from Hyde Park Corner to Piccadilly Circus, the charge treble today, and everywhere is so crowded, there were *dreadful* blocks and crowds and crowds on foot. Carpenters and decorators hard at work. Went to see the wonderful additional west front built on to the Abbey as a robing room, it is exactly in colour and style like the Abbey itself. On up Whitehall where Canada has erected a splendid arch of different grain, to be illuminated, costing five thousand pounds. Miss Dodge and Jem Barlow came in after dinner, the former firmly believes there will be no coronation.

June 24. Met Isabel just as I was getting into a bus and went with her to Harrods and then took a bus to South Kensington. The busman took our breath away altogether, that there *would be no coronation*, he had seen the news in the City and the Lord Mayor had given it out. The King was ill and undergoing a dangerous operation today. Everyone talking of the postponement of coronation and what will happen. All the guests and royalties here and every preparation.

June 25. Mama and I got up early and out before 8 and took a bus to see the decorations on London Bridge. Everything in the eve of readiness and it seems half pathetic to see the tinsel and paper flowers and gaudy hangings now and the stands all ready; the poor King ill in bed. The busman was of opinion it was really too much fuss to make over one man and that the procession ought to take place, but the general feeling of the people seems to be intense sympathy for the King and Queen. Bulletins are issued several times a day and though he had a restless night there are no bad symptoms. It is curious that Miss Dodge *was* right, after all, and there can be certainly no coronation now under three months. The odd prophecy she had heard was that no king will be crowned till a boy king comes to the throne.

On June 29 and 30, Frank met Kathleen in London; he was on his way to Aldershot to take a course in signaling. This would make it easy for him to come up to town or see Kathleen elsewhere at weekends.

Letter from Frank, July 9, Mandora Barracks, Aldershot:

My dear, do come on the river on Saturday. It is so much nicer than sitting up in Kensington Gardens and settling our plans. I am a very hard-worked man at present and want to be greatly petted and to have a chance of petting you too! You can't do that in Kensington Gardens!

. .

On Sunday, July 13, Kathleen met Frank at Reading. They went on to Goring, where they lunched in a punt on the river.

Letter from Frank, July 14, Aldershot:

My dear, I have been thinking so much of our short little burst of confidence to one another yesterday evening in the train and I think what I said must have seemed harsh and disagreeable, or do you realize that I don't want to say anything to stifle your doubts and hesitations about marrying? Even at the last moment it would be much better for you to give me up than to chance ruining your life—*and mine too.*

Marriage must mean the end of what one calls 'the good time' of one's life but I have learned to think that it's the beginning of 'the better time'. I've had my doubts too, but I have come out of them onto the marriage side. If you emerge on the other, you won't be the least afraid of saying so, will you?

I wish so much you could talk it over with 'the dearest Mama' or do you feel it's a thing you must decide for yourself? I want to make you happy, but if I can't do it I would much rather not try and fail. And I can't help being a man and not a woman! (You wouldn't like me to be an imitation of one either, would you?) And being a man is quite a different thing to being a woman. I don't mean better or worse or any nonsense like that.

But you will understand, won't you, why I have written this? I have that picture you suggested of you sitting up alone at Wybersley longing to be back with the dearest Mama, and I don't like it at all. You mustn't let that ever come true. Whatever happens I shall always be your devoted Frank.

Letter from Frank, July 17, Aldershot:

My dear, nobody but you would have understood quite what I meant by my letter and I was so glad to get yours assuring me that you did. I ought to be ashamed of myself for not being quite sure that you would.

We mustn't forget our old dream of having all our interests together—all the little excursions and jaunts with which we are going to enliven our everyday life but which seem to have rather been forgotten lately under the trials of getting formally engaged, and of this rather unsatisfactory state of affairs at present. I *hope* we'll be able to get things settled up directly now.

On July 22, Kathleen writes in her diary: "Letter from Marple and discussion." The letter was from John Isherwood to Frederick:

My dear Sir, my eldest son has returned and I have had a talk with him about what we can do to make a settlement on the marriage of Frank and your Daughter. He will join me in agreeing to pay two hundred pounds a year and continue it in case of Frank's death to his widow and their children. I am now having Wybbersley Hall repaired for them to live in and when they leave it I will give Frank the rent received for it, if let to anybody else, for my life. The farmer has had the hall as well as the farm and buildings and has sublet it for years and the house is in very bad repair and it will be very expensive to make it comfortably habitable for them. This is all I have power to do, for, as you know, I only have a life interest in this estate.

The discussion resulted in two letters being written: one by Frederick to John, the other by Kathleen to Frank. Frederick uses almost the same tone to John as to Frank himself, condescending and dictatorial; perhaps he feels that the whole Isherwood family has sunk to Frank's level through association with him:

As to the rent of Wybersley, or an equivalent, I don't think that it should cease at your death, but there should also be an undertaking from yourself and your eldest son to allow not less than fifty pounds a year for house rent, in the event of your son Frank leaving Wybersley and moving elsewhere. As the house is now being improved for his benefit (and ultimately for the estate) it is only fair that he should reap every advantage during his lifetime. It would be impossible for them to manage without a house rent free, or its equivalent, for which fifty pounds a year is a moderate amount. I presume that, in the event of your eldest son not marrying, your son Frank is the heir presumptive.

Kathleen's letter—as is shown by Frank's reply to it—urged him to appeal personally to Henry to guarantee the amount of the Wyberslegh rent. No doubt she wrote this under pressure, direct or indirect, from Frederick and Emily. But it isn't surprising that Frank takes it as an act of disloyalty to him, an alignment of herself with the Smiths against the Isherwoods; especially since Kathleen evidently got carried away by her private resentment and attacked Henry. How dare he not help them, he who has everything, far more than he can possibly need, he the unjustly wealthy eldest son, the pampered selfish globetrotting idler, the social butterfly who stayed at home in luxury while Frank risked his life at the war—one doesn't have to have read Kathleen's letter to know how she must have put it. Her violently partisan approach to life always requires a villain; Buller has now left the stage, and Henry is the nearest available replacement. Besides, Frank himself has taught her to criticize Henry, a fact which he temporarily forgets in his present indignation.

Letter from Frank, July 24, Aldershot:

I am inclined to give you rather a lecture about your last night's letter. What you said about my Brother was a bit strong! Do you quite realize that my People are doing a great deal to help us to get married, indeed everything in their power. I don't quite understand why you are making such a point about the Wybersley rent. I rather dislike pressing Henry about it personally. Don't think me unreasonable and cross, but you mustn't say things about my People till you really know them.

Kathleen probably wrote an outwardly submissive reply to this reproof, but the friction between them continued, as will appear.

On August 1, Kathleen, Emily and Frederick went up to Cheadle to stay with the Sykeses. Kathleen was still hopeful that their financial problems would be solved during this visit, in which case Frank would come to Marple and the engagement would become official. Frank was much less optimistic, however; he thought it a bad sign that Henry hadn't yet given an answer to Frederick's conditions.

Letter from Frank, August 3, Aldershot:

My dear, I have had a day that you ought to have had a part in. I always feel if I am in town without you that you are absent without leave and that I am being defrauded.

I went the first thing to Deightons in the Strand and asked them if they would like some African pictures. They didn't seem very enthusiastic. Then I thought it would be a good thing to go and look at some amateur work, so I went to the Dudley which rather staggered me. People who paint a lot better than I do do not show up to advantage there. Dear old S. had three which looked all viridian, and awful. I walked as far as Robersons. I had meant to go in there but the man looked so dreadfully patronizing (seen through the glass door) *that I funked it.*

Letter from Frank, August 4, Aldershot:

My dear, I am sorry to say that I got a letter from Henry this morning and that he does not feel it feasible to promise anything further for Wybersley. I have written to ask my Father to write to yours at Cheadle, which I hope is right, and you can talk it over with him before he goes. Until I know what he and you think and say, I don't know what to propose further, but I do wish this question had never been raised. I feel dreadfully sorry for you. I know how wearing it all is from bitter experience.

Letter from Frank, August 6, Aldershot:

I do not feel that I can ask Henry anything further, as he expressly told me his decision was quite final; and indeed I think, as far as he is concerned, you are looking at the matter from a wrong point of view. He has done a very great deal in allowing my future income to be increased and settled on my widow and children, and when you consider that he looks upon me as one of his brothers and sisters who may all make like demands upon him, you can understand his hesitating to grant anything or everything I may ask. However, my Father and your Father will, I suppose, correspond and it is much better for us not to discuss this, on which I dare say we shall always disagree.

I am wondering if your Father would think it sound if I saved a sum of money to be kept and spent in case of contingencies. I could save this by economy during the winter or perhaps in the furnishing or if necessary by postponing our marriage until the autumn. I do not think that, if my Father did not live until my adjutancy expired, my Brother would kick us out or charge us rent, and if we lasted that out and had two hundred pounds, it would last us four years, by which time I am absolutely certain to have my majority.

I fancy, myself, that we could also save a little money at Wybersley. Of course it will mean a little self-denial all round but if we want to be married we are the people to pay for it. I hate thinking of you miserable, so let us be brave and make up our minds that if other people won't pay for our being married we will do it ourselves.

August 7. [At the Sykeses'.] Found another worrying letter by second post and collapsed into despair at the hopelessness of things and the tiresomeness of a certain person. To bed early feeling everything so hopeless that there simply must be a turning point! This is particularly vexing as I had set my heart on everything being settled this week.

("The tiresomeness of a certain person": another of Kathleen's ironical circumlocutions. Frank has told her not to criticize Henry, so she won't mention his name even in her diary!)

August 8. Marjorie and I started out at a quarter to three and drove to Marple, then over the Ridge which was looking lovely in spite of the day, past Wybersley into Disley and tea at the pink inn, The Ram's Head. A sweet garden and Disley quite a nice little place with church on side of hill. Back to Stockport along an uninteresting road.

August 9. CORONATION DAY. The King really got crowned at last. In a way his illness has been a good thing and made him far more popular and created a greater feeling of loyalty than ever before. His message to his people had the first ring of sincerity of any of his messages, and, though I could never feel the least spark of loyalty like one did to Queen Victoria, one admires his courage. In the evening the house was illuminated and all from the road looked lovely, two three and four candles in every window and nearly a thousand little lamps. A crowd came to see it and twentyfour people to supper and drink the King's health. It was very amusing and did not get to bed till nearly twelve.

Letter from Frank, August 12, Aldershot:

It seems to me so curious that you all seem not to believe in my saving powers. My life has been an alternation of extravagant periods and saving periods. I had a big one of the first at Cambridge and after that I was tremendously economical for years and did not finally pay off my debts until I had been in the service for a year or two. Since you have known me, I have been pretty well off. It seems to me so obvious that the largeness or smallness of an income depends so entirely on the tastes of the people who have it to spend, but I think this is what you mean when you say that I am so extraordinarily young in so many ways.

Anyway I am dreadfully sick of this scheming and planning and wish we could simply be in a boat together and forget the whole thing except one another. I have a vision of all the illuminations and glare and a noisy supper and the Cheadle populace, and poor you, worried about our affairs and obliged to smile the whole time. My dear, I do feel so sorry for all the trouble I have caused you. I really quite agreed with your Father at last when he said that I should have thought of all this before I thought of an engagement. But you will forgive me, won't you? Your lover, Frank.

August 12. Started for Marple in trap via Hazel Grove and got over in three quarters of an hour. Found Mrs Isherwood very poorly with swollen foot on sofa in her sitting room. Mr Isherwood came down and we had a long talk. Left after tea.

Letter from Frank, August 13, Aldershot:

We have done our best and fired the last shot in the locker. We can only sit up and wait for results, but don't let us think of them. My Mother liked your coming so much and spoke of you as looking very well and pretty (in the ostrich feather hat?).

Did I tell you I had a letter from my servant, who got home the other day? He was dragged up from the station, which he enjoyed tremendously, and his banns were asked in church the next Sunday. I suppose he is not bothered with settlements. I shall have to give him a wedding present. I thought of one of those small oblong gilt and glass clocks in a leather case which I could put a little plate on, with a small inscription.

August 13. Drove over to Wybersley which was full of workpeople. But there is a bathroom and servant's room added and it is getting on. The group of trees in the garden and the wide open view and the nice little tangly garden are full of possibilities and the house itself is nice and quaint and oldfashioned.

· ·

(Kathleen used to tell Richard that she had fallen in love with Wyberslegh at first sight and that she had even had a psychic sense of having known the house in some previous existence. There is no hint of such a strong emotion in the entry quoted above or in that of January 31, 1901; but perhaps Kathleen, with her usual superstitiousness, was afraid to admit to it until she felt quite certain that she would be able to live at Wyberslegh one day. When she writes about her next visit there, less than a month later, her tone is already warmer.)

On August 15, Kathleen and Emily left Cheadle and went to stay in lodgings at Cambridge. "Pleasant sitting room with tiny balconies full of flowers. Felt very tired out."

Letter from Frank, August 15, Aldershot:

I have just heard from Henry who consents to I or my widow and children having Wybersley or the fifty pounds (if we did not wish to live there) until both your Parents' deaths, upon certain conditions which he has submitted to my Father—these conditions having nothing to do with us. If he consents I understand that this will meet your Father's views and all will be settled at last. It seems now too good to be true that by next week we may be able to settle everything finally and tell people and begin again with the furniture lists and even fix *the* day.

You have had a long trying time and I can never thank you enough for sticking to me as you have done through it, not forgetting the dearest Mama and all her wonderful goodness and kindness. You will neither of you ever regret it, I trust. I am going to be *such* a good boy to make up for it all to you.

August 16. Heard from F this morning. His Brother makes certain conditions about Wybersley which his Father must first agree to, and it may all end in nothing again. I am quite tired of hoping, good luck and I seem to have long ago parted company. Took the dearest Mama to her lecture, and she seemed so brisk and happy it was a pleasure. Did some shopping and back by

Kings Parade. It is a nice old place and though not a patch on Oxford has a delightful collegiate sort of atmosphere.

They spent the next six days sight-seeing and going to lectures. Kathleen enjoyed herself, but maintained a patronizing attitude toward Cambridge: "We walked along the Backs. Of course it is very pretty, but then no one ever mentions Cambridge without saying how pretty the Backs are." On August 22, Frank joined them for a two-day visit. While there he got letters from John and Henry saying that they had come to an agreement on Frederick's terms and would guarantee the annual fifty pounds which he required. So even Kathleen had to admit, "It really seems as if at last things might be settled." Before Frank left Cambridge, she wrote to Frederick asking him if he agreed that the engagement might now be officially announced. She also asked if he would now be prepared to meet Frank socially, as his future son-in-law. The question was urgent because Frederick, Emily and Kathleen had arranged to stay at Nether Hall that very next weekend, and Frank was also invited. Frank seems to have expected that Frederick would write to him directly about this, but Frederick never did; he merely sent an ungracious message in a letter to Emily that Frank could do as he liked.

Letter from Frank, August 26, Aldershot:

My dear, thank you for your kind little letter—'kind' in the way that 'Silvia' was kind exactly describes you, I think: 'For beauty lives with kindness'. I like to think of you in those charming Cambridge rooms.

I never thought that *you* wanted to get married, but I do think and shall continue to do so till the day of my death that women want to marry more than men do. They think about it much more than men do, at any rate I don't think many men want to marry till they see *the* woman whom they fancy. And a great many women do!?!?! At any rate, *we* never talk about it!

We have been out all day signalling, our last scheme, and now are just going out to read the lamp. Tomorrow there is an exam at 9.30, two papers. On Thursday and Friday there are tests in reading the lamp and helio and flag. I shall be delighted to get done with that beastly little blue book. One never feels that one can sit down quietly to read or write, but that one ought to be reading the horrible little thing.

I wonder if I shall get the Dearest Papa's letter tonight. It will be rather annoying if it comes just before the exam tomorrow morning!

Wasn't that a nice moment when we leaned over John's bridge together? I have thought of it so often. Make a little pilgrimage there tomorrow evening; if you can't think of your lover, *I* shall think of you there.

Letter from Frederick to Kathleen, August 26, Cranley Mansion:

In answer to your letter of the 24th, you need hardly have written to ask me whether your engagement should be made public, as you must know that I do not approve. Consequently I am not likely to say anything now, and leave that to you. I expect you will find that it has been suspected or expected for some time. I quite agree with you that it would have been a much happier state of things if I could have regarded it with pleasure, but as I have not been considered much in the matter it is rather late to express regrets. I can only say that I wish it had been otherwise for all our sakes. Your affect. father, Fred. Machell Smith.

Thus Frederick withdraws from the battle. His opposition, which once looked so formidable, now appears to have been nothing more than a rear-guard action to delay inevitable retreat. His raising of financial objections to the engagement now seems an unwise bluff which the Isherwoods have called by agreeing to his terms. His moral objections, whether sincere or not, have become irrelevant, since Kathleen and Frank are going to get married in spite of them.

Could Frederick possibly have prevented this marriage? Per-

haps; if Emily had remained loyal to him and had brought her tremendous influence to bear on Kathleen. Emily too has been basically opposed to Kathleen's marrying, but she is deeply shrewd and has an eye to the future. She now knows—and has probably suspected long before the operation, even—that she will outlive Frederick. So she has chosen a safer policy than opposition to the lovers. By becoming the Dearest Mama, adopting Frank as her son and blessing the union, she has bound the two of them to take care of her for the rest of her life.

It may be argued that Frederick still has one last opportunity. He could still turn his defeat into a moral victory by pretending to be won over. He could pretend to forgive Frank: "I was testing you, I had to be sure you were the right husband for her, I may have seemed harsh sometimes, but it was necessary and now I am convinced—bless you, my son." Frank might be suspicious at first, but he has always felt a certain sympathy for Frederick and would gladly make peace. As for Kathleen, she would weep tears of gratitude. Frederick's previous behavior would only heighten the effect of his transformation; he would seem to have become a saint almost; he would indeed be the Dearest Papa.

It isn't likely that Frederick even saw this possibility, much less entertained it; he is too stupid, too obstinate and too vain. But Emily must surely have seen it and seen also that her new role demanded that she be recognized as the lovers' only champion, the only martyr to their cause. If Frederick were to transform himself into the Dearest Papa, then the Dearest Mama would lose much of her glamour and power. Which would be intolerable.

Therefore Frederick must never change. He must go on making Emily suffer. What did Emily do to ensure this? Probably, very little was necessary—only a word dropped from time to time, a meaning silence in answer to a question, a quick tragic glance, a patient sigh. How consciously did Emily do it? That no one can ever know.

So Frederick retires into the psychological hinterland and opens a guerilla campaign which he will wage for the remainder of his life. He will harass Kathleen through Emily, and Frank through

Kathleen, *menacing them with his broken heart and his breaking wound and generally doing his utmost to make them all feel guilty of ingratitude, betrayal, unnatural selfishness, inhuman cruelty, even intent to murder. His campaign will be fairly effective but also, because of the weapons he is using, ultimately self-destroying. Frederick will end by pitying and sulking himself to death.*

Letter from Frank, August 27, Aldershot:

I am writing to you to please return to London. I think you will understand that I cannot force my presence upon your Father at any time. Until you have seen him and learnt what line he means to take, it would be rather rash to go to a house where he was staying.

I hope most sincerely that he will now consent to behave kindly to you in this particular and receive me with civility at any rate, but I think it must come from him although I am of course anxious and willing to meet him halfway.

I am very sorry his letter was so depressing for you, but it is a great step getting it known and the force of public opinion may settle him down. I am most sorry for the dearest Mama who I am afraid it does worry terribly.

I feel that I cannot meet your Father at Nether Hall unless he consents to my doing so or gives up going there himself. I am awfully sorry but I feel certain that he would resent my presence and I think not unnaturally under the circumstances.

On August 28 Kathleen wired Frank, giving him Frederick's indirect message to him and urging him to accept the invitation to Nether Hall since, after all, he and Frederick must meet sooner or later. That afternoon she and Emily left Cambridge and went to stay with Katie, a married daughter of Walter Greene, who lived near Ely. She found letters of congratulation on her engagement waiting for her there from Aggie, another of Walter's daughters, and from Walter himself.

Next day, Frank's reply to her wire arrived, much delayed be-

224

*cause it had been forwarded by mail from Cambridge; it said that
he was going to Nether. Kathleen hastily sent telegrams to Aldershot and London, telling Frank that she wouldn't be arriving at
Nether until the thirtieth and that Katie had invited him to spend
the night with them at her home. Meanwhile Emily left for
Nether; she was meeting Frederick en route and traveling down
with him. Later in the day, Kathleen got another wire from
Frank. Her telegrams had missed him, he was at Nether already
and begged her to come as soon as possible. Kathleen writes that
she, Katie and her husband "spent the evening in vain speculations
and commiseration for Frank's position, as he did not know one of
them. Mama would get there at seven, but then so would Papa!"*

August 30. Katie suggested coming with me, so as to be introduced to Frank, and we met him at Bury, where he had walked to
meet me, and we went on by train together. Aggie and L were in
the garden and they all said nice things about Frank who seemed
to have got through the ordeal of his arrival among complete
strangers very well indeed. The only solemn person was poor
Papa.

*Throughout the next day, Frederick continued to be solemn
while Frank continued to be approved of. He submitted to the
inspection of relatives and family friends and played the organ in
the evening. On September 1 he left for Marple; Kathleen returned to London, where there were already many more letters of
congratulation to be answered.*

Letter from Frank, September 3, Marple Hall:

My dear, I wrote you such an unsatisfactory sort of letter yesterday. I think I was rather in the dumps last night. It all seemed
so flat after the excitement of the last few days and being with
my dear little K. Marple is so dark until you have got your eye
focussed to it. The only time of day there is any light is the early
morning, so last night I didn't go to bed, just lay down in flannels

and was ready to get up at six and have been painting and getting pictures ready ever since. I can't copy them somehow, so I shall have to send the originals. I don't suppose they'll sell so we shall get them back all right. I can't quite decide whether they are good or awful. Sometimes I think I am only making a fool of myself, sending them.

Kathleen has told Frank in a letter that two of the guests at Nether Hall, out of ignorance or sheer tactlessness, "gushed" over Frederick, congratulating him on his charming and admirable future son-in-law. Frank comments: "I expect he put on that parroty look which frightens one so dreadfully. How they dared to go on, I can't think."

On September 6, Kathleen went to stay at Marple for three days. While there, she visited Wyberslegh with Frank and they discussed where the cupboards should be put. She writes: "It looked very pretty and is a dear little place."

September 10. [Cranley Mansion.] Papa returned from Suffolk. Things looked very gloomy in evening. It is *most* sad to see him like this, with perverted ideas and no affection or happiness left in him.

September 12. Announcement of our engagement in the *Morning Post*. By middle day advertisements from various firms began to arrive! Wedding orders solicited, bouquets, trousseaus. News-office offering to send cuttings, shops offering to print wedding cards, etc!

September 13. Sad discussion at breakfast. It is so terrible and miserable to see poor Papa like this.

10

About this time, Frank took up his duties at Stockport as adjutant of the Fourth Volunteer Battalion of the Cheshire Regiment; he usually refers to them as "the Volunteers." He describes to Kathleen how he was introduced to their officers and noncommissioned officers during an exhibition drill:

It was rather formidable as there was a large audience sitting all round the room and all the NCOs fallen in in the middle, and the Colonel said, 'now we will walk slowly round and they will have a good look at you'! The officers are not so formidable, as they are all frightened of saying and doing the wrong thing themselves, they really wouldn't notice it if one stood on one's head.

Frank was told that he would have to attend a "camp of exercise" for a week, beginning on September 13. This worried him, because he would be expected to pay certain expenses out of his own pocket; it would cost him at least ten pounds. "I think I must give up going to London to make up for it, as we really must be economical. I think we have rather played at being so, so far." However, Moey had at last sold one of his watercolors, for ten shillings. "I can now honestly call myself a professional, I think."

At the camp, Frank met an officer who was about to get married and who told him:

. .

227

that if his girl wished him to stand on his head in the middle of Piccadilly he would do it. His wedding is going to be a marvellous show—six bridesmaids in Empire dresses and bouquets and long blue wands. Each of the bridesmaids is to have a Kruger half sovereign dangling on a curb bracelet. The men who walk with them are to have a pin with half a merrythought on it. The other half of the merrythought is to be presented by the man to what this fellow called 'his best girl'. It all sounds most vulgar and Sykesy, I thought.

Less than two weeks later, this officer was brutally jilted. His fiancée sent him a telegram calling off the wedding only ten days before it was due to take place; that was the last he ever heard from her. Perhaps Frank is ashamed of his snobbish comments, for he now tells Kathleen, "I feel very sorry for him," but he can't resist baiting her by adding, "and think the heartlessness of most women is awful."

Letter from Frank, September 21, Marple Hall:

I am not at all on joking terms with the Volunteers. They never call me anything but 'Captain Isherwood' or 'Sir' and their whole conversation consists in asking one military conundrums.

I do wish you could bring the Dearest Mama here. You really ought to get her away from your Father. I hate to think of his bullying two defenceless women, and although I admire beyond words your goodness and patience in being able to think that perhaps you are in the wrong, and feel how sweet and womanly and divine your forgiveness is, *still* to him I should like you to be more hard-hearted. I'm sure it would be better for both of you.

Old Standen said of my pictures that he felt there was a want of quality and that the outlines of the distant hills were too hard, but—that seems to me *the* distinctive feature of South African landscape—so what's a fellow to do?

September 22. Busy answering letters and received my 80th one of congratulation!

Letter from Frank, October 1, Marple Hall:

I am so sorry I couldn't write to you yesterday but I was out all day and I will give you two thousand guesses as to what we were doing??????? Are you guessing all this time? Well, the correct answer is—shooting grouse! Lord Newton rode over himself, an unparalleled act of civility, on Monday, to ask Henry and I to go, and Mother said he was so civil and seemed to think it would be an excellent thing to make friends with him, so we said yes. I think another reason why Mother was so keen on our going was that Lady M. whom she hates was coming over and she wanted her to have a slap in the face and be put off.

I don't know who shot worst but we managed to mop up forty braces, and the moors looked lovely although it was a drizzling dark day but the colour of the bracken and the various moorland plants was most brilliant and the moors always, I think, look more mysterious under a grey sky.

Letter from Frank, October 12, Marple Hall:

It makes me so angry when I hear people running down Japan. I always feel more drawn to it than ever when I hear Henry talk about factory chimneys and a want of colour, etc etc. I think that sort of person with what I call professionally good taste hasn't very often any real taste at all. They only see beauty where they expect it.

Henry calls the opposite of this, the finding of beauty in unexpected places—which he thinks is done for effect—'pressu'. I don't know how you spell it or what language it is. Have you read a book called 'Gleanings in Buddha's fields'? If not, you must. It was à propos of it that he first said that the author was 'pressu'.

These little tattling oldwomen men are most irritating sometimes, I think. You see how angry it makes me. This grievance has been smouldering for quite a week.

(It seems obvious that the offensive word used by Henry was précieux, *meaning affected. Frank was a little too fond of using French words himself, and it can only be affectation on his part which makes him pretend not to recognize this one. No doubt Henry did pronounce* précieux *"pressu"; that was the way he talked. The truth is, Frank is envious of Henry because he can afford to visit places which Frank longs to visit. Frank feels that he, not Henry, deserved to go to Japan, because he could have appreciated it, while Henry didn't. This is what Frank's "grievance" is really about, but he is embarrassed to admit it, so instead he vents his spleen by sneering at Henry's effeminacy. Later in the letter he refers to himself as being, by contrast, "Early English," that is to say virile, uncomplicated, down-to-earth. Such posturing seems unworthy of Frank, who has been man enough to confront the enemy in uniform and the audience in a skirt, and to confess to the girl he loves that he is "rather like a woman in many ways.")*

Letter from Frank, October 19, Marple Hall:

I woke up feeling in such low spirits and that there were so many beautiful things in life that I was missing, useful things I mean, that I could do so much better than soldiering. It seems rather hopeless to have to keep what talents you have in a napkin and go pounding away at something one isn't fit for particularly. I suppose that lots of men have to do it and it's only childishness on my part to think it's so much worse for me than anyone else.

However there are moments when one feels quite military. Did I tell you about the little man who rushed up to me the other day and told me that he had made enquiries of the sergeants in the Volunteers and he heard that I was likely to be most popular—that what the men liked was a real officer who, when they came in from drill, said something which made their bosoms swell. I can't imagine myself doing this at all!

(Frank was probably depressed because of some tiresome examinations which he was working for at this time. As a grown man

and a combat veteran, he must naturally have resented having to study such academic details as the correct dimensions of a sandbag.)

Letter from Frank, October 29, Marple Hall:

Jack comes back tomorrow. We have got an enormous pile of duets from the circulating library and we hope to play on two pianos and one piano until all's blue. Do you really, *really* realize how musical I am? A little playing sometimes in the evening wouldn't content me a bit. Are you sure you realize what musical friends mean?? I always remember poor Mr Hall (at Cork); when he used to come home and find me playing duets with his wife, how trying it must have been, we went on till dinner time. He used to be very kind and ask me to stay to dinner and then after dinner my train didn't go till eleven o'clock!! Duets, duets, duets, duets. Of course we enjoyed it up to the tips of our fingers, but *he*, poor man?? I didn't care at all for either him or his wife, and it was only the duets which made a bond between us, so one's one idea was to get back to the piano.

(Music was a strong bond between Frank and Jack, who was a fine pianist, undoubtedly the better of the two; but the brothers enjoyed each other's company apart from this—they were much alike, physically and temperamentally. This may have been why Kathleen in her later years felt closer to Jack than to any other member of the family.

Born on October 21, 1876, Jack was the fourth of the Isherwood children, senior only to Esther. He was good-looking; not as handsome as Henry, but far more attractive. He lived to be eighty-five and kept his youthful figure and blond hair throughout much of his life. He had the eyes and mouth of a humorist, with big teeth, a dry witty voice and the air of being always about to say something amusing; he frequently did. His humor was cheerfully unkind, but not bitter or vicious. When he laughed he laughed violently and his otherwise pale face flushed crimson.

Jack didn't get married until he was in his middle forties. When

231

Christopher was growing up, he liked to picture Jack's earlier bachelorhood as the kind of life he himself hoped to live someday. For Jack had known the genuine London bohemia, where musicians, artists, writers and their lovers roamed free and fearless outside the cage bars of conventionality. He had mixed with them at exotic studio parties and joined them in the practice of occult disciplines, such as hatha yoga. He had not shrunk from experimenting with spiritualism or the use of the stomach pump. He had enjoyed the friendship of a real composer, the fascinating and enigmatic Cyril Scott. That Jack had spent his working hours dealing with death duties and property deeds only made him more romantic in Christopher's eyes; he seemed to have led a daringly double life.

Jack was actually less daring and more sensible than Christopher cared to admit. Instead of gambling everything on a musical talent which might or might not have been adequate to support him, he preferred to remain a lawyer with a steady government job. He could thus keep one foot in bohemia without having to rely on its doubtful mercies.

In 1902 all this still lay ahead of him. He was obliged to live at Marple Hall on a tiny allowance from his Father while he prepared for the civil-service examination which could get him into one of the legal departments of Somerset House. Jack's whole future was at stake. He stood to win escape to London and independence or to fail and face an antibohemian provincial existence and a job in a Stockport law office, obtained through his father's influence, if he was lucky. So Jack had to win. When the examination results were published that December, his name was third from the top of the list.)

October 30. Finished 'Love and Mr Lewisham' which irritated me beyond words, selfish, blindly priggish, would-be proper sentiments. I could have thrown the book at his head, as if we were just put here only to continue the wretched human race. I don't fancy we should hear much of these fine ideas if the man had to change places with the woman.

Kathleen must have also expressed her indignation against H. G. Wells in a letter to Frank, for on November 3 he replies:

I can't remember about Mr Lewisham, except that it was a very dull book. However if you are going to throw books at the heads of all the people who make rules for other people to live by, your library will be rather knocked about. (I suppose you'll stick to your own books and not think of throwing mine.)

Kearsey is to come next week. He is writing a regimental book about the war and wants me to write the chapter about Pieter's Hill. I think I could write one, more or less—all the emotions of the thing, the smells and the sensations—but I'm sure I couldn't do a dull record of brigades and divisions and plans and maps. I feel inclined to throw them and the books about them out of the window. However I'll keep them for you to shy about, as you are in the book-throwing line.

(Kearsey's book has already been quoted from. In the introduction to it, he thanks several of his brother officers, including Frank, "for the interesting papers which they have each contributed." If Frank did indeed write its terse soldierly account of the attack on Pieter's Hill he must for some reason have decided to omit 'the emotions of the thing' as well as those descriptive touches of the watercolorist which fill his South African letters.)

On November 6 Frank writes from Chester, where he is taking his military examination: "Today we are going out to do the practical fortification, which is more or less of a farce." He adds that he has spent the previous evening with a fellow candidate and had to listen to his sexual reminiscences, of the "she was a fine woman in her time" type:

You would have been amused to hear what a frightful 'rip' I appeared to be. These fellows always tell me long yarns about their adventures and because I don't reciprocate, *really having nothing to tell*, think I am a very dark horse and that my experiences are too bad to relate!! It makes me feel, when I think it over the next morning, that you and I are the only two really nice people in the world!

Letter from Frank, November 12, Marple Hall:

I am reading a book on Esoteric Buddhism which is very interesting but rather difficult to understand. It doesn't seem to be incompatible with Christianity exactly, either. It appears that, though we shall not really spend Eternity together, we shall each think the other is with us! Do you think that satisfactory? They go too much into detail altogether to be absolutely believable, and profess to *know* these things as a matter of fact. Goodbye, my dear. I do hope we are going to have a *very* long happy time together, even though we don't get Eternity.

On November 18 Kathleen came up from London to visit the Isherwoods, and she stayed until December 2. She and Frank spent much time over at Wyberslegh, deciding what additional furniture they would need and how the rooms should be painted and papered. Meanwhile, the entries in her diary reveal that the charm of the countryside is growing on her, no doubt because she sees it more and more through Frank's eyes:

Lovely day, bitterly cold and bright. Frank drove me up to Mellor, in the hills. There is the old church and Mellor Hall and a few cottages. It is most romantically situated, so high up and such splendid views and so lonely.

We walked by the canal, the hills and mills down to the water and picturesque barge 'The Hilda' painted in queer ornate patterns. Most lovely reflections and the pretty bridges across the water and then Marple church high up on the hill.

Along the canal towards Hyde, past Woodley station, near which is a wonderful old red and yellow mill; seen through the arch of the bridge, quite Venetian.

We walked to Romiley church and back by the aqueduct and

234

viaduct, a great splendid looking old arched bridge over a very pretty valley, quite Roman in appearance, such grand arches, very tall and high and fine, and the old bricks a beautiful rich colour. This country is full of colour and immensely varied and attractive.

The day after Kathleen's return to London, she notes with secretive vagueness in her diary: "Everything seems most extraordinarily unsatisfactory and miserable." But it is clear from Frank's next letter that she has told him she has had a candid talk, perhaps even a quarrel, with Frederick about his ugly behavior. Frank writes:

My dear, I am very glad that you had it out with your Father. I don't quite know if all the things we imagined you saying to the D.O.D. included any remarks as to his treatment of the Dearest Mama. I rather hope you gave him to understand that your Husband will have the right to look after his Mother-in-Law as well as his Wife, and to stop all nonsense and bullying.

(D.O.D. = "Dear Old Dad"?)
That Kathleen's outspokenness didn't have much effect on Frederick is also clear, however. Frank writes (December 5):

I am very sorry to hear from your letter of your difficulties. As far as I can judge, I think you must get the Dearest Mama out of it in spite of herself and suggest your writing either to your Uncle Walter or any other of your Mother's trustees and telling him the facts of your Father's behaviour, pointing out how terribly the trial of living in such a tempestuous atmosphere is weighing on her and begging him to see your Father and insist on his going away, or arranging for your Mother going away, or his controlling himself. I suppose it would do if he were forced to give up letting loose his feelings in her presence. Poor you. I wish we were peacefully at Wyberslegh, all three of us, if you can think it possible to be peaceful with a man in the house. I don't think you have had very good experience of us, up to date!

(It will be noted that Frank has just changed his spelling of Wyberslegh. This seems to have been his idea; Kathleen immediately adopted it.)

Letter from Frank, December 6, Marple Hall:

Jack and I walked up to Mellor this morning to church. It's rather quaint, the singing is excruciating but that's the case everywhere. There was a large congregation of young men which is unusual, great broad-shouldered farmers, a much more interesting class than the people of the plains below. It was rather an awful moment when we went out before the sermon, as we couldn't get the door open. I banged and pushed while Jack went into fits of laughter behind the curtain. At last in the desperation of despair I felt we couldn't go back beaten to our pew, I banged it open with a loud crash and we fell out of church.

Frank goes on to say that he has been reading Conrad's Youth, which has just been published; he compares it with the latest novel by Venus:

Venus's book so very much the woman's point of view and his so very much the man's. She with her implication that love, and all that, is the solution of the secret, while he seems to find it work and adventure and a sea life etc. Do read it and see if you aren't delighted with the scene where the boy from the wreck woke up and found himself at last in the East. There's one side of me that thrills in response to all that—and that sometimes makes me a little difficult for people at home to manage. Do you understand?

Kathleen certainly understood that this was another of Frank's mischievous male provocations. Man's basic threat to Woman is that he will run away from her; Woman's basic retort is that those who run away are children, not real men. In her diary (December 13) Kathleen notes that she has now read Youth: "very cleverly described, the breeziness and hope and joy of life (in the first) of youth." Conrad is a producer of escape literature, therefore he cannot be treated as an adult writer; Kathleen tells him, as woman to child, that he has described things "very cleverly." ("Oh, of course I can see that it's desperately clever," *she would say twenty years later, when putting down the "modern" writers whom Christopher admired.)*

To judge by the handwriting of this diary entry, Kathleen drew the parentheses around "in the first" as an afterthought, for extra emphasis, lest she should seem to have admitted that there was any breeziness, etc., in this, the last of her youth. Sometimes she is exactly like a lawyer detecting an unintended, hitherto unnoticed concession in a contract!

On December 12, Kathleen was visited by a Miss L., a lady who was supposed to have once had romantic feelings for Frank. Kathleen writes of her that she was "very amusing and full of what tremendous friends Frank and she had been." A few days after this, Frank sent Kathleen the letter Miss L. had written him about the visit:

My dear Frank, yesterday I went to London shopping and I went to call on Miss Machell-Smith. As good luck had it she was at home and I had the most pleasant visit. I am quite charmed with her, I remember her sincere and pretty eyes perfectly, and I think you are a most fortunate person. I am sure she has a perfect disposition, she is so calm and friendly. The room seemed full of such pretty things. I gave you an excellent character, you may like to hear.

To enjoy the full flavor of Miss L.'s condescension, it must be remembered that the word "character" was then used, much more commonly than nowadays, to mean "a formal statement by an employer concerning the qualities and habits of a former servant." Only, in this case, Miss L. appears to be recommending two servants to each other!

· ·

I had an awful night last night, as I had a little touch of influenza and very weakly told my Mother and she nearly worried my life out and actually about ten o'clock sent off for the doctor. I am afraid I lost my temper completely, but I do so loathe being fussed over—*please note.*

I don't seem to have read anything except the little theosophist books, which impressed me very much. I wonder, if I got them for you, if you would read them. They seem to give one such a very definite grip of life and the importance of every thought and action in forming oneself for a future state, and are I don't think inconsistent with Church teaching. They certainly aren't inconsistent with Christianity, which I think is a very different thing. I should rather like to go to their place in London and hear one of them speak about it. I suppose you would hardly care to go there with me. It would, though, be very much better if we could share all those things, wouldn't it? I don't like your taking the attitude that it is silly and you can't bear to think of it, and even if your own ideas are settled I should like you to sympathize with my attempt to settle mine, which the Church will never succeed in doing. I feel it would always be a great barrier between us if we felt we couldn't speak of these things and if I had to go to church and pretend, and hide books from you that I was interested in.

On December 24, Frank, who had come up to London a few days previously, traveled down with Kathleen and Emily to spend Christmas at Nether Hall. Frederick was already staying there and had consented to endure Frank's presence, while reserving the right to sulk. Emily was demonstrating her martyrdom to Frederick's behavior by a swollen gland and a mysterious crick in her neck; the doctor had forbidden her to travel when the wind was in the east. Kathleen was unhappy, worrying about Emily. Frank was the only one of them who seems to have been looking forward to the holiday season with enjoyment. Referring to Nether in one of his letters from Marple, he had written:

Somehow it's more amusing playing the engaged couple there than anywhere else, before an admiring audience. It's so very amusing to let them think that we are the ordinary ridiculous pair in love, who will quarrel directly the wedding's over, when we know all the time that we aren't, and are so far superior—*so far superior!*

And about Frederick:

Your Mother wrote to me quite pathetically that the Nether Hall party was so large that he needn't spoil my pleasure. He won't, you may be sure of that—indeed I think he adds a spice of excitement to the visit.

December 25. It did not feel the least like Christmas. We walked over to Thurston to church and stayed second service. It was a nice day.

December 27. The others went shooting and Frank and I drove into Bury in the pony cart. They declared the shops would be shut, but we went to Bests and managed to bring back in triumph a Braysworth chair and copper coal scuttle.

December 28. Very cold. In afternoon we walked by the fens to Ixworth. It was more or less settled in the evening after some discussion that the wedding is to be here, on March 12. Went to the Smoking Room after prayers to tell Papa, though he did not take any apparent interest.

December 29. Mama very poorly. Saw Dr who ordered her to bed. The gland will not discharge freely and he ordered hot linseed poultices every hour.

December 30. Went to interview Mr B. about the wedding. A week's residence in the parish beforehand and a bag left the re-

239

maining week will count alright, so our banns will probably be published next Sunday and will hold good three months, and we needn't 'reside' again before wedding.

In Kathleen's 1903 diary there is no list of Things I Want. (It will be discontinued for the next three years.) There is a list of "Poor Ladies" who can be helped by giving them employment—with substandard wages, no doubt! And the usual bookbinding instructions, knitting and crochet recipes, rules of bridge, invalid foods for Emily.

January 1. Heard the bells ring the New Year in. Bright frosty morning. Frank left. Busy with poor Mama who has to have little compresses of lint dipped in hot boracic water and changed every hour, on her gland. It is discharging much better and bled a good deal, which Dr thought good.

January 3. Dr came and thoroughly looked me over, sounded and punched me and says I am perfectly healthy, lungs and heart sound etc, but not robust and far too thin! And that I must take a cup of Benger an hour before getting up, jelly or beef tea at eleven, the same thing during the afternoon and milk before I go to bed—about eight meals a day, in fact.

January 4. *Our banns were given out* at Thurston and felt disappointed that I had not been there, but I thought Mr B was not going to begin till next Sunday.

Letter from Frank, January 4, Marple Hall:

My People have gone to All Saints to hear our banns. I told my Mother every eye in the church would be glued on her back, but she didn't seem to mind. I went down to St Martin's to the communion this morning. I like that the best of all the services.

I thought a great deal of you and how I must make up my mind now to merge myself as far as I possibly can in you, and how we must share our thoughts and feelings together, without irritation, over differences of opinion. It is very difficult to start and the feeling so has often made me tiresome and cross. I know, though, you will help me all you can and we must feel that we are making a fresh start together. I know so certainly and have never doubted that marriage must be for *my* good at any rate, in the way of making life so much more serious and full of deeper meaning. I am afraid sometimes it will be a disappointment to you, but you mustn't expect too much!

Letter from Frank, January 7, Marple Hall:

My Mother means to go to the wedding all right. I am persuading her to wear grey, and lace. I liked the Mama saying we had had a 'long Lent' and that she thought we were entitled to a rather earlier Easter than most people. I read that to my Mother and she was visibly impressed.

Letter from Frank, January 10, Marple Hall:

I went to the ball last night and did my duty thoroughly, dancing with all sorts of people, wives and daughters of Volunteers, and really some of them were very nice and, if they were Lady Gaggs or the Duchess, would have been considered charming. They all seemed so astonished at one dancing the 'hopwaltz', as they called it. One woman asked me if I thought it would become general?

I am going to lunch with Murray. He is most amusing on the subject of matrimony and was dreadfully upset when he heard we were coming straight home. He kept on saying in a dreamy voice, 'take her away as far as possible, oh take her away, Frank, it makes such *an impression* on them!' Switzerland *had* made such an impression on his Wife. He is, I think, such a very nice chap and a tremendous enthusiast for married life, indeed they are a most encouraging pair, and we both want encouragement(?)

. .

241

January 11. Lovely bright day. Drove with Uncle Walter to church. Heard my banns published. Felt very frightened when the second lesson came to an end! However, it didn't sound very surprising, after all.

January 12. Snow on the ground. Uncle Walter gave me a *most* handsome cheque. Mama and I left by the 12.20, most regretfully —all the bustle and hurry begins tomorrow of shopping. Also it is rather alarming to be saying goodbye to Nether and feel that the next time—

January 14. To Miss Harrison's about teagown and wedding train and the gown to be fitted. Settled on going-away blouse.

January 15. Madame d'Alessandri came to fit Mama's dress for the wedding. Bronze green velvet.

Letter from Frank, January 15, Marple Hall:

'The Man' as a thing doesn't exist. Some men imagine things and are afraid and irresolute, and others—don't. That's the long and short of it. Both sorts have the defects of their qualities, and if the other sort don't worry and imagine etc, they would probably annoy you just as much because they didn't. So cheer up! Or do you wish you had got one of that sort? No, I see you say.

So—if there is any throwing over to be done, you must do it because *I* am not going to. Do you like to know (or not?) that I have thought it all over many times and I have even imagined a little scene—taking place, I think, after a long morning's shopping with a certain rather alarming and managing young lady—in which 'the man' did say goodbye to the M.Y.L. . . . but, as she turned the corner, he seemed to see his old friend Miss Machell Smith of Oxford days and his K, his young woman of later, going out of his life for always—and, when she looked back, they . . . I thought then that, if the little scene did take place, the M.Y.L.

mightn't look back—and then! I should get left. I shouldn't like that—so, you see, 'the man' hasn't any doubts after all!

Shall I meet *my* K. at the carpet shop on Saturday? P.S. Don't bring the M.Y.L.

Frank came to London that Saturday, the seventeenth, and met Kathleen at Harvey and Nichols, where they chose some of the carpets for Wyberslegh. He left for Marple two days later. On February 3, Kathleen and Emily went down to stay at Ventnor. Kathleen remarks that the place is "looking as sulkily grey as ever." They were to have bad weather during most of their visit.

On February 4, Frank writes that he has been digging in the garden at Wyberslegh and planning how to plant it, and that he has been visited while there by his old nurse, whom the family called "Chew."

When she went into the cellar she said, 'do you know what this puts me in mind of?' Of course we none of us had the slightest idea and she said triumphantly, 'Lancaster Castle'. She supposed the walls there were in parts twenty feet thick.

On February 12, Kathleen got a letter from Frank which, she says in her diary, "worried me a good deal." This is puzzling, because the letter which Frank wrote her on February 9 could have worried nobody; it is chiefly about the excessive amount of household silver which they have already received in wedding presents and how much of it could be exchanged for other things they need.

The next letter in the packet is undated but must have been written on February 12, because of its reference to the wedding:

My dear, a month today! We shall have started off on our journey together. I do hope it will be a successful one for you and that we shall get to the end of it all the better for travelling together. We are both good travellers in the real sense of the word, so I hope my using this expression is a good omen.

Can you imagine that a month today it will be all over—the

church, and all the compliments and jokes, and we shall really be ourselves again? I can't. I expect you have had some shivers over it.

This too sounds absolutely unworrying; indeed, it is reassuring. Yet Frank must have written in an altogether different tone only a day or two days before, on the tenth or eleventh. It is very strange that his letter of the twelfth, quoted above, gives no hint of anxiety about Kathleen's possible reactions to that earlier letter, for he must still have been awaiting her reply. When he finally got it, probably on the thirteenth, he answered in a way which shows how seriously he has been concerned:

My dear, thank you in every possible way for your kindness and patience. There can be no doubt as to what my answer must be. I should simply be a fool to throw away such a real friend and companion for life, and if you can be happy in marriage with me there can be no further questions as to whether we shall go on.

But I *do* want you to be happy and so you mustn't deceive yourself about me or think I have got all sorts of imaginary noble qualities and all that, because you've really seen every square inch of me and it's a poor show, I'm afraid.

I can honestly say I want to marry you as much as ever I did, and care for you more than any other woman—in fact, I don't care for any other woman in the least! And I feel sure that when all the vexations and worries of the engagement are over, and we shut the Wyberslegh gate on the *trio* of friends, I shall be really happy and I know that I hope you will be able to be so too.

I own to having felt in the past that you did expect and want more than the close friendship we originally made our ideal—and I feel that it was partly my own fault if you had expected it. But I shall know better now and can promise that I will never (I don't think I have ever done so in the past) show you any feeling that isn't perfectly genuine. I believe you know that I shall make a much better husband than a lover, and when it comes to everyday work, and our lives are going on side by side all the time, I believe affection—which I think cannot arise except in that way—will intensify out of the germ which I am sure is there.

Thank you again for your letter. What you show me in it of the nature of a good kind woman is a lesson for which a man can never do enough in return—and I hope *most* genuinely that I shall be able to do something.

Anyhow I am still and always your Frank.

As Frank's letter of February tenth or eleventh is lost, one doesn't know exactly what he wrote and can only guess at his motives for writing it. Frank's letters are so often ambiguous in tone, a mixture of "Early English" outspokenness and subtle teasing, half playful, half hostile—jokes which seem to imply threats, threats which may be merely jokes. For example, his jokes about "the managing young lady" (January 15) seem to show a real resentment against her; but one can't be quite sure. Kathleen can never have been quite sure, either. Whenever Frank talked like this, she must have been worried.

However, one thing is made clear by Frank's indirect description of the lost letter in this later one: it wasn't written jokingly, its tone was absolutely serious. What worried Kathleen, perhaps, was that his seriousness might not mean what it pretended. If he said more or less what he says again here, that he is "a poor show" and that she is crediting him with "imaginary noble qualities," she may well have found such exaggerated humility a bit suspicious.

Kathleen has expressed her own doubts about her fitness to become a wife. But the raising of doubts and difficulties by separated lovers is actually a way of lovemaking; by creating tension they keep their relationship alive. That Frank should raise similar doubts now, within sight of the altar, is an altogether different matter. No one in Kathleen's position could help asking herself, Is he hinting that we should break off our engagement?

It is improbable that she did believe this, but she evidently put the question to him. His answer sounds miserably lukewarm; it is also not a straight answer. He doesn't say what he did or didn't mean by his previous letter; he only implies that the kindness and patience expressed by her reply to it have moved him to reconsider his attitude. He now realizes that he "should simply be a fool to throw away such a real friend and companion for life . . ." Even chillier and more ungracious than this statement is his assurance that he cares for her more than any other woman because—he doesn't care for any other woman in the least! And then he offers her this icy crumb of consolation: he is "sure" that there already exists between them a "germ" of affection!

That Kathleen wasn't even more seriously upset by any of this must prove that she understood what had made Frank write it. Indeed, she seems to have grown, lately, in wisdom and common sense. Her former doubts about marriage appear to be resolved. Despite some ordinary stage fright, which will bring on physical reactions later, she is basically calm. She still doesn't want to be a hausfrau, but she has prepared herself to run a house; she still doesn't want to be a babymaker, but she is quite ready to have one or two children. Her greatest fear, that she won't be able to see enough of Emily after the wedding, has been set at rest by Frank's assurance that, at Wyberslegh, Emily shall have a second home and be a member of "the trio of friends."

Frank's apparent lack of feeling can be understood only in reference to his own character, not to his relations with Kathleen —which are, one suspects, much more normally romantic than either of them will admit. Frank is, and will always remain, intensely fastidious. He is repelled by the bragging of men to each other about their sex life and by the insincerity of their pretty speeches and flirty behavior in the presence of women. Therefore he prefers to use words like "companionship" and "affection" and shies away from the word "love." His natural approach to sexual emotion is gradual, through friendship. He is afraid of being rushed.

But now the ominous impersonal tribal ceremony is finally before him, with its awesome gathering of the folk, its sly whispering of elders, its indecent inspection of the stud bridegroom and brood-mare bride, its legal documents binding the unborn. There is much here to disgust a tougher man than Frank; there is nothing here which does not seem right and proper to a woman of Kathleen's class, even to one as sensitive as Kathleen. Kathleen is nervous now because she must play the leading part in this ceremony, but she accepts the inevitability of it without question. How could she not? She has been conditioned to it since child-hood.

Why did Frank write to Kathleen as he did? Probably because he had realized, with sudden appalling clarity, what was about to happen to him, and for a moment lost his head. So, perhaps, behind his frigid ill-chosen phrases there is nothing more (but nothing less) than a last desperate male cry of terror at the closing of the tribal trap, the cutting short of his long bachelor boyhood. Having uttered that cry—and acknowledged its futility—he pulls himself together and turns, like the soldier he is, to face the organ music. It is significant that the main section of his next letter (February 15) begins, "Now to business!"

"Business" includes: the traveling bag they are to take on their honeymoon—Kathleen is to buy it at Asprey's, since the whole-salers aren't offering it much cheaper; the prayerbooks to be given as presents to the bridesmaids—they are to be decorated by a man at Bath who paints designs under vellum which has been rendered transparent; Michael Halford, who, although Frank was so fond of him in South Africa, is dreadfully casual and hasn't answered his invitation to be best man—Frank must ask Captain Clemson to act as substitute, though he feels this is "rather a cool thing" to do; the four more screens needed for Wyberslegh— "Mama's bedroom will be uninhabitable without one"; and the wedding ring—Kathleen must send the measurement of her finger ("it is the sort of ceremony which ought to have been per-formed in the Nether Hall boudoir with Aggie superintending") and say if she would prefer it to be thick or thin.

February 19. Left Ventnor. Home about 5.30. Found the sofa *stacked* with presents!

Letter from Frank, February 19, Marple Hall:

I hope you have got back to London all right and received a fairly good welcome from the D.O.D. I think the Mama will rather feel it if he doesn't come to the wedding? So you had better encourage him to do so!! I had a scheme of writing to him and asking him, now that we had come to such close quarters, to bury the hatchet. I should like him to do so so much, for her sake, but I expect he would only think it was a put-up job and it might make things worse.

Letter from Frank, February 25, Marple Hall:

What did 'Papa' see in the paper about the wedding? It really is absurd, his being annoyed about it at this stage. I should like him to come if it is any pleasure to the dearest Mama, but if he is going to be tiresome and annoy and depress you both, I should tell him to stop away.

March 3. Went in afternoon to try on wedding dress. Wrote letters of thanks in every spare interval. Had a bad headache and felt very sick. Went to bed soon after tea and could not eat any dinner.

Letter from Frank, March 3, Marple Hall:

Don't you think we could get the dearest Mama down from Friday or Saturday till Monday?? I should love to have her. I know it's not the usual thing to have (or want to have) your Mother-in-Law on your honeymoon, but we need not tell Aggie or the outside world, and we always have our best times when we are all three together. So *do* get her to come.

I found myself talking to the grocer, who came to bother me about custom, about 'Mrs Isherwood'. You will very soon be that now and I do hope it will make you happy.

March 10. Rained all day in a miserable half-hearted way. Had excellent journey, reaching Bury at 1.5, where they kindly sent to meet us. Only Aggie here so far, so had a nice quiet evening and the plan of table and who takes in who was discussed and worked out.

March 11. Lovely day and felt afraid it would never last over tomorrow. Aggie, Mama and I sat in the kitchen garden enjoying the sunshine. A dinner party of thirtyfour in evening, I going in with Frank. We signed papers after, and there was great talking and amiability and feeling of unreality!!

(This was the day on which most of the guests arrived. Frederick was among them, having decided that it was less humiliating to seem to sanction the marriage than to allow Walter Greene to give the bride away and thus usurp his place as The Father.

John, Elizabeth and Henry Isherwood had come; Moey was ill, Jack was probably too busy, Esther could hardly have been expected.

Elizabeth brought Kathleen a note from Frank, scribbled on the train. Frank was no doubt forbidden by etiquette to talk to Kathleen in private before the wedding; they could meet only at the evening dinner party. Frank writes:

My dear, I am writing you a line to go to you by my Mother, just to assure you how glad I am. The train journey—this seems to be most fitting, as it was our love of travelling that first brought us together—has somehow seemed to smooth away all the difficulties and brought back the old feeling which I am afraid I had partly lost lately, the realization of what life with you as a constant companion and friend will be. The spring seems to be coming in too, in earnest. I feel that I shall be a better happier man and a more useful soldier, for being your husband, and I hope most earnestly that you will find no reason to regret our joining forces. A rivederci this evening!! I am and shall always be your lover and friend, Frank.

Etiquette also forbade the bride and bridegroom to spend the night under the same roof. Since Kathleen was at Nether, Frank and Henry were invited to stay at the house of a neighbor. Their hosts had naturally prepared the better guest bedroom for the bridegroom, but Henry blandly took it for himself, as a matter of course, and Frank didn't protest!)

March 12. My wedding day, and brilliant sunshine with no wind. Stayed in bed till about 10, though breakfasted with Mama in her room, and then partly got up and Lilla came and did my hair and the others all paid me little visits during the morning. Dear Mama most wonderful. We had lunch together, and Lilla came and pinned on my wedding veil and wreath. Auntie Annie lent me the former, of old Brussels lace. Mrs Pickin and the servants left in the house came in to look at my dress, which looked nice. Drove with Uncle Walter to the church, such a glorious day and did not feel so frightened as I expected. Church crowded. Papa met me in the porch. Everyone very kind and *quite* enjoyed the wedding! Frank and I left a little before 4 and were driven to Bury station. Got to Cambridge at 6.

(A local newspaper adds some details of costume. The bride was "attired in ivory satin trimmed with Honiton point lace and accordion-pleated chiffon around the skirt, and train of silver gauze and chiffon with silver embroidered net frills," the bridesmaids wore "tucked cream silk voile with insertions and medallions of guipure, scarlet sashes were at their waists and their three-cornered toques were of black tulle and jet ornaments." When "the happy pair" left to spend their honeymoon at Cambridge, Kathleen was dressed in "dark blue serge and a picture hat to match, trimmed with tucked chiffon and a large white feather; her travelling cloak of Parma violet cloth was lined with fur and she wore a sable pelerine and muff.")

March 13. [Friday!] Same wonderful brilliant weather. We slept with our window wide open all night. The University Arms is charming, so clean and comfortable and light, and south windows looking on to Parker's Piece.

We went out about eleven into the sun and wandered into the R.C. church and then along Kings Parade and into Kings and enjoyed the glass, and back into St Mary's where there is a very nice east window, modern, full of angels giving praise. In afternoon we wandered along the Backs and sat in the sunshine basking. Went to Buol's for tea and then to a beautiful service at Kings College Chapel, no organ and the boys' voices sounded most lovely. Back to the Varsity Arms, dressed and drove to Buol's to dine. Had a very happy day, almost too much so, to be real!

March 14. Another brilliant morning, the sun streaming in to our windows. Down to the station to meet the Dearest Mama. It was so delightful to have her and see her so bright and happy. We all three had a cheerful little lunch at Buol's and sat about along the Backs, after going into the Market and the garden of Trinity Hall. We went again to service but liked the effect of voices less well with the organ. Dined at hotel and sat in drawing-room in evening.

March 15. Lovely sunshine. We walked across the meadows in the Grantchester direction. Rested after lunch at the hotel until it was time to get ready for the afternoon service at Kings. We all three dined at Buol's at eight o'clock. It seems quite extraordinary, after the turmoils and worries of the last months, to feel so happy and everything to be so bright.

March 16. We had meant to return 'home' today, but we seemed to like Cambridge so much that, as Frank's leave extended over, we wired to put off our return till tomorrow.

We saw the dearest Mama off. Frank and I lunched at Buol's, and then he made me rest before we went down to the station and caught the two-something to St Ives, a most charming little old town with market place dominated by Oliver Cromwell, who was born there. Had a little farewell dinner at Buol's. Another perfect day of happiness.

March 17. Rainy. Journeyed via Kettering to Marple station. Drove round by Marple and had tea with Frank's People and then on to our own home, via the Ridge.

The Coopers had the flag flying and Mrs Orchard and her husband were all ready to receive us. The house looked absolutely enchanting. The bright red hall paper and dark wood and the cosy little dining-room with its blue and white paper and blue carpet and our mahogany and the table all gay with daffodils sent by Mrs Isherwood, and as a surprise the drawing-room more or less furnished and we spent a cosy evening round our own fireside. My room is simply lovely.

Marple Hall

Emily

Kathleen and Christopher outside the front door of Wyberslegh,
Christmas 1905

LEFT: *Frank as a cadet at the Royal Military College, Sandhurst, aged about 21*

BELOW: *Frank at Cambridge, August 1914, just before leaving for the front*

RIGHT: *Kathleen in her early twenties*

BELOW: *Kathleen, aged 27, dressed as 'a girl of 16'*

Kathleen and Richard, March 1917

11

The title "Hall," in its Old English meaning of the residence of a territorial proprietor, may belong to a pretentious mansion or to a plain farmhouse; all you can say with certainty about a Hall is that it must be old. Wyberslegh Hall was at least three, perhaps four hundred years old when Frank and Kathleen moved into it in 1903.

During the previous eighty years the whole of it had been leased from the Isherwoods by a family named Cooper. They farmed its fields, lived in its rear wing and sublet rooms in the front to a succession of tenants. But now the alterations made by John for Frank had divided Wyberslegh into two dwellings without any interior communication. The front, with its lawns, flower beds and carriage drive, had become a residence for gentlefolk; the rear, with its barns, cowsheds and dairy, remained a working farm. The Isherwoods had a door in their kitchen which opened into the Coopers' farmyard, but the Coopers had no such access to the Isherwoods' garden, and if they wanted to talk to the Isherwoods they had to come to their back door, like social inferiors. All in all, the partition displeased the Coopers and wounded their pride. Relations between the two families were strained for a long time.

Wyberslegh stands just above the village of High Lane and between the larger villages of Disley and Marple, on a chain of low hills. One of these is called the Ridge. The house commands *two dramatically different views. From the front you look south-west across the flat Cheshire plain and can see the Welsh mountains if visibility is good. The foreground is crowded with red brick slate-roofed villas which multiply year by year, usurping the meadows. High Lane, on the road from Buxton to Manchester, is already a suburb with a bus service into the city. Away to the northeast and north spreads a vast spawn of houses, Stockport merging into Manchester, Manchester into Salford and beyond. In 1903, Manchester was busy and dirty and grim. Today it is idler and rather cleaner; its grimness remains. You can still wander through streets which bear the stamp of a Puritan industrialism so classic, so absolute in its denial of all joy to their inhabitants that they make you smile with horror.*

From the back of Wyberslegh you look out across the farmyard to Cobden Edge, a big bare windswept hill crisscrossed by low walls of loosely piled stones. A few farms are dotted over it. In the background, across the Derbyshire border, the moors of the High Peak climb over dark outcroppings of rock to a boggy plateau covered with heather. This is Kinder Scout. There is a cascade from the rocks called the Downfall which you can see when its spray is blown upward and catches the light or when in winter it is frozen solid and shines. This great empty view, unlike the other crowded one, hasn't changed at all since Christopher was a child.

If you stand directly in front of the Hall, so that its rear farmhouse wing is hidden, it looks quaintly small and compact. Its gables and parapet are ornamented with the projections known as crowsteps; they resemble battlements and give it the air of a miniature castle. Wyberslegh is a homely cheerful house, but it is chronically damp. Bed linen feels clammy there, mold forms on books, wallpaper peels off. Its rugged but porous stone walls soak up the wetness of the climate.

This country never really dries out. The sense of weather is overwhelming. Every view is a watercolor, dripping with melancholy. The desolation of the nearby city seems to relate naturally to the desolation of the moorland. One may call this a suburb, implying that it has been tamed, but the dominant impression is of wildness. These bleak hills may be much less than mountains, but how hugely they impose their presence!

"I wonder what lies on the other side—is it the sea?"
"No, Miss Cathy. It's hills again, just like these."

From here you could follow the high ground up north into Yorkshire and reach Haworth without crossing any urban area; so Disley may claim to belong geographically to the land of the Brontës, although it is nearly forty miles from their home. When Christopher in his youth first read Wuthering Heights and Emily's poems, he at once superimposed their myth upon Wyberslegh, Disley, Cobden Edge, Ridge End Farm, Jackson's Edge woods, and even upon the surrounding modern villas:

Cold in the earth—and fifteen wild Decembers
From these brown hills have melted into spring . . .

It was as Heathcliff that he rode his bicycle uphill and down, through the familiar but transformed landscape, dreaming of death and despair and hopeless love. As Heathcliff he imagined himself standing all night in a storm outside Catherine Linton's window; Catherine being for the moment a blond boy with a charming grin and long legs, who played hockey. Christopher was eager to love hopelessly, desperately, fatally. When he discovered that the hopelessness was not only unnecessary but less fun, he had to give up the role of Heathcliff as lover.

But Heathcliff is also the traveler who returns, after mysterious wanderings, to the scene of his youth. The elderly Christopher still enjoys playing this role, every time he comes back to Wyberslegh. Walking up the old coaching road into the hills, with the rain clouds blowing in over the ridges and the rooks cawing fatefully around the gold ball on Disley Church and the tower in Lyme Park standing up black like an omen against the sky, he is unfailingly moved to tears. That the tears are pleasurable doesn't

*make his emotion less genuine and strong. Christopher is thankful
for it. But even more thankful that he isn't stuck, like Heathcliff,
with Wuthering Heights and its tragedy. He is firmly resolved
to die somewhere else.*

*The three-mile journey from Wyberslegh to Marple Hall was an
almost continuous descent. You came down off the Ridge into
Marple, kept on downhill through the village to the gates of the
park and the driveway which led across it, then suddenly dipped
into the hollow where the Hall itself stood hidden within a walled
garden surrounded by trees.*

*Marple was much bigger and more impressive than Wyberslegh;
it had the self-assured charm of a "country seat." The house was
built of warm red sandstone and heavily clothed in ivy. It was
there to meet you with a picturesque seventeenth-century brick
clock tower in attendance on its right, rising above the stables.
Its sheltered garden made, nearly all through the year, a welcoming display of flowers.*

*Because of many alterations and additions, Marple was a mix-
ture of styles: an E-shaped Elizabethan mansion which had kept
its decorated lead rain pipes and about half of its mullioned
windows, while the rest had been converted into sash windows or
bricked up to avoid the window taxes of the eighteenth century.
The original gables had been removed from one side of its façade
but not the other; this gave it a pleasing individuality, like a
crooked but attractive face. The nineteenth century had seen the
insertion of two huge bay windows at the back of the house and
the addition of a Victorian Gothic conservatory, opening out of
the library. Also, an odd-looking little balcony with squat pillars
had been put up over the front door.*

*Coming into the house, you felt at once that you were in a
showplace. The entrance hall was paved with big white flag-
stones inlaid with black marble tiles at each corner. The front
staircase, somewhat lopsided through the warping of age, was
built massively of black oak and had heavy baluster heads carved
to resemble goblets full of fruit. There was richly colored stained
glass in the windows. Around the walls were family portraits,*

suits of armor, dower chests, pewter dishes, antique weapons. There was an immense fireplace, from which boy sweeps had started their dangerous and filthy climb right up the chimney to the roof (this wasn't effectively forbidden until 1875). On either side of the hearth stood a tall hooded chair, rather like a hansom cab, which had a hole under its seat cushion to allow the use of a chamber pot. These chairs had been for menservants to doze in while waiting to unbar the front door to late-arriving guests.

The adjoining library offered rows of ancient leathern volumes; Foxe's Book of Martyrs was the only one of these that anybody ever opened, because of its gruesome woodcuts. The arms of the Bradshaws, the Isherwoods and all their kin by marriage had been painted on the oak-paneled walls and embroidered on the seats of the chairs; a typical touch of mid-Victorian vulgarity.

The dining room, at the far end of the hall, was hung with Flemish tapestry. Over the sideboard was a portrait of Queen Elizabeth in ruff and jeweled stomacher, with one hand on a sieve, the emblem of chastity and justice. ("Justice without mercy," Elizabeth Isherwood used to murmur automatically whenever she looked at it.) The painting was inscribed with three mottoes in Italian: "The good falls to the ground while the bad remains in the saddle," "I see everything and much is lacking," "Weary I rest and having rested I am still weary." (Christopher had been taught to render the last of these as "Weary rest and restless ease"—which is inaccurate and almost meaningless, but the beauty of the phrase still haunts him. In his teens he often showed visitors around the house and could rattle off facts and legends and dates like a professional guide.)

When the visitor had admired the show rooms upstairs—the Bradshaw Room with its excessively carved four-poster, the drawing room with its Gobelin tapestry—he would be taken out onto the terrace at the back of the house. The terrace was a big surprise to those who had so far seen the Hall from the front only, apparently standing deep in a hollow; for the terrace wall was built along the edge of wooded sandstone cliffs which were at least two hundred feet high.

Between these cliffs and the woods of a hill which rose steeply opposite, there was a narrow valley of meadows and a pond with an island in it, the Grotto Pond—probably so called because a summerhouse on the island was decorated with patterns of seashells, like the artificial grottoes of the eighteenth century. This valley had once been entirely under water and was then the "Mere Pool" from which Marple took its name. If the pool was part of a small river, it must have flowed into the River Mersey, which passes close by, rapid and foaming yellow with chemicals from the mills.

In 1903 there were active mills all over this district, their chimneys befouling the sky. Even out here, in what was seemingly still the countryside, they made the air sooty. Charming and romantic by contrast were a few surviving ruins of the original "dark Satanic Mills" raged against by William Blake, in which children had died slowly of tuberculosis or suddenly by falling into the machinery.

Despite the open view from the terrace, Marple Hall was apt to make you feel shut in, below the surface of the land. In winter, its surrounding hills cut off the light earlier than elsewhere. Many corners of the house were in continual twilight; the dark furniture and paneling absorbed most of what filtered through its narrow windows.

When John Isherwood became Kathleen's father-in-law he was in his early sixties. He was an easygoing amiable lazy man who had suffered, though not seriously, throughout his adult life from the effects of the stroke already referred to. It had forced him to leave the Army when he was barely twenty-one, after four years' service with the York and Lancaster Regiment. Since then he had done nothing professional, except officiate sometimes as a justice of the peace. As he grew older, his speech had become less and less distinct, until he could be understood only by those who were accustomed to it. He had also become messy in his habits, dropping food and tobacco ash over his clothes and wetting his armchair; the smell of it, rank but by no means unpleasant, like straw in a stable, is one of Christopher's basic memories.

John had never been handsome, but he had a pleasant good-natured face; its babyish pinkness, which did not leave it in later life, went well with his silver hair and moustache. He often looked amused, as if he were having private fun somewhere deep within the ponderousness of his slow body with its impeded reflexes.

Elizabeth Isherwood was now beginning to age rapidly. Christopher remembers her only as an ancient-seeming woman, tiny and shriveled, with a shockingly white wrinkled pallor. She was full of concern for her children and for all visitors to the house and could fuss them maddeningly. One of her favorite fussings was to express fear that you were straining your eyes by reading too far away from the lamp; she kept urging you to change your chair. Her memory was weak, and this caused her much distress. She spent her days in pitiful anxiety, searching for names of people and places, as she wandered around the big dark old house. As she wandered and searched her mind, she hummed to herself, not a song exactly but a kind of anxiety-noise.

John was not only generous, he was a childishly extravagant spender of whom many local shopkeepers took advantage. Jack, because of his legal knowledge, was frequently called upon to cope with the chaos of his Father's finances. This he did ably and patiently. Once, after a particularly trying session, he relieved his feelings by remarking to Kathleen, "Considering Father, it's a wonder we're not all congenital idiots." Kathleen laughed at such remarks, taking them in the spirit in which they were made, but she herself, as befitted a newcomer to the family, tried to dignify John as much as she could. She even tried to see him as the Squire of Marple.

The role of squire can be played only within a group of people who still instinctively approve of feudal relationships. A squire is head of his village by virtue of being its most prominent land-owner. He is expected to lead the village in political opinion, organize its charities, preside at its ceremonies, know and concern himself with every member of the community and represent it when its interests are threatened from outside. In return, he expects to be supported, honored, even loved. In 1903 there were still a great many squires functioning more or less adequately in the rural areas of England, including some villages of eastern Cheshire.

John certainly had the right to call himself the Squire of Marple; he was the present head of the family, and Marple had recognized Isherwoods as its squires for generations. But that was beside the point. By 1903 Marple had already rejected the squirearchy and all it stood for. You had only to walk through the village to sense that.

It was a tame charmless place, architecturally too dull to be even ugly; its former weathered gray stone had been supplanted by new brick, dark red or salmon pink. At the top of the main street there stood a big pink mill with a tall chimney; and that, not the Hall, was now the center of Marple. You were very far from the Brontë land here; very near Manchester.

Manchester businessmen and their families had been moving into Marple in increasing numbers since Kathleen had known it. She regarded them with distaste and dismay. From her viewpoint they were loud and rude, aggressively pleased with their Lancashire accents, contemptuous of all tradition and culture, utterly unashamed of the mess they had created around the scene of their operations; "Where there's muck there's money" was their slogan. These people lived in houses as vulgar as themselves and scorned to put on airs of gentility to go with their wealth. (If they had shown any desire to assume "the purple of commerce," Kathleen would have probably found them easier to understand and tolerate.) With all their faults (and considerable virtues, which she refused to recognize) they were psychologically very close to a certain type of urban North American, many of whose ancestors did in fact emigrate from this part of England. There is a town called Marple in Pennsylvania.

As for John, he couldn't have filled the exacting role of squire if he had wanted to. And he didn't want to. He was perfectly content with his agreeably passive life and its daily outing. Every morning he was driven up into the village, where he looked in on the grocer, chatted with the bank manager, who often had to remind him tactfully of an overdraft, got his hair cut sometimes and always bought the latest crime and mystery novels from the stationer's; Guy Boothby, William le Queux and E. Phillips Oppenheim were his favorites. At these establishments he was treated with the utmost respect and referred to as "the Squire," for the simple reason that he was an excellent customer. Most of the boys and girls who saw him as they came out of the mill knew who he was. Some of the boys touched their caps to him, and why not? He was old, familiar, harmless. He wasn't exploiting them. He wasn't even a mill owner.

But Kathleen, with her obstinately cherished mystique, read the situation quite differently. For her, John's daily outings had the significance of a royal progress; it was enormously important that he should show himself in public as much as possible. She was convinced that the people of Marple, even these deplorable nouveaux-riches, felt a subconscious need for some human link with the traditions of the Past, since a life without tradition becomes meaningless and finally unbearable. Therefore, according to Kathleen, John was sustaining, singlehanded, the psychic health of the community. He didn't have to fulfill the functions of a squire, he was The Squire. He didn't have to turn Marple Hall into a center of village social life, he had only to live in it. He didn't have to do anything, only to be. The same idea is expressed in the Analects of Confucius: Shun, the great sage, rules the country simply by remaining seated, gravely and reverently, in the position of the ruler, with his face turned toward the south.

(In 1932, Christopher published a novel called The Memorial which contains a candid though basically affectionate portrait of John, as well as two characters named Lily and Richard who are offensively dull substitutes for Kathleen and Frank. Elizabeth doesn't appear. Instead, Christopher has mated John with Emily—a union as monstrous as any imagined by the Greek mythologists. A few members of the Family found this portrait of John in the worst possible taste; they had apparently forgotten the remarks they had made about him themselves. Kathleen had far more reason to dislike the novel, but she never once complained that it *had hurt her feelings. Indeed, she became highly indignant when some critics gave it bad notices.)*

It is significant that Kathleen was psychologically unable to adopt John and Elizabeth as parents. In her diary she refers to them as either "Mr and Mrs Isherwood," "Frank's People" or "Frank's Father and Mother." Later, when she begins to regard them in relation to Christopher and Richard, she will write "Grandad" and "Granny." But, whereas Emily will thus become "Granny Emmy" and Frederick, posthumously, "Grandfather Frederick," John will never be "Grandfather John" and Elizabeth will never be "Granny Elizabeth," only "Granny Isherwood."

Kathleen wasn't expressing hostility in this, only an absence of sufficient affection, which was probably due to her doubts about the Family as a whole. If she consented to think of herself as the daughter of John and Elizabeth she would also have to accept their children as her brothers and sisters; and she couldn't. There was something about them—their manner, their dry faintly patronizing voices, the way they looked at you: they kept their distance, not only from outsiders but from each other. Rightly or wrongly, that was how Kathleen saw them; she had glimpsed this attitude in Frank himself. She didn't want to dwell on it, she tried to ignore it, but her sense of a barrier was always there. And once, in May *1915*, when she was under terrible emotional strain, she relieved her bitterness by writing it out in words: "I don't think the Isherwoods have much real feeling."

Kathleen's love for Wyberslegh and its surroundings is expressed over and over again in her diary during the months which follow her marriage. Characteristically, however, she manages to push the Present halfway into the Past by reminding herself that she and Frank won't be able to stay here indefinitely:

It is eighteen weeks since our wedding day, and I grudge thinking that even so much has gone of our time here, the most absolutely perfect little house that ever was or ever will be, the most delightful country—and great happiness.

262

June 2 and 3. Garden so gay with wallflowers and forgetmenots and orange and tawny tulips and the trees so green and the house looking so fresh and so pleased to see me back! Hot but refreshing air. The garden and the fresh green of the trees looked *indescribably lovely*. Never outside a novel or dreams was there such an *absolutely perfect house and garden* with such a wonderful charm about it all. . . . . such *a human house!*

Emily came up to stay with them and clearly voiced her approval of Wyberslegh and her disapproval of the Coopers. On May 25th, Kathleen went to London, planning to go on from there to France with Emily. This was her first separation from Frank since the marriage. He had to remain at Wyberslegh and go to camp with his Volunteers in North Wales.

From Frank's letters it is clear that Frederick has begun behaving badly again:

What a silly ass the D.O.D. is, indeed what silly asses we all are, we never seem to know when we are well off!! If Mama is dreadfully tried by him she had better come back here after abroad, otherwise she will feel that she has Cranley Mansion hanging over her head all the time she is away. If she goes on with that life of worry and anxiety it will kill her, quite literally.

I am sorry the D.O.D. has been so odious but you ought not to mind. I daresay you toss your head and think that you look quite indifferent but I am sure he knows all the time that you do mind, and redoubles his efforts to be disagreeable. I hope, though, he clearly understands that I don't care a curse.

Frank is now beginning to feel dissatisfaction with his job. Before leaving for camp he attended a regimental dinner which was "a great success":

I sat near Clemson and Michael Halford and we all giggled and talked rot and were very happy. Lots of other fellows I knew were at the dinner and I felt very sad at turning my back on them and coming back to Volunteers.

Furthermore, Frank's work as adjutant is being criticized by his superiors:

It appears that they have got rather a down on me at Chester. I was afraid it would come to that, as the Regiment has got a bad name and they don't appear to see that it has made great advances in the last year. It is very disheartening to be treated as if one were a regular scrimshanker when, as you know, I have worked as hard as anyone, all the drill season. The Colonel was very kindly but it is very annoying to be discussed and reported on by a man of that class. If it wasn't for 'our dear little home' etc etc, I should be inclined to chuck the whole thing.

This added threat to her tenure of Wybserlegh made Kathleen nervous and hostile. When Lord Newton, who was opposed to the Volunteer system and favored conscription, remarked casually that of course Frank could easily rejoin his regiment at any time if Volunteer adjutancies were done away with, Kathleen comments indignantly: "I wonder how he would like it if anyone proposed turning him out of Lyme, which he can't care for a bit more than I do for Wyberslegh."
Frank had probably encouraged Kathleen to dislike Lord Newton. He had motives for doing this of which he was scarcely aware; they will be discussed in a moment. In a letter written nearly a year earlier, he tells her:

Newton told me he had been up to Wyberslegh. He is a person who always runs down everything in a very gruff voice. He began by saying he was so disappointed in the view. So I said it was such a blessing you couldn't see any chimneys, so he then said that we should find the blow holes from the tunnel a terrible nuisance.

(The "blow holes" were ventilation shafts in a railway tunnel on the line between Chinley and Manchester; it passed under the

*fields behind Wyberslegh. They were anyhow too far from the
house to be a nuisance. And the successive puffs of white vapor,
bursting suddenly out of the earth as a train went through, created
an effect which was magical and pleasing; at least, Kathleen and
Frank always thought so.)*

Again, on November 25, 1905, Frank writes:

I played golf with the noble Lord. He is a trying person to play
with as he always stands just in front of you. It is a mercy he
hasn't been killed before this. Poor man, his manners leave much
to be desired, if you can call them manners. S. (the lawyer), who
was also playing, seemed an extraordinarily well-bred charming
person beside him.

*These playful but spiteful remarks all seem aimed at proving
that a lord isn't necessarily a gentleman. Unkind as they are to the
memory of Lord Newton, who was a great local benefactor and
a distinguished figure in politics, they are worth quoting simply to
illustrate an interesting social prejudice often held by the untitled
landed gentry. People like the Isherwoods tended to sneer at
members of the peerage, regarding them as upstarts and themselves
as the real aristocracy. This kind of snobbery made at least a little
sense when it was directed against some merchant who had bought
himself a title by contributing to his party's funds. It made none in
the case of Lord Newton, whose family, the Leghs, was far more
anciently "landed" than the Isherwoods; they had been living at
Lyme since the fifteenth century or even earlier. But a prejudice
is a prejudice.*

*That Henry didn't share it is interesting, too. Henry adored all
titles of nobility and their possessors, both English and foreign.
But then, Henry wasn't quite a gentleman, though he certainly
thought of himself as being one. His contacts with European high
society, the Catholic hierarchy and the homosexual subculture had
somehow subtly combined to declass him, endowing him with a
shamelessness which could be truly shocking and was nevertheless
his most likable quality.*

Christopher inherited the Isherwood snobbery and inverted it. As a young man, he threw lords, landed gentry and all the rest of the ruling class together into the lower depths and exalted the workers over them. But this arrangement was unsatisfactory, because it left him nowhere. He soon found that he needed an aristocracy with an eventual place for himself in it; so he declared a private aristocracy of the arts and proceeded to create his own peerage.

During the nineteen-thirties, Henry had an encounter with one of Christopher's art lords. At his club he got into conversation with a stranger and found that he knew Christopher, slightly. Thus the two became acquainted. The man seemed unwilling to talk about himself (which Henry thought unnatural and affected), but he admitted to being the editor of a minor literary magazine. His name was T. S. Eliot. Henry soon began complaining to Christopher that Eliot kept asking him to do crossword puzzles; Henry regarded himself as a crossword expert, and Eliot was hopelessly out of his class. When Christopher told Henry that there were many people in London who would count it the greatest honor of their lives to be invited to do crossword puzzles with Mr. Eliot, Henry was at first incredulous, then he roared with laughter: "That awful boresome man? You can't be serious! Why, he's so stoopid! He's such a bore, don't you know? I have to tell him all the clues!" Mr. Eliot subsequently murmured with distress to a mutual friend that he was having the most trying time with Isherwood's uncle, who would corner him whenever he came into the club. It was a case of misplaced politeness on both sides.

On September 21, Frank developed mumps. Emily, who had been expecting a visit from Kathleen, responded with characteristic emotion when she heard the news:

My own darling, angel, pet, I am so *awfully awfully* sorry both for you and poor Frank; mumps are so painful, though not, I am thankful to say, dangerous (I have been reading up about them). Be *very careful*, precious lamb, not to take his breath.

266

I had been so happy this morning, getting my Lamb's room ready, and a nice new long glass and rose soap, but I hope you may come ere long. The D.O.D. has just gone off to Bury till Wed. I told him about Frank and he said quite sympathetically (*for him*), 'Mumps, has he, that's a nasty thing'.

I stayed in all yesterday and am not going out today on account of the bitter east winds, as a small gland has gathered and is discharging but isn't the least painful like the others, only uncomfortable. When I told the D.O.D. he said quite cheerfully, 'I don't think your glands will ever be cured, they are constitutional'. The D.O.D. so far has been better and more like himself to me than ever before. Of course he only shakes hands and never calls me anything (but these are details).

I do hope dear old Frank has had a fairly good night. I almost envy him, having you all to himself all day!! It is an unspeakable comfort to me that dear Mrs Isherwood is at hand. *Promise* not to keep anything from me about yourself or Frank, or I shall come up and stay at Disley. I am not in the very least afraid of mumps.

When Emily wrote to Kathleen that this disease is not dangerous, she may have done so in ignorance. Or she may have known, but wished to spare Kathleen's feelings by not saying, that the infection can spread to the testicles or the ovaries and cause sterility. In this case, there were no complications. Kathleen got the mumps, too, but both she and Frank recovered in a few days. Less than two months later—about November 17, according to subsequent calculations—she became pregnant.

Meanwhile, how was the marriage working out?

One can say, very well indeed. Certainly the fears expressed by both Kathleen and Frank in advance now seem absurdly theoretical. And even a far less compatible couple could have enjoyed living with each other under such optimum conditions.

One can't help feeling, however, that Kathleen had the best of the bargain. In addition to Frank, she had acquired a home of her own which she found "absolutely perfect" and a round of not too demanding household activities sufficient to satisfy her sense of duty. She could still see Emily in London and have the added delight of entertaining her at Wyberslegh. She didn't have to see much of Frederick and was anyhow no longer in his power. Frank was away a good deal; being with him was always a pleasure to be enjoyed, not a daily habit. Her diary shows her happiness whenever he is unexpectedly free to spend an evening at home.

But this is not to say that Frank was at all discontented. He was getting just what he needed from the marriage, someone to return home to and to think about lovingly while they were apart.

On November 27 he writes to Kathleen, who is visiting Emily in London:

I think the way you always seem to understand me is so wonderful, and your patience too. There isn't any woman in the world like you, I feel certain. I often think how dreadful it would be to have a wife one couldn't be thoroughly proud of, always.

Frank had to be constantly occupied; his energy was immense. Nearly every day, he went into Stockport to his Volunteers, often on a bicycle, and returned at all hours, sometimes drenched to the skin. He seemed to revel in the rigors of north-country weather. He took long walks over the moors, ran on paper chases even when it was snowing, played tennis, hockey or golf according to the season. He still acted in theatricals now and then. At home he gardened, read, painted, played the piano. With Kathleen he went to concerts in Manchester (which she did her very best to enjoy) and made expeditions to neighboring places of interest.

When a series of lectures on English literature was given in Disley and the audience was asked to write essays on their subjects, Frank chose "The wit of Goldsmith compared with Thackeray's" and attempted to prove that Thackeray's was the bachelor's point of view and Goldsmith's that of the married man. The lecturer was so impressed that he read parts of Frank's essay aloud, saying that its author's style reminded him of "the best in Sterne" and that he hoped she would continue to write. Frank had signed it "Edith Boyle"!

Their few mild quarrels were about religion, specifically church-going. Nowadays it seems incredible that a hard-worked husband should have been expected by his wife to go to church twice on Sundays; but to Kathleen Christianity meant traditional worship publicly shared and churchgoing was its essential expression. "No one can stand alone," she told him on one occasion when she had asked him to come to evening service at Disley Church and he had replied that he wasn't in the mood and would rather play bowls at the Ram. This argument touched on a real difference between them. Frank had had too much public religion in the Army; to him, churchgoing was too like church parade. So he was tempera-mentally attracted to the philosophy of Hinduism and Buddhism—as expounded, somewhat confusingly, in his theosophy books—be-cause it taught a private religion of self-effort, self-knowledge and solitary meditation. Christopher and Richard were later to follow Frank in this. Both grew up, largely because of their experiences of public religion at school, with a horror of the Church. So Christopher took to Vedanta, Richard to the Rosicrucians.

On May 14, 1904, Kathleen at length makes a direct though cryptic reference in her diary to her pregnancy: "Told Mrs R. about 'August.'" A few days later she went to stay with Emily at Barmouth in Wales. Frank was in camp with the Volunteers at Towyn, nearby. On May 25 she got a letter from him which upset her, although she was ready to admit to herself that her reaction had been exaggerated. The letter is lost, so one can only assume that Frank had made one of his ambiguous remarks and that Kath-leen, in her present overemotional state, had misinterpreted it. She evidently wrote to him about this, for he replied soothingly on May 30:

We are going to have a good time during June and July, I hope. The garden will be nice and we can get some amusing people over. I am so sorry you have got this business to put up with. It's no good my saying 'I wish I could share it with you', though, is it? I feel so indecently well and strong and as if I could stand anything! It does seem hard luck on you that it should be so. You can certainly dismiss the idea of your life having been a failure out of your head for ever. It hasn't from any point of view—except perhaps your own?

June 28. [At Wyberslegh.] Extraordinarily tired and to bed after dinner. As long as I remain in garden here I seem to feel quite well, but going about at all finds one out sadly.

July 7. Did not feel up to the drive across Ridge to Marple, it is so uneven. Lay out under the Stone Parlour window nearly all day.

July 8. Signed my will and sent it off to Jack.

July 11. Felt much revived and busy all the morning. Unpacked cot and some things from Harrods. The cot is a present from Frank's Mother and is a charming one, all white spotted muslin and satin ribbon. How I wish it were already occupied and me about again as usual! Frank and I lunched garden and practically sat out till 10 p.m.

July 16. Frank and I sat out all the evening and saw the new moon. I do hope before another comes that . . .

August 1. Feel a perfect mountain now and the nights are so restless and hot, although the room is beautifully airy.

August 3. Had my bureau moved up to my bedroom and settled various things in anticipation of coming events! Mrs Macmillan arrived. F and I drove over to Marple to dinner.

(*Mrs. Macmillan was the nurse who had been hired to look after Kathleen during her lying-in. Kathleen later wrote of her, "She*

270

has been so *kind and delightful and sympathetic and bright, one of the dearest and best of women.*")

August 12. Birth of a son to the Czarina. Walked up to the quarry before lunch.

(*When, on September 15, the Queen of Italy gave birth to a son, Kathleen wrote in her diary: "Christopher is a fortnight younger than the future Czar and three weeks older than the future King of Italy." Obviously she regarded these royal births as favorable omens for Christopher's future. They could not have been more sinister. The "future Czar" was to be murdered in 1918, just before his fourteenth birthday; the "future King of Italy" was to be deposed and exiled in 1946 after reigning for one month!*)

August 19. Disagreeable day, so grey and chilly. Did stores and a few things about the house. It doesn't seem worth starting anything fresh and one can't help hoping every day is the last that one has to toil about with effort!

August 25. Another day gone and *still* about. Slept rather badly and felt very disheartened! Mama came round and we both read, I 'The Queen's Quair'. Maurice Hewlett has such a very graphic descriptive mediaeval atmosphere that he carries conviction against one's will though giving a very different idea of Mary and one that entirely takes her off a pedestal. Mama and I had tea on verandah of Golf Club. Frank read out loud to me in evening Macaulay's History of England. We had a fire.

August 26. BABY BORN. Felt uncomfortable with bearing-down pains from after 5 a.m. but had a good hot bath and breakfast as usual. Same pains continued and Mrs Mac felt really hopeful, as they came on worse at intervals and never left off altogether (though quite endurable). Mama came round and we sat outside the Stone Parlour window with books. Dr Nall came round just to see what I was doing and said the longer these preliminaries lasted the better and easier it would be in end, so quite hoped to go to tea at cottage without letting Mama discover anything different. However after lunch had to retire upstairs and every fifteen minutes pangs came on rather bad. Undressed and lay on bed. Frank so kind. Doctor sent for and gave me whiffs of chloroform on lint (the weakest stuff!) every time a bad pain came. Things got very indistinct later. I believe Frank fetched a Dr Anderton from New Mills and more chloroform but all the world was one great pain culminating in fearful throbs and my piercing screams. Then the text on the opposite wall faded and the room and the lights went out in a mist and at 11.45 p.m. Dr Nall's kind voice saying how sorry he was he had had to stick me, as if that or anything mattered—for there on the next bed was the *Baby*, a little crying bundle. I felt I could never thank God sufficiently for bringing me safely through, the Baby well and strong and a son. Frank and Mama came up for a few minutes, and though it is a lie, or at least in my case, that a woman forgets 'her anguish in the joy' etc, yet to see Frank's pleasure and to feel that it was *our* son was *intense* happiness—and made all the rest seem worth-while. Mrs Mac and the baby slept in south room with electric bell between us. The stitches made a tiring pain but had a fair night on the whole.

August 27. Frank over to breakfast to Marple to tell the news. The greatest delight and pleasure at its being a grandson. Flag flying in honour and Coopers had up their flag here. Felt so proud and happy and thankful. Dr Nall came, just felt pulse and looked on tongue but did not disturb me. Baby had sugar and milk. He screamed loudly but is the most delightful creature with amusing long slitty eyes like a Japanese baby but lovely skin. Mrs Mac says the image of his Father with a voice like mine!! Many wires of congratulations.

12

During the next twelve days, Kathleen and Frank were trying to make up their minds what to call their son. Louis was considered, in homage to R. L. Stevenson, but soon rejected. Alexander was another possibility, after Lieutenant Kearsey, whom they had asked to be one of the godfathers. But the four final choices were Frank's John or William and Kathleen's Christopher or Henry. The reason for John is obvious. William was a favorite because of Frank's friend William Bradshaw and because William was the name of the father of the Henry Bradshaw who had bought Wyberslegh for the family (this second, farfetched reason is mentioned by Kathleen in her diary and must surely have been discovered by her). Kathleen admits that she chose Christopher because she liked the name, though she justifies her choice by citing Christopher Machell, a great-uncle of hers, and Christopher Clayton, the father-in-law of the Henry Bradshaw referred to above. Henry was a recurring family name.

Henry Isherwood finally forced them to decide. He had agreed to be the other godfather, and now he said he would give the baby a silver christening mug. Since the baby's names had to be engraved on it, he asked to be told what they were as soon as possible. So Frank and Kathleen settled on Christopher William. (Frank preferred to call his son William, and Kathleen sometimes used this name; but Christopher never thought of himself as anything but Christopher. At one time or another he was to blame

Kathleen for almost all of her decisions affecting his future, but about Christopher he was never in doubt. It has always seemed to him to be his name, the only one which really describes him. This doesn't, however, prevent him from finding the name pompous-sounding or even revolting in some other combinations. Christopher Marlowe yes, Christopher Robin no!)

September 27. Baby christened. The cab came for us about 11.30 and Mrs Mac, Frank, the Baby and I drove to Disley Church. An ideal autumn day, very still, and a bright hazey sunshiney morning and very warm. The Baby wore the robe that I wore at my christening and a bonnet and sash from Mama, 'something old, and something new, something borrowed and something blue'. Mr and Mrs Isherwood came, we had no one else. Mr Isherwood stood sponsor for Henry and Frank for Mr Kearsey and Mama and I for his godmother Aggie [Agatha Greene]. The font was full of white lilies and it was all very quiet and solemn. C.W. protested slightly, as is required of all orthodox babies, and the day ranks among the days of Great Events.

It was 249 years since any of the Bradshaw family have been baptized at Disley—the last was the youngest son of Col Bradshaw. 'Joseph, sonne of Henry Bradshaw of Wybersley and Ann his wife was baptized April 25, 1655' (saw this in the old Disley register).

We walked down to the cab after and Mr Isherwood said I had done my duty and done it well!! To which I quite agreed. Sat out on long chair after lunch in garden and then rested till tea and Mama came up and had dinner with us. I got into a proper evening dress again!! The blessing it is to be one's own size again and the event over.

(The above description is taken partly from Kathleen's diary and partly from The Baby's Progress, *a record of Christopher's growth and doings which Kathleen now began to keep. She*

decorated it elaborately with floral designs and fancy lettering and later bound it between hard covers of blue-and-green wallpaper which had a pattern of cornflowers and poppies.)

If the day was indeed a Great Event in Christopher's life, it was an equally great event in Kathleen's. For this was the day on which she was for the first time fully recognized as a member of the family. Kathleen certainly realized this; and, despite her irony ("I quite agreed"), she accepted John Isherwood's approval with pleasure, even though her feminist spirit must have resented his masculine use of the word "duty." She had produced the first male Bradshaw-Isherwood (this was no time for dropping hyphens) of a new generation, her name would be recorded in Disley Church in kinship with "Ann his wife," she was part of the hereditary chain, she belonged. This belonging didn't mean that Kathleen felt an increased affection for her in-laws; it did mean that she felt she had now won a place among the Isherwoods and that she would begin to identify herself more and more with the Family and its history.

John Isherwood had been born on August 27, 1841. That Christopher had missed sharing John's birthday with him by a mere fifteen minutes was a disappointment to Kathleen's sense of historical fitness. During the years of Christopher's childhood, his birthday was always celebrated on the twenty-seventh. Kathleen even found a justification for this, saying that Christopher had been born a quarter of an hour before midnight only because the doctor had intervened surgically to assist the delivery; if the birth had been allowed to proceed naturally it would have taken place on the twenty-seventh. As the years passed, she went further and began to say that she really wasn't sure, it was either fifteen minutes before midnight or fifteen minutes after. This was disingenuous, for she had simply to consult her own diary!

In thus establishing an extra link between John and Christopher, Kathleen showed a sound instinct, for it was clear already that John was the only functioning grandfather Christopher would get. Frederick showed no inclination to join the family group. It wasn't until more than a week after Christopher's birth that he even condescended to mention to Emily that he knew of the occurrence: "I hear Mrs. Isherwood and child are doing well. It must be a relief to you."

Kathleen's next problem was to find a permanent nurse for Christopher. She had begun interviewing applicants as soon as she was well enough. Her first experience was not encouraging:

After lunch, H.J. came to be interviewed, the most objectionable young miss—apparently only interested in her own comfort and how much one could save oneself by proper discipline to babies, but she hardly glanced at him—and told Mrs Mac she should like to come and live with a young mother who did not know all the tricks.

There were several more disappointments after this one, and it wasn't till October 27 that Christopher was given over to the care of Annie Avis.

Kathleen doesn't say in her diary exactly how she came to hear of "Avis"—or "Nurse," as she later called her—but it may well have been through some member of the Greene family, for Annie was a Suffolk girl; she had been born near Bury St. Edmunds and was the only unmarried daughter of a large family (she had had a fiancé, but he died). She had been brought up by an uncle and aunt. (Richard remembers her telling how this aunt, when dying, had the illusion that she was in an enormous railway station, with rain falling on the roof.) When Annie came to look after Christopher she was about thirty years old—that is to say, at least five years younger than Kathleen.

Nanny (as Christopher was to call her throughout the rest of her life) was small and sturdily built. She was quite pretty when young. Her bright eyes and general air of alertness used to remind Christopher that avis is Latin for a bird. She was reliable and a good worker, and had a curious talent, perhaps psychic, for finding things that had been mislaid or dropped. She smiled a great deal and grumbled without ceasing. She flattered Christopher; he was always her favorite. She got terribly on Richard's nerves with

276

her fussing. Kathleen was never unreservedly fond of her but came to rely on her increasingly and continued to employ her, as a combined parlormaid and housemaid, after Christopher and Richard had grown up. They were together for forty-four years.

Nanny had a standing grievance which she declared whenever she felt put upon: she claimed that she might have married if she hadn't stayed with Kathleen; she had sacrificed her life for the Isherwoods, she said. This would provoke Kathleen almost to the limit of her patience. "Oh, really, Nurse!" she would exclaim, smiling because she longed to shake Nanny's tubby little body until her false teeth rattled, "how can you go on like that! You know perfectly well we'd never stand in your way if you felt you could do better somewhere else." On one occasion, in 1937, when Nanny had complained bitterly about some unsuspected need, Kathleen writes in her diary: "It was all very upsetting, the unfriendliness of it all and resentment, for I honestly try and save her in all the ways I can and she behaved as if she was a hard-driven slave instead of an old and valued friend."

Nanny had really no intention of leaving. She knew she couldn't do better elsewhere, and soon she was too old to look after young children with their demands and tantrums. Besides, she had broken her arm skating on a pond in Marple Hall park and the doctor had told her she would never be able to hold a baby with it again. In later life she became increasingly accident-prone; this seemed to be one of her methods of tormenting Kathleen. During the nineteen-thirties she expressed a superstitious belief (or determination) that she would have an accident every February; and she did, for several years running. Christopher remembers the faint smile of gleeful triumph which she smiled, lying on the floor after falling off a stepladder (which Kathleen had implored her not to use) and getting a compound fracture. There was always an underlying glee in Nanny's complaints to Christopher, and sometimes a touch of real poetry, as when she called the stairs "the wooden mountains" or described a mysterious noise in her head as being "just like a train—puff, puff, it goes, and then it gives a little whistle, woo!"

In 1909, when Nanny was away on holiday and Christopher was

nearing his fifth birthday, Kathleen records that she helped him wash and dress himself for the first time. *This admission would make many a modern psychologist shake his head reprovingly over Kathleen's failure to provide "tender loving care" for her child.* During the Age of Nannies such a state of affairs wasn't unusual in upper-class homes, however; and in this case Emily and Frank were chiefly to blame for it. Between them, they took her away from home a good deal; she had to be a wife and daughter first, a mother second. Under the circumstances she was wise to leave Nanny supreme in her own sphere, instead of competing with her as a nurse and inviting comparisons.

Nevertheless, Kathleen's frequent absences had their effect; particularly on Richard. He recalls that when he was four years old Kathleen was "a semi-stranger of whom I was a bit in awe. It was Nanny who came first by a very long chalk in those days. At the same time it must have hurt poor Mum when I said I liked Nanny best."

And it must have pleased Nanny. She was quite sufficiently a bitch to enjoy family discord. Many years later, she asked Richard teasingly how he would like it if Christopher and she went away together. No doubt Christopher had told her she could housekeep for him when he got a place of his own; this would have been a probably excellent arrangement, but he hadn't at that time the slightest intention of settling down in England or anywhere else. When he and Kathleen were on bad terms he would bait her by showing favor to Nanny, so such suggestions were apt to have an ulterior motive.

Nevertheless he loved Nanny dearly. He bullied her and ordered her around but rewarded her by telling her his secrets. When he started smoking, she was the first to know of it. He let her see him coming home drunk at night and complained to her of his hangovers in the morning. He even made it obvious which of his friends he was going to bed with by the strict instructions he gave her not to disturb him when they came to the house. Sometimes she pretended a little clucking disapproval, but she was never really shocked, never dreamed of seriously criticizing his behavior, *was incapable of preaching to him. He treated her as a familiar with whom he could be shameless and at ease, as a servant with whom he could league himself against his own class. Though it may not have been true that Nanny really thought of herself as "a hard-driven slave," their relationship did rather resemble that of a white child of the old American South with his colored mammy. And, oddly enough, the first song she ever taught Christopher was "The Old Folks at Home"!*

November 29. Foggy thaw, cold and rather dismal. But for all the bad weather, this always seems to me the most romantically fascinating country in the world! It has the most extraordinary charm which every other place lacks—it is more like the charm of places one sees in one's dreams and which never exist in real life. It's partly the hills and the thorough country, yet all within the beat of life and work, and the big towns round it. It is quite wonderful walking down the drive to see beyond, down in the plains at night, the thousands of lights. (This comes of talking over possibilities of where and what we shall do in 1907, when the time is up!!)

December 17. To shop in Stockport. It looked so pretty and mysterious towards evening, the flaring lights in the markets and the deep shadows and gay stalls of oranges. The narrow steep streets are wonderfully picturesque too.

That autumn it had been decided to put in electric light at Marple Hall. A generator had had to be installed, so the work had taken a long time; it wasn't finished until shortly before Christmas. On December 20 Kathleen walked over with Frank to look at the result:

All the lights were turned on, from floor to attics, and it may be very convenient but it dreadfully does away with the shadows and the mystery and the charm. The light seems to pry into everything and I don't like it one bit.

(Christopher remembers the thrill of visiting the engine room to watch Coyne, the gardener, start the engine. This always seemed exciting and dangerous, because Coyne, who was muscular but small and light, had to climb onto the great flywheel and use his whole weight to get it moving, leaping off again before it kicked back.

The wiring within the house was no doubt poorly insulated, by modern standards. On one occasion at least, it started a fire in the cellar, or rather a slow charring of one of the huge oaken beams which ran under the house. The oak was too tough to burst into flames, luckily; it smouldered for many days before it was discovered.)

Letter from Emily to Kathleen, sometime in February 1905:

Darling, the D.O.D. got into the drawing-room today and is in every way stronger, but the running about which the poor thing causes is extraordinary, what with constant food, fomentation and medicines!! So cheered by the Doctor's report that I felt I might go and see dear Sarah Bernhardt. I always feel she may never come again. Mrs Patrick Campbell is as graceful as ever but aged in the face (I shouldn't advise looking at either of them with glasses!!) I know Frank will scoff at S.B. but oh her voice was as lovely as ever and her acting, to me, the perfection of art.

Emily then returns to the subject of Frederick and admits, "His attitude to me tried my nerves more than I can say." This is followed by one of Baby Mama's obliquely threatening demands for attention. She tells Kathleen that she begged a mutual friend "to tell everyone, had I got ill or departed, that it wasn't your being gone, but wholly him, poor man—that your happiness was my one bright spot and comfort. I couldn't have borne your being made ill and wretched by it, my darling."

1905. March 12. Our wedding day. We have been married two years—a lifetime, and how quickly it has gone.

280

May 6. Beautiful day. C.W., Nurse and I went to Marple. Frank came over in the afternoon and some of the officers with about eight hundred Volunteers who drilled in the park and ate pork pies. The officers in to tea at Marple after. C.W. very excited and pleased. Sergeant Jackson, whose baby was born the day after, says C.W. is a good deal heavier and the men were heard to remark that the Captain's baby looked as if it was fed on Mellins' Food, which was considered a compliment.

Frank confirms what seems to have been a general impression of Christopher's sturdiness, in a later letter: "I hope he is not going to be one of those big beefy men. They are always so stupid." Christopher was to disappoint these expectations. He grew up to be below average height, less than five foot seven, and of a small build.

The Baby's Progress *records many other details:*

At six months, Christopher still lay down in his pram when out, but tried to sit up and see what was going on. "It is a source of regret to his Grandmother Isherwood that he is not fonder of lying on his back and kicking! And there are still greater lamentations when at nine months he sat up on the floor of his pram and on his rug but refused *to* crawl!"

There is huge exasperation between the lines of this entry. Elizabeth's fussing has at last begun to get on Kathleen's nerves. So much so that she writes to Emily about the crawling. Emily reassures her: "You can't make him crawl if he won't. What does poor Mrs I think will happen if he doesn't crawl? What could happen?

Kathleen adds: "At 14½ months he staggers alone across any room. . . . At 16 months he runs about all over the room. When excited always stands on tiptoe and waves his arms and hands tremendously." Then she adds, triumphantly: "He never *crawled!"*

Christopher's eyes are said to have changed at the age of nine months, from hazel to clear gray-blue; a small light-brown patch in the right eye was noted—with pleasure, because such patches are said to be lucky. When Christopher grew up, he described his eyes in his passport as "greenish grey"—this to tease Kathleen, who of

*course thought green eyes horrid. He didn't mention the patch,
though it was still there.*

Under the heading "First Words":

At 15½ months he began to say, 'Dad, Dad,' laughs and coos
and notices everything. At 16 months can say the name of various
things, 'shoe', 'tea', 'book', 'but' (for bread and butter). Also,
when nursery rhymes are said, can say the right word to end each
line in a good many of them. *Will look at books for hours and
likes being read to.* . . .

At two years old can string together quite long sentences, saying each word very carefully and distinctly. *His vocabulary very
varied and large,* can say little verses of four lines. He is very
interested in the names of flowers. Though he talks distinctly, he
uses *d* instead of *l*—as 'dike' for 'like' and 'dove' for 'love'; and *u*
for *i*—as 'hull' for 'hill'; and *a* for *u*—as 'narsery' for 'nursery'. All
through his childhood he never seemed at a loss for a word and
was generally rather happy in his choice of words to best express
his meaning.

*This last sentence can be seen, from the handwriting, to have
been written in much later; so can the underlinings of the sentences about looking at books and having a large vocabulary.
They must be hindsighted references to Christopher's emergence
as a writer. The very last entry in* The Baby's Progress *is: "On
January 5, 1928, Christopher's first novel accepted by Jonathan
Cape, it came out at the end of May."*

*This is at the end of the section called "First Lessons," which
covers Christopher's schooldays from kindergarten to college,
with a record of his marks, places in class, term reports and prizes
—so that the acceptance of his novel seems to be just another prize,
awarded by the publisher instead of the headmaster. Note that
Kathleen doesn't find it necessary to mention the novel's name;
what matters to her is that it is the* first *novel and thus in the same
category as the first step alone, the first word and the first tooth!*

. .

On June 8, Kathleen, Nanny and Christopher went to stay at Penmaenmawr in North Wales. (This was to become the scene of many of their seaside holidays.) Emily joined them there. Frank remained at Wyberslegh because he was about to leave for camp with his Volunteers.

On June 10, Kathleen and Emily went for a drive in a carriage, along a pretty but narrow road high above the sea. A motorcar came up behind them and hooted ("perhaps meaning well," Kathleen concedes), with the result that their horse was frightened, turned, reared and put its forelegs on the wall. Emily "expressed her mind" to the driver of the motorcar, "emphatically." She and Kathleen walked the rest of the way home.

That same day Frank wrote:

My dear, I am very glad Mama has got away from that D.O.D. As far as I can see, he really enjoys particularly good health and ought to be very thankful, considering the awful amount of sickness there is around us. I am fairly well this morning except for a pain in my back which I think came from my dressing too quickly, and as I write I have also a pain in the third finger of my right hand. I hope this is not a symptom!

I'm afraid you will be dreadfully annoyed when you hear that the second cupboard in the dining-room is left unlocked. It has the blue teacups in it which my dear Father gave me on my last birthday. The other cupboard is locked all right, but it would be very easy for the Coopers to break through the wall at the back. However there is a decanter of sherry there, one glass of which is certain death. So they will meet their deserts if they try that. Otherwise the house is fairly safe and properly bolted and barred, though I'm afraid we can't prevent people from burrowing under the walls and getting in that way. The pain has shifted from the 3rd to the 4th finger of my right hand. I am afraid this is a very bad sign.

I am glad William is having such a success. However, tell him the type of young men one sees at watering places are not at all in good style and I hope he won't develop into that.

N.B. The part about the pains in my finger and back is a joke. Haven't any in either place.

One wonders how Kathleen reacted to this letter. (It reads as if Frank may have been slightly drunk when he wrote it.) He actually seems to be sneering at all sickness as hypochondria—which would be a direct dig at Emily, utterly unlike his usual tact. Frank also suggests that Kathleen is becoming too possessively anxious about the safety of Wyberslegh and its contents. He is obviously afraid that he may have gone beyond the limit in making fun of her, however. He doesn't rely much on her sense of humor. He is still a little bit afraid of her, even now.

But if Kathleen was upset by what Frank wrote, she soon had reason to forget it and rejoice. On the fifteenth he wired her to say that the Regiment had extended his permission to hold the Stockport adjutancy for another two years. So Kathleen's dreaded parting from Wyberslegh was postponed.

June 18. Very worrying and aggravating letters from Aunt J, thinking Mama ought to go home as soon as possible. She wants to send the D.O.D. back as soon as he can travel. She thinks 'the dear man cannot live many months'. How she can write such humbug after the way he has behaved—and neither the London or Bournemouth doctors thought it was at all a question of dying. She also suggests Mama ought to do everything she can 'to make his last days happy', which I call *exceedingly* impertinent.

Yet Kathleen was forced, before long, to agree that Aunt Julia had been right. Emily sent bad news from Cranley Mansion, and when Kathleen went down there on July 21 she admitted: "I think he is very ill . . . He received me quite affably and talked more or less all the evening. It is a very wearisome hopeless business, I think."

July 22. The D.O.D.'s wound broke again, which has disheartened him very much. Dr L looks on it as a safety valve and considers that, if it healed, abcesses would probably form internally and have to be cut. But the worst of it is, he can't get about while it is open (because of the leaking) unless he has a tube in, which he won't consent to.

From the terminal gloom of Frederick's sickroom Kathleen returned with relief to Wyberslegh and her happy life:

August 2. Joined Frank on the canal. To the same wood on the bank that we went to before. It was very still and pleasant, except for one extraordinary and sudden gust of wind, just after we had started to sketch, which seized the sketch I did yesterday and whirled it up into the sky til it disappeared, a small black speck smaller than the birds. I never saw anything so odd as the suddenness and the height and the total disappearance, almost as if invisible hands had snatched it away!

August 3. C.W. downstairs all the time. I never saw such a cheerful baby, or so full of smiles, and the fattest and most comfortable of laughs!

At the end of August, Kathleen and Frank were off again. Kathleen went to London to be with Emily and Frederick, Frank to Suffolk to study watercolor painting with an artist named Lenfesty. Lenfesty had a sketching class which had been recommended by one of Frank's artist friends.

Letter from Frank, August 29:

I am very much pleased with Lenfesty's work and teaching. It is of the severest type, and there is something quite grand about his drawings. They are extremely restrained and simple in colour and style—no prettinesses. And his teaching is the same, a very few very simple colours, strict attention to values. No running of colours so as to make delightful and gaudy bits of colour and none of that block style of painting so dear to the amateur. I think as far as I have seen he is quite first class. As a man he is dull, a small chubby looking youth.

I painted all this morning. If you are at Harrods will you get me a cake or two of dry raw sienna. It is the colour which Lenfesty uses in a perfectly ogre-ish manner. Thank heaven it's cheap. That and Leitch's Blue and a little Rose Madder are his principal terrestrial colours, and for the celestial Cobalt and Sepia—and you would be astonished with the effect he gets from these. Any little bit of bright colour he puts in besides tells at once.

September 5. [In London.] Suddenly remembered Dr Lambert was coming this morning. After seeing the D.O.D. he came out of his room with the disheartening news that the wound has given way again after being healed for six weeks. There really seems nothing to be done and Dr L evidently felt the outlook very hopeless and likely to go on in the same way for months. The poor D. took it very pluckily, I feared he would have been terribly upset, and asked me to go down to Cannon St Station to a particular fruit shop there where he fancied the fruit was very good, so I did before lunch.

Letter from Frank, September 6:

I'm afraid you are having a ghastly time and feel rather a beast to be enjoying myself so much. One is very lucky to have a second profession to fall back upon when one is on leave, only I am not sure that I don't wish that I was a professional artist and a volunteer soldier. It would be a bad look out for you and William, though, if I was. It must be rather a trying and anxious way of earning one's bread. The Lenfestys haven't got a house yet or anywhere to go when they leave this place, and he says he thinks his Wife will be much happier in lodgings than in a house of her own. I told him that he was very young, or words to that effect. He is 33!

Letter from Frank, September 7:

I am rather disgusted with 'The Way of All Flesh'. He is so frightfully down on the parents, and I look at dear innocent William and wonder if we shall hit it off so badly, and if he too will one day 'find his parents out and never forgive them' as Oscar Wilde says. I think very few people do ever really forgive their parents!

On September 27 Frank and Kathleen left for a holiday in Spain. While in Burgos, Kathleen remarks: "I never realized before how much colour there is in black. All the women in the town, nearly, wear it." In Madrid she finds "a great air of gaiety and royalty. I think that helps to make Paris so depressing, the thoroughly Republican dullness which envelops it. There isn't any earthly pleasure or excitement in seeing a president!" In Madrid they visited the Prado and were both greatly impressed by "a painter quite new to us, called El Greco." (Kathleen and Frank were not betraying unusual ignorance here, for El Greco was only now beginning to emerge from more than a century of neglect; his work had been exhibited at the Prado for the first time in 1902.)

When they got back to London on October 30, Kathleen found that "the poor D.O.D. has lost much more than half his hair since I went away and is actually slightly bald. Has no moustache and a short white beard. He is very altered but rather better, I think." Next day, she and Frank returned to Wyberslegh:

Rather grey and damp but very English and homelike and the house looked a picture, and as for C.W., he was so grown and so marvellous and so astonishing we could not tear ourselves away from him! He stands alone and makes rather uncertain steps like a mechanical doll, and says several new words and laughs and smiles and seemed delighted and in the best of spirits and an absolute picture of health.

November 18. Wire from Mama to say the D.O.D. suddenly worse and unconscious, thought I had better come. So I caught the three minutes to four. Found Uncle Charlie there. There had been no change. Doctor came in after dinner and said if the temperature (103–104) went down he might rally and become conscious again. We went in to see the poor thing, it was so pitiful, he looked so worn and old and tired and breathing very heavily.

November 19. Cold east wind, neuralgic day, very long and sad. The poor D still unconscious and breathing heavily, terribly sad to see. The doctors said there was absolutely nothing more could be done and that he would not rally or regain consciousness now. This Mama felt very much, but I hope it was more peaceful for him, poor dear. He had seemed so entirely his own self and quite bright on Friday, she said. Had talked much of me all the week and seemed glad to have her back again and been affectionate and interested in everything. On Saturday he sent for her in the morning, complaining of a headache, and soon after he became unconscious and never regained it. They say blood poisoning set in but both doctors never expected anything so sudden. Mama sat in his room most of the afternoon and we were both with him at the last, the end was so peaceful, we could hardly realize the actual moment he passed away, for which thank God.

There were some painful and dreary days for Kathleen after this—Frederick's funeral, the packing up of furniture and the sorting through of letters and papers, anxiety about Emily's constant headaches, and then the farewell to Cranley Mansion.

Miss Robins came up after tea to say goodbye. She feels it very much, poor dear, losing her old neighbours of so many years and it makes one feel very old when one looks back and remembers oneself as a child and one's schooldays and first balls, all connected with our time here. We looked on the lights of London from here for the last time—and the drawing room, the prettiest London one I know, and so full of past ghosts.

The New Year of 1906 brought more unpleasantness, over Frederick's will. During his period of maximum hostility to Kathleen, Frederick had willed his money away from her to some cousins; they were to inherit it after Emily's death. In the last

weeks of his life he had relented, however, and had told Emily
and others that he meant to alter the will again, in Kathleen's
favor. He had died without doing this.

The family lawyer wrote to the cousins, telling them of Fred-
erick's intention; but they refused to give up what was legally, if
not morally, theirs. Kathleen comments in her diary (January 5):

They are evidently aware they are behaving badly. One thing
is, it would have been hateful to have it returned in any other
spirit than as my *right*, and I needn't have anything to do with
them now. They were so good as to say they might 'reconsider
the matter' if I am left badly provided for. Thank heaven I needn't
descend to that!

After some discussion with the lawyer, Kathleen wisely decided
not to contest the will.

Meanwhile, Emily was hunting for a new flat and in March she
found one in Buckingham Street, which runs down from the
Strand to the Embankment Gardens, near Charing Cross Station.
The flat was on the top floor of number fourteen, where the street
ends at an old water gate. You could take a boat from its steps
before the river was narrowed and embanked in the mid-nine-
teenth century. This area was once the estate of the first and
second Dukes of Buckingham; hence the names of the adjoining
streets, George, Villiers, Duke, and Of Alley (now renamed York
Place). And Samuel Pepys had lived for fifteen years in a house
on the site of the present number fourteen. So there were enough
historical associations to satisfy even the Authoress of Our Rambles. *Like Pepys, Emily was to spend fifteen years here. They*
were to be the happiest years of her life.

13

On August 19, 1906, Kathleen refers in her diary to "the history of the Family I am making for C.W." This is a handmade book, like The Baby's Progress, but a much larger one. Most of it is written in Kathleen's clear elegant script, with occasional ornamentations. The book contains a history of Marple and Wyberslegh Halls, a life of John Bradshaw the Regicide, an extract from the diary of the Reverend Charles Bellairs describing Marple Hall and its occupants in 1838, a newspaper report of the coming-of-age festivities of Thomas Bradshaw-Isherwood in October 1841, a note on Moll of Brabyns the Marple Ghost, a diary of a journey made by Anna Maria Bradshaw-Isherwood from Marple to London in July 1831, a family tree of the Bradshaws and Isherwoods of Marple, some extracts from the Survey Book of Henry Bradshaw of Marple dated 1735, a plan of the ground floor of Wyberslegh Hall, some details about the marriages of Mary Bradshaw to Messrs. Pimlott and Isherwood, footnotes on the Bellairs family and the Orrells of Mobberley, a list of farms belonging to John Isherwood in 1831, and various newspaper clippings relating to subjects mentioned above. It is illustrated by Kathleen with watercolors and drawings in pencil and in ink; these include a view of Marple Hall from the Grotto meadows, two exterior views of Wyberslegh, pictures of several of the Wyberslegh rooms, and copies of portraits at Marple Hall of Mary Bradshaw, Dorothy Bagshaw and Moll of Brabyns. Kathleen worked on the book for many years; one portion of it was written as late as 1918.

Kathleen did no doubt start out with the intention of writing a simple family history for Christopher and any other children she might later have. But her researches seem to have fascinated her so much that she let them lead her far afield. What she has produced is a sort of private museum. Many of the exhibits in it are directly related to her theme, others appear to have been chosen merely because they evoke the Past for her in some special way. How else can one explain the trouble she has taken to list by name all the tenants of the Isherwood farms in 1831, with the exact number of acres, roods and perches of land belonging to each? Or the evident relish with which she quotes passages of such absolutely irrelevant information as: ". . . married at Twickenham, 30th May, 1811, to Dorothy Parker Mackenzie, youngest daughter (and co-heir with Mary, first wife of the Earl of Strafford, and Sarah, wife of Captain Carmichael of the 9th Dragoons) of Peter Mackenzie of Grove House, Twickenham, Middlesex and of Harmony Hall in the Island of Jamaica"? (Kathleen herself was often unable to explain her mysterious romantic preferences; she could only say, "I like the sound of it.")

The original Marple and Wyberslegh Halls were probably both built in the last quarter of the fifteenth century. They had belonged first to the Vernon family and then to the Stanleys. In 1606 the Stanleys sold both houses to Henry Bradshaw, who had been living at Marple Hall as a tenant for the previous twenty years. This Henry Bradshaw will be referred to here as Henry One—although there was at least one earlier Henry in the family—because it is with this Henry that the Bradshaw history begins to be worth retelling.

(The early Bradshaws probably all wrote their name with an e at the end of it; John Bradshaw signs himself thus on Charles's death warrant. But most modern historians spell Bradshaw without an e. Their example is being followed here.)

For some years before Henry One bought the two houses, his son Henry Two had been renting Wyberslegh. So it is to be assumed that Henry Two's children, including John Bradshaw, were born there. Kathleen was determined to believe that John was, in spite of a tradition that he had been born at Marple, in the room which was therefore named the Bradshaw Room. John's christening at Stockport on December 10, 1602, is recorded in a parish register. Against the entry someone has written "traitor."

Henry Two had three sons who lived to be grown men: Henry Three (the eldest), John and Francis. When John was a schoolboy he is supposed to have scratched the following lines on a tombstone in Macclesfield churchyard:

> My brother Henry must heir the land
> My brother Frank must be at his command
> Whilst I, poor Jack, shall do that
> Which all the world will wonder at.

The coincidence of the three names thrilled Kathleen, of course. The modern Henry would "heir the land" almost certainly, the modern Frank was already "at his command" in the Army, and the modern Jack was already a lawyer, like John—so perhaps he too would make the world wonder!

By 1648, John Bradshaw had become Chief Justice of Chester. But he was by no means a nationally known figure. He had always been a strong supporter of the Parliament (which had now won the Civil War and taken Charles I prisoner); indeed, he wanted to see England turned into a republic. Milton, who was a friend and perhaps a relative by marriage, praises his integrity and learning. A portrait of him by Peter Lely shows a handsome long-faced man with a large sensible nose and mild eyes who looks honest and quite unfanatical. He has a certain resemblance to Frank.

When Cromwell and the Army decided to try the King for treason, many leading members of the bar, Parliamentarians as well as Royalists, refused to have anything to do with the proceedings, declaring that they would be illegal. Bradshaw did not refuse, but he stayed away from the first two meetings of the commission which was to conduct the trial. In his absence, he was chosen Lord President of the High Court; Dame Veronica Wedgwood in A

Coffin for King Charles calls him "an undistinguished choice but . . . the best man available." At the third meeting of the commission, on January 12, 1669, Bradshaw appeared and was persuaded to accept the presidency, after making a speech in which he said he felt himself insufficient for so great a task.

The trial was a fiasco. Bradshaw and his colleagues were unable to establish convincingly their right to try the King or even their right to represent the people of England as his accusers. The proceedings lasted a relatively short while, January 20–27, yet they seem cruelly drawn out, because of hesitations, changes of tactics, tedious public rantings and long arguments behind the scenes. John Cook, who presented the case against the King, was a raging fanatic; he denounced Charles as an enemy of the human race. Bradshaw was almost polite by comparison, though often irritable and schoolmasterish. He must have been more timid than he appeared, for he wore a hat lined with steel plates for fear of attempted assassination. Neither Cromwell nor Cook took such a precaution.

Charles had far more style and presence than his judges; and he was much cleverer. Saying that he did not recognize the authority of the court, he refused to plead either innocent or guilty. According to the law, refusal to plead in a treason trial was equivalent to a plea of guilty. But the court did not want to invoke this rule; for propaganda purposes, it had to find Charles guilty after presenting a case against him which would impress public opinion. Bradshaw could do nothing with Charles, except to order him removed from the court. This happened three times and it made Bradshaw look like a weak frustrated judge obliged to use force. At the end there was more confusion. Lady Fairfax (in a mask) shouted from the gallery that Cromwell was a traitor; she was taken out after the guards had pointed their muskets at her. One of the commissioners, John Downes, was overcome by feelings of guilt and cried to his colleagues, "Have we hearts of stone?"; he had to be browbeaten into submission by Cromwell during a recess. At last Bradshaw made his prepared address to the prisoner. His speech was unconvincing at first—he compared the trial of

293

*Charles to the overthrow of Caligula, Edward II and Richard II—
but it became impressive when he pointed out that the contract
between king and people was reciprocal and that Charles had
broken it. After this he "pressed the King in a sweet manner to
repent of his sins." Charles wished to speak now, but Bradshaw
refused him: "You disavow us as a court. The court needed not to
have heard you one word."*

*So Bradshaw declared Charles guilty and ordered the clerk to
read the sentence: "that the said Charles Stuart, as a Tyrant,
Traitor, Murderer and a public enemy, shall be put to death, by
the severing his head from his body."*

Charles: "Will you hear me a word, sir?"

Bradshaw: "You are not to be heard after the sentence."

*He ordered the guard to take Charles away. Suddenly the King
seemed to realize fully what had happened—he was to be taken to
his death unheard. He had refused to speak, and now his judges
refused to listen. He was overwhelmed and began to appeal to
Bradshaw in broken phrases: "I may speak after the sentence . . .
by your favor, sir, I may speak after the sentence ever." Then, as
the guards surrounded him: "By your favor, hold! The sentence,
sir—I say, sir, I do—" But when the guard prepared to take him
away by force, he made a coherent and telling protest: "I am not
suffered for to speak; expect what justice other people will have."*

*Three days after, on January 30, Charles died as every martyr
should. Fearless, forgiving, full of trust in God, assured of his
rightful place in heaven and in history, he uttered the reverber-
ating word "Remember."*

*After the King's execution, Bradshaw was made a member of
the Council of State and later its Lord President. He presided at
the trials of several Royalists and sentenced them to death. He was
appointed Attorney General of Cheshire and North Wales; Parliament voted him an income of two thousand a year derived from
the estates it had confiscated from Royalists. Bradshaw's behavior
in court has been criticized so severely that it is well to remember
what William Penn writes in his character sketch of George Fox
the Quaker (he is referring to the persecution of the early
Friends): "Through the tender and singular indulgence of Judge*

Bradshaw and Judge Fell, who were wont to go that circuit, the priests were never able to gain the point they laboured for, which was to have proceeded to blood and to have cut them off and rooted them out of the country."

On April 19, 1653, Cromwell, who had just dissolved Parliament in a famous hysterical scene, went to break up the Council of State. He found it in session, with Bradshaw in the chair. "This is no place for you," Cromwell told them, "and since you cannot but know what was done at the House in the morning, so take notice that the Parliament is dissolved." To this Bradshaw replied, "Sir, you are mistaken to think that the Parliament is dissolved, for no power under heaven can dissolve them but themselves, therefore take you notice of that."

Bradshaw thus rebuked and defied the man who was his chief hope of future advancement, and he remained an uncompromising opponent of Cromwell for the rest of his life. If Bradshaw had been the mere contemptible careerist that some historians have thought him, this loss of Cromwell's favor would have been the end of him politically; he could have found no other friends. In fact there must have been many people who admired and supported him, for he was returned for Stafford in the Parliament of 1654. This led to another clash: Cromwell summoned the members to the Painted Chamber and told them that they would not be readmitted to the House until they had signed a promise to be faithful to the Lord Protector and the Commonwealth and not to alter the government as settled in a single person and a parliament. Within a few days, three hundred of the four hundred and sixty members signed this pledge. But Bradshaw was among those who refused to do so and went home.

In 1656, Sir Henry Vane was brought before the Council and imprisoned for writing a seditious pamphlet. Bradshaw was thought to be involved in his sedition, and an attempt was made to deprive him of the office of Attorney General of Cheshire, but the Council changed its mind. Cromwell's influence was sufficient to prevent him from obtaining a seat in the Parliament of 1656 and Cromwell had no further trouble from him.

Bradshaw hadn't given up politics, however. After Cromwell's death and the abdication of his son Richard in 1659, he again entered Parliament, became a member of the Council of State, and on the third of June was appointed a commissioner of the Great Seal. Bradshaw must have known by this time that a restoration of the monarchy was almost inevitable and that he could expect no mercy from a royalist government. Yet he remained as active and as outspoken as ever. Perhaps he knew that he would not live long. In his last public speech he declared his abhorrence of the Army's arrest of William Lenthall, the Speaker of the House of Commons. He died of a quartan ague on October 31, 1659, and was given a state funeral in Westminster Abbey.

Less than seven months later came the Restoration. Charles II was not vengeful, but the Parliament insisted on punishment for the actual regicides, those whose names had been signed to the death warrant. They and a few others faced the death penalty. Some had already escaped abroad. Some were able to excuse themselves, claiming that Cromwell had forced them to sign; these had their sentences commuted or were even set free. Thirteen only were executed.

King Charles had died painlessly from the single stroke of an expert headsman, who had addressed him as "Your Majesty," in the presence of an awed and largely sympathetic crowd. Nine of the regicides had to suffer the law's obscene punishment for traitors: being half hanged, then disemboweled and cut to pieces while still alive. The onlookers jeered at them, yet they too died as martyrs should. "I followed not my own judgment," said Thomas Harrison, "I did what I did as out of conscience to the Lord."

Bradshaw's name stood first on the death warrant, Cromwell's third, Ireton's ninth. Their bodies had already been deprived of their graves in the Abbey. In 1661, on the anniversary of Charles's death, an act of ritual vengeance was performed upon them. They were "dragged upon a sledge to Tyburn and then taken out of their coffins and in their shrouds hanged by the neck until the going down of the sun. They were then cut down, their heads taken off, and their bodies buried in a grave under the gallows." This account is from the diary of John Evelyn. The sight caused

*him to praise "the stupendous and inscrutable judgments of God."
The grave was the common pit used for the bodies of criminals.
The severed heads were taken to Westminster Hall, the scene of
Charles's trial, where they were publicly exposed. They were to
remain there for more than twenty years.*

*According to Kathleen's history, a member of the family whose
name was also John Bradshaw emigrated to America about this
time. He passed himself off as the judge and was greatly honored
in consequence. She continues: "Some years ago, a man came to
Marple Hall saying he had seen the Judge's grave in America and
would like to see his birthplace." Though Kathleen doesn't actually say so, she implies that it was this same man who told them
that the alleged Bradshaw grave was in Maryland, near Annapolis,
and that there was a cannon placed at its head which bore the
following inscription:*

> *Stranger as thou pass contemplate this cannon, nor re-
> gardless be told that near its base lies the deposited dust
> of Judge Bradshaw who nobly superior to selfish regards,
> despising alike the pageantry of courtly splendour, the
> blast of calumny and terror of regal vengeance, presided
> in the illustrious band of heroes and patriots who firmly
> and openly adjudged Charles Stuart tyrant of England to
> a public and exemplary death. Thereby presenting to the
> amazed world and transmitting down through applaud-
> ing ages the most glorious example of unshaken virtue,
> love of freedom and impartial justice ever exhibited in
> the bloodstained theatre of human action. Oh Reader,
> pass not on till thou hast blessed his memory and never
> never forget that Rebellion to tyrants is obedience to
> God.*

*(Research in the archives of the State of Maryland has failed,
so far, to confirm any part of this story.)*

*Henry Three, Bradshaw's elder brother, became a colonel in
Cromwell's army; he was wounded at the Battle of Worcester in*

1651. (*This was the defeat of an attempt by the future Charles II to invade England from Scotland and make himself king.*) *In 1654, Henry Two died and Henry Three inherited Marple Hall, which he proceeded to rebuild almost completely in 1658. A black-and-white gable, now become part of a wall in one of the bedrooms, remained as the only visible trace of the original house. To commemorate the rebuilding, Henry Three had its date carved, with his initials, in the stone above the main door to the terrace. Wyberslegh also may have been rebuilt or added to at this time.*

In 1651 Henry had been a member of the court-martial which sentenced the Earl of Derby to death for his support of Charles II. After the Restoration, Henry was summoned before the Lords committee to answer for this, but was allowed to go unpunished. He died a year or two later. His son, Henry Four, succeeded him.

Henry Four died in 1698 and was succeeded by his son Henry Five. But now a blight fell upon the Bradshaws. Within a comparatively short space of time the male line died out in the various branches of the family, first in Lancashire and Derbyshire and finally at Marple, where Henry Five died childless in 1735.

So the estates passed to Henry's sister, Mary Bradshaw, and from her, in 1761, to Nathaniel, her son by her second husband, Nathaniel Isherwood. This Nathaniel Isherwood was a felt maker from Bolton, Lancashire. Mary's first husband, William Pimlott, had been a timber merchant. Both of them were therefore "in trade," and Mary's relatives had looked down on them, considering that she had married "much beneath her."

(They might have thought better of the name Isherwood if they could have known that it would be dignified by Sir Joseph William Isherwood (1870–1937) the British shipwright, and by Benjamin Franklin Isherwood (1822–1915) the American naval engineer. In commemoration of the latter, there is an Isherwood Hall in the United States Naval Academy at Annapolis; there was also, until recently, a destroyer named the Isherwood *in the United States Navy.)*

·   ·

*With the succession of Mary Bradshaw's Nathaniel, the Family
begins to call itself Bradshaw-Isherwood, though not invariably.
The hyphen appears, disappears, reappears; so does the e on Bradshaw. According to the family tree in Kathleen's book, Nathaniel's
nephew John restored the e and John's son Thomas dropped it
again.*

*While this Thomas Bradshaw-Isherwood was up at Oxford in
1837, he made friends with—or rather, was made friends with by—
a fellow undergraduate named Charles Bellairs. There is no need
to describe Charles, he is so vividly self-described in the extract
from his diary which Kathleen has copied into her book. In later
life he became a clergyman. If he remained as honest with himself
about his motives as he is here, he must have been a remarkable
one:*

> *In the year 1837 I became an undergraduate at Oxford,
> and, being the younger son of a country clergyman, I
> went there on a small allowance but I was determined
> not to lower myself by making inferior acquaintances.
> My rooms were poorly furnished but I made up for it by
> adorning them with some tolerable knick-knacks, so that
> I got the credit of being as cosy as my neighbours, who
> had spent twice as much at the upholstress.*

Now Thomas Isherwood appears:

> *I soon became friendly with the best men of the col-
> lege, and amongst them was a young lad, only just eigh-
> teen, the only son of a country gentleman in Cheshire
> whose income I afterwards understood was about four
> thousand a year, and who resided in a curious old man-
> sion where his ancestors had flourished for many hun-
> dreds of years, in much the same social position as they
> enjoyed at that moment. . . . I soon became very inti-
> mate with this specimen of the favoured class. He was
> amiable, good-looking and generous but he had seen
> little or nothing of society and was a good deal laughed*

at for his peculiarities. He was not at all conceited or uppish or purse-proud, but he showed ignorance of the ways of the world.

In the summer of 1838, Thomas Isherwood invited his Mother and two of his sisters to Oxford for the Commemoration. Charles Bellairs made it his business to be with them whenever possible, at breakfasts, boating parties, concerts and dances. With the result that he was invited to visit Marple Hall during the long vacation.

Just before Charles's visit was due, Thomas wrote to say that he was in bed with an inflammation of the lungs and so unwell that he would probably miss the next term at Oxford, but that Charles was to come to see them anyway. So Charles took the train from Liverpool to Manchester and went to the Royal Hotel, where he was met by "a high spare antique chariot of the colour of mustard"; its doors were almost covered with an enormous coat of arms and the crests of the Bradshaws and the Isherwoods (a stag under a vine tree and a boar's head). On arriving at Marple, Charles noted disdainfully "the shabby looking park without much ornamental timber," but was impressed by "the ample Elizabethan mansion without any modern additions, the sort of house you would expect for an oldfashioned country gentleman."

It was the old-fashioned gentleman who welcomed him. Charles noticed that Thomas' father, John, was "rather stout and rosy, he had the smallest hands and feet I ever saw."

He held out his hand and said, 'I am glad to see you, Sir! You are a friend of my only Son's. I am sorry he is not well enough at present to come down stairs to receive you but he will see you in his own room. He is my only son, Sir, and it is of great consequence that he should live till he is of age, for the property is strictly entailed, and if he should unfortunately die before he is twentyone it will go to the Salvin family and not to my daughters. I have however directed my lawyers to get everything ready against his coming of age, and the very moment the clock strikes twelve, Sir, this disagreeable

*entail will be cut off, so I hope he will get better. I have
the principal physician to see him every other day from
Manchester, whose fee is six guineas.'*

This opening speech must have reassured Charles; it certainly
showed that John and he had much in common. John may even
have guessed at Charles's long-range intentions already and approved of them, for he went on to speak of his daughters and
their accomplishments: "Anna Maria is fond of riding spirited
horses. Miriam . . . is a good accountant, I much wish she had
been a boy. Magdalene plays on the harp and sings with taste."
Then, as if he feared that Charles might prefer a Miss Davenport
who was staying at the house, he casually let fall the remark that
her father's estate was mortgaged—"I am afraid he is at times in-
convenienced."

No doubt Charles was thoroughly enjoying the situation. When
he went up to his room to dress for dinner, he admits that "as
there were four young ladies in the house and I was the only
young gentleman, I probably took some pains with my toilette."

Next morning, John showed Charles some more rooms, most of
which he found gloomy and depressing. But one amazed him:

*'This small apartment', said the old Man, 'is vulgarly
called by my Wife "King Charles's Closet". I do not at
all approve of it myself, but I have to put up with many
things which I disapprove of, of far greater importance
than this. I have not told you before, Sir, that my Wife is
of a very romantic turn and it frequently leads her to
excess. That extraordinary and indeed ludicrous figure on
its knees in the centre is intended for the Martyr King
Charles I, and he is supposed to be kneeling before that
little table, perusing his death warrant.*

*'You are perhaps not aware that Judge Bradshaw who
presided at his trial was born in this house, and that I am
descended from his eldest brother. I am not proud of the
connection, Sir, though I believe he left considerable
wealth to the family, but my Wife considered that it*

ought to be illustrated by that ridiculous figure before
you. She selected several pieces of old armour from the
collection in the hall and had a kneeling block made on
which they fitted. The hair, (which flows over the shoulders from beneath the helmet) was cut off her own head
when she had a fever. The purple velvet bag breeches
were made from the skirt of a worn-out dress, and the
leathern jack-boots were made by a neighbouring shoe-
maker, and as the figure is kneeling you can see at once
that the soles have never been used. I do not like to remove it, Sir, as it would cause discord in the house, but I
assure you, Sir, I am ashamed of it.'

John's eccentric wife Elizabeth was not at home during Charles
Bellairs' visit; she had gone off to the seaside with her maid. "She
frequently goes off for two or three months together," John told
Charles, "but I have so many home occupations I do not much
miss her."

In the spring of 1839 Charles Bellairs returned to Marple to
attend a funeral—not Thomas', as John had anticipated, but John's.
At the end of his previous visit Charles had written in his diary:
"I felt on leaving that on the whole I had made a good impression
on my Host." He had not been mistaken. John, on his deathbed,
had told his eldest daughter, Anna Maria, that he wished her to
marry Charles. They were married the following December.

In 1840 Thomas Isherwood became doubly a brother-in-law to
his friend by marrying Charles's sister, Mary Ellen Bellairs. Next
year, Mary Ellen gave birth to her first child, John, who was to
be Frank's father. 1841 was also the year of Thomas' coming of
age. The elaborately staged celebration is described (without using
either the hyphen or the Bradshaw e) by the Stockport Advertiser
of October 7:

The dinner was held in the entrance hall which was
most splendidly lit and decorated for the day. The imperial crown was suspended from the ceiling and the

*entire room was decorated with pillars, festoons and
tastefully variegated floral emblems of which the motto
was 'Speed the Plough'; this had a good effect and was
highly characteristic of the occasion, the company being
comprised principally of those engaged in agriculture.*

The six-weeks-old John Isherwood was brought into the hall
by his nurse while the band played "See the Conquering Hero
Comes." A neighbor proposed John's health and the health
of his parents, and then observed that "when he looked around
him and saw the high, the low, the rich and the poor (he meant
nothing invidious) met together, it looked like the return of the
good days of Old England." Actually, England was just about to
experience the bad days of radical Chartism, with their bloodshed
and burnings. Before long, the mother and child whose health was
now being drunk would be confronting the crowd at the gates of
Marple Hall.

Since Thomas had come of age, his mother was called upon to
hand over the management of the property to him. When her
accounts were audited they showed a deficit of two hundred and
sixty pounds. Being informed of this, she at once put in a counterclaim: "two hundred and sixty pounds—for wear and tear of mind
and body." Kathleen doesn't say how this dispute was settled.
Mary Ellen was quite strong enough to stand up to her Mother-in-
Law; but no doubt she could do this only by urging Thomas to
demand his rights, and Thomas was sickly and weak-willed.

He must have had his stroke three or four years later. One
doesn't know just how serious this was. Richard remembers being
told that although Thomas had lost his speech he was still able to
go for walks and play the piano. Kathleen says in her book that
"his mind gave way." In any event, he lived to be seventy-five.
John and Elizabeth came to live at Marple Hall in 1886, while
Thomas and Mary Ellen were still alive.

It is evident from Kathleen's book that she had difficulty in
finding any material for romance in the history of the Bradshaws

and the Isherwoods during the past two hundred years. And when she went back to the seventeenth century her loyalties became confused. John and Henry Bradshaw were romantic, but they were anti-Royalist. Charles I was romantic but, in Kathleen's eyes, a carrier (so to speak) of the Catholicism which would break out in his sons. So she couldn't really support either side in the Civil War. She did, however, tell Richard she believed that if Frank had lived in those days he would have been a Cavalier.

Christopher's feelings were more violent but just as confused. He loathed Puritanism and Puritans, which made it impossible for him to side wholeheartedly with the Parliament. He rejoiced in the Restoration because it did away with the Puritans' kill-joy ordinances and brought back whores, orgies and sexy plays. But he hated nearly all monarchs—William Rufus, Elizabeth I and Charles II were possible exceptions—and would have been happy to see any of them executed; Charles I, in his opinion, deserved it more than most.

According to Christopher, ancestor worship was vile; it belonged to the cult of the Past. But Bradshaw wasn't an ancestor, Christopher decided; he was the opposite, the Anti-Ancestor, who could be revered without shame. The Anti-Ancestor can never be glorified officially; the only valid tributes to him are the insults of his enemies. He is branded a traitor on his birth register; after death he is flung nameless into the grave of criminals. In being dragged from the respectable Abbey tomb and exalted to the gibbet, he achieves his highest political honor.

Even today, Christopher seldom misses a chance to boast of being descended from the Regicide. He thinks with proud emotion of the heads at Westminster Hall and with amusement of Cromwell's disgust if he had known that Bradshaw's would be one of them. Not long ago at a dinner party in Australia, he found himself getting into a quite heated argument with a descendant of Fairfax, about the Lord General's refusal to take a share of the responsibility for Charles's execution!

In contrast to the Anti-Ancestor, there are the squalid and grotesque creatures of whom Baudelaire writes in his Intimate Journals: "*My ancestors, idiots or maniacs, in their solemn dwellings, all victims of terrible passions.*" When Christopher read this, as a young man, it inspired him to create a new myth about himself which he acted out for the amusement of his friends. The father of one of them, a doctor, had said that there must be madness in the Isherwood family, they had such oddly shaped heads. Encouraged by this professional endorsement, Christopher took to describing John as a slobbering incoherent idiot, Elizabeth as a mumbling witchlike crone, his Great-Grandfather Thomas as a staring schizoid, his Great-Great-Grandmother as a religious maniac with delusions of grandeur. His prize exhibits were the two cousins who really had been arrested as "wandering lunatics" (this was how they were charged in court); the husband had been told in a dream to strangle his wife, so he had tried to but failed, perhaps from an inability to concentrate, for she hadn't resisted. (Later, at the police station, she said she wanted to be burned at the stake.) Before being taken into custody, the husband had threatened the police with a gun, announcing that the end of the world was at hand. . . . And so, Christopher would conclude, he himself was obviously the offspring of a doomed line and must expect to be dragged off, some day soon, screaming in a straitjacket. When he talked like this, Kathleen would protest, but only mildly. She had no fears for his sanity. And, indeed, she must have realized that he was trying, in his own peculiar way, to do just what she had tried to do, make the Isherwoods seem a bit more interesting.

While Christopher was a child, he established a physical contact with Marple Hall, learning the feel and smell of the house by clambering over it on his hands and knees. He did this when accompanying the housemaids on their daily tours of cleaning.

Since Marple had many visitors in those days, some of them unexpected, its show rooms had to be kept dusted and polished—even the library and the drawing room, which John and Elizabeth never used unless there was company. Elizabeth preferred her small cheerful sitting room. John liked to hide himself away in *his snug attic den, where he sucked on a wet smelly pipe and blinked half asleep at a volume of escape fiction which was often upside down.*

Going into the show rooms when they weren't on show was unlike walking onto the stage of an empty theater. For these rooms resembled shrines rather than stages; they were permanently activated. The front staircase had the atmosphere of a dark old church; it made you feel deeply "indoors." Breathing the perfume of beeswaxed oak, you climbed its thickly carpeted steps in massive silence, until your weight on a sensitive spot caused a loud sacrilegious creak.

The housemaids were young and lively and exuded healthy sweat. They treated "the young master" with amused familiarity, sensing something girlish in his liking for their company. They treated the furniture familiarly, too, being quite unintimidated by all this enshrined history. During spring cleanings, they would haul the tapestry out onto the lawn and thrash it heartily with carpet beaters. Generations of them had done this, until parts of it had become threadbare; they had to be rewoven by experts, at great expense, when the time came for the tapestry to be sold.

Guests who stayed overnight at the Hall and thus saw some of its backstage arrangements would discover that it had only one bathroom. This certainly didn't shock the majority of them; at that period, many far statelier mansions were equally primitive. Guests bathed in their bedrooms, before a blazing fire, in large portable tin baths—which was pleasant enough, as far as they were concerned. It simply meant that the servants had to carry the baths and huge cans of hot water up flights of stairs and along passages—which was a lot of hard work. Christopher couldn't understand this, of course; their work was his play. As long as he was trotting around after them or doing play jobs which Cook invented for him in the kitchen, he was like a stagehand behind the scenes in a theatrical production, he was part of the show. But when the curtain finally went up and some of the maids put on starched aprons and became actresses who served lunch in the dining room, then Christopher was excluded. He had to sit still at the table and be waited on. He was just a member of the audience.

When you had climbed to the head of the overfurnished front staircase, you walked out of the set scene and passed suddenly into a bare backstage area, the attics of the top floor. The attics led out of each other, and the furthermost was known as the Glory Hole. You entered it by a very low doorway (an adult had to stoop to get through) and found yourself in semidarkness, amidst trunks and unwanted objects. The Glory Hole itself was at the far end of this attic. It was a shaft which dropped the whole height of the house and down to the bottom of the cellars. It must have been formed by the construction of an outer wall in the 1658 rebuilding, but legend preferred to regard it as having been an oubliette for dealing with the unwelcome; hence its name.

The attics were related in Christopher's imagination to one of his great early myth books—The Roly-Poly Pudding, *by Beatrix Potter. This is a story about a Mrs. Twitchit and her three children, who live in a north-country village among the hills. (To look at, Potter country isn't unlike the Brontë land; but it belongs to a different world, in which there can be tears and even death, but never tragedy.) The Twitchits are cats. They wear clothes like humans and speak English. Other animals of various kinds live in this village; so do a number of humans, including Miss Potter herself. Its householders, animal and human, treat each other as equals, though they are perfectly aware of the biological differences between them.*

Samuel and Anna Maria Whiskers wear clothes and speak English, but they are not householders; they live in a hole between Mrs. Twitchit's chimney and her attic. They are rats, and Mrs. Twitchit regards them as a cat regards rats. They reciprocate. When they capture her son Tom, who has strayed into their territory while exploring the inside of the chimney, they prepare to turn him into a roly-poly pudding. Tom is rescued by John Joiner, the local carpenter, who is a dog. Mrs. Twitchit gratefully invites Mr. Joiner to dinner, to sample what is left of the pudding

307

after Tom has been extracted from it. But he declines because he has to make two hencoops in a hurry for Miss Potter—who, apparently, regards hens simply as hens. (Although the Authoress doesn't attempt to explain these social inconsistencies, she does seem to be apologizing for them by dedicating her book to Samuel Whiskers!)

Mrs. Twitchit's home is described as follows:

> *It was an old, old house, full of cupboards and passages. Some of the walls were four feet thick, and there used to be queer noises inside them, as if there might be a little secret staircase. Certainly there were odd little jagged doorways in the wainscot, and things disappeared at night—especially cheese and bacon.*

Christopher loved this description, because it could so easily be transferred to Marple. Some of Miss Potter's illustrations actually looked like rooms in the house; particularly the one which shows the attic and the exact point on its skirting board behind which Tom fell through the hole onto the Whiskers' bed. The Marple walls were even thicker than Mrs. Twitchit's and there were hollow places where you could squeeze your way along inside them. Since the electric light had been installed, Coyne had to do this now and then in order to repair wires which had been gnawed through by rats.

But Christopher hoped to discover something more mysterious than Samuel and Anna Maria. He began to tell himself that somewhere, in the innermost depths of the walls, there must be a place, a back-of-backstage—not that he could possibly have used such an expression. He never even tried to picture what it would be like, beyond feeling that it must be thrilling and secret and safe. Someday, he told himself, when he was least expecting to, he would come upon one of its "odd jagged little doorways" . . .

The Family, in its preoccupation with John Bradshaw, had very naturally hit on the idea that the Hall must be haunted by the ghost of his "victim." From which it followed, of course, that King Charles must appear carrying his head under his arm. But it is not recorded that anyone ever claimed to have seen him.

Marple Hall was also made the scene of a much more interesting ghost story; it is retold in verse in Leigh's Lays and Legends of Cheshire. The story takes place in the sixteen-forties, during the Civil War. Three of its characters are Colonel (Henry Three) Bradshaw, his wife and his daughter "Esther." (Henry Three had no daughter named Esther; Ann, the most likely candidate for the role, wasn't born until 1652.)

The Esther in the story is loved by and in love with a young man named Legh, of the Leghs of High Legh, who were kin to the Leghs of Lyme. Young Legh is in the Royalist army, but he and his family are still on good terms with the Bradshaws, despite their political differences. So when his commanding officer gives him some dispatches to deliver to the King, who is encamped near Chester, he finds it quite proper to call in at Marple Hall and ask if he may stay the night. (Judge Bradshaw did in fact remain friends with the Leghs of Lyme, who were also Royalists, and once signed a safe conduct for some of them, at this period.)

Warmly welcomed by the Bradshaws, Mr. Legh tells the Colonel of the dispatches he is carrying and adds, truthfully, that he has no idea what is in them. Mrs. Bradshaw is suspicious, however. So, while Legh is being entertained with songs after supper, she and her French maid take the dispatches out of his saddlebags and open them. Sure enough, they recommend that her husband and his friends shall be arrested at once and charged with treason.

Mrs. Bradshaw sends for her old and trusty manservant Christopher and tells him to cut the straps of the saddlebags halfway through, so that the current will carry them away, by seeming accident, while Legh is fording the Mere Pool on horseback next morning. It conveniently happens that the Pool has been turned into a raging torrent by a recent storm.

Next morning, Mr. Legh rides down the path to the Mere Pool, guided by the trusty Christopher, while Esther waves to him from an upper window of the house. Unfortunately for Legh, Christo-

pher is even trustier than Mrs. Bradshaw requires him to be. With-
out saying anything to her, he decides not to rely on the doubtful
success of this trick with the saddlebags—why not get rid of
all the evidence? So, instead of showing Legh where the ford
really is, he points to the place where the water is deepest and
Legh rides trustingly in. Caught in the powerful current, he still
has a chance to survive if he can stay on his horse. But Christopher
has foreseen this and cut through the girth of the saddle. Legh
loses his seat and gets drowned. Esther, who is watching, shrieks
wildly and goes mad. Henceforth, her ghost haunts the wood
below the terrace, causing it to be called the Lady Wood.

There was no convincing record that this ghost had been seen,
either. However, when the Mere Pool was drained in 1810, a
helmet, a bridle and spurs of the Civil War period were found in
the mud. And it was romantically taken for granted that they had
belonged to Mr. Legh.

So much for stories. What follow are happenings. Stories have
a point and make dramatic sense; their truth is of secondary im-
portance. These happenings do not seem to make any sense at all.

On the outer wall of the front staircase, facing you as you
began to climb from the middle floor of the house to the top, hung
an unframed picture, a canvas on a wooden stretcher. In view
of all the circumstances surrounding it, one hesitates to describe
it as sinister-looking; that sounds too subjective. The woman it
represented did have a sour harsh-featured face; but no sitter looks
her best in an eighteenth-century painting which hasn't been
cleaned.

The painting was of Elizabeth Brabins, wife of Nathaniel, the
first of the Bradshaw-Isherwoods. Their marriage was a short one,
and it was childless. When Nathaniel died in 1765 without an
heir the Hall passed to his brother Thomas, and Elizabeth had to
leave it. She went to live with her father at his house on the other
side of Marple, called Brabyns Hall—this explains part of her
nickname, Moll of Brabyns. Moll was supposed to have resented
the loss of Marple so passionately that her ghost came back to

haunt it, looking for her wedding ring. (There was no ring on her finger in the portrait.) Moll was also supposed to hate children, as being usurpers of "her" property. So she wanted to scare them off the premises. She had appeared to John's aunts, it was said, while they were in their teens.

Moll was shown wearing a voluminous dark garment with a severe-looking white collar. Over her head was a silk kerchief. A little black-and-white dog with floppy ears like a spaniel's was on her lap and in the act of pawing her dress.

At the end of June and the beginning of July 1907, Kathleen did the pencil drawing of the portrait which was later bound into her family history. Since that wall of the staircase was so dark, she asked the maids to move the portrait into the sitting room, which had plenty of light. The maids didn't like to see the portrait moved; they were convinced that Moll resented it, and they assured Kathleen that strange knockings and creaking noises were heard in the house every spring after it had been taken down from the wall to be dusted. Kathleen seems to have been skeptical about this; but after the portrait had been brought down to the sitting room twice and the noises allegedly heard, she humored the maids by finishing her copy while it hung on the wall.

Later that summer, Christopher and Nanny went to stay at Marple Hall. Meanwhile, Kathleen and Frank were visiting Oxford with Emily. When they got back to Wyberslegh on August 10, Nanny and Christopher had already returned. And Nanny had a tale to tell them. How she must have reveled in the telling of it and in the knowledge that she was forcing her mistrustful mistress to believe her! That night Kathleen writes:

Christopher looking very well, though they seem to have had considerable experience of the *Marple ghost*, Moll of Brabyns, who is said to haunt the big N.E. room at the top of the house, where they slept. She took the opportunity of being very unpleasant to him and annoyed him every night during the week he was there, August 2nd to 10th.

The very first night, Christopher woke up between 12 and 2

and sat up in bed, not at all frightened but complaining to Nurse of the 'muzzy old woman' sitting at the end of his bed, 'I don't like her, Nanny, no I don't'. This happened every night about the same time. Sometimes he said, 'now she's going down the steps' or 'out of the window'. Sometimes he mentioned a little dog she had, and remembered her in the morning as 'the muzzy old woman in the bonnet, with curls' who he didn't like, and imitated her sour face.

Nurse said she could see nothing and had never believed in the ghost before, but was quite certain C.W. saw *something*. He was *quite* wide awake each night. She herself felt conscious of a third presence in the room. Though she was not nervous, she said every night she woke up in a perspiration and there were strange knocking and creaking noises. Moll is supposed to have been especially lively since I took her down to copy. Frank thinks there is no doubt Christopher saw her.

On October 22, Frank and Kathleen started on a five-week trip to Spain. Nanny took Christopher to Marple, where they were given the same room as before. This seems odd, in view of what had happened in it; perhaps all the other rooms were occupied. Kathleen sometimes calls this room the Nursery, and that name will be used to identify it here—though "Anti-Nursery" would be better!

This is Kathleen's account of the happenings of October 29, written months later and based on what she had been told about them by Jack Isherwood and others:

Nurse had gone down to supper, leaving Christopher fast asleep in his cot, the sides of which were up. She left only a nightlight burning and shut the door of the room. One of the maids was in the room next and promised to go to him should he wake up and call out.

Just as they had finished supper, the maid came down and said there was no sound in the nursery.

Almost directly after, they heard a strange noise outside on the terrace, described as a sort of shuffling and deep sighing. All started up alarmed. A moment later, Christopher's voice was heard from the anteroom to the Servants' Hall, calling 'Nanny'.

She ran to the door and found him standing there with nothing on but his nightshirt, but *perfectly* warm and pleased with himself, and he said he thought he would now go back to bed. As Nurse opened the door on hearing his call, she said there appeared to be something behind him which vanished.

When asked how he got down, he said Daddy came and popped the lights on and carried him down. (*Frank was that evening at Segovia, suffering agonies of toothache!*)

The strange thing about it is, that Christopher is naturally a nervous child, and if he ever does wake and find himself alone, shrieks almost hysterically for 'Nanny' but never attempts to leave his bed, yet in this case he would have to get out of a crib with high sides, open a difficult door, descend two flights of stairs, go along a stone passage and across a stone hall—and, in spite of all these difficulties, there he was outside the Servants' Hall, not in the least frightened and quite warm although his feet were bare and he only had on a little nightshirt.

Then they took him upstairs to put him back to bed and Nurse said, to her surprise, she saw through the space above the door that there was a bright light in the room and fancied she saw something moving against it. On attempting to go in, they found they could not open the door and all fled down to the Oak Parlour. They met Mr Isherwood coming up and he at once went for Jack, who was in the Drawing-Room.

Jack wrote to Frank in answer to our wish to know what he thought of these experiences. He told the same story that Nurse had done and added that he should not have believed it all had he not been there. His Father fetched him, saying that Christopher had had a fright. He then went up to the Nursery and found the door fastened as the others had done. He managed however to force it open a little way and discovered that what prevented it opening was a chair which had been jammed in between it and the chest of drawers. He said that it would have been impossible to get out of the room and leave the chair in that position. The lights had been turned on, on the dressing table, and the sides of the cot had been let down, an impossible thing for Christopher to have done.

Jack's theory is that whatever it was that carried Christopher down, put on a semblance of Frank in order that the child might not be frightened, and that his guardian angel, if such it was, had removed him from the room because there was some influence in it harmful to him—and that what was done to the door, the lights and the cot was done to emphasize the fact and to insure notice being taken of it.

We slept in this room the following Christmas 1907, but neither of us saw anything.

The only reference Christopher made to it was to wonder if Mummy and Daddy would see the 'muzzy old woman' who tried to pull him out of bed.

To begin with, some architectural explanations:

The servants' dining room, known as the Servants' Hall, was on the ground floor next to the Kitchen and separated from it only by a small windowless lobby, just an area between doors. The Servants' Hall looked out on the terrace at the back of the house. So did two of the windows of the Nursery. The obvious way to reach the Servants' Hall from the Nursery on the top floor was to go down the back stairs. When you got to the bottom of the stairs, the lobby leading to the Kitchen and the Servants' Hall was on your right. On your left was the Oak Parlor, a paneled room overlooking the garden at the front of the house, in which John Isherwood often sat for a while before or after dinner. Ahead of you, as you stood at the bottom of the back staircase, was a stone-paved passage leading into the entrance hall.

There is a puzzle about Christopher's route down from the Nursery to the Servants' Hall, if Kathleen's account is to be accepted. Richard clearly remembers having been told that Christopher was discovered in the lobby between the Servants' Hall and the Kitchen, and this would be the logical place for him to have arrived at. But Kathleen writes of his going "along a stone passage" (*the passage from the bottom of the back stairs*) *and* "across a stone hall" (*the entrance hall*). This means that he must have been discovered in the anteroom which connected the entrance hall with the other end of the Servants' Hall; a strangely unnecessary detour. If Christopher had come down the front staircase, his entrance through this anteroom would have been the direct route; but, to get to the top of the front staircase, he would have had to pass through two of the servants' bedrooms. Kathleen can't be suggesting that he came this way, because if he had done so he couldn't have used the stone passage as she says he did. (Of course, this is anyway only her conjecture.)

Jack states positively that it would have been impossible to leave the Nursery by the door without moving the chair from its position. Could a person have left by the window or the chimney? This particular chimney, though small, was probably just wide enough to get into, but its stack was almost certainly too narrow to let you out onto the roof; also there would most likely be a fire burning in the grate at this time of year. The windows of the Nursery were mullioned; although some of their panes were made to open, the apertures between the stone uprights were so narrow that an adult could barely have squeezed through them. If he managed to do so he would then have had to climb down the wall from the top of the house to the bottom, holding on to the ivy; possible, but dangerous. (The "shuffling and deep sighing" heard outside on the terrace does suggest noises made by someone who had fallen and hurt himself.) When Nanny described how they all reentered the Nursery that night, she used to say that Jack immediately searched the two narrow tunnellike closets which were built into the walls of the room. Though Kathleen doesn't mention it, he must surely have taken this obvious precaution; he was always practically-minded. And even if the closets weren't searched, it is hard to believe that anyone who was hiding in them could have escaped unnoticed or not been missed by the others.

For the next twenty years the Nursery remained more or less as it had been in 1907. There was nothing sinister about its appearance, or even particularly ancient; it was spacious and comfort-

able, with plenty of light despite its mullioned windows. The Victorian furniture was solid and reassuring. When Christopher was older, he used to examine the chest of drawers and demonstrate to himself how the door had been jammed with the chair. But by no means could he stimulate any memory of what had really happened to him on October 29, though he tried hard to do so.

The fact that he spoke of "the muzzy old woman who tried to pull him out of bed" doesn't prove that he remembered, even as a child; he was obviously referring to the happenings of August 2–10. It was Kathleen who chose, without any evidence, to connect Moll of Brabyns with October 29—perhaps because she felt an instinctive need to give meaning to the apparently meaningless.

Christopher may have used the word "muzzy" for private reasons, because its sound seemed descriptive, and in ignorance of its dictionary meaning. However, it is significant that "muzzy" can mean gloomy and also (figuratively) blurred. Sometime in the winter of 1907, Christopher dismayed an elderly woman visitor to Marple by suddenly turning and running from her offered embrace, exclaiming that she was (or looked like) the Muzzy Old Woman. (He does dimly remember this scene; it took place in the stone passage.) The woman was wearing a hat with a veil, so her face was "blurred."

Since the happenings of August 2–10 are vouched for only by Nanny and Christopher, they must be regarded with suspicion. For all her apparent self-control, Nanny was a hysteric, and Christopher was an imaginative precocious child. The two of them could have worked each other up into believing almost anything, scaring each other and yet enjoying their own fright. The picture of Moll was always on view to stimulate them. Nanny must have known Moll's story, and Christopher no doubt overheard parts of it from the servants' whisperings, which would have made it sound all the more fascinating. Nevertheless, Christopher is now inclined to believe that he did see something, which Nanny then interpreted in her own way and helped him to describe to other people.

Nanny may have added some improving touches to the October 29 account: the presence she saw behind Christopher in the anteroom and the figure moving in front of the light inside the Nursery. But these are unimportant. The main facts are confirmed by at least half a dozen witnesses.

What took place on October 29 was either a paranormal event or a hoax. A hoax, even a pointless and crazy one, is an act of which almost anybody is capable, given the right mood and circumstances. Therefore, everyone who was at the Hall that night must be suspected and required to produce an alibi.

Nanny has an alibi. So have all the servants, with one exception. So have Elizabeth and Jack and two male guests of his who were staying at the house; these four were together in the Drawing Room when John came to ask Jack to come up to the Nursery.

John has no alibi. Neither does the maid who had been upstairs in the neighboring bedroom until just before Christopher's appearance downstairs. John was infirm, slow on his feet, lazy and unenterprising; one must surely rule him out on physical and psychological grounds. The maid was presumably young and active. Her character is unknown. She is a much more promising suspect. But the problem is the same, however one chooses. Neither John nor the maid could have perpetrated such a hoax without two accomplices.

The first accomplice must have been Christopher. It is impossible to believe that he wouldn't have seen through anyone who tried to impersonate Frank. So he must have been persuaded by the hoaxer to join in the game and tell everybody that it was Daddy who had carried him downstairs. Meanwhile, the second accomplice, who was probably a young agile man, could have jammed the Nursery door shut from the inside, climbed out of the window and down the ivy, fallen or not fallen—for he could have made the noises on the terrace simply to frighten the servants—and then run away and hidden himself.

Well, the reader is free to believe that this is more or less what actually happened. If he can.

.   .

On October 26, 1914, Kathleen came up to Marple from London, where she had been staying with Emily. Richard and Nanny were already there; since the outbreak of the war and their return from Ireland, Marple had become their temporary home. Christopher was away at school.

That evening Kathleen notes in her diary: "Richard curlier and better looking than ever, but was sorry to hear he has begun to see the old woman who haunted Christopher at his age."

As Richard was seven years younger than Christopher, the correspondence of these dates was astonishingly close.

Next morning, when Richard came early to Kathleen's bedroom, Kathleen questioned him while they sat together looking at a picture book of trains:

I asked him if the old woman had said anything to him, and he said, 'she says "you muft go away" and she come and look at me in bed, and I say "I don't want to go away" and she say "Oh, but you *muft*" ' (he still talks indistinctly). He repeated this several times but did not appear frightened. He also said that she sits in the corner by the chest of drawers and has a pussycat with her and a sash on.

Kathleen arranged that Richard and Nanny should be given another bedroom; it was on the same floor, at the front of the house. That Richard should ever have been put into the Nursery isn't really so surprising. Kathleen may not even have known that this had been done; in any case, she had much more serious anxieties on her mind, for Frank was already at the front. John had grown increasingly apathetic and Elizabeth was no longer capable of running the household; neither of them would have interfered in any domestic matter. Nanny probably rather enjoyed being in the Nursery; her need for excitement was stronger than any nervousness she may have felt. When Nanny and the servants realized that Richard had been frightened by something in the room, they took it for granted that he had seen Moll. So they described her to him. Which accounts for the story Richard so convincingly told Kathleen.

Nearly forty years later, Richard told Christopher the sequel to that story—the happening which his story had concealed. It was on an evening in the winter of 1951–52 when they were together in London. Their talk had touched for some reason on Moll of Brabyns and suddenly, with a dreamlike sense of oddness, Christopher found himself taking part in (approximately) the following dialogue.

Richard: "I didn't tell Mummy what really happened. I said it was an old woman for the sake of peace, because I wanted to leave the room next day. I was afraid she wouldn't believe me."

Christopher: "Then you didn't see anything? You mean nothing happened?"

Richard: "Oh dear no, I didn't mean that at all! I didn't see an old woman. I saw a dressmaker's dummy."

Christopher: "A dressmaker's dummy? You mean a dressmaker's dummy?"

Richard: "Yes. It was very odd. I saw it as plain as I see you now."

Christopher: "But . . . did it have a head?"

Richard: "No, not a head exactly. There was some kind of screw sticking out of the top of it. It looked so funny, with the screw sticking out of it, jumping up and down."

Christopher: "It had feet, then?"

Richard: "I don't know. I couldn't see. I could only see the upper part of its body. I suppose it had feet. You see, when it jumped up and down, I could hear the noise of feet on the wooden floor."

Christopher: "Where was this thing when you saw it?"

Richard: "It was near the door."

Christopher: "Was the door open?"

Richard: "Oh dear no, the door was locked. It had got in through the locked door. That was what terrified me."

Christopher: "Did you scream?"

Richard: "No, I didn't scream. I tried to wake Nanny, though, but I couldn't. She was sound asleep."

Christopher: "Did it speak to you?"

Richard: "Oh no. I don't think it saw me, thank goodness. Well, not exactly. But it made me feel it knew I was there and it wanted to drive me away. It was threatening me."

Christopher: "And you made that up to tell Mummy in the morning—about what the old woman said?"

Richard: "Well, I had to tell her something. I couldn't tell her I'd seen a dressmaker's dummy, could I? Of course I don't expect you to believe me, Christopher. But I can't help it, that's what happened."

The relations between Richard and Christopher as adults had never been complicated by pretenses or concealments. Christopher would have said without hesitation that he couldn't imagine Richard ever telling him a lie. But this story of the dummy did bother him at first. Surely Richard must have dreamt it? He suggested this to Richard. Richard was certain he had been awake. Still, unworthy suspicions lingered. Christopher even stooped to the trick of cross-examining Richard one evening when he was drunk. But Richard wasn't to be shaken; repeating every detail, yet obviously redescribing the experience rather than parroting his previous account, he showed both patience and sympathy with Christopher's skepticism: "Of course I don't expect you to believe me . . ." And thus, gradually but finally, Christopher found himself forced to believe.

. .

Between the ages of nine and seventeen, Christopher spent a large part of his holidays at Marple and slept at one time or another in most of its bedrooms. When he was alone at night, there was always a background of fear in his mind. Not fear of the dark; fear of the something that had manifested itself in the happenings and might manifest itself again at any moment. For now, without trying to explain his belief to himself, he took it for granted that there was something. In certain rooms his sense of a psychic menace was related, quite inexplicably but definitely, to a particular feature of that room—to the black-and-white gable embedded in the wall or to the lemon-colored silk shades of the electric lamps over the dressing table. His fear never approached

320

panic and was never likely to, now that he had accepted it. He was getting accustomed to the menace, as one would to the presence of wild animals in a jungle at night.

Once or twice, when his schoolfriends came to stay, he played "ghosts" with them. They put on sheets and ran around the pitch-black passages or peered in through the kitchen windows from the darkness outside, wailing to scare the maids. From Christopher's point of view the curious thing was that as long as he was playing this game he lost all his fear of the psychic menace; indeed, he felt that he was part of it. *This suggests that he subconsciously recognized the relationship between the menace and himself, between haunter and haunted, as being also a sort of game—terrifying and sado-masochistic, but a game nevertheless. By trying to scare the maids—even though they weren't a bit scared and he knew it—he was reversing the roles and becoming the haunter.*

Christopher grew up with an aggressive anti-romantic attitude toward the happenings at Marple Hall. He had developed this attitude in opposition to what he chose to regard as Kathleen's. He accused her of being able to find the Marple happenings romantic because she was determined not to believe in them, to dismiss them as exaggerations by Jack and Nanny. (Just as you could find slums romantic as long as you were determined not to believe the reports on slum conditions.) Christopher declared that he did believe in the Marple happenings and therefore couldn't find them romantic or Halloweenish or fun; they were squalid, he said, and a public offense, like bad drains. The more he hated Marple Hall as the archsymbol of Kathleen's Cult of the Past, the more its condition of being "haunted" appeared to him as a disease. It was a sick house, he said; a psychic slum. It ought to be burned down. (He never felt like this about Wyberslegh—and nobody has ever suggested that Wyberslegh is haunted.)

Poor old Marple Hall—Christopher repents now of having hated it. He remembers it with pity; for it was doomed anyway, without his ill wishes. After the First World War it was already obsolete, because it was too big. You couldn't maintain it without a large staff of servants, and servants had now become prohibitively expensive—that is to say, they were being adequately paid. Those who could afford them preferred to live in convenient modern houses rather than uncomfortable antiques. There was some talk of a school taking the Hall over; but this would have meant a reconstruction as drastic as Henry Bradshaw's—walls knocked down, rooms combined, bathrooms added, plumbing modernized, central heating installed. It couldn't even hope to be accepted as a public monument and museum by the National Trust (as Lyme was in 1946); too many magnificent old mansions were competing for this guarantee of survival, and Marple wasn't a quite good enough specimen of its kind.

When Henry inherited Marple, he didn't for one moment consider settling down in it. In 1929 he sold most of the furniture that had any value. (The suits of armor in the entrance hall were subsequently rented to a film company and used, appropriately enough, in René Clair's The Ghost Goes West!) Henry then put caretakers into the house; a succession of them looked after it until 1953. Less than a week after the last of these had left, one of the chimney stacks collapsed, crashing down through John's attic sitting room and the Bradshaw Room below it onto the floor of the entrance hall. So the house was condemned for habitation by the local authorities.

Nevertheless it still stood. And the portrait of Moll of Brabyns still hung on the wall above the front staircase. Later that year, Richard found that it had been taken down and was leaning against the stairs, half torn from its wooden stretcher. Richard hung it up again. A few days after this, he discovered it lying rolled up in the Glory Hole, minus the stretcher. A few more days passed and it disappeared. (Richard and Christopher wonder if anything out of the ordinary happened to its thief.)

One evening in September, while it was still daylight, Richard visited the house with a friend. They had just let themselves in by the kitchen door—which, like all the other doors, was kept locked

—when they heard a heavy thud from somewhere upstairs; as if, Richard said, "something filled with sand had been pushed over." This thud was followed by "slow heavy purposeful" footsteps. Richard and his friend grabbed pokers and ran up the back staircase. They searched both the upper floors but could find no explanation of the sounds.

About six months after this, Marple Hall began to be broken into and wrecked, with that mysterious ferocity which is vaguely described as vandalism. The lead rain pipes were ripped from the outer walls, the windows were smashed, the woodwork of the front staircase was hacked to pieces, the bathtub was dragged out of the bathroom and halfway down the back staircase, where it stuck. To Christopher, it was as if these youths from Stockport or Manchester had been possessed, without knowing it, by his own ugliest fantasies and were acting them out to shame him.

On February 5, 1956, while he was staying at Wyberslegh, he had his last horrifying glimpse of the Hall; Richard and he went over to look at it. Seen from the outside, it looked like a gutted ruin, stripped naked of its ivy, with black staring window holes. Richard led the way inside and up the back staircase; the front stairs were unsafe. They climbed over the wedged bathtub and went along the bare corridor to the drawing room. Strangely enough, the pink marble fireplace which Henry had brought back from Italy was still intact. Christopher remarked that it ought to be salvaged, and Richard agreed; but they both knew that nothing would be done. Things had gone too far here. The inertia of hopeless damage was too heavy. When the two of them came out of the house again, quite a number of people were wandering peaceably around, taking photographs. It suddenly struck Christopher that Richard and he had also become Marple ghosts, just for this moment. But ghosts are often mistaken for human beings. No one screamed.

During the next three years, the roof and floors continued to give way as the weather rotted them. Signs were put up warning tourists not to go into the building, but many did. Richard was

323

advised to hand it over to the Marple Council, lest he be held liable for some fatal accident. The Council was ready to carry out the demolition because it was taking the adjoining land for a school. So, in 1959, the Hall ceased to exist.

In October 1966 Christopher was back in England again and staying with Richard. When he suggested going to see how the site of the Hall now looked, Richard said no, he couldn't face it. Remembering their last grim visit, Christopher wasn't surprised. He went off by himself in a taxi.

The entrance gates to the park were gone, and the side of it which ran along the Stockport road was built up with new villas to a depth of several streets. What the Family had called "the private drive" was now officially Marina Drive. Christopher was taken along this, past the Marple Hall Grammar School, two big airy buildings, one for boys and one for girls. In the classrooms the children were sitting at their lessons. Over in the field beyond where the barns had once stood, boys were playing football. It was a beautiful autumn morning.

Christopher's driver had told him, in the ungracious north-country way, that he couldn't wait long, he had to pick up another customer (who had more important business than Christopher's, he implied). So Christopher got out of the taxi and began walking hurriedly but aimlessly back and forth—a Proust who was limited to fifteen minutes for his Recherche and didn't know where to begin.

He could barely trace the mounds and hollows which had been the foundations of the house, they were so thickly grassed over. The Hall seemed to have sunk bodily into the land, and this bumpy surface was like the commotion of waters above a ship which has just gone down. The area between the terrace and the garden wall was marked only by the two great copper beeches. Amidst the grass lay the headstone of the terrace doorway, inscribed "H.B. 1658." And that was all.

There was no grimness or sadness today. Christopher felt wonderfully joyful. For him this certainly wasn't the end of an

*ancient enemy, but it did seem to be the lifting of a curse. What-
ever here had exercised an evil power seemed appeased now and
buried, like Heathcliff in Gimmerton churchyard. He summoned
Emily Brontë to say goodbye for him to this place and its dead:*

> I lingered round them, under the benign sky, listened
> to the soft wind breathing through the grass, and won-
> dered how anyone could ever imagine unquiet slumbers
> for the sleepers in that quiet earth.

14

*As far as Kathleen was concerned, the last months of 1907
were darkened by the shadow of the impending move from
Wyberslegh. Frank had now to leave the Volunteers and rejoin
the Regiment at York. A house had to be found there and arrangements had to be made for moving the furniture. Then came the
question, Who would commit the sacrilege of occupying Wyberslegh? Their successor proved to be someone whom Kathleen
felt she could forgive, because he was taking the house for the
sake of his old mother and because he had said he would regard it
as an honor to live there. The Volunteers surprised Kathleen and
Frank (and perhaps rather shamed them for the things they had
said and thought about them) by presenting them with a clock,
"such a beauty, mahogany inlaid with brass, and lovely chimes
and big deep strike." Kathleen kept this with her for the rest of
her life.*

*On October 1, Kathleen was told of an important and utterly
unexpected family event, which she received with very mixed
feelings:*

Henry arrived on his horse with a great piece of news about
himself. He had been over yesterday to see Miss Muriel Bagshawe.
They had not met since Egypt three years ago this winter. I remember when he came home he talked a great deal about her, I
thought then there was something in it and it seems he *did* propose

but she refused on the score of religion. However finally she wrote the other day to say if he was still of same mind she had reconsidered her objections and would he come over? So he went, and said he could not help thinking all the while of Queen Victoria's account of herself proposing to Prince Albert! She has given in on the children being Roman Catholic and all points, and he seemed particularly pleased with the size of the dining room, the niceness of the house and the old iron gates to the Park, also that there was a rookery. She has two places which bring in five thousand pounds a year and is quite independent of all relatives. Poor Christopher William, his nose already seemed out of joint and his charms to have grown less, in view of Bagshawe cousins to be!

October 4. Henry's fiancée has written, hopes his Mother will think her worthy of him!! She thinks him such a beautiful character. Certainly most people are much nicer away from their own families. Esther says she is quite delightful, very simple and unspoilt, and it does seem *the* most perfectly satisfactory marriage from every point, as far as Henry is concerned.

October 5. Drove over to Marple. Muriel Bagshawe had already arrived. I do not think he could have found anyone possibly nicer or more likely to be nice to all his family. She has a very pleasant sympathetic manner, is utterly unlike an heiress or in any way spoilt, and evidently admired Marple tremendously. So I do hope that after all they may live there some day in spite of having places of her own.

Of course it couldn't help being a little sad when I thought of C.W., as his Grandfather had always talked of him there some day. And I can't think now why anyone believed Henry when he said he would not marry! She seems so fond of him and I do think he is lucky. She wrote to Mrs Isherwood that she hoped she would grow more and more worthy of her dearest Henry and hoped his Mother would not mind sparing him to her! She loved him so enormously. I saw the letter. She was very nice to us. I liked her.

October 12. Letter from Miss Bagshawe about our going there on Monday and saying how more than fortunate she feels in having the love of her dear Henry and only hopes she will always make him happy and be worthy of him, for he has been so true to her all those sad years they have been parted, but she feels it only makes their love more perfect now and how Henry had always spoken of our happy married life and she hopes and feels sure theirs will be just the same! I wonder if Henry and she both honestly believe he has been in mourning for her since they parted!

October 14. We met Henry at Marple station and went by the 11.12 to Dore, where Miss Bagshawe sent the carriage to meet us. Her home, Oakes, stands on high ground in a park, a comfortable square stone house with stone terrace and urns designed by Chantrey, who was a native of the village, Norton. Delightful view from terrace which faces south and though only eight miles from Sheffield appears to be in depth of country. House full of nice oldfashioned things and fine tapestry in the dining-room.

Henry and Muriel were married at the Bavarian Chapel in London on November 21, while Frank and Kathleen were still away on their Spanish trip. John and Elizabeth Isherwood, Christopher and Nanny all came up from Marple for the ceremony.

Henry and Muriel then left for a honeymoon in Paris and Rome. After their return, there was a big dinner at Marple Hall on January 3, "to entertain our tenants." Nanny and Christopher went to this. Kathleen writes:

They were the first to drive under the arches of welcome in the Park. There were nearly a hundred and they sat at two long tables in the hall and the house party dined there too at a separate table placed by the front door, coming down when they were all seated. C.W. entertained a small overflow party in the dining room by a speech on his own account, beginning 'Ladies and Gentlemen, I rise on this auspicious occasion—' I don't know if it extended much beyond. They seem to have enjoyed themselves,

328

he and Nurse, in spite of being ignored by his Uncle and new
Aunt, who kept their attentions for the Toogood children. Nurse
very bitter and described Muriel as looking worn and old and ill!
For which, of course, there may be a reason. . . .

*Frank and Kathleen were not at the dinner, however. On Janu-
ary 1 they left Wyberslegh to join a house party of friends at
Mow Cop, south of Macclesfield, and didn't return until January
4. This caused great offense. Henry wrote to Frank (January 8):*

I must say, I think the absence of yourself and Kathleen was to
say the least of it very unfortunate and I am certain this would
have given everyone the impression that you did not wish to have
anything to do with my Wife as a person you did not consider a
fitting addition to your family circle, were she not already too
well known in our district to require recommendation. I do not
think any engagement should have stood in the way of your being
at the dinner, if only for the fact that you were absent from our
wedding and are still the occupants of one of the houses on the
Marple Estate and you made your action too the more tactless in
returning home the very morning after the dinner. That my
opinion of your behaviour is not singular I am convinced from the
comments that were made by the guests of my Father and Mother
on your absence.

It is amazing to read the words of your Wife to mine when she
wrote congratulating her on our engagement: 'I can never forget
the cordial way in which Henry welcomed me into the family.
I hope that you will feel you receive from us an equally hearty
welcome'—or words to that effect! I left the Bay of Naples instead
of failing to be present at your wedding. You go off twenty miles
to avoid our homecoming. There it is 'in a nutshell'! Yours, Henry
B. Isherwood.

This enraged both Frank and Kathleen. Frank commented:

Even if he has a grievance it is needlessly offensive. If he is
suffering so badly from swelled head, the less we see of him in the

future the better. He writes as if we were in some way his dependents. . . . It is really rather hard that your little efforts to gush back to Muriel should be quoted against you 'with amazement'! 'The guests of *my* Father and Mother'!!!!!

Kathleen reacted similarly: "His letter is really beyond anything! He must either want to pick a quarrel or be very hard up for a grievance, or perhaps all these receptions have turned his head. His tone most high and mighty."

Henry's tone may be high and mighty, but the fact remains that they ought to have called off the Mow Cop visit; their hosts would certainly have understood. Kathleen must have been the one who was determined to stay away from Henry's dinner. She was trying to like Muriel, but when it came to celebrating the marriage publicly at Marple Hall—which Christopher should have inherited and which he was now probably going to be cheated out of—that was more than she could stomach. Frank, who felt less strongly about this than she did, does seem to admit they are in the wrong when he writes "Even if he has a grievance . . ." He finally returned a more or less apologetic answer to Henry's letter, signing himself "Your affect. Brother." But the feud wasn't over.

*In the back of Kathleen's 1908 diary there is a rough sketch in ink of the front of Wyberslegh. A frame is drawn round it, at the bottom of which Kathleen has printed her full name. Along the top, on a scroll, is written "*GLAD MEMORIES NEVER FADE.*" This must be a design for a bookplate, but she never had it made.*

Frank was now up at York a good deal of the time and had been house-hunting for them. He found a cottage at the village of Strensall, a few miles north of the city. Kathleen traveled up to see it.

January 14. Colonel very kindly lent us the trap to drive out to Strensall which made getting there much pleasanter. There are six miles of quite flat road but Strensall itself is quite a nice little place. There is a big wide common with gorse and I believe woods which are full of daffodils in the spring. The Cottage is the size of a big dolls house and stands in the village street with white front and square projecting windows on either side the front door and prim plain ones above, a garden path up to it and plots of grass the size of a large pocket handkerchief on either side! At the back a straggling yard leads to a small orchard and the river beyond. The orchard is a distinct feature and I noticed some rooks' nests in trees near. The bedrooms are tots and the only large thing is the rent. She asked at first two pound five a week.

Frank later got the owner to come down to two pounds a week, or seven pound ten for four weeks, which Kathleen still thought "fairly enormous"; but they agreed to it.

February 9. I simply can't realize that this house for me will *all* have vanished in three weeks time. In some ways it will be almost a relief when the move is over, though I grudge each day as it passes and the feeling of having no home in front of me seems horrible.

February 14. That Mrs Duncan who was giving fortnightly lectures on novelists has thrown in her career with the suffragettes and went up to London last Thursday and managed to get herself arrested and is now in Holloway Gaol for six weeks. Mrs H said it did seem to her so unrefined to allow oneself to be mauled by men!

February 23. Bright but high wind and storms of rain all day. In spite of it all, saw the *first snowdrops on the bank at last*. I felt I *must* stay on till they appeared, so now have no longer any excuse, though wish I could have seen it golden with crocuses.

February 28. *Woke to heavy snow*, quite thick and white on the ground and drifted up all round the windows. Heavy snow showers on and off all day with sun for a little while between. Managed to get the remaining carpets shaken. The kitchen things were packed together in a box, the curtains taken down, folded and done with keating powder and pepper, ditto blankets, and the cretonnes packed away into the sofa of my room. It was all very melancholy and the poor house that has given me so much happiness seemed very sad and forlorn. Nurse and Christopher went to Marple soon after four, and Mrs Ashton and I were left to keep house together. The coming here was so very joyful and the going away so sad and I shed a tear over the dear house and the happy times and felt very miserable.

Letter from Emily to Kathleen, February 28, No. 14 Buckingham Street:

Ownest Darling, when this reaches you, my Darling Pet will have left her first home, than which *no other* place can ever come up to it. It is something however to have had five happy years, a treasure always to look back to and a harbinger of Hope for many more happy years to come, though *never* the same over again, but when one thinks the happiness of one's life is gone, it comes again in some other form.

February 29. LEFT WYBERSLEGH. Everything white with snow. Mélisande brought me up my breakfast about a quarter to eight and the men came about eight thirty.

(*Mrs. Ashton was called Mélisande by Frank and Kathleen because she had the habit of speaking many of her "lines" twice over, like the character in the play.*)

It was a bitter night and a cold day but Mélisande lit me a fire in the drawing room and I sat there as the things disappeared around me. *It was unspeakably melancholy.* I thought the work people odious, no manners, humming whistling and smoking all over the house and in and out of everywhere, so different to the nice men Mama and I had in London when she moved. Mélisande made them a steak pie (three pounds) with potatoes and pie crust and they had cocoa and tea but barely said thank you for that or a tip (ten shillings). After they had gone, soon after three, Mélisande and I went through the poor lonely rooms together and I couldn't help saying 'Oh, Mrs Ashton, wasn't the house lovely?' and she said, 'Oh it was, Mam, noble—splendid'!!! And so we wandered through everywhere, she forming a sort of Greek chorus to my Tragedy! And I felt she was the only person really in sympathy and who understood my sorrow at leaving. I told her how much I should miss her and she said she should miss me far more—an outburst of eloquence such as I had never heard from her in the four years of our acquaintance! I said I hoped we should meet again and she said she hoped so, but one could never tell . . . one could never tell . . . and vanished into the house with her shawl over her head as I drove away. The snow was heavy on the hills and as I drove over the Ridge it looked just as it did long ago when in the happy times we drove over first to see the house. It seems like the passing away of Romance and Youth—and so much. Felt very tired out.

The move to Strensall was all the more distasteful to Kathleen because she knew in advance that it would be temporary. Before the year was over the Regiment would be moving again; this time to Aldershot, which was then, as now, the largest permanent military camp in England. And, after Aldershot, other moves were inevitable. Kathleen was now "an Army wife," much as she hated to accept the fact. Henceforward, Wyberslegh was to be obstinately mourned as her first and last "real" home. Frank knew how she felt, and he did his best to sympathize, just as Kathleen (sometimes) did her best to see some good in their nomadic habitations. But Frank couldn't help feeling the charm of a wandering life; he even ventured to justify it to Kathleen in a letter, suggesting that each move into a new home would be like "another honeymoon" —a masculine view, to say the best of it, since it would always be Kathleen who would have to take care of the move itself.

Of Kathleen's three "nomadic" homes, Strensall would be the one she liked least. Here are some of her early impressions:

The roads are very wide and straight, even across the common, and a desolation of flatness. I feel like the Israelites journeying across the desert, only it can't be for forty years and anyway our tent is a pleasant little place and I suppose one gets used to wandering.

The hopeless flatness everywhere makes walking most uninteresting.

A Capt Marsh of the Border Regiment at the Camp came to call. It must be the first time I've had a man to call since I married!!

A Captain Birch came to call with a dog and stayed to tea and ages after. Then the Doctor came and then Captain Mobberley of the Eleventh Hussars. It does seem so funny, these endless men!

Fine and sunny early, but the sharpness in the wind gives me constant neuralgia and I hate the air!

Head ached and felt sick all day. This is a *most deadly* little hole and there seems no object to go out for! Nothing to see and nowhere to go! I *hate* the prim little house opposite, and the air and the whole atmosphere! My poor romantic beautiful Wyberslegh and the hills seem all a dream.

I think this is a *most utterly detestable* climate, in fact it is an odious place. I dreamt about Wyberslegh last night and then to wake up and find oneself here was really unbearable.

Kathleen didn't merely complain, however. In the back of her 1908 diary, dated April, is a list of "THE ONLY advantages at Strensall!!!" Some of these are that both sitting rooms, the nursery, the bedroom and the dressing room get sun all day (when there is any); that the cottage is compact and convenient; that grocer, dairy, post office and butcher are all very close; that the roads are good for bicycling (if there happens to be no wind); that the sweet peas do well here; that there are two posts a day; that one can go into York. Kathleen adds, "The disadvantages are too many to mention!" At the end of her list is one more negative advantage: "The intense pleasure of getting into large airy rooms when one goes away—instead of minding leaving 'home' one is glad to go!!!"

Kathleen left Strensall as often as she could manage, that summer. Her first trip was with Frank, to look for a house in the Aldershot district. The neighborhood made a very bad impression on Kathleen: "half-built villas, market gardens, cemeteries and later heather, camps, pines and soldiers. Horrid atmosphere of soldiers nearly everywhere and nothing intimate or restful about the country. How can anyone like living in this restless sort of atmosphere!" Of the houses they looked at, "Frimley Lodge seemed the least villary, and older and more self-respecting." It was at Frimley Lodge that they would finally decide to live, though only after grave misgivings.

At the end of May, John and Elizabeth Isherwood came to spend two weeks in York. John showed a nostalgic interest in the various trophies of the Regiment's history. He took Christopher into the Minster and showed him the flag which he had carried as a young officer. On another day during John's visit to York, he insisted on paying the difference between third- and first-class railway fare back to Strensall for Nanny and Christopher, because "Christopher didn't like travelling in an ordinary carriage with no carpet. Mr Isherwood said it was so like himself."

Shortly after this, Frank went on a walking tour with Jack in Switzerland while Kathleen, Nanny and Christopher went to stay at Nether Hall. Frank and Jack enjoyed themselves, although the weather was bad and although Frank was prevented by his vertigo from following Jack up the glacier on the Jungfrau. Christopher and his Great-Uncle Walter took to each other hugely. As Kathleen puts it, "All his little jokes are well within C's intelligence." Walter was a practical joker of the kind called infantile by those

335

who are not amused and surrealistic by those who enjoy seeing others made ridiculous. He had been known to give specially designed fireworks to his guests instead of cartridges when they were going shooting. The smoking room at Nether offered explosive cigars and trick lighters. (Walter did not smoke.) And there was a stuffed rabbit which a concealed gamekeeper would drag across the lawn on a wire. "There's that confounded rabbit again!" Walter would exclaim when the drawing room was full at tea-time; whereupon the male guests excused themselves, ran to the gun room for weapons and blazed away.

From Nether, Kathleen went to London to be with Emily.

June 21. Quite cool. Mama and I went into Hyde Park to see the Procession of Suffragettes (who are the more violent contingent of the Suffragists). They arrived in seven processions from all parts of London and England, about thirty thousand of them, and nineteen or twenty platforms were erected in the centre of Hyde Park just sufficiently far apart for each speaker not to interfere with the other. It was wonderfully orderly on the whole and I was surprised to see so many well dressed people among the crowds. At five, the *great shout* 'votes for women' went up.

Kathleen, that born feminist, was obviously thrilled by the emotion of this gathering. But she could never bring herself to join the movement or directly support it in any way. Perhaps she instinctively felt the dangers implicit in equality of the sexes: the withdrawal of male respect and male protection and male responsibility for everything that is wrong with the world.

In July, the feud between the Henry and the Frank Isherwoods broke out again when Frank discovered the terms of Henry's marriage settlement. This had been drawn up in the autumn of 1907, shortly before the wedding, and it contained an agreement between John Isherwood and Henry that the Marple property could be inherited by either a son or a daughter of Henry in the event of Henry's death. Until this change had been made, the

336

*property was inherited through the male line only. In other words,
under the previous arrangement, Frank (and hence Christopher)
would have inherited the property from Henry even if Henry had
died leaving a daughter or daughters.*

*What angered Frank and Kathleen was that they had never
been officially told of the terms of this settlement. The news
leaked out to them by the roundabout way of gossip, which was
why it took eight months to do so. Furthermore, when they asked
John Isherwood about his part in the agreement, he expressed
surprise and dismay and told Kathleen that "he would sooner have
cut off his right hand than injured little Christopher." Kathleen
was disposed to believe this and make allowances: "The unfortunate Mr Isherwood, who wishes to please everyone, falls completely between two stools. Of course he always has and does
consent to anything from Henry, though I don't think for a
moment he would have done it if he had fully understood."*

*Jack Isherwood did his best to help Frank and Kathleen. He
went over to Oakes to see Henry and Muriel and present Frank's
grievance to them, but Henry was unabashed. As he put it in a
letter to Frank, "I am in no way prepared to cry 'peccavi'!" Henry
implied, though he was careful not to say so unequivocally, that
it was all the doing of the lawyers. He had wanted to keep the
Marple inheritance in the male line, but the lawyers had told him
that this was impossible, since Muriel's property could be inherited
by either a son or a daughter. (Yet Kathleen remembered Henry
telling her this, last October, and saying that nevertheless the
Marple line of succession wouldn't be altered!) According to
Henry, John Isherwood had understood the situation perfectly
and had even protested at first against the proposed change, but
had agreed to it in the end. Henry denied that anything had been
done behind Frank's back. "The whole matter was pushed on
because the time before our marriage from the time of our engagement was short, and not with any idea of keeping you in the
dark." (Jack, however, told Frank that Henry, in conversation
with him, had hinted that if Frank had been kept in the dark it
was his own fault; instead of going off with Kathleen to Spain he*

337

should have stayed at home to protect his own interests—and attend Henry's wedding!) Henry concludes his letter thus:

Of course the contingency of my having a daughter only is one that has not yet become a matter of practical politics. Muriel is at one with me in saying that, in the event of that possibility becoming an event, we should do all we could to make it up to Christopher if he required it and opportunity was given us.

How strangely, sadly unnecessary these anxieties seem, sixty years later! Henry's marriage won't make one pennyworth of difference to Christopher's financial future. Christopher will inherit the Marple estates, but without the consequences of which Kathleen now fondly dreams: a new Squire at the Hall and new heirs to carry on the old traditions. Even death, to which all lawyers refer so lightly, won't play its expected part. Christopher will remain alive while another Isherwood succeeds him, one whose existence isn't yet foreseen. John will outlive Frank—and Henry's marriage. And Kathleen will outlive Marple Hall.

On November 9, Kathleen and Frank moved from Strensall to Frimley. "No regrets at this move!" she wrote. And Frimley Lodge proved better than she expected.

November 13. The place begins to look so nice and homelike and oldfashioned, *quite* unlike a soldier's house!!

November 15. Nurse has worked splendidly and been quite invaluable. After lunch Frank and I went along the canal which is quite lovely, with all the bracken and high wooded banks with autumn leaves.

November 18. In the afternoon we walked across Frimley Green. The dark ridge of Farnborough and the Mausoleum ahead of us.

. . .

(Farnborough was then the home of the exiled Empress Eugénie, widow of Napoleon III. The mausoleum contained the bodies of her Husband and her son, the Prince Imperial, who was killed in the Zulu War when he was twenty-three. Farnborough had also lately become the headquarters of British aviation. It was there that Colonel Cody had just made the first powered airplane flight to be officially recognized in England.)

November 28. I altered some sleeves in blouse. Everything is out of date in present fashion.

November 29. We went to church in the evening at the tin church. Nice earnest clergyman.

On December 8, Frank and Kathleen went to London, Nanny and Christopher to Marple for Christmas.

December 11. To see 'Hannele' [Gerhart Hauptmann] translated from the German. It was acted in the semi gloom and as a child's dream. But what with drunken father, fighting paupers and cheap German angels, thought it at moments almost unbearable.

December 13. Frank and I went to Sloane Square to the new Christian Science church lately opened there. It is severely simple but in good taste. It lasted just under an hour altogether and was very simple and dignified and restrained, the whole tone and teaching being on the great love of God. We both liked it very much.

On December 18, Frank and Kathleen went up to Marple. Kathleen became ill there with a bad cold and went to bed. On December 22, she notes that Henry and Muriel motored over to lunch from Oakes. "Muriel came up to see me after lunch, carrying a little scented dog." The two women were now face to face for the first time since Muriel had become Mrs. Bradshaw-Isherwood-Bagshawe. The offense over the tenants' dinner and the marriage settlement was still an unspoken reproach between them, but they obviously behaved with adequate politeness. Indeed, Christopher was used as a peace offering; he and Nanny were invited over to Oakes along with Esther Toogood and her two children. Kathleen conceded that the invitation "seemed well meant."

Kathleen was finding it painful to be so near Wyberslegh:

December 30. Drove by the lanes to lunch with Miss S. Fortunately the roads were too bad to go over the Ridge but it was all I could do to face High Lane and Disley. That five years was heaven to me, no one knows how I miss it all, Wyberslegh and the hills, and how *awfully* homesick it made me feel, even going near them.

But, despite Kathleen's nostalgia for Wyberslegh, despite the worries and anxieties which sometimes beset her, the three years she spent at Frimley were certainly happy. Frimley Lodge became, if not a home, at least a place of comfort and, in retrospect, a historical monument, for her son Richard was born there. Here are some glimpses of her life:

1909. February 3. Amateur theatricals. *Their Bitterest Foe, The Compromising of Martha* and then *Brown with an E.* Frank very good in rather an uninteresting part. The soldiers of course were a rather trying audience and inclined to laugh in the wrong places.

February 17. Sat in the greenhouse. It really is delicious there, quite 'summer-land' as Christopher says and we have long chairs and get all the sun.

February 20. In afternoon, Frank, Christopher and I into the pine woods to dig up baby Christmas trees and plant in pots to help furnish the green house. After tea, C illuminated the biggest of the baby Christmas trees with six candles for a penny and gave a party to puppy and the china ornaments. He has started having 1½d a week pocket money but so far has the most hazy ideas on the value of pennies and what they will buy!

February 28. To Farnborough to see the Mausoleum. A very disinterested amusing monk took us down. The old building cost the Empress Eugénie one hundred and twenty thousand pounds to build, but he complained bitterly that she did not spend anything on the monks, though worth seven millions. The tomb of the late Emperor and that of the Prince Imperial stand one on each side of the altar and were loaded with sham wreaths.

April 3. In morning I bicycled to Camberley, calling for my bicycle basket made by the poor blind ex-soldier. It was very nice but too little room inside. However I hadn't the heart to tell him. Had to get a chicken extra as I found two subalterns were coming to supper tomorrow.

April 11. Most beautiful Easter Day *imaginable*. C to our room early to look for his Easter parcels, a gorgeous red satin egg with chocolate from Cousin Rose, a shop with chocolate man and hot cross buns from Granny Emmy, an egg containing pigs from Frank and one with a purse from me, a white cock from Nurse, a nest of sugar plover's eggs from Jack Isherwood, box of chocolate cigarettes from Moey, an egg with soldiers from Grandad. Frank to military service with the men. C said his Easter hymn very nicely.

June 1. A big field day, got up for the benefit of Mr Haldane and the Imperial Press delegates. We found ourselves in the middle of a terrific battle, Aldershot supposed to be evacuating and the other side attacking. We looked down over a big valley and miles and miles of country, and the big cannons booming off all round us were awful. C and I hated them, and the guns in the trenches made a fearful noise too. A very fine sight and horribly realistic. At the end we waited to see the March Past which was nice and peaceful.

June 3. Poor C stung by a wasp or bee and very much frightened because he remembered it had said in the Children's Nature

Book that stings were poisonous! However the blue bag afforded relief, he lay down for half an hour. We had tea in the garden early and then all went out in the punt on the canal.

July 1. The first time C had been out to play alone with children. He enjoyed it very much till tea time, when a hot little figure suddenly appeared at the drawing-room door, calling for Mummy very agitated, but he played again with them after tea.

July 9. The distant sound of troops and drums returning from manoeuvres. Frank did not get in till just on 7, covered with dust and tired after twenty miles march and *four nights out*.

July 26. Blériot flew across the Channel yesterday in 37 minutes in his aeroplane, the first man to fly across.

July 28. To London. To Selfridges Stores in Oxford St to see the BLERIOT MONOPLANE. It is on view for four days only, thousands going daily to see it. There was something strangely thrilling and yet pathetic at the sight of this frail looking little weird birdlike machine. I looked and looked and came back twice more to look again. It looked so slight, the framework, so amateur and rough the outstretched wings, so simple in construction and so small—to think of it risking wind and weather and ever getting across from France to England. The official time given was 31 miles in 43 minutes, the length of the machine 26 feet 3 inches, span of wings 25 feet 7 inches, the engine 20 horse-power. Wooden frame of wings composed of ash covered with water-proof linen.

August 28. Nurse weeded paths and I beds and in afternoon picked a box full of filberts out of garden. Every day we have had delicious black grapes out of the greenhouse, they should last us all through next month too.

October 1. Going to Hawley Hill we met the Empress Eugénie driving. A very handsome alert looking old lady with keen dark eyes and white hair. A carriage and pair and black liveries.

October 2. We dined at the Colonel's. I recognized one of our own dinner napkins, sent there by mistake by the laundry, and bore it off triumphantly!

November 5. [At Marple.] C went out on Dolly, the little dapple grey pony Mr Isherwood has so kindly hired for him, Dobson running by the side with a leading rein and Nanny panting behind. After tea, C dressed up as Guy Fawkes and Daddy let off Bengal lights.

November 6. In the afternoon we drove in the waggonette with Frank's Mother to Stockport. It struck me afresh how quaint it all is, the steep cobbled streets, the women wearing shawls over their heads and clogs on their feet. It might well be some old foreign town that people made a great fuss about. After tea, C dictated a story called *The Adventures of Mummy and Daddy*, chiefly about himself!

December 27. C very full of who shall be asked to his party, especially desiring some of 'the goodlooking girls all in white with mittens' at Mrs F's party!

1910. January 13. [At Ventnor with Emily.] Ventnor just the same and full of memories. Last time I was here, seven years ago, was just before I was married. What a happy seven years it has been.

Letter from Frank to Kathleen, written while she was still at Ventnor:

I always begin to lose confidence in myself when I haven't you to back me up. I am glad you like our 'busy' life. I was rather afraid you didn't and wished sometimes to be more settled and comfortable. I am afraid it is only what books call your 'sweet sunny nature' that has made the last seven years always very happy ones, but really when I look round I come to the conclusion that most men have their drawbacks and that I am not such a bad husband after all.

January 26. Travelled up to London with Mrs K. She has been with regiments and mixed up with the Army since she was two, so no wonder she is military to her finger tips; and *I* have only been with it two years and despised it the rest of my life from a society point of view, and can hardly be expected to be 'like a soldier's wife', though I couldn't help being secretly delighted to hear her say I wasn't!!

February 12. Saw the Army airship up in the sky. (Col C in charge, though of course we could not see him!)

February 26. Frank heard that all three of his pictures have been hung at the Old Dudley Art Society. Very satisfactory.

March 15. Mrs M is *bent* on getting up a subscription dance to which *none* of us want to go, but just because she is 'Mrs General' we have *got* to go! I hate the whole class of military bigwigs and the ridiculous way they are played up to.

March 16. The secretary of Dudley wrote to say Frank *had sold one of his pictures for four guineas*. Feel so pleased! Tried the curdled milk cure for him but for some reason the milk would not curdle!

(*Ever since the Boer War, Frank had suffered, on and off, from the after-effects of enteric fever.*)

March 28. Christopher had a cold but we played William Rufus in the wood, because Daddy had seen the stone in the New Forest recording where he was killed. Then, having shot Rufus, (Teddy Bear), we became the old charcoal burners who found him and carried him to the summer-house, where he was buried—the summer-house being really Winchester Cathedral.

April 9. Frank and I bicycled to North Camp and caught the 1.45 to Gomshall. Jack's cottage is about three quarters of a mile from the station. He has just taken it and furnished it and has it for three years, *Orchard Cottage*. It has a large dining-room and pretty little bow-windowed sitting-room looking down the garden. In the garden is an old timbered cottage dating from 1214, used formerly as the village prison. Jack intends using it as a sort of summer house. It is only two or three minutes' walk from the Duke of Northumberland's park. There are the weirdest old spanish chestnut trees looking like bad human beings transformed. The park is lovely.

(*Jack Isherwood had previously been living in London, sharing rooms with Cyril Scott. Orchard Cottage at Shere was now to become his home; later he bought it and lived there with his wife, Freda, and their son Thomas until his death.*)

April 12. Mama still undecided about maids. There are two in hand, a rather young one, seemed capable and quick, but Mama was afraid her appearance might be a responsibility, she has very noticeable hair. The second belonged to the thoroughly grand lady's maid type, used to travelling. Quite young also and a perfectly odious manner, I thought.

May 4. After lunch, Christopher and his Grandfather went out along the Common and had the luck to see *an aeroplane in the air*. Christopher recognized it from having seen pictures of Blériot's and was much impressed. He described it as having wings and a long body and rather like Blériot's. He and Grandad very excited as they had neither of them seen one before.

May 6. The papers this morning announce the King's illness, an attack of bronchitis which seems to be very severe. We drove back to the hotel with Frank's Mother for dinner. It seems to me *so* pathetic the way they cling to us but unfortunately Frank is

345

getting very tired of hotel meals and I rather long for evenings at home. His Mother strikes me as very feeble and her memory, poor dear, *so* bad. I think his Father is really better for the change.

May 7. Heard of *the King's death* when we were called at 7, which took place in the most tragically sudden way a little before 11 pm last night. It seems almost paralysing and a terrible loss to the country. He has shown such infinite tact and savoir faire and always on the side of peace. The Prince of Wales gives one the feeling of being feeble and hating his position, none of the tact of his Father and, they say, obstinate.

(The funeral of Edward VII was on May 20. Both Kathleen and Frank saw it—Kathleen from a balcony, Frank from the side of the street which he and his men were lining. Frank thought Queen Alexandra looked "quite dazed but wonderfully young and handsome." Kathleen writes that the coffin, "covered with white satin, rose colour and purple, looked too gay, I thought," but she was touched by the sight of the Highlander leading the King's little dog.)

May 22. We saw a misty big blurred star after dinner, all that is visible of Halley's Comet.

May 29. We motored to Shere, had tea with Jack. Cyril Scott, his great friend, there. Thought him very conscious and bad manners, the usual long hair of musicians but healthier appearance. Jack's walls covered now with Japanese prints. They look very well but I fancy I might personally find them monotonous.

(In his autobiography, My Years of Indiscretion, *Cyril Scott tells of the various diets and disciplines which he and Jack tried while they were living together: simple vegetarianism was followed by the Fletcher cure, the cold-water cure, exercises, fasting, and the herb teas of Benjamin Foster, so it was no wonder he looked healthy!)*

May 30. By three o'clock, Frank's Father and Mother appeared. There is something most pathetic about them both but one could wish they were a little more independent! I don't want them to cut short their one yearly holiday, but it is very difficult to go on every day giving up so much time, yet unless we do they seem disappointed.

May 31. Really the Army IS . . .! 'Derby Leave' is a recognized thing yet this year can't be had, and we had settled to go off for three days' sketching at Winchester tomorrow. The change would have done Frank good. They offer leave next week when Mama is coming, it *is* vexing. You can never make a *single* plan in the Army without having it upset and never can be sure of anything—indeed that is the *only* thing you *can* be sure of.

June 14. Lovely morning but a disappointing day. First, la cuisine dit que sa homme veut beaucoup le marie dans septembre. Then the list of the seven selected for the Cheshire Constabulary appeared in the Times and Frank was not amongst them. And lastly Fletcher, much the best soldier servant we have ever had, is going to be bought out and is going into business.

(*The habit of speaking French—usually as incorrect as the above —to conceal information from the servants was a characteristic vulgarity of the period; both Emily and Kathleen were guilty of it. What is baffling here is the question, Why does Kathleen use French in her diary? She must have supposed that Nanny was reading it. But surely, if the cook was being pressed by her young man to get married in September, Nanny would have known all about it anyway. More of Kathleen's secretiveness!*
Frank was now seriously considering leaving the Army altogether. His application for a post with the Cheshire constabulary was the first of several attempts to find civilian work.)

July 17. To call at the Forbes' and ask Mrs F and Arthur to tea. We picked strawberries for Arthur. There are only a few left and

347

Christopher was very inhospitable and I am afraid the art of 'giving in' and 'giving up' is quite unknown to him. He is, besides this, *jealous* which distresses me.

(*Arthur Forbes is the first subject of* The History of My Friends, *which was begun sometime during the winter of 1910–11. It is a tiny book made of cut-down sheets of notepaper fastened together with a pin. It is in Kathleen's script and presumably written at Christopher's dictation. But did Christopher literally dictate it? It reads like an attempt at collaboration between a child and an adult, in which each is trying to mimic the tone of the other:*

I first met Arthur Forbes in December 1909 when we returned from Frimley to Marple. He was just going to be four. He made up all sorts of wonderful things that he meant to do when he was five, just as if five was when you were grown up. I have not seen him since he was five, as the regiment his Daddy was in had to go away to Alderney, so I do not know if he finds himself feeling a great deal older. When we went for a walk we generally had fights, because he used to find all sorts of grublets and sticks that I wanted, he rootled in the dirt and always saw them first and then we used to fight when the Nannies weren't looking. I am afraid the fighting consisted in snatchings and tears. . . . I have got some laurel bushes in my garden and sometimes we had games there too, we each had our own branches. Now that Arthur is gone I begin to feel very sorry and perhaps I shall put up a monument to him and hang it on his branch where he got.)

July 24. Frank amused Christopher drawing him little figures representing Anne Boleyn etc on Tower Green—the scene of her execution (this painted round the three sides of an old bootbox).

July 29. Delightful to be in dear Oxford again. Mama in purple velvet teagown and band of sparkling violet in her hair looked a perfect picture and so young.

August 12. [At Marple.] It cleared as the day went on and the hills looked very beautiful. The towers and chimneys at New Mills with their background of hills form a group far more beautiful than the towers of San Gimignano that people rave about!!

August 13. Caught the 12.55 to Disley and then went a pilgrimage up the dear wellknown road to the quarry with the wonderful view. Sat there some time among the heather. It always seemed to feel like the top of the world there. And then I actually went to Wyberslegh and saw Mrs Cooper. The family were all away and she was very anxious I should go over the house but of course I didn't do that, but the dear garden seemed so gay. Then I walked back along over the Ridge with the beautiful view that was once so familiar and now seems so long ago. Glad I went again to Wyberslegh.

December 3. [In London.] Went with Frank in morning to see the Post Impressionists at the Grafton, in which the select few see marvels and the others jeer! The first room has Manets and the others even wilder exponents, indeed a great many of the pictures seemed to me sheer impertinence. Frank liked them enormously and stayed on to gloat!

In October, Frank and Kathleen went on a trip to Italy, Bosnia and Dalmatia. From Banja Luka they brought back "an absurd little crockery horse which was also a whistle"; it is the only relic of Christopher's childhood which he has kept to this day.

In December, according to The Baby's Progress, *"his Father started teaching him French words and also drilling and continued his instruction in reading by publishing a paper called 'The Toy-Drawer Times' every morning, illustrated!" What Kathleen calls drilling was nothing military, just physical exercises. Frank himself exercised every morning in his dressing room, naked except for his undershorts. He let Christopher come in and watch him. Christopher can remember taking a pleasure which was definitely erotic in the sight of his father's muscles tensing and bulging within his well-knit body, and in the virile smell of his sweat. But when Christopher began to masturbate (which he did while at Frimley), his fantasies weren't about Frank. He imagined himself lying wounded on a battlefield with his clothes partly torn off him, being tended by a woman; Kathleen, no doubt, in disguise. The mood of this fantasy was exhibitionistic; Christopher's own nakedness was what excited him. His "wounds" were painless.*

Frank kept up The Toy-Drawer Times *in various forms until Christopher went away to school in 1914; it evolved into a kind of comic strip. Christopher can remember how Frank used to come back from the barracks in the late afternoon (this would have been during the Limerick period) still in uniform but with his tunic unbuttoned and his pipe in his mouth—no longer a figure of parade-ground authority. The soldier who was his orderly would bring in a bunch of official papers for his signature. Having signed them, Frank would turn the duplicate copies over and begin drawing on their backs. He could draw very fast and also write in block capitals (which were easier for Christopher to read) as quickly as most people could write longhand. He told Christopher the story as he did this. The stories were mostly adaptations from Dumas, Henty, Stevenson, Conan Doyle, H. G. Wells.*

As a teacher, Frank was fairly patient. But sometimes he would fly into rages with Christopher and shake him till his teeth rattled. Christopher may have been frightened a little, but this too is a sensual memory for him: his surrender to the exciting strength of the big angry man.

By March 1911, Kathleen had to face the fact that she was again pregnant. This dismayed her, and with good reason. She was now forty-two. Her first childbirth had been delayed and difficult. And this seemed the worst moment to have another child, Frank's future being so uncertain. However, she soon made up her mind to accept the inevitable.

· ·

March 31. Christopher had a special tea party, mostly of his own choosing. He insisted on reciting and got very excited and I am afraid rather forward and objectionable, though of course it amused the onlookers, except me.

April 2. About 10.30 heard or thought I heard coming down the road some *very extra* heavy and noisy motor van, far louder than any ordinary one or even a train. Stood watching at the drawing room window for something to appear along the road when suddenly overhead swooped a huge black thing from behind the house and flew very rapidly in a direct line over the fields making a dreadful humming! Flew screaming to Frank and Christopher who thought I had gone mad! *The first aeroplane we had any of us seen so near in motion.*

April 25. [At Shere.] Jack Isherwood, very full of the perfect health produced by the use of a stomach pump once a week.

May 1. Christopher and I walked to Mr Penrose's arriving very punctually at 10.30 to SCHOOL, his first school! It consists of a class of five little boys and is only to last for an hour daily, Mr Penrose having undertaken teaching them to write and read and do the simplest of sums. C can write quite nicely for his age but cannot read yet, though he can spell a great many words. It seemed such a great day, this start, and as if it was a final farewell to babyhood. I fetched him again and he was in the highest spirits and delighted at the thought of going daily. Brian Wynne, Reggie Bullock, Edward Lewis and Jack Biddulph make up the class.

May 4. We saw the new Lebaudy Army airship (a huge thing like a monster caterpillar) making its trial trip. Thought it turned in rather an uncertain way. Finally it appeared to descend somewhere at Farnborough. They say it is over 300 feet long.

May 5. This morning is the account of the total wreck of the airship we saw flying last night. In descending, control was lost and its huge carcase crashed over a house at Farnborough, quite enveloping it. Mercifully none of the men in it were badly hurt.

(*The wreck attracted crowds of souvenir hunters. One of these brought Christopher a bit of the silvery rubbery envelope which he had cut off with his penknife. Christopher kept it for many years.*)

May 6. Fine and sunny. Took C to school and fetched him. He came out in great spirits, each child with a piece of paper announcing their place in class, and he was the top!

May 9. Read Christopher Lamb's version of Midsummer Night's Dream, he had seen pictures of the play in the illustrated papers and anything to do with plays he is wild about.

May 16. The new (and hideous) statue of Queen Victoria in front of Buckingham Palace to be unveiled with great ceremony today.

May 17. Frank off to London, the first day he has had off for ages. Sent me a wire from Waterloo to say he is *gazetted as Major* today. So glad. Frank back about seven. The Nursery decorated in his honour and the dolls and teddy bears in their best with devices 'Welcome to the Major', 'Congratulations to Major and Mrs Isherwood and their little boy' etc!

May 24. C. to tea with Jack Biddulph and came home in triumph, the paper snake which J.B. *would* frighten him with and which he threatened to destroy if it was thrown on him again, he had torn in two. I got in London one of those compressible wire snakes which spring out when let go of, and trying to get used to this has prevented him minding the smaller one.

(*Kathleen herself was terrified of snakes, and she must have communicated her fear to Christopher. He had a recurring night-*

mare in which he struck at a huge cobra but failed to hurt it; the cobra then followed him along streets, through houses from front door to back and even—this was his last desperate line of defense —through the ranks of Frank's soldiers lined up on parade. It never caught him, of course; if it had, he would presumably have died in his sleep from shock. As a schoolboy he read with horrified fascination Kipling's "Rikki-Tikki-Tavi" and Conan Doyle's "The Speckled Band," also the scene of Cleopatra's suicide with the asp; when younger, he had believed that she actually swallowed it and that it bit her inside, which seemed to him superlatively loathsome. After he had grown up, one of his friends assured him that his fear was nothing but a repressed longing to submit to anal intercourse. "You want it to crawl into your arse." They were all amateur Freudians in those days, and such theories were part of their group-humor. Still, even a joke can point the way to a cure.

Cure or no cure, when Christopher later settled in California and found himself actually exposed to reptile life for the first time, he wasn't unduly repelled by it. He even set up housekeeping with a young man who kept nonvenomous snakes as pets, and soon he was handling them with only mild distaste. If he found a dead rattlesnake, run over by a car on the road, he would dare himself to pick it up by the tail and throw it into the bushes. With his friend he sometimes visited a snake pit where the owner would grab a live rattler, holding it fast behind the head, carry it over to the barrier and offer to let it lick your bare arm with its tongue. His friend didn't mind at all; but Christopher never felt quite ready to pass this final test.)

June 15. To see Dr Wheeler. From various tappings and soundings he concludes that all is as it should be and the inmate undoubtedly alive. Said medicine should be able to prevent the much greater nervousness I feel this time.

June 27. C. very nervous state about thunder, otherwise he is looking well. I wish he could hold his own better and retaliate when the boys tease. Boys really are little fiends but he seems to like school very much, though as far as playing is concerned he is much happier with his plays and his theatre made out of a Quaker Oats box. Anything to do with the stage or theatre seems to interest him more than anything in the world.

Toward the end of July 1911, a seemingly trivial affair of red tape and conflicting interests developed into a grave domestic crisis for Kathleen and Frank.

The Regiment was due to be transferred to Ireland and stationed at Limerick immediately after its September maneuvers. Kathleen was expecting her baby late in September or early in October; therefore it was out of the question for her to make the move at that time. Frank planned to get leave, so that they wouldn't have to go till later. The Colonel said, however, that he must have a major with him when they settled into the barracks at Limerick. Only two majors were available, a Major Ashton and Frank. Major Ashton was the senior, so he had first choice of leave. He said that he wanted his leave first, thus obliging Frank to go to Limerick—or to "send in his papers," resigning from the Regiment. That was his only alternative.

The situation seemed to prove how right Kathleen had been about Army life; its caprices were intolerable. Only a dedicated professional or a carefree bachelor could go on indefinitely accepting them. Frank couldn't live from day to day as he had done before he married. However much he might still like being a nomad, he now had two children as well as Kathleen to think of. He couldn't submit unquestioningly to the Colonel, saying, "His will is our peace." Although Frank had never known any other life than soldiering, he wasn't a single-minded soldier. For he was now daring to hope that he might become a "serious" artist, which would hardly be possible as long as he stayed in the service. He had realized all this for some time. He had become used to the idea of leaving the Army. Yet this crisis found him emotionally unready.

It is a great compliment to Emily that he consulted her about

354

the problem. Emily quite rose to the occasion. She advised him definitely to resign. Her reasons: the expense of a move to Ireland, the uncertainty of conditions in Ireland because of impending Home Rule and consequent trouble with Ulster, the wisdom of entering civilian life while he was still young enough to get employment. Frank's retirement from the Army would be in Emily's own interests, of course. If he had a steady job and was settled in one place in England, Kathleen would be that much the more available to her.

But now Kathleen herself was confused and deeply disturbed:

August 4. Mama and he think it is the right moment to take the plunge *if it is to be taken,* but it seems so awful that I should be the cause of it all. It seems inconsistent, when I have often been so horrid about soldiering, that I begin to realize the fascination of the life, even to see there is a certain excitement in *not* knowing what will turn up next! Frank is simply saintly about it. I know he feels it a desperate wrench though he won't say so—no longer to belong to the Regiment, the daily meeting and working, men one has always known, the feeling of being one family. There is charm even in the grumbling (for which they certainly have cause!). Though, apart from me, Frank *declares* he is sure it is the wisest moment to go, all the circumstances considered. The only comfort is, Mama and he are of the same opinion, and she seldom makes an error of judgment.

Letter from Emily to Kathleen, August 6:

I quite understand your feelings, darling, inconsistent as they may appear to your dear self, and most extremely sympathize with your regret at the thought of never seeing Frank in uniform again!! (Though I fancy they wear it, don't they, at Regimental dinners.) Most of all I feel for you about the papers having to go in so soon, one hates being hurried, unless one wants a thing desperately like I did to leave Bury, a step which even the poor D never regretted afterwards, though he flung a book across the room years afterwards because it spoke disrespectfully of Bury!!

It is most trying for you darling that this question should have arisen just now, but *do do* try to be your own calm and sensible self, for the sake of *us all* and for yourself. Remember you probably don't see things *quite in focus now*. We are all trying to act to the best of our judgement, one can't do more, we must leave the rest in higher hands. Take [word illegible, presumably a homeopathic medicine] any time in the day, no matter when, if you feel the least tearful. Don't keep anything from me. It is the worst thing in the world to keep things to yourself.

I do think, as you say, it is wonderful the way in which Frank has entered into his duties. I think his *personality* will always be a strong force in his life, and when you think of his artistic temperament and of his upbringing, the way in which he has fulfilled all his duties is nothing less than marvellous. C.W. ought to do something with such parents and such a grandfather above all and greatgrandfather on your side!

Early in August, the transport strike which had begun in June seemed likely to grow into a general strike. Kathleen was now at Marple, but Frank had to stay at Frimley because the Regiment was being held in readiness for action. Then the situation eased for the moment, and Frank joined her. On the fourteenth he sent in his papers and began writing a children's story about Christopher's two Buster Brown dolls, Bobbie and Albert. That evening he was recalled by telegram to Aldershot, since more violence was feared. On August 16 Kathleen records that soldiers had fired on a crowd in Liverpool and killed two men. On August 17 the Regiment was ordered up to London; they bivouacked in Regent's Park. In a letter written on the nineteenth, Frank says: "This is really rather a good finale to one's service as it makes one long to be out of it and not subject to be let in for such utter boredom again." He adds that he came away in such a hurry that he forgot his sketch book and had been reduced to reading Seton Merriman's The Velvet Glove; "I never could bear late Merriman." A day or two later they were sent to Nottingham and quartered in a skating rink. "We passed through a crowd who booed us in a goodhumoured sort of way." From Nottingham Frank went to Doncaster, then to Trent and Alfreton, always in pursuit of rock-throwing crowds and other disturbances which melted away before they arrived. Windows were broken in signal boxes all along the line and there were no signalmen or lights. Frank remarks that his men are quite happy as long as they have a football to kick around: "It quite frightens me sometimes when I see that all men except myself share this extraordinary taste." His comment on the ending of the strike is: "Now we hear that it was all for nothing and that the Masters have caved in. It is I am afraid a great triumph for socialism and we shall be in the hands of the mob who will strike whenever they don't get what they want." Frank was accustomed to say that "a soldier has no politics," and no doubt he sincerely believed this was true. In a war, he was fighting "the King's enemies." In putting down civil unrest he was "restoring law and order." No need for the soldier to ask who the King's friends were or whose law and order was being restored!

While strike-hunting, Frank charmingly demonstrated his political muddle-headedness by writing a story for Christopher which is not merely anti-establishment but downright revolutionary:

Mrs Nanny looked out of the window in the early morning. Good gracious, she said with a scream, there are pigs in the garden and they have eaten all the gooseberries and carrots. Whatever will the Master say? Master Christopher jumped out of bed and rushed to the window and there he saw an old Lady Pig in a blue bonnet sitting up in the middle of the bed with six little pigiwigs round her, each with a carrot sandwich in its hand and drinking the most delicious gooseberry wine out of tin mugs. Mrs Nanny leant out of the window and said shoo, shoo, go away. Go away indeed said the old Lady Pig and she got up and instead of going away she walked straight into the house with the six little pigs after her, climbed up the stairs with many grunts and groans and came straight into the nursery without so much as knocking. Good morning, Nurse, she said condescendingly, I'm Mrs Porkington Pigiwig of Ham House, Cambridge, and these are my six children: Nellie and Aggie, Susan and Charles and Arthur and this is my youngest, John Willie. Mrs Nanny and Master Christopher were too flabbergasted to speak, and untying her bonnet strings Mrs Porkington Pigiwig threw herself back into a chair and smiled affably. Kiss your little friend, dears, she said, and to Master Christopher's horror, all the little pigs advanced towards him and gave him a great smacking kiss with their great mouths and then began to dance round him in a ring. Children claim children, said Mrs Porkington Pigiwig, and I like to see it. After all, we were all young once.

(The story goes on to tell how there were sausages for breakfast and how Mrs Pig called Christopher a savage and a cannibal and how she told her sad story of her husband's loss and her escape with the children from the Cambridge sausage-machine.)

September 9. Frank found a very good art school at Reading which he will be able to attend during autumn.

September 20. Invitation to Frank to farewell dinner to him by Regiment tomorrow.

September 21. Frank to farewell dinner, wearing his uniform for the last time. A desperately trying evening for him.

September 22. Christopher introduced to the idea that it would be very nice for Nanny to have a little baby to look after, as it would 'keep her so amused and happy' and these little garments he considers may be hopeful signs that we shall have one sent us, if we pray for it.

September 24. Am so *desperately* sorry. I should have liked to do one more station and seen what Ireland was like and I know Frank is simply *hating* leaving though he does not say much.

September 26. The Colonel said how sorry he was we were not coming to Ireland. I said so was I and what a muddle the whole thing seemed to have been. Felt very severe to him. He might either have done without a major or insisted on Major Ashton taking second leave, as in the end he has had to do. He asked hurriedly if Frank was coming to see the Regiment off tomorrow, but I said I thought there was a limit to what he could bear.

September 28. Frank started going to the life class at Reading.

September 29. Christopher very excited at hearing of the arrival of the Plumptree baby and that I had seen Dr A. there and had said I hoped he would soon bring us one. He thought this such a 'board hint' that Dr A. really might, perhaps.

September 30. Woke up just before daybreak to feel myself very wet and wondered if this could possibly be the breaking of the water. Dr came at midday and thought nothing likely to occur for at least another week. Increased ache and dragging pain after tea. Played poker patience till nine thirty. Pains by then were every five minutes. Frank's presence the greatest support and comfort. Nurse helped me to bed and then F went for the doctor and sat holding my hand until he and a sister from the Cottage Hospital arrived. A sharp time of pain followed but I had whiffs of chloroform till it was quite unbearable and then I went right off and a son was actually born by 1.15 October 1st, rather a disappointment that it was not the longed-for daughter, however Frank prefers sons. Dr and Sister left soon after two and Frank slept in my room, Nurse taking the baby, a dear little lusty noisy thing. *Deeply* thankful it was all over and so quickly and no complications or stitching. C came to my bed when it was all over and was introduced to his new brother, with whom he was delighted.

October 2. The saint for October 1 is ST REMIGIUS, Bishop of Rheims. I think Remigius would make such a delightful second name, it sounds so like foreign churches and a tour abroad, and yet nice and strong. Richard Remigius could not fail to make his way in the world, but Frank thinks the baby would not like it.

(Richard was actually given the second name of Graham, after his godfather and cousin Sir William Graham Greene, who had an important post at the Admiralty. Graham Greene the future novelist, then a small boy of Christopher's age, was also a cousin.)

October 6. Frank not very well, saw Dr again. I do wish he could get a good change. The Regiment going and the Baby coming all combined have been *very* trying, I know. I begin to think how much nicer a son is than a daughter, who would probably have been very modern and not what I like!!

October 7. Nasty grey damp day but such a happy birthday all the same. In the afternoon Mama came to tea and my 'youngest' son came and snuggled and grunted in bed beside me and brought me a little lock of his hair done up in tissue paper as a birthday offering. I had no idea a second baby could feel so unspeakably precious.

October 8. Most glorious autumn morning all sparkling and sunny, but had the worst day since I was in bed, feeling so weak and worried. Nurse came in and said how ill the Major looked, which of course upset me dreadfully, and then the Dr saw him and thought it was due to giving up his work and my illness and I felt as if I had quite ruined his life and I couldn't help crying and crying. Frank came and sat by me and was so kind and cheery and said he really so far hadn't missed the Regiment at all and liked going to the studio far better than to Barracks and that it was absurd to say his upset came from worry.

October 9. A bomb from Ireland this morning, a letter from the Colonel enclosing communication from War Office. Frank's retirement not accepted unless he goes to the Militia for five years.

This means a month's training each August and might interfere with his taking another job, also it is not easy as a major to get a nomination in a militia. However the Colonel has put in for leave for him till November 30th which gives time to make enquiries and decide, and he will get his pay as Major all the time, so, after all, his staying here with me will not even prevent his still going to Ireland and I need never feel it is my or the Baby's fault. Am so very very thankful. Frank went to talk matters over with Col Kilpatrick. He has been through so much I think he hardly knows if he wants to go back or not, now.

October 11. Darling Richard came and snuggled quite a long time. I wouldn't change my new son for any daughter in the world.

October 12. Letters from Colonel Broughton (of the York and Lancaster Militia) and Major Clemson, the first to say no vacancy in their battalion and both to say, under the altered state of affairs, why not stay on with the Regiment.

October 16. Frank to London to War Office. The Military Secretary sympathetic as regards his claims not to have to go to Militia, promised to push his case. If it fails, we go back to Regiment and Limerick, if not, Frank retires on his pension.

October 17. Richard out for his first airing in the garden accompanied by Christopher, who decorated his brother with flowers.

October 28. Richard is looking splendid, a nice white skin now, dark blue eyes with darker rims, Frank's mouth and the family cleft in his chin! The nose, which is very pronounced, is considered like mine!

October 29. In a coat and skirt my figure wonderfully slim! Frank quite surprised at its appearance!

November 3. Frank to London to the Dudley Gallery private view, has five pictures hung.

November 7. Despairing letter from Major Ashton to Frank. He says Limerick is the most Godforsaken dirty hole he had ever seen, that he is absolutely miserable, nothing to do and surroundings in which a decent-minded English pig would be ashamed to live.

November 8. Letter from Major Clemson. He had seen the Military Secretary at the War Office and it seems, in spite of the very strong case Frank had, they won't let him off going to the Militia if he resigns. So this decides it and we go to Limerick—and after all the 'wear and tear to mind and body' we are just where we would be had we quietly been given first leave at the beginning of things. Felt very depressed all day, so many plans to be made, and things to meet and 'lions to pass'. Limerick, apart from the distance from Mama and civilization, does *not* sound delightful.

15

*Now that Frank was to stay in the Army, they found them-
selves under pressure again. There was much to be done, and
time was short. Kathleen was still suffering from the aftereffects
of childbirth and often felt "bruised, tired and tearful," but she
had to keep on her feet.*

*Richard was christened on November 14. Frank played Handel
on the organ at the beginning and the end of the service. Richard
"cried quite properly, just when he should." Kathleen notes that
his godparents gave him a silver mug, a check and two silver
spoons—"so the darling has done well."*

*On November 27 Frank went to visit his parents at Marple, on
his way to Ireland. So Kathleen was left alone with barely two
weeks in which to get ready for the move from Frimley Lodge.
On November 30, Frank was already in Limerick. He wrote to
her from the so-called New Barracks:*

My first impressions are rather favourable. The station is quite
near barracks. You go along a typical Irish street, passing Perry
Park on the way which is rather like a decayed London square.
The barracks are very quaint and old-fashioned and rather attractive and I can't see that they are in such a bad state, however
I haven't seen much of them yet. Everyone seems pleased to see
me back.

. .

On December 6, Kathleen took Christopher up to London to spend an unforgettable day. In the morning they visited the Christmas sideshows in some of the big stores. There was a mechanized model of London in the sixteenth century: coaches and sedan chairs moving across the frozen Thames, and people skating, and an ox being roasted over a fire on the ice. And there was Lilliput Land, over which the sun kept rising and setting, with the houses lighting up at night. In the afternoon, Kathleen and Christopher went to the variety show at the Coliseum. This was his first experience of a theater. Its high point was a playlet called The Slum Angel. Seymour Hicks and Ellaline Terriss were in it, but what mattered to Christopher was that a real motorcar and a coach with live horses were driven onto the stage. Christopher can remember his almost frantic delight at this. Why was it so wonderful to him? Perhaps because it seemed to destroy the barrier between everyday life and make-believe. If this *could* happen in a theater, then anything was possible anywhere!

(Christopher has an earlier memory which is even more exciting. It is connected with some theatrical show at Frimley in which Frank was appearing. Christopher wasn't allowed to stay up for it, but they let him peep into the hall just before the performance began and see the audience and the lighted curtain. What he so vividly remembers is the thrill this curtain gave him, with its infinite promise of what it would reveal when it rose.)

On December 13, Kathleen supervised the move. It took place in a downpour of rain. She writes in her diary: "Left without one pang of regret, feeling only sorry to think I shall not wake up any more to the view out of my bedroom!"

On December 21 Kathleen went up to Marple, to spend Christmas with John, Elizabeth and Jack Isherwood and Christopher and Richard.

Kathleen's 1912 diary is the first of her diaries without quotations or other matter of an inspirational or romantic nature. Instead, there are names and addresses of Irish neighbors and lists of *officers and their wives who have been invited to dinner on certain dates. Kathleen seems to be concerned only with her obligations as an Army Wife, and painfully conscious of calls and invitations which haven't yet been returned.*

January 1. New Year's Day, a momentous day! Left Marple soon after 9.30 with rather a sinking heart at leaving the children behind, just when Richard is in that state of adorable babyhood, changing so from week to week. The paper said 'smooth to moderate' but for all that a *very choppy crossing*. Mothersill remedy a great success. Frank met me on the pier at Kingstown. Walked across to Rosses Hotel, clean and friendly. It all feels strangely foreign and incapable. Everyone so leisurely and talkative.

January 2. Rosses Hotel great success, kept by father and two sons. One son has a farm outside and supplies them with milk, eggs, butter and poultry. The father is in the hall and talks to anyone who will listen. Bill fifteen shillings for bed, dinner and breakfast. Left Dublin 9.15, flat green meadowland and rather dull journey except for passing Kildare and getting good view of the old church with its round tower, the first I have seen. Arrived Limerick 1.15. Jolty slow train to Barrington St. Limerick is rather a picturesque and dirty-looking old place with many big Georgian houses.

January 3. It appears that yesterday was a fine day in Limerick, a fact I had not realized till I saw the rain today! It went on more or less without ceasing, sometimes heavy, sometimes merely a thick wet mist. Mrs Mott came round in morning and we went together over some of the town houses. All with cavernous kitchens and mysteriously dark, and a rabbit warren of places for which there seems no particular use. The servants supposed to sleep in dark roomy cupboards, the only outlook or ventilation being into the kitchen itself. The upstair living-rooms fine and large, two on each floor. The backyards of unutterable gloom.

Mrs Mott has lodgings in a house the size of a palace and the paper peeling and the blinds torn.

January 5. Have now been over sixteen houses!

On January 7, Kathleen saw Roden House, her seventeenth, and this, as she wrote later, proved to be the very one she wanted:

There wasn't *a doubt of it* from the first moment, when the woman who had the keys came across with a shawl over her head and let us in mysteriously through a gate in the wall, followed by other shawled people waiting to see what we should do! High grey walls bounded the house on two sides, covered with creepers —really the backs of the cottages in the lane, but only one had a window on the garden, discreetly wired over, where the nice peasant (who had the keys) lived.

(Yes indeed, Kathleen really does write "peasant"! Is this the romantic influence of Yeats and Synge? Partly, no doubt. Partly also an indication of her willingness to be pleased with her sur-roundings. She wants to picture these town dwellers as retainers on a phantom feudal estate.)

In front of the house were prim little beds with box borders and a fountain and an apple tree, and a long glass verandah ran the whole length of the house and above were seven windows in a long row. Inside, it was the quaintest place. Downstairs only a kitchen, servants' hall, pantry, dining-room. But upstairs it was all surprises—little passages and endless doors running in and out, giving one the impression of a network of rooms, some quite a good size, you hardly knew where you were—so unexpectedly did rooms thrust out in all directions, going right through to another lane at the back, looking to the Barracks, in the midst of the most slummy cottages where everyone threw everything out of the window!

I suppose it must have been much larger at some time, as

evidently blocked-up doorways must have led into the adjoining cottages and been part of the original house. And it belonged to two old Miss Warmleightons who had lived here from their childhood when the Military Road was nothing but fields, and instead of the big Technical School nothing but a big orchard led away from the upper garden, but still the steps are left leading down into the onetime orchard, and the old iron gate and the square pillars and urns guarding it. I have always wanted *urns* on pillars and an old iron gate! And the Technical School is quite a long way off. There was something very romantic too and un-obvious about it all, and so unlike the regular soldiering house. Indeed, no soldier has ever discovered it.

January 27. Bright and sunny but very cold. News that the furniture had reached Cork but I suppose it won't come on till Monday. We went for a lovely walk to Lax Weir over the fields, where a raised path above river and bogs winds away to the weir, lovely views of Limerick looking back, the cathedral tower etc and flat green meadows in every direction away into blue and misty distances.

January 30. Bright and frosty. The foreman from the Junior A and N turned up at 8.30 having come yesterday by sea and train direct. To our disgust a great many of our things were travelling loose, the rest packed in two smallish vans. The Foreman found some ruffianly looking men to help by about midday and the first van was there then. The men made a dreadful mess all over the house. Of course having to walk up the garden added to the dirt.

February 3. Mrs O'Callaghan and her box came in the afternoon. Her idea of cleaning her bedroom seems to be to sweep the dust out of it on to the stairs and she made all the floors shake as she walked. She is rather like an Irish cook in a book, but her amusing side would be much more apparent if she was someone else's cook not mine! She is a most imposing figure-head for any house and very impressive in a jetted bonnet with a rose and a velvet dolman and furs!

February 5. The dining room and my bedroom look so like home and pleasant. Mrs O'C came in course of the morning and she and Mrs Riley lunched off pigs feet and tea! Dreadful consternation, the water has stopped—this severe frost has frozen everything and in Barracks there is only water to be had in one of the wash-houses. We had to let the fire out in the range. Dined with the Bs. It was gay as we sallied forth from our new front door. The bells were pealing and the Technical School at the front of the garden all lights, and then to come home to a fire and one's own bed and pictures, no words can describe how nice it seemed!

February 11. Did not go out all day and spent a day of rest and leisure in our new drawing-room watching the birds from the sofa and reading. Such a cheerful lookout—the iron gate with the urns on the top of the crumbling pillars, and the spreading apple tree close to the window and the quaint box-bordered beds below, and trees in the distance and the Technical School and a church spire, and seagulls and blackbirds and sparrows and chaffinches all flying, hopping and making nice noises.

February 19. Dreadful day with smoke, the chimneys were bad yesterday but simply outrageous today. The Nursery and Drawing-room were unbearable and the whole place was covered with blacks. I took C to school and fetched him and we went into the town after. He is going to the Girls High School where there are also a few little boys. I like Miss Mercer the head, also Miss Croston in whose class C is.

February 21. Christopher very pleased with his school which I hope will make him much more independent and tomorrow he is going to walk there alone. When C came out of school we went down to the town and back along by the river to watch the loading and unloading of the ships.

February 22. Smoke, though less violent, continues to cover everything with smuts and the rooms are cloudy with smoke, it is *so* tiresome. C to school alone from the Technical School and walked back all the way by himself.

February 24. Bright day. Christopher has whole holiday on Saturdays. He and I went to do Sunday marketing and looked into the old Market which has sort of cloisters running all round supported by Doric pillars and behind which a great trade in old clothes is done, a great deal of colour and clusters of women in funny little donkey carts. The women manage to arrange their black shawls to give an almost eastern effect, often folding them across the lower part of their faces so that little more than their eyes are visible. Frank ran with the men in afternoon, 8 miles and came in about 150th out of 600. We again had to sit in the ante-room, the man never came to put the chimney pot on and the bells have all ceased ringing again!

March 3. Took C to the garrison service. In afternoon gave him commission to pick up all the dirty pieces of paper flying about the Technical yard and then we made a bonfire. Richard slept in his pram while F sketched the house. A fire in the drawing-room but it was not a success and smoked! Richard wore his first socks and shoes!

March 22. Doyle came to look at Chimneys. *He* declares they never smoked before! But seemed half-hearted as to any remedy, saying old flues were so difficult to deal with! I heard from Mrs Senior who lived here 8 or 9 years and I am sorry to say she gave the chimneys a very bad character and appeared to have suffered from them much as we do now!

March 25. C top of his class. Man about chimney has suggested another chimney top that the smoke came out of at the side only, or else taking the chimney to pieces which probably would be the most satisfactory thing, only it is a big order. F painted in the glass room out of the dining-room which is very pleasant. The hedges are all getting quite green and the pink of the apple blossom is beginning to show in the big old tree outside the window. I love the house.

March 28. A Mrs Townsend called just as the smoke was puffing out at its worst into the nursery where there was a fire and into the drawing-room where there wasn't one. Feel quite tired out with the chimneys and the gloom. Poor C's one idea being that if only it would smoke into the drawing-room and spare the nursery and Nanny's displeasure!

April 6. It really seems as if there was no end to the worries here and even going to London loses half its pleasure with that awful journey across the sea and now it seems as if, even if I go, I shall feel worried about the children all the time.

April 17. [In London.] Eclipse of the sun about midday. All down Sloane St saw people looking up at it through smoked glass. It was too dazzling for me to see anything, not having a glass. M and I to see *Bunty Pulls the Strings* by the Scotch Company. Coming back saw the crowds still waiting poor things outside the office of the White Star Line to get further news of those saved off the Titanic, but alas it is feared there were at least 1400 lost. The wreck was from floating iceberg off America.

April 27. In afternoon Frank drove me with his new trapper in the Col's cart to pay calls. She goes well and looks smart but has a nasty habit of cocking her ears and looking as if she was going to shy. She has a light mouth and behaved well.

(*This was Kitty, later to be referred to as "the little mare."*)

May 4. F, C and I walked to the sports ground to see regimental sports, races, etc. C and I sat retired by the hedge and watched from a distance. It is the sort of entertainment that makes me feel thoroughly shy and out of it and I never have an idea what to say to the officers, especially the subalterns, all of whom were there. Mrs Gardener and Mrs Mott also there, the latter really is more than half a subaltern herself!

May 5. F took the soldiers to church. F and I up to the band after, which means sitting in a row in the barracks square. A Mrs and Miss Hickey came up, it seemed quite pathetic how much they appeared to enjoy it. They are having a little season in Limerick and usually live in a castle on the Shannon about 11 miles from a station. Mrs H is English, poor thing.

May 6. F and I by the 11 o'clock train to Limerick Junction, thence to Goolds Cross, thence to Cashel. As soon as you step out of the train you see the big rock in front of you, with the wonderful ruins within the encircling walls at the top. The rock is 300 feet high, rising out of rather flat country, stretching away for miles and miles and distant mountains in all directions. I never saw anything quite like this Rock of Cashel, the home of the Kings of Munster.

May 8. Mrs O'Callaghan left, the most amusing cook I ever had!

June 3. Christopher is having a Shakespeare week at his toy theatre! Tonight it was Macbeth which he read extracts from, different china animals taking the different parts.

This theater had been given him the previous Christmas. It must have been made in Germany or Switzerland, for its cutout cardboard figures were characters from some romantic German drama, by Schiller probably. Its two sets were a banqueting hall in a castle and a dense pine forest. This basic indoors and outdoors did well enough for all Christopher's purposes; he anyhow preferred to keep the stage in semidarkness, with big shadows cast by a candle in the wings. Thunderstorms occurred in every production; Frank had shown him how to simulate lightning by blowing rosin through a tube into a candle flame. He seldom used the cardboard figures, even though his Schiller-type leading lady

—being, after all, in the Shakespearean tradition—could easily have passed for Lady Macbeth. Instead of her he cast a china rabbit in the role, and he made up the rest of his company with other china animals which stood on the nursery mantelpiece. (Does this preference prove that Christopher was at heart an Expressionist? Or that he was a pioneer of the Theater of the Absurd? Probably the former, for he was a deadly serious director and hated to be laughed at.)

When he held a theatrical season, the announcing of it was a great part of his pleasure. He pinned posters on the nursery door and expected Kathleen, Frank and Nanny to attend every performance. Frank was ready to be helpful, but Christopher soon grew impatient of advice. Sometimes the two artistic temperaments clashed and Christopher closed the show in a huff or Frank walked out.

Christopher cut the Shakespeare plays drastically. His Othello was simply the strangling of Desdemona, accompanied by screams and groans. Macbeth, his favorite, was the longest, but even this ran for less than fifteen minutes. Nothing was left of it but bits of Duncan's murder, Banquo's ghost at the feast, and the sleepwalking scene, which some childish puritanical whim caused him to expurgate, so that "out, damned spot!" became "out . . . spot!"

Since the Frimley Lodge days, Christopher and Kathleen had played at dressing up; they pretended to be taking part in a ball, in which the dance was Sir Roger de Coverley, the first dance that Christopher learned. It would have been logical for him to put on something representing a masculine white tie and tailcoat, but that would have been no fun. Dressing up meant the excitement and safety of disguise, you had to transform yourself as much as possible, so it was natural that you should change your sex. Kathleen didn't discourage this at all; she draped him in a silk petticoat and let him wear her furs and necklaces and even her switch—not false hair, as she was careful to explain to him, but a lock cut from her own hair which she sometimes used to give body to the elaborate hairdos of that period.

By the time they moved to Ireland, dressing up for its own sake had ceased to satisfy him. He wanted to be an actor, like Frank.

Sarah Bernhardt was his model—by this time he must have been told about her and the sort of plays she performed in by Kathleen, Frank and probably Emily as well. A Bernhardt play had to be tragic, of course, and it had to be in French; Christopher's Bernhardt play had also to be for one character only, a middle-aged lady.

The play Christopher composed was called La Lettre. *A lady enters holding a letter which she has just received. She opens it and reads it, with increasing horror. It tells her that someone has died—the audience is expected to guess that it is her son. The Lady: "O, il est mort!" She falls to the ground in a swoon. End of play. Christopher scrambles to his feet and bows.*

The indulgent applause of his captive audiences went to his head. He wanted more and more of it. One afternoon when the drawing room was full of people, he walked in and began his performance without previous announcement or permission. This embarrassed and annoyed Frank. He ordered Christopher to leave the room at once, and the play was thenceforth banned.

July 4. The usual grind of shopping. Never in any place has the housekeeping been so tiresome as here. In afternoon we drove up to the Market Fields for the Church Lads Brigade sports. A most fortunate afternoon for it. Frank inspected. I gave away the prizes!

July 17. Interviewed policeman about the children in the lane, lawless little hooligans who bang at the door (which we have to keep locked, now that Frank is away) and dash in the moment it is open to try and steal the apples and pick the flowers for sheer mischief's sake, not for the love of either! The Irish seem most *hopelessly* lawless and murders are overlooked in a way to make an Englishwoman's blood boil.

July 26. An interesting talk with Miss F, who told me quite mediaeval stories about the state of things in Ireland. They think if Home Rule really comes they will be too much at the mercy of all sorts of incapable and dishonest people to make it possible to go on living here.

(*When Christopher taught at American colleges, after the Second World War, he sometimes likened his position as a child in Ireland to that of the son of a Nazi officer in occupied France. This comparison was intentionally melodramatic—to startle the students into attention—and didn't, of course, imply that the York and Lancasters behaved like the Nazis or that the Irish of 1912– 14 reacted to them like French civilians of the Resistance. The English soldiers were certainly hated by many Irishmen as invaders. But, during that period, religious hatred was still uppermost. When street boys shouted insults at the children of the garrison, their epithet wouldn't be "Dirty Englishman!" but "Dirty Protestant!" Irish Catholics hated all Protestants, English and Irish, and they were quite capable of turning on their own countrymen when the quarrel was religious (as will be shown by Kathleen's October 17 entry). It was only after the Easter Rising of 1916 that Irish nationalism began to prevail over religious differences and Irish hatred focused more sharply upon the English as English. Thus a situation arose which was indeed somewhat like that of the French collaborators after the Nazi withdrawal: many of the Irish families who had shown hospitality to the now withdrawn English garrisons found themselves in trouble, some had their houses burned and were frightened into leaving the country. Miss F. may well have been one of these.*

While Christopher was at Roden House he took the hostility of the street boys for granted, as a part of daily life, along with the caressing foreign charm of their eyes and voices, the music of their accent, the filth of the picturesque lane and the stink of sewage in its puddles and gutters. However intensely Kathleen may have thought of herself as an Englishwoman with boiling blood, she wasn't the sort of mother who would try to teach the same attitude to her children. When Christopher got angry with the boys and girls he played with, he accused them of many things, but never of being Irish.)

August 8. Mirabel Cobbold came round early for Christopher. She is aged eight and quite a head taller and very self-possessed and patronizing. They do 'nature study' together, which means collecting the most unpleasant insects and keeping them in a box. This morning, however, they went to sail their boats in some puddle and fell out. But they seemed to be as good friends as ever in the afternoon.

(Mirabel's father was the Captain Cobbold of the photograph described in Chapter Four. He had just arrived in Limerick as the Regiment's new Colonel.)

August 10. Christopher had Mirabel to tea. It is extraordinary to me the charm Mirabel has for him! She hits him and teases him and gives him things and takes them away but he seems to have no sense of retaliation, and never attempts to hit back, does just as she tells him and apparently has no pride either.

August 12. Christopher and Richard and Nurse with Mirabel Cobbold to tea with the Gs and I grieve to say C and M teased Nancy and both behaved abominably, it seems so *mean* when he dare not touch Nancy if he is alone (though she is smaller and younger) and *never* attempts to stand up for himself. It is quite extraordinary the influence Mirabel has on him, how he believes all she says, and how he follows her like a dog even though she hits him and makes him cry.

August 26. C's eighth birthday. Frank gave him a magic lantern and he could not contain his delight and enthusiasm, *never* had he imagined anything quite so delightful. The birthday tea consisted of Nurse pouring out and Richard very vigorously thumping his fat hands on his high chair, Frank, Major Clemson, C and myself. After tea there was a performance of the magic lantern up in Frank's dressing room which gave enormous satisfaction.

375

August 31. Mirabel and C played *Swiss Family Robinson* (which he is now reading) in the yard of the Technical School, fighting wild beasts and sailing on imaginary rafts.

(The yard, despite Kathleen's efforts to keep it tidy, remained a resting place for every piece of lumber or hardware which the Technical School discarded. It was therefore an ideal playground, full of props for games of make-believe, such as planks, barrels, packing cases, detached doors, broken laboratory apparatus, wire, rope, plumbing fixtures, sheets of glass.)

September 28. Nurse and C to the moving pictures at The Gaiety, the new place of entertainment at St George's Street about which C has been excited for weeks.

(Thus Christopher's lifelong devotion to the movies began, as an indiscriminate appetite for any two-dimensional happening on a lighted screen in a dark theater. He finds it hard to remember individual film actors or films from the Limerick days, but he is certain he saw John Bunny, Francis X. Bushman, Lillian and Dorothy Gish, Annette Kellerman, the Keystone Cops, Mae Marsh, Mabel Normand, The Spoilers, Judith of Bethulia, *the Italian version of* Quo Vadis? *and episodes from many serials, including Pearl White's* The Perils of Pauline.*)*

October 16. In afternoon took C across to the Gym with Mrs Cobbold and Mirabel, and the first drilling class started. Colonel Cobbold came and conducted the proceedings.

October 17. To the town before lunch. Every other shop, nearly, has suffered from the riots of last week and has smashed glass. From starting politically on the grounds of the big Unionist meeting, it ended by being a religious riot. The Roman Catholics especially attacking all the Protestant shops and the Archdeacon's house and the church next door, into which they threw nearly a thousand stones. The Archdeacon was chased and cut about the face. The priests finally came out on Saturday and addressed the people, imploring them to cease, and they did.

October 29. In afternoon to Patrick Punch Corner to see the men return from their fortnightly run, six miles across country. Frank's company second and he very well to the fore, far ahead of most of the officers and men. Then at four Mrs Cobbold had her first monthly tea to the women on and off the strength—jam roll, bread and butter, ham sandwiches etc. I think it went off well and I increased my acquaintances! Though it remains to be seen how I shall ever remember all the names and faces.

(*Mrs. Cobbold was a brisk cheerful strong-minded woman and a first-rate Colonel's Wife. "On the strength" was a term applied to those soldiers' wives whose marriages had been approved and officially recognized by the authorities; "off the strength" described the unofficial remainder. This distinction no doubt affected claims to pensions and other benefits and privileges.*

Kathleen was becoming involved in Mrs. Cobbold's projects, though unwillingly; for her, this was Jennie and Limehouse all over again. She acknowledged the obligation, but felt unequal to it. She wrote to Emily for advice—and got no uncertain answer:

I will *never* believe you are a bore to those poor vapid creatures, tho of course they are to *you*. The Barracks entertainments must be dreadful and the solitude of the country far better. I should mix with them as little as possible and what does it matter what they say, the real thing is that you like your home and garden and Limerick, and have Frank and C.W. and R. *Nothing else matters.*)

November 4. Very busy with Nurse's and Bell's help moving the drawing-room things into the spare room and making it into a temporary winter drawing-room. The present drawing-room fire is generally befogged with smoke from the nursery. So it means practically we only have the dining-room to sit in and the ante-room at night. It is too dark for a day room. It all looked very cosy when done.

(Bell was the soldier-servant. Christopher remembers him as a good-natured docile young giant who did all the heavy work around the house. He was to die as a prisoner of war in Germany.)

At the end of November, they all left for England. This was quite a long holiday; they didn't return to Limerick until February 5. They went first to Marple, where the children and Nanny would remain throughout. Kathleen thought Stockport "looked indescribably clean after Limerick, such white clean-looking streets and no mud!" Frank and Kathleen then went up to London, where they saw Fanny's First Play *("very like Shaw, indeed it could hardly have been by anyone else, and one is getting a little tired of his tactics by now"). Frank and Emily offered to buy Kathleen one of Joseph Pennell's etchings of the Panama Canal, and she chose "The Bottom of Gatun Lock"; the Pennells and Emily were neighbors and friends. Speaking of the London traffic, Kathleen remarks that "a four-wheeler feels quite a survival from other days now," presumably because of the great increase in taxis.*

Frank and Kathleen returned to Marple for Christmas with the children. Moey was there, too. She had been trying in some way to help Frank get appointed as chief of the Colchester constabulary. In mid-January, the news came that the post had been given to one of the other applicants. Kathleen comments: ". . . so that castle in the air is shattered, but it is better than not knowing and going on in uncertainty, though I had given up hope some time ago. Frank of course is really rather glad." This was to be Frank's last attempt to get himself a job in civilian life.

1913. February 19. Took C to his first dancing class at the George. Thirteen children and a very alert little teacher from Cork.

March 17. To see Miss Mercer in morning. She is giving up the High School on account of her health. Talked of Christopher and I told her of our intention of sending him to Miss Burns on account of the society of a few other little boys. She said as far as education was concerned she feared it was time wasted and that to send him to England would really be better. We parted very solemnly. His education is a great problem and difficulty here. If only—!

(*Miss Mercer had previously written to Kathleen that Christopher was "so straightforward and reliable that I often think he would make an ideal clergyman." After other equally complimentary remarks, she concluded, "Please forgive my talking about him, you must know all this better than anyone." Kathleen, who knew Christopher better than Miss Mercer, must have thought her a very innocent soul.*)

March 20. Mrs Cobbold disturbed me a good deal about Christopher, he so easily gets overexcited and frightens himself over the stories he tells himself, and he is always telling himself stories. She thought him very overexcited when he had tea with Mirabel yesterday, indeed they are *not* suited to be together.

April 7. Took Christopher to Miss Burns's school, Mount Saint Vincent Cottage, up the Military Road next to the Convent, only six or seven children but the majority are boys. Do hope it will be a success.

This change of schools was, of course, made in the hope that Christopher would become more masculine in male society. Kathleen took it for granted that his growing interest in girls was due to a girlishness in himself and nothing more. But perhaps she was wrong. Perhaps Christopher was actually exhibiting slight heterosexual tendencies which could have been strengthened and confirmed if he had been sent to a coeducational school in his teens. Perhaps he could have worked his way up to a George Sand-

Alfred de Musset type of affair with a girl like Mirabel! Well, thank goodness for St. Edmund's School and Repton, if they did indeed have anything to do with tipping the balance in the opposite direction. Despite the humiliations of living under a heterosexual dictatorship and the fury he has often felt against it, Christopher has never regretted being as he is. He is now quite certain that heterosexuality wouldn't have suited him; it would have fatally cramped his style.

The pupils at Miss Burns's included a pair of brothers named Jack and Bob Armstrong, whom Christopher had first met soon after arriving in Ireland the previous year. They are dealt with in The History of My Friends:

I used to go and play with Jack and Bob a lot when we first came to Limerick. A governess called Miss Smith was with them till last Christmas and she made things very nice when I went—but after she left there was a great difference and somehow we did not seem to get on so well.

My personal opinion of Jack is that he is rather boasting and is very fond of saying 'I'll wrestle you' to other boys without carrying it out. At school he made a lot of plots in a loud voice against me which were useless and even babyish. He said he would build large trenches, fill them over with earth for me to tumble into a lot of tar. He also said he would send me up in the kite with a fuse attached to which he would set light to blow me up. He evidently appears to be insane but at times very amusing.

Bob is always glaring at me and calling me little baby, to this I laugh in his face which annoys him greatly and the days of our great friendship is now over.

In the History, *the Armstrongs are followed by Eddie Townshend:*

I first met Eddie at the drill class last year. It was then our great friendship began, before this I did not know anything about him.

I think it first started by my having a long talk with him after gym and Mummy asked him to tea. He used to tell me long tales about his boxing. After that, we used to make sham flying machines out of the heap of old forms and wires and boxes out in the Technical yard, he soon became very great friends. I cast off Jack, who had long been cool, presently I told him I had entirely cast him off, that his chances were gone and I was now best friends with Eddie. I think this annoyed him. Eddie is twice the size of Jack and of me, but that doesn't make any difference.

The wrinkled monkey-face of Jack Armstrong and the hot red button-nosed face of Bob, both of them towheaded, are still dimly printed on Christopher's memory. Eddie's face has disappeared. But he was probably one of those big dark pale good-looking Irish boys. No doubt he needed someone smaller and weaker than himself to boast to and protect; later it would be a girl, later still a son or a daughter. Once, when they were in the cinema together —it was a long narrow hall and they always sat right up in front, far from the entrance—Eddie said that if a fire were to break out he would take Christopher on his shoulders and carry him to safety, jumping over the backs of the seats. This boast must have charmed and thrilled Christopher particularly, since he chose to remember it. But his attitude to Eddie seems domineering and possessive rather than affectionate. He talks like a despotic little monarch, making and unmaking his favorites. What did his coauthor and secretary Kathleen think when she had to record such expressions as "I told him I had entirely cast him off"? Did she find them merely childish and funny, or did they alarm her for Christopher's character and future?

April 25. Frank made a study of the apple tree from the drawing-room window, it is now in full bloom. C. played at Swiss Family Robinson. Read *The Aran Islands* by John Synge. C. top this week at school. They think him very forward in reading but backward in arithmetic.

· ·

(Frank's tiny watercolor of the apple tree is now with Christopher in California. Once in a while, someone who comes to the house will notice it, amidst the many moderns on the walls, and ask with admiring surprise who its painter is. Frank has let the white paper show through between his touches of pink, thus making the blossom seem to shine with its own light against a dark vague background of trees. He was at his best when he tried for quick impressions like this one. Too often, apparently, he didn't have enough confidence in his instinct to stop when it told him to; for his teachers had drummed into his head that a picture had to be properly "finished.")

April 27. C wore his first stiff Eton collar and a new grey suit, cleverly made by Nurse! Took him to church.

May 1. [In London.] Walked along Oxford St and down Regent St looking at the shops—anything like the fashion in hats I *never* saw, tiny little things with a bow or a scraggy feather sticking out at some extraordinary angle.

May 4. Mama and I walked to the Savoy Chapel. When we walked out at the end, every eye turned to gaze at Mama, all wonderful in her velvet and furs and looking such a personage!

May 8. Mama and I went to the quaintest little place for a *Poetical Reading*. They have them twice a week at the back of a bookshop kept by a Mr Monro. Everyone present was very serious and intense and Sturge Moore read his *Rout of the Amazons* very well. He is a serious looking man with a beard, dressed in a frock coat. It was very enjoyable and quaint.

(This was of course Harold Monro's Poetry Bookshop. Kathleen's air of being on an art-slumming tour would have enraged Christopher if he had read the above entry during the nineteen-twenties. For the bookshop had then been made sacred to him by the wartime visits of Wilfred Owen.)

Kathleen returned to Limerick on May 14. From May 24 to 26 she and Frank made an expedition to Dingle, via Tralee. Kathleen notes that men in mourning wore black bands of crape around their caps with a bow at the back, instead of around their arms (as Christopher would be wearing his, before very long; it seems rather uncanny that she should have chosen to mention this particular detail). They found a bog plant which was new to them, called pinguicula, and inspected many Celtic remains—forts, pillar stones, crosses, cromlechs, beehive huts and ogham inscriptions. They saw the Blasket Islands in the distance, and Bray Head on Valencia, which is the westernmost point in Europe.

Kathleen was recalled to England in June by a carbuncle which Emily had produced on the back of her neck. The area of infection was "quite the size round of the top of a good-sized teacup and swollen red and raw in the centre." It went away as soon as it had shown itself to Kathleen and warned her to be ready and waiting at all times to obey Baby Mama's next summons.

July 4. [Limerick.] Eddie Townshend to play with C, also Mirabel who left in a huff. When later C. and E. went across to see if she would come and have tea, Mrs Cobbold blew them up and told C. he had been very crabby and disagreeable to her. But if Mirabel doesn't get it just her own way she always resorts to tears and Mrs C. thinks it is the other child's fault.

July 18. C practises the piano for half an hour daily and does his tables and catechism and we are reading Kipling's Child's History of England. Eddie Townshend went away. C to tea with his long-neglected Armstrongs and returned after an hour as he was offended over something, but Frank promptly sent him back!

July 23. A lovely day and really hot, just as it was for the sports last year. We all went. Richard dressed to the nines in a white embroidered frock and pale blue linen and white embroidered jacket, looking angelic! C also in white, flannel shirt and knickers and a blue tie, and I wore black chiffon over blue with blue in my hat. All Limerick was there.

On July 24, Kathleen and Frank went off for a week to Connemara. Here Kathleen saw genuine peasant women, wearing "deep bright crimson" skirts. They traveled through a country of bogs, with peat stacked beside them, passing Croagh Patrick, where Saint Patrick expelled the toads and snakes from Ireland, to Achill Island. They stayed at a happy-go-lucky, sometimes amusing, sometimes infuriating hotel, where nothing was done punctually and there was never quite enough to eat. On Achill they admired the luxuriant hedges of fuchsia, Slievemore Mountain, which Kathleen describes as having "a tender blue mistiness" and looking like her idea of Mount Fuji, and Keem Bay, which she calls "the most beautiful small bay I have ever seen." Other features of the island were the jig dancing, "the nearest public house to America," and the Protestant Stores, which were then being boycotted. Their manager had to have his supplies brought to him under a police guard. Kathleen was told that he had already tried to escape from Achill but had been recognized and stoned; she wasn't sure if she believed this. Anyhow, she boldly visited the Stores, which sold groceries, postcards, secondhand books and whales' ears— there were whaling stations in the neighborhood. After listening sympathetically to the Manager's grievances, she bought a whale's ear for Christopher; it was a small rounded bony object which you could hold easily in your hand.

When the day came for them to leave, Kathleen and Frank discovered that the hotel bill was "anything but happy-go-lucky, one pays heavily for the atmosphere of irresponsibility and Irishness."

On August 7, Frank left with the Regiment to take part in maneuvers, and Kathleen, Nanny and the children went to Marple. A week later, Kathleen visited Aggie, who was now married to a Major Harry Trevor, at her home in Wales. While there she encountered a member of the smart young 1913 set:

. .

384

We simply gasped at K's appearance when she arrived. She is the latest thing in modernness and is exceedingly pretty but gets herself up like a Gaiety actress, such a pity as she is only a little over twenty and needs no artificial aids. Aggie rather anxious as to the effect on the natives of her little ladyship's appearance, when she appeared in a dress cut V-shaped open at the neck (as they wear in London this season) and a hat jammed down over one eye! Harry Trevor refuses utterly to be seen with her at the Shrewsbury Show, which adds to the difficulties of the situation!

August 21. [At Marple.] Richard and I drove up the village with his Grandad, where the 'moke' from the big chimneys gave him infinite and endless satisfaction! We drove round by Wyberslegh. The garden looked so gay with flowers and altogether worthy of that hallowed spot. After lunch, C and I drove up to the village to have the Brownie camera explained to us. Grandad and Granny are giving him one.

August 24. C and I struggled to understand how one develops the Brownie film in the Brownie developing box.

That autumn, after their return to Limerick, Kathleen comments on the growing tension in Ireland. The Home Rule Bill was now almost certain to become law, and Ulster was determined to resist it, fearing the rule of a government of Irish Catholics.

They have appointed all the members for their own government should Home Rule come in force and intend governing themselves should Ireland separate from the Imperial Parliament. They are backed by funds and a trained army of volunteers who mean fight without any doubt.

Meanwhile, in Limerick (October 12):

The statue in the Crescent is decorated with mottoes of FAITH AND FATHERLAND and a dozen or so young men dressed in saffron coloured kilts and stockings appeared in a long procession which with many bands marched through the chief streets, representing the Home Rule demonstration. They were afterwards addressed by Redmond. The general opinion seems to have been that they were rather a disappointed looking band, but the day was depressing.

October 26. To my great pleasure the two Miss Warmleightons came to tea. They were passing through Limerick on their return to Dublin. They were so nice and oldfashioned and very pleased to go over the house. The ante-room they called the Music Room and had little concerts in it and the Nursery was the Blue Room and there they used to sit and do needlework. Indeed they seemed to have lived just the quiet lives with their music and their books and their work that I had imagined—which was most gratifying!

October 27. C gave a performance of his version of 'Sealed Orders' (now being performed at Drury Lane) at his toy theatre, which was rather a failure.

(*No doubt because the technical demands of the melodrama were too much for a toy stage—an airship had to be shot down in mid-air! Christopher must have seen an account of the production in a magazine.*)

October 29. One of the popular ideas is that, if Home Rule comes and the English leave, the Irish American millionaires will then come back and flood the country with money, build mills and have fine ships up and down the Shannon.

On November 1, Frank and Kathleen were invited to stay at Curragh Chase, once the home of Aubrey de Vere, the schoolmate of Byron whose sonnets (e.g., "The Rock of Cashel") were called by Wordsworth "the most perfect of our age," and of his son Aubrey Thomas de Vere, also a poet ("Florence MacCarthy's Farewell to Her English Lover"), who had entertained Tennyson, Coventry Patmore and Watts; Watts had done an outline on the

stairs for a fresco of Dante meeting Beatrice. Kathleen admired
the house, which was built in the grand manner:

The long room which opens out of the hall is called The
Saloon, there are busts all down the room and tall french windows
open on to the broad stone terrace, just now the woods beyond
the lakes are perfectly gorgeous with the colouring of autumn and
the mountains to the south the most wonderful blue.

The present owners of the house had what seemed to Kathleen
and Frank an amusing eccentricity: they ran it on Daylight Saving
Time:

All through our visit they kept explaining what the time was,
according to *them*, which made the hours of meals very con-
fusing! They get up at 7 and call it 8, go to bed at 9 and call it 10,
or at 10 and call it 11. Of course the scheme is that it should be
universal, even so it seems unnecessary to put the clock on!

November 6. To party at Fred Clares'. Wore new yellow dress,
so tight round feet could hardly walk across room. Never another
fashionable skirt!

November 13. To the Literary Class. Frank gave short lecture
on Bernard Shaw, very good, and then the play of Candida was
read, it went so well. Frank the poet, Mrs Yates Candida, Mr
Hardy the husband.

On December 3 they all left for England again; Nanny and the
children went to Marple, Frank and Kathleen stayed with Emily
in London. While they were there they visited Hindhead in
Surrey, where there were two preparatory schools which might
be suitable for Christopher; they had decided that he must start
being educated in England next year. They finally chose St. Ed-
mund's School, which was run by Cyril Morgan Brown, his sister

Mona, his daughter Rosa and other members of his family. The Morgan Browns were cousins of the Isherwoods:

Was agreeably impressed by Miss Mona Brown, who seemed practical. It seemed human but rather big and a very cold house, supposed to be heated with hot pipes. Horrified at lunch to see several of the boys playing with their forks and spoons and balancing balls. No one said anything. Still it felt kindly. Cyril Brown rather dreamy.

December 24. [At Marple.] In the evening the carol singers came and sang carols in the hall. Jack and his friend Mr Sprangue arrived soon after nine.

December 25. Mild damp Christmas. C arrived in our room between seven and eight to look at his presents with which he was *very* delighted, especially with a box of conjuring tricks from Frank and a wonderful engine which makes electric light. A box of Meccano to build models with also a great success. Frank, Jack, C and I drove to St Martin's to church, Mr and Mrs Isherwood to All Saints. Christmas dinner with plum pudding on fire, turkey and champagne in middle of day and Richard came in for dessert and C and he sat on each side of me. R looked angelic with his shining curls and for once behaved angelically! Frank gave me a lovely new velvet evening dress which I wore! A thoroughly successful and enjoyable Christmas Day. C said it was the best he could remember.

December 29. Snow on the hills and everything white but not deep. Christopher himself suggested sleeping alone in his Father's dressing room, so with electric torch, a supply of books and a clock, he went off very grandly to bed. *The first time he has ever slept alone.*

December 31. Frosty and fine. After C had finished his lessons he went out tobogganing and again after lunch. After tea I read him *The Talisman*. Richard seems quite fairly reconciled to the idea that Nanny has gone to see her Mum Mum. C slept alone again, getting up at six and dressing himself. Carol singers came to sing in the hall after dinner round the big open fireplace.

Kathleen's 1914 diary has the morbid fascination of a document which records, without the dishonesty of hindsight, the day-by-day approach to a catastrophe by an utterly unsuspecting victim. Meanwhile, as so often happens, this victim expects and fears a different catastrophe—civil war in Ulster—which isn't going to take place.

Two poems are quoted at the beginning of the diary: Robert Bridges' "Christmas Eve," some skillful uninspiring lines addressed to the King in Bridges' capacity as newly appointed Poet Laureate, and "Prayer" (author unidentified):

> *The weary ones had rest, the sad had joy*
> *That day and wondered how?*
> *A ploughman singing at his work prayed*
> *Lord help them now.*

Besides these, there are some items which Kathleen must have added much later. There is a list of officers' names, with crosses against some of them. In a few cases, it has been possible to confirm that the men thus marked were killed in 1914 or 1915, but this may be only coincidence and the list may refer to something else. There is also a list of things to be sent to Frank or to others at the front, including a four-ounce box of Navy Cut, medium, Van Houten cocoa prepared with milk, Peters chocolate, Maggie soup squares, socks. And there is a code, evidently worked out by Frank and Kathleen for use in his letters, which will tell her where he is without breaking the censorship rules: "quite safe" means in England, "safe" means abroad, "safe up to date" means at the front.

On January 23, Kathleen left Marple and went down to stay with Emily at Ventnor. Kathleen was scornful because some of

*Emily's previous visitors had been over to Bonchurch to lay a
flower on Swinburne's grave; her comment was that she would
much rather lay a flower on the doorstep of Lady Ritchie, the
novelist and daughter of Thackeray, who lived at Freshwater.
Kathleen loved the "delightful style" of her book* From the Porch.
  Frank wrote from Marple:

Christopher managed to tumble over a rake in the barn and tore
his stocking very badly and scratched his knee slightly. He thoroughly enjoys walking lame. Father is completely taken in by this
and woke up constantly at teatime to ask how he was. The Baby is
all right but very ill-tempered. My Mother seems better. She really
is wonderfully strong, in fact I wish I had hers and Father's
digestions. The way they pour down jugged hare and pork and
toasted cheese etc is astonishing. It is very pleasant to feel that we
shall be back in Limerick today fortnight.

February 14. [At Limerick.] An excellent film of Hamlet, acted
by Forbes-Robertson last year, just before his retirement. Ger-
trude Elliot as Ophelia and a very good cast. As it was done out
of doors, the scenery was far superior to any I ever saw on the
stage. Only, under the searching light of photography, poor
Forbes-Robertson looked far *too old*.

February 18. Mrs Rogers arrived from Tipperary. Heard about
their time at Stockport and how they were never free from the
Volunteer officers coming in at all hours and dropping in even to
lunch, of course none of them gentlemen and no idea how far
they could go, and then to crown all, after all their kindness, one
of the wives said, 'we never saw much of Mrs Isherwood but then
of course she was a real lady'!

February 21. In afternoon Christopher to the pictures. Jem
Barlow and I followed later. They always start with events of the
week and the opening of Parliament was excellent, King and
Queen driving in their state coach. A certain amount of hissing

but a good deal of clapping. This followed by exciting detective dramas!! Jem gave an exhibition of table-turning after dinner and 'William Isherwood' told Frank he would die 'rich and happy'. It is very queer but I think the answers must depend on the thoughts!

(*The psychic information which Kathleen got about Frank, both before and after his death, was always either false or inconclusive. She was skeptical in her attitude toward table-turning, yet it fascinated her as a forbidden and possibly dangerous kind of prying. Richard remembers that Miss Barlow and she had another sitting in June 1931. The table kept rapping out messages as long as the radio played a tune called "I'm Happy When I'm Hiking"; when the tune stopped, it stopped, too. After Miss Barlow had gone, Kathleen said to it playfully, "Oh, you wicked little thing!" as though she felt that the table itself had seduced them into committing a sin.*)

March 18. In afternoon to the dancing class with C who was much excited at Miss Miller's costume, black satin cut low in a V-shape, very tight, disclosing a black chiffon petticoat and a good deal of very neat silk stocking. A sort of pleated lampshade of black satin went round the waist!

March 21. *Very warlike news*. It seems as if the Government were trying to bully Ulster into making the first move. Of course Ulster is in absolute readiness and backed by such leading men as Sir Edward Carson, Lord Roberts, etc etc and thousands of volunteers have offered themselves from England if they need further help. Some say numbers of cavalry officers at the Curragh have already resigned their commissions sooner than fight against Ulster.

March 22. Perhaps, having brought the country to the verge of civil war, the Government will at last see they are incapable of governing. Practically, England is now governed by the Irish, as

Asquith sold himself to Redmond, promising him Home Rule in exchange for the Irish votes—however he reckoned without Ulster! Took Christopher to the cathedral and Frank brought the soldiers to church. Everyone was wondering if they would come, but the town seemed peaceful.

(General Gough, commander of the Curragh camp, and some of the officers under him had indeed just handed in their resignations. This forced Asquith to compromise and declare that Ulster would not be coerced into Home Rule—at least, not for the present.)

It was now time for Christopher to leave for England and the beginning of his school life at St. Edmund's.

April 23. C and I left by the 8.15, Frank driving us to the station in the trap. It seemed dreadful to feel that this is C's first start away from home, and Nurse felt parting with him, I know, very much. The apple tree was a picture and the wallflowers and forgetmenots, and the sun shone on our departure—I hope a good omen. We found a very good cabin with berth alongside a porthole which we were able to have open all the time, it was so smooth. Stockport 8.55, and found a taxi which took us to Marple.

(Frank later wrote to Kathleen: "I felt inclined to cry, myself.")

April 24. C did not go out but played to his Granny and drew and did conjuring tricks. Very much on his dignity in his new clothes; arrived with his hair wonderfully damped down and flattened in my room before breakfast. He dined downstairs as a special treat and bathed and put himself to bed, scorning any help!

April 25. Reached Euston 2.10. Found dear Mama looking better than I expected. We chatted, and then C and I up to our rooms to unpack. He so important and pleased with his room and felt very gay, I think! After tea, we went out to see if we could find a bookshop open to buy 'The Air King's Treasure' but did not manage to get it.

When Christopher thinks of the Buckingham Street flat, his memories are chiefly of Emily's drawing-room. This could have been an uninterestingly cheerful light airy room with a view of the Embankment Gardens, the Thames and Charing Cross railway bridge. But Emily preferred to keep the light reduced by blinds and the windows closed. The air felt languidly heavy and still; it was perfumed by potpourri which lay around in china bowls. Some of these stood on the tops of stoves which warmed them and increased the odor. The stillness seemed all the greater because you had just come down the street from the noisy Strand and Trafalgar Square, the spinning center of the town. There was also mystery. When you advanced from the door you had to make your way around two or more screens, placed so that you could not see the whole room at a glance; you discovered it by stages, as you turned each corner. Its furniture was crowded and its pictures were hung close together, almost entirely covering the walls, but the crowding wasn't oppressive; the general effect, so unlike that of Marple Hall, was of blond satiny wood, creamy marble, alabaster, gilt frames, pink and sky-blue fabrics. The pictures were mostly watercolors, etchings and quick modern-looking charcoal sketches, not oils. Many of them were foreign scenes, places Emily had visited, Venice, Granada, Avignon, which stirred in Christopher a desperate longing to travel—all the more so because here you were right beside the railway which led to the harbor and the river which led to the sea.

The final discovery, as you came around the last of the screens, was Emily herself; she usually received you lying on her couch in the alcove. She was like a great actress resting after the emotional demands of the matinee and preparing to give herself even more utterly to the audience of her evening performance. There was often a bottle of champagne on the table beside her, as if to strengthen her for the latter ordeal after the little vials of homeopathic medicine had repaired the damage done to her nerves by the former. The odors were different here: you sniffed the faint pleasing bitterness of the medicine, you were enveloped in the aroma from Emily's furs. In California, Christopher has found, most people take it for granted that the smell of a skunk is unpleasant. He has always liked it (in moderation); it reminds him so strongly of Emily.

Since Emily's co-star Frederick was unavailable, Christopher never saw her in her greatest role, the Martyr-Wife. Despite her ailments and fatigues, she was now quietly gay, indeed her life was entirely devoted to pleasure. In her presence he never felt awed or bored, as young people are by woe; she stimulated and interested him and was quick to respond to his interest. He became one of her most favored courtiers. Emily knew how to reward her favorites: she could be marvelously gracious at almost no cost to herself, which is the mark of true professional royalty.

Emily's flat wasn't a flat, strictly speaking; it had an upper floor on the level of the roof, reached by a tiny staircase. This, for Christopher, was one of its greatest charms. For the staircase seemed to turn the flat into a miniature house, a house within a house, a place which was out of scale with the external world and therefore a place of safety—like Christopher's fantasy-retreat within the walls of Marple Hall.

All Christopher's memories of Buckingham Street are happy and exciting because he always visited it on holidays. It was the base from which he set forth to shops, theaters, cinemas and other entertainments and to which he returned to gloat over the books he had bought and the programs of plays he had seen.

On this visit to London, he and Kathleen saw Granville-Barker's production of A Midsummer Night's Dream, *in which the fairies wore gold and had gilded faces, and a magic show at Maskelyne and Cook's. They also went to Madame Tussaud's, the Natural History Museum, Westminster Abbey, the Zoo and, most importantly, to Hendon Aerodrome, where they watched some Graham White biplanes demonstrating bomb-dropping and aerobatics, including that enormously fashionable maneuver "looping the loop."*

Christopher's last requests had now all been granted. On May 1 he could no longer put off remembering that he was a condemned man:

The train went from Waterloo at 3.45. Found the second class saloon and some of the boys already assembled. Cyril Morgan Brown taking them down, very incapable and dazed! Poor C—till we actually were sitting in the train I do not think he realized, but it was a most trying moment—the other boys all knowing each other and he a stranger and alone for the first time. It was all we could do, both of us, to put a good face on it, but he just managed to keep back the tears. It was a truly dreadful moment to me, seeing him go off so small and inexperienced into the unknown.

May 2. Wondering so all day what my dear C is doing.

May 3. Warmer. We could hear Big Ben strike again and knew the wind was out of the East. Wondered *much* how Christopher was getting on.

May 4. Could hardly sleep, so anxious to get C's Sunday letter! Apparently yesterday, 'they ran to the gate and back before breakfast, after which they had chapel and in the afternoon played cricket'. He said he 'liked school fairly' and thought 'the Masters looked nice' and 'rather liked the boys but none specially' and he 'was fairly happy sometimes' but did not think he would ever like games. It was a rather pathetic little letter though very restrained, but of course it is early days yet and I trust and believe he will like it better when he is more at home.

Letter from "Miss Mona" (Monica Morgan Brown) to Kathleen, May 4:

Dear Mrs Bradshaw Isherwood,
   Christopher seems quite happy and friendly and I do hope that he wrote home a cheerful newsy letter yesterday. He seems a very jolly little chap and one feels very friendlily disposed towards him, over and above the fact that he is a relation. He sits next me

at meals. He has begun his lessons very nicely and certainly reads and writes and spells well up to the average. He has, with a little encouragement sometimes, finished up his platesful so far, though he has not yet asked for a second helping. But perhaps that will come, it is wonderful what the force of example does for them. I think that he has slept quite well so far. I have never heard him call out and I usually do hear them at once, my room is so close, and he is always asleep when I come up to bed.

Letter from Frank to Kathleen, written a few days after the above, from Roden House, Limerick:

I was very glad to see Mona's letter. I think, if you can bear it, you should ask them to call you Kathleen. They are people who think a good deal of it and Mona at any rate is really very nice. I like Cyril too, myself.

What nonsense about your not being a satisfactory mother. I think you are absolutely ideal in that relation and indeed in every other (except perhaps you were not quite successful with the D.O.D.) and I am sure Christopher will always think so too. I am sure your companionship has done more to develop him in the right way than anything could have done, and if he has got any airs and graces from being at home these will soon disappear at school. It is much better for him to have a high ideal of you and your sweetness and goodness than to remember you by your severity, and indeed you were quite severe enough with him too. I can't see that you failed in any way and I feel certain that every day he lives he will admire you more and more—as I do. I am rather surprised that Mona only says he is quite up to the average. I really think he is an unusually well-educated child. With Mother, Son and Husband (to say nothing of your Father- and Mother-in-Law) at your feet, you can't call yourself a failure exactly.

May 6. Another letter from C. This time he writes, 'I am enjoying myself much more. I was lonely on Sunday and a nice master called Mr Sant was kind to me. I am very happy now. I have liked it much more since lessons started. Today I swallowed a huge piece of fat, ugh! It was quite a shock to my nerves. I am afraid I have no more to say'. Felt so cheered.

On May 9, Kathleen went down to spend the night at St. Edmund's, met the staff and some of Christopher's schoolmates and came away feeling that the school had "a most friendly and kind atmosphere."

How did Christopher himself feel about St. Edmund's? The images in his memory aren't painful or ugly, merely rather drab: battered boot-lockers, ink-stained wooden desks, narrow dormitory beds, lists of names on notice-boards, name-tags on clothes, names read out at rollcall—names which make you less, not more, of an individual, which remind you hourly that you are now the household darling no longer, just one among many: Bradshaw-Isherwood, C.W. This feeling of lost importance is at the bottom of so-called homesickness; it isn't home you cry for but your home-self.

Still, Christopher had been to school already, even if it was only day-school, and knew how to cope with other boys. Before long he was making friends and enemies in his accustomed manner. Later he added two portraits (the last ones) to his History:

Russell-Roberts. He was among the new boys who came to St Edmund's at my first summer term. The first funny thing I heard about him was that he was seen dodging about Miss Mona's garden (which is not allowed). He is always rather an ass and violently passionate but I quite like him. He is very cheeky to the bigger boys, but last term he took me out twice. The second time I met his sister (a gay young thing!) who flirted atrociously. I suppose Russell-Roberts will always be the same as long as I know him.

Abrahall, (Major). This acquaintance began in the winter term of 1915. He has a passion for secrets and enjoys scandal! He became violently attached to me all at once, but threw me off, mainly I suppose because of my want of appreciation of secrets, also because of the arrival of Murray, a red-haired boy of sly countenance. Then ensued frightful coldness. Abrahall quarrelled with Murray and came back to me.

Christopher found the staff much harder to cope with than the boys. There were only three of them he really liked: Mr. Sant, with whom he used to talk about Sarah Bernhardt; Miss Lowe, the deaf music mistress; and kind weatherbeaten Miss Mona, who unfortunately went away to teach elsewhere at the end of his first term. He might have liked Miss Rosa—who was full of energy and fun and very attractive, with beautiful thick hair, on which it was said she could sit—if she had liked him. But she didn't. And neither did Cyril.

Cyril Morgan Brown, known officially as "Mr. Cyril" and called "Ciddy" behind his back by the boys, was a big handsome flatfooted man with gray hair and a gray moustache. He preached a gospel of thoroughness, exactitude, levelheadedness, persever-ance—all of the virtues recommended by Kipling in If. *(It is amazing that Kathleen thought him "incapable"—so amazing that one suspects her impression may have been a flash of true insight!) Kathleen ended by disliking both Cyril and Rosa but was ready to admit, in their defense, that it had been unfair to send Christopher to a school run by cousins. The relationship made them expect more of him than of the other boys; it also made them afraid of seeming to show him any favor.*

Cyril couldn't have picked a less suitable cousin than Christo-pher if he wanted one who would measure up to his standards. This weird little creature had a voice and a precocious way of expressing himself which were marvelously irritating. Once when Rosa had asked him a question and he answered, "I haven't the remotest idea," she lost control and slapped his face. He was a tireless chatterer, a physical coward who lacked team spirit, a bright scholar who soon got bored and lazy, a terrible showoff. He hated cricket because it hurt to catch the ball; he was timid at football because he didn't like being kicked in the shins. But it was chiefly the seriousness of organized athletics which daunted him and damped his enthusiasm. Unorganized physical play always appealed to him. He loved tearing around with the other boys, screaming, laughing, scuffling. Wrestling soon became a conscious sex pleasure. He found boxing sexy, too, even though he usually got knocked about. If they had played Rugby football instead of soccer, he would have enjoyed the body contact of the scrums and perhaps not so much minded the kicks.

At the Sports, which were held in the middle of the summer term, the quarter-mile handicap was the one compulsory event for every boy in the school, big or little. It must have been because Ciddy already had such a low opinion of Christopher as an athlete that he was the only boy to be given the maximum start of a hundred yards; the next runner was placed at least five yards behind him. This was a mistake. Christopher, even then, had unusual strength in his legs, inherited from Frank. When the race began, he didn't lose his lead. Soon he was being tailed by one of the older boys, who had come up from near scratch. Christopher kept glancing anxiously over his shoulder as he ran. This amused the spectators, and some of them ran beside him, shouting to him not to look back, laughing and cheering him on. He passed the winning post first and received the silver cup which was given for the event. Kathleen, back in Ireland, was delighted when she heard the news. But Christopher's victory must have disgusted Ciddy— it was victory of the wrong kind, unearned, fluky, farcical, a sort of send-up of the Morgan Brown way of life, and all the more stinging for being unintentional.

May 25. Richard announces his intention of leaving me soon and going away for a long long time in a big 'shrip' to look for 'Bubbie' (Christopher). I think he misses him a good deal.

May 26. The third reading of the Home Rule Bill passed yesterday and last night there was a good deal of shouting and playing of bands and it is said the effigy of the King and Queen was burnt!

. .

June 12. Those *fiendish suffragettes* have placed *a bomb beneath* the coronation chair in Westminster Abbey as their latest outrage, having burnt down two old churches a week or so ago.

June 14. Jack Isherwood had been down to see Christopher. The Browns said he has settled down with them and with the boys and that he makes a great impression on the latter with his long words and large range of topics!

June 21. Richard *in tunic and knickers for the first time,* looked sweet but alas for the departure of his baby frocks.

June 23. C's weekly letter. He writes of the half-term exam results being read out, 'Mr Cyril announced who had passed with honours and among the names he read was my name!! Whereupon someone gave me such a violent slap on the back I nearly fell off the desk I was sitting on'.

June 28. The Regiment goes off on Tuesday. Some say the town nationalists are only waiting till they are gone to raid the guns and ammunition left behind. However the General won't hear of the Regiment not going on manoeuvres.

July 3. In the north they say the priests are selling lottery tickets for the big places now belonging to Protestants, which they tell the people they will get when Home Rule comes.

July 10. In afternoon to the town to get another trap for we are now infested with rats and seven have been killed the last few days. Fearfully close and heavy and the air full of oppression and smells.

July 13. The papers look fearfully serious. Ulster is an armed camp. Sir Edward Carson says 'if it be not peace with honour it must be war with honour'.

·   ·

July 15. Another rat caught, the fifteenth. Richard and I met a huge one in the hall!

July 21. Got out things for packing and Nurse packed.

July 22. Had smooth crossing. Reached Buckingham St at 9.30. Very close and airless but Mama looking fairly well.

July 25. To the National Portrait Gallery to see Chamberlain's portrait just added since his death. Carlyle's frame still hangs empty and the very thick plate glass smashed, with a photo of the picture as it was—all slashed by one of those mad and wicked suffragettes.

July 26. Stayed in till lunch which we had at the Strand Palace Hotel. Then on to church at the Temple. Singing very good but both felt sickly! In evening newspaper men calling out loudly, but we could not hear what. . . .

July 27. The Nationalists tried to land arms at Howth near Dublin and police were sent to prevent them. There was a row and shots were fired on the police. Then the soldiers appeared, the crowd hustled and threw things at them, injuring several, and finally the soldiers started firing. Of course the outcry of 'murder' on the part of the Nationalists is tremendous.

(*This is a garbled account of the events, which is hardly surprising, considering the kind of newspapers Kathleen read. She seems sarcastic about "the outcry of 'murder,'" but in fact four people died and thirty-five more were wounded.*)

July 28. To take ermine to be altered, to Harrods to change books and to the ticket place to get C's ticket. The evening papers announced that Austria had declared war on Servia.

· ·

July 29. To Hindhead. Christopher looked very well and seemed very much the same, not grown but very untidy! Ink on his coat and a dirty collar!

July 30. A wire from Frank to say the Regiment were returning home today, so I suppose they are afraid of rows in Limerick. Nurse also wrote she would be glad when we were back, that two soldiers had been nearly killed on Monday and that the guard at the barrack gate had been doubled and armed.

(Nanny, as always, must have exaggerated the alarms. Because of the sensational stories she later told him about their life in Ireland, Christopher grew up believing that the Regiment had been sniped at on its way to service at the cathedral on several occasions. He only recently discovered that this wasn't true.)

July 31. Left the flat at 7.45 and got to Paddington 8.5, so was able to get corner seats the moment the train came in. Such crowds, more people going on cheap excursions to Ireland than ever. We had a crowded journey to Limerick, where Frank met us. They had been expecting all day to mobilize, to be ready by the 5th if required, as France can't mobilize so quickly. It seems *so appalling*, one can't take it in. I never thought of Irish troops being called upon. The only hope is that Germany does not want to fight, but they have asked Russia why they are mobilizing, and if it is to assist Servia then Germany is bound to help Austria. It seems so extraordinary that in a few hours Home Rule and Ireland have sunk into insignificance. Unionists and Nationalists alike agree to throw in their lot with England.

August 2. Showery. C and I to the Cathedral as Frank was taking the soldiers to church. No definite news. To the band after church. Mrs Cobbold there. Mirabel bigger than ever.

August 3. Germany has not only declared war on Russia but crossed the French frontier at three different points. It is impossible for England to be neutral. The fleet are to mobilize and the army are awaiting orders. All the men went through their medical exam today to be in greater readiness.

August 4. Down the town with Frank who wanted to get various things in preparation. All available horses are being called for. Flour and sugar have gone up but there is enough wheat to last four months. Paper notes are to be issued and the banks are closed till Friday. At six pm came a message from the Barracks that the troops are *to mobilize at once*. On the fifth day they will be ready to go. It is simply crushing, the suddenness and awfulness of it all.

This is the moment which Christopher's memory has chosen to retain, not only as a picture but as a playback of Frank's voice. Kathleen and Christopher are together in one of the rooms of Roden House and Frank looks in, only for a moment; he must hurry back to barracks. He says, "The order to mobilize has come." His tone is quiet, gentle, almost reassuring. Then he is gone.

16

August 5. Showery all day. In the town to get an aircushion for Frank. *England has declared war on Germany*, and now seven countries are at war. Mrs Cobbold came round with plans about the women. Met various people, all very kind and sympathetic. Gave a month's warning of the house.

August 6. Made Frank a housewife in morning. Various rumours but it seems pretty certain that the Germans and English are having a naval battle in the North Sea. In London Mama writes sugar is a shilling a pound. In the Isle of Wight they are expecting the proclamation of martial law and all arming in anticipation of an attack from Germany. Various German spies have been arrested.

August 7. 300 reservists arrived between 7 and 8 pm. 300 come tomorrow. Rumours that eight German battleships are sunk, also that the English flagship has gone down.

(*No naval fighting of any kind had actually taken place so far.*)

August 8. Hurried off to a ship's chandler on the quay to get some canvas to make a new holdall for Frank's bedding. Bell and I made it while Nurse finished lengthening the sleeping-bag. It was packed and the name painted on it by 3 pm and then we found it weighed 40 lbs instead of 35 lbs, which is the allowance, so that amount has to come out.

August 9. Service at the Cathedral for the soldiers. They marched down a thousand strong. The Dean, with a great want of tact, assured the men their widows should be looked after! They had 'Jesus Lover of my Soul', 'The King of Love' and 'Oh God our Help'. The psalms were the 23rd and the 27th. Somehow it was as little impressive as was possible, which was a comfort considering the terrible solemnity of the occasion. In afternoon the troops were reviewed by the Colonel and all their kit inspected.

August 10. The Dean came after lunch to pay a sort of farewell and condolence visit and say how sad it was to think that perhaps half of the men in the Cathedral on Sunday *would never come back*, so cheering and tactful!

August 11. No real news. Felt rather seedy and faint all afternoon as I ran two staylace tags into me by sitting on them. Christopher to the Gaiety pictures in evening.

August 12. A beautiful day and very warm. To sketch view of King John's Castle. The men inoculated against typhoid. Frank done and it made him feel wretchedly sick and gave him a bad head. Some of the men fainted. Everything now is just waiting. . . .

August 13. Frank very busy with final arrangements. Did not go out beyond the 'Technical' for fear further orders came. They came later to say they were to start tomorrow in two lots, leaving at 12 and 1.

August 14. At 4.20 am Nurse came in to say Bell had come to say they were starting earlier. It seems a wire had arrived at midnight to tell them to be ready to go at 9 and 10 am. Breakfast 6.30

and parade at 7.45. Close heavy day. Christopher and Richard and Nurse and I to the Barracks after saying goodbye here to my dear —he looked so tired and his arm is hardly well. We went to the station, there were a good many people to see them go, and it was just heartbreaking. They only knew that half were to embark at Queenstown, half at Cork, no orders further till they get there.

Postcard from Frank, August 14:

Arrived Queenstown. At first we were told there were no transports and we were not expected. However they have found us an awful old boat on which we are crowding but we are luckier than other regiments who are hanging about till tomorrow. The mare will not go on board and hasn't been got on yet.

August 15. Very close and heavy. Heaven only knows when one will have a home again. It is sad to think of leaving our little home here for ever. I love this house and its quaintness and our happy time—but now Frank is gone it is all different. C had a fancy to have his tea on the roof so we had it there and got a slight breeze.

Postcard from Frank, August 15, Holyhead:

Arrived this morning. 'Quite safe'. Going off this morning into the unknown. The poor little mare wouldn't go on board yesterday, so a sling was constructed *very badly* and she was hoisted in the air. The sling gave way and she fell in between the boat and the quay and lay on the ledge and gradually slipped into the water. She then swam right round the ship and was headed off by a boat. She wasn't hurt at all but had to be left behind. I have got a spare horse but I feel so sorry about her.

Letter from Frank, August 17, Cambridge:

We travelled right across England yesterday and finally arrived at the place where we had our honeymoon! No one seemed to expect us. We didn't get settled in till about midnight and every-one was very tired and hungry. Managed to get a sort of meal off bloater paste and dog biscuits. You have no cause for anxiety and we aren't so very uncomfortable and very lucky to have got across without delay or losing anything except indeed the poor little mare. She is so associated in my mind with you and it is dreadful to think of all the fright and indignities she had to put up with. It seems such ages since we parted and you are in another world to which I long to get back. In the afternoon Sandys and I went on the Backs which were looking lovely. I thought so much of you and the time we sat there on the seat together. Went to tea at Buol's, another of our old haunts.

August 18. Mrs Cobbold called and we went together to the meeting of the SSFA at the Strand Barracks, held in an upper room looking across to Arthur's Quay and so associated with Frank and happy days that I nearly wept. It looked so lovely, the still reflections in the water, but no one saw it.

(*The SSFA was an organization which helped the families of Soldiers and Sailors.*)

August 19. Henry wrote yesterday that if I could not find an escort for the children, he would come to Holyhead or Dublin and take them to Marple and have his reward in feeling he had relieved me of one of my anxieties—a really kind unselfish offer.

Letter from Frank, August 19, the Union Society, Cambridge:

My dear, you see I have penetrated into the Union. We are all honorary members. I am glad to say that the mare turned up today. She is rather bruised and cut about, but nothing at all serious. She walked on board the ship she came over in quite coolly. I suppose she realized how silly she had been to make such a fuss. We really have been having a peaceful not to say gay time. We dine either at Sidney Sussex, where we are honorary members, or at one of the other colleges. Sidney is Oliver Cromwell's college. The Master and other dons are authorities on his period and very much interested to hear about Bradshaw. The way we are being feted and lionized is quite funny. An old lady came up to me in the street yesterday and presented me with a rose which she said she hoped I would carry. I don't quite know where.

I don't know when we shall start. I suppose we shall come in as a reinforcement if the Germans don't see the folly of their behaviour before we get there. Except for you I don't really very much care. One gets very reckless and devil-may-care in this atmosphere, but I feel dreadfully sorry for you and the dull anxious time you are having. However at the present moment you have absolutely no cause for anxiety except that I may undermine my constitution by eating and drinking too much!

August 20. The Barrack gate at the top of the lane locked. Mrs Cobbold and I to the Strand Barracks and she began going into the cases needing relief. Mirabel came and as usual she and Christopher managed to fall out before the end. Felt very very tired.

Letter from Frank, August 21, Cambridge:

Had a very polite note from the Head Porter of Emmanuel, saying he was Nurse's brother-in-law and if I cared to go down to the college and get a hot bath he would see that I had one. He afterwards showed me a portrait they have there of John Bradshaw which represents him as a very goodlooking young man with a long pointed face and curling chestnut hair. I feel I am having an unfairly gay time but I dare say I shall make up for it before I have done!

Letter from Frank, August 22, Cambridge:

My dinner at Christs last night was most interesting. McClean took me to his rooms afterwards with two others and all three were radicals and Home Rulers and we had a tremendous conversation. One of them had lived a good deal at Marple. He was very amusing about it and said he had always looked upon us as sort of Feudal Lords, and seemed quite surprised that I was a human being at all. The other fellow who was there was going out with Shackleton to the Antarctic but I thought was rather a foolish youth.

(*It seems strange to think of these two, the "rather foolish youth" and the middle-aged soldier, meeting for this one evening and then parting, each to encounter his adversary, with half the world between them. Shackleton's ship, the* Endurance, *was crushed by the ice and abandoned in November 1915; his party drifted on a disintegrating floe for more than four months, then managed to reach an island on which they endured exposure, disease and near-starvation throughout the antarctic winter. They were rescued at the end of August 1916, after Shackleton and five others had sailed eight hundred miles to South Georgia to get help, in a small open boat.*)

Shortly after writing the above letter, Frank must have got some assurance that they would not be ordered to leave Cambridge for several days at least, for he wired Kathleen to come if she possibly could. Kathleen packed in haste and left Limerick on August 24. Nanny, Christopher and Richard traveled with her as far as Crewe, on their way to Marple. Kathleen got to Cambridge on the evening of August 25. Frank was at the station to meet her. Next day, Emily joined them.

Kathleen's diary says nothing of her feelings during this visit; probably she did not want to make them even more painful by writing about them. She and Frank saw each other whenever it was possible; he had to spend much time out at his camp or on marches and training exercises. The war news was bad, with the Germans steadily advancing on Paris. There were rumors (absolutely false) of Russian troops passing through Cambridge at night on their way to France. Mrs. Cobbold collected over a thousand pairs of socks for the regiment. The weather was perfect. The colleges "looked most beautiful, so shady, so peace-

ful and so far from war, the trees so green and the lawns so velvety." Kathleen decided it would be very nice if Christopher became a don.

Then suddenly, in the early afternoon of September 7, came the order for the troops to leave that night. Kathleen and Mrs. Cobbold went to see them off.

(More than a year later, October 6, 1915, Kathleen would be writing in her diary: "Heard from Mrs Cobbold that Major Robertson was killed last week. This completes the casualties to those travelling on the seventh of September in the same carriage from Cambridge as Frank. Nothing has happened to any of those in the same carriage as Colonel Cobbold.")

Letter from Frank, September 8, Southampton:

We arrived here about 5.30 am. I feel like an animal, and what the men can feel like who have been in a carriage with eight in it all night, I can't imagine. We don't know where we are going but report says to St Nazaire, which I think is on the Loire. It is a voyage of about 26 hours. I have taken my Mothersill.

I did so appreciate all your kindness. It makes it so different, leaving someone behind who really cares about you—and be sure whatever happens I shall *go to you at once*. Think of me at night and perhaps you will be able to realize whether I am all right or not. I will try to make you. I am writing in an awful din, so it is rather difficult to express myself.

September 9. Left Cambridge 11.15, getting to Marple 5.15. Moey and Christopher met me. Very close and heavy.

Letter from Frank, September 10, St.-Nazaire, France:

Our arrival was very amusing. The ship had to go through a narrow channel, right through the middle of the town, this was lined with a crowd, very enthusiastic, partly composed of the seediest-looking French soldiers I ever saw. When our men threw them coppers and hat-badges etc the sentries deserted their posts and scrambled with gamins on the quay for them. The men sang what now seems to be the National Anthem, 'It's a Long Way to Tipperary', and 'Everybody's Doing It', amidst applause and clapping. I have just read through all my Company's letters to censor them and they evidently find the same difficulty that I do in writing when you know that your letter will be read. I think of you so pretty and clean in your pink dress. I am fairly clean and we hope to get a bathe in the sea this afternoon. We haven't much news but everything seems reassuring and I really think we may look forward to that Christmas dinner after all! You ought to be very thankful that we were not out here in the retirement a fortnight ago. They seem to have had a most terrible time.

(*This refers to the British retreat after the Battle of Mons, August 23.*)

September 14. Had a good crossing. Reached Limerick at 10 am. Up to the house after lunch, sadly overgrown and deserted. Packed things away. We were attacked by legions of fleas and so bitten!

Letter from Frank, September 14:

We were in a delightful little town last night in a very clean house belonging to a very nice woman. She sighed dreadfully, poor thing, over our dirty boots but was so thankful to have got rid of the Germans she didn't mind us. They stole everything and smashed what they didn't take and they killed all the waiters. Cowley was on outposts in a village and met a man who had all his children bayonetted and his wife carried away and he didn't know where she was. Tonight we are quartered in a cafe. We are warned not to drink anything out of any opened bottles as they have left poisoned drinks about, aren't they swine? There is no low trick they aren't capable of. We have heard no guns today and the report is they are retiring fast. The country about here is

411

very pretty, wooded ridges and rivers and the most charming little villages.

(They were now in the neighborhood of La Ferté-sous-Jouarre on the Marne and moving northward toward the Aisne.)

September 15. To Roden House soon after breakfast. Wrote letters in the verandah keeping an eye on the men. One big van filled by dusk.

September 18. Furniture all out last night. The King to give the royal assent to the passing of the Home Rule Bill today, which we concluded he did, from the shouting in the late evening.

Letter from Frank, September 18:

We have been billeted in a series of farms, really beautiful old buildings with enormous barns. One has seen France in a sort of way one never could again. We are now very near the fighting and hear the big guns going off a few miles ahead of us, but when we shall be in it I don't know.

September 21. Very smooth crossing—my twentyfirst! The Allies seem to be holding their own and the dreadful casualty lists keep appearing. Frank's Mother, Richard and Nurse met me at Stockport.

(This was the day Frank's unit reached the front. They were in trenches near the village of Vailly on the Aisne for the next three weeks.)

September 22. Up the village in the victoria with Mr Isherwood who had a longer talk than usual with 'the man at the bank'. After that to see Fanny Hudson at Brabyns. She is still waiting for convalescent soldiers. A party of refugee Belgians are arriving today at Marple. Two cottages have been furnished and made ready for them.

September 23. Left by the 10.6 for London.

September 24. Sent off first parcel to Frank. Three pounds go for a shilling. It contained 2 packets chocolate, 2 oz tobacco, 4 packets soup, 2 tins vaseline.

(*On September 25, Kathleen went to Hindhead and saw Christopher at St. Edmund's. He must have gone back to school earlier in the month, but Kathleen's anxieties and preoccupations were such that she doesn't even mention this in her diary. While there, she found rooms for Emily and herself in the neighboring village of Grayshott, into which they moved next day.*)

Letter from Frank, September 25:

We are living the queerest life. Our company headquarters is in a cavern, where we have a fire and are quite warm. Westby our cook is a wonderful person and manages to pick up all sorts of luxuries, fowls and rabbits, etc. Today he has been down to the village which has been shelled to pieces and found a sweet shop still open, so he brought back a packet of sweets which were most welcome. As he pops one into his mouth every time he passes the bag, we shan't get many, I am afraid. We spend most of our time digging in the trenches. It is a queer life but one gets into the way of crawling about on one's hands and knees to avoid getting sniped. I am quite well and really in no particular danger. I can't think this will last very long. I am sure we shall appreciate our home life all the more for having had it broken up for a time.

September 28. Kind letter from Frank's Father saying I was to be *sure* to make Marple my headquarters and leave the children there whenever I wish to go away.

• •

Westby goes foraging and has battles royal with other people who are shopping. One officer tried to take his things away from him but he said 'nay, nay, my officers want it as much as thine' and refused to give it up. People pretend they want the things for the General or the hospital or something.

September 30. Called for Christopher and we drove round by Frensham. On the common were tents and soldiers, mostly in scarlet jackets when they had any sort of uniform, having run out of khaki.

Letter from Frank, September 30:

It is dreadful to think you are terrified by the Daily Mail account of battles when really I am not in any particular danger at all. The battle of nowadays is such a drawn-out affair that most of the time the people on either side are doing nothing at all and all the wild charges and murderous artillery fire that one reads about doesn't come in *everyone's* way. However I know it is of no use to tell you not to be anxious and of course in a way I can't help feeling glad that you are.

Letter from Frank to Christopher, October 4:

My dear old thing, I was very glad to get your letter. You would be very much interested in the aeroplanes here. The British ones have a Union Jack painted under their wings, the French a tricoloured target and the Germans a black Maltese cross but I think some of the latter carry the French colours to deceive us. The Germans however are rather a different shape and have the wings curved back behind. It is very pretty to see the guns firing at them and they fly about among the shells in a very daring way. There is a British one that the men call 'Cheeky Charley'. I hope you are having a happy time. I am sorry to hear that you don't care for football. I think myself it is much more amusing than cricket.

October 5. Round to see Christopher in the 10.45 break. Also interviewed Cyril. He spoke of Christopher as having plenty of brain but rather slack over work that did not interest him. Said he was as good as gold and he thought as happy as a king, and that though he was no good at games (Mr Sant spoke of him as being quite pathetic in the cricket or football field) the boys admired him for the things he knew and could tell them and he got on quite well all round. Felt so glad. Mama and I left by the 2.25.

Letter from Frank, October 9:

The artillery had a great fight. The shells whistled over our heads but I sat comfortably in the bottom of my trench knitting, surrounded by the men who thought it a great joke. They really are marvellous and the older ones are very sensible in the way they look at things, and I think they are showing themselves and their class in a very favourable light, one really can't help loving them. I'm afraid the people who think that the war will be over by Christmas are rather optimistic. I think Lethbridge has gone home. He really behaved rather well and deserves any fuss that is made of him. Active service does bring out the best of a fellow's character (and in some cases perhaps the worst, selfishness and so on). There is a certain amount to put up with.

(*Mr. Lethbridge was the first officer to be wounded. He had been hit on September 21, their first day in the trenches.*)

October 10. Very interested in the weird searchlights which illuminate the darkness from the top of Charing Cross station and we fancied now and then we saw dim objects scouring the skies as well. Mrs M in after dinner, took a most gloomy view of the danger we are in, not only from zeppelins but the numbers of Germans still in this country. *Antwerp has alas fallen.*

We are still sitting here. The place is getting a very worn appearance but by moonlight still looks fresh and beautiful. I sat on the bank last night during my watch looking down a little avenue of poplars with the moon showing through brown clouds at the end and enjoyed it very much. We feel rather left here as the fighting seems to have moved away. Not that I particularly pant for blood. I am prepared to do my duty, as Sandys very grandly said in one of his letters. He writes pages to his Mother and his Brother and all his female friends every day, full of old-fashioned pious sentiments, rather the sort of letter that Nelson wrote home to Emma. One of his ladies sent two large parcels of tobacco and matches and a hundred pipes for the men. I tell him he will have to propose to her after this.

Mrs H sent a very good parcel of socks and balaclava helmets. The helmets really are wanted as the nights are very cold and you can't sleep in your cap. I tie my head up in old socks! I am longing for a piano and a paint box and to be settled somewhere with you again. I wonder what will happen to us when the war is over. I sometimes feel that this is the end of my soldiering and that I have earned a little peace. However I don't suppose they would let me go very easily.

October 12. War news very depressing. With Antwerp for a base, the Germans talk of being able to take Ostend and being in England at the end of the month.

(*On October 12 the Regiment left Vailly and began a round-about journey by train: Etaples, Boulogne, Calais, St.-Omer. From St.-Omer they marched via Cassel into the area south of Armen-tières. (All this was part of a general movement to check the German advance toward Calais and Boulogne.) On October 18 they had their first fighting in the open. They attacked Radinghem and suffered heavy casualties. This is the action referred to in Frank's next letter.*)

October 14. In morning to take pictures to be framed in Fetter Lane. Every other person seems to be talking French and two thousand more Belgian refugees arrived yesterday.

October 15. Interviewed the cellars in case of bombs and having to retire into them. The Military Expert of The Times today said we ought to be all prepared.

Letter from Frank, October 22:

The Sixth Division is right in it and we are fighting and digging day and night. It is really much less alarming than you would think, only very fatiguing and unpleasant and rather dull. We have in the last week dug or commenced to dig five different lots of trenches, and are going to dig another tonight. I think we have rather a reputation as diggers and certainly the men are very good. We got it rather hot last Sunday, as we advanced on a village rather prematurely, in fact I lost 60 killed and wounded in my company and I think if we had gone a bit slower it might have been avoided. Our excellent Westby was wounded. He cooked and looked after us and is a great loss. Do tell Henry if you write that Westby also lives in Sheffield and if he could go and see him and help him in any way I should be awfully obliged and he would find him very amusing.

Yesterday I went out of the trenches to a farm about 300 yards back and had breakfast. The woman was living there all alone. She said she wasn't going to turn out and she was a good catholic and if she was going to be killed she was and there was an end of it. (Since writing this the farm has been shelled and burnt.) The French women are delightful and splendid, so calm and brave and so extraordinarily women of the world, for their station. Most of the men seem to me rather silly. The French troops we have seen are all right at attacking but seem to be quite incapable of keeping still and quiet, and the French cavalry in front of us are rather an embarrassment. We shot one of them by mistake the other day.

Letter from Frank, October 24:

We are still right in it. You will have seen that Sandys is wounded and missing but I am afraid there is little or no doubt that he is really dead and Bell is the same. It is all dreadful but somehow one goes on. Not that I am in the least frightened but it is all so boring and deadly and all the things I like have disappeared for the present. I feel sure that I shall see you again and I hope before long.

October 25. To see Major Robertson, wounded by a bullet that passed through his left wrist and a second one that went in below his ankle and came out at his heel, shattering the bone. Said the Germans took special aim at officers, according to the Kaiser's instructions. Frank well when he last saw him.

Letter from Frank, October 27:

I have got two warm coats now as I annexed the fleece-lined Burberry which poor Sandys was so proud of. However I really never felt so well as I do. I shall have to live on a diet of bully beef for the rest of my life. It suits me extraordinarily well. Cullen got wounded yesterday. It was his own fault as he was walking about at the top of the trench and a sniper hit him. I asked him to let you know his address if he was in London. Lethbridge's picture appeared in the Daily Sketch, he is at the Empress Eugénie's house and was taken in a group of the Empress talking to the convalescents.

I hope some of them will come back soon, as there is only Cowley left to me now. The Colonel told me he had sent in my name for mention in despatches but I fancy he sent a good many so I don't suppose we shall all get in. I am not conscious of having done anything very remarkable in any case, but the really important thing is to stick it. 'He that endureth to the end . . .' is the useful man. But oh, let it be soon!

.   .

(For the next three days and nights they were very heavily shelled without being able to knock out the German guns. The General complained bitterly to his superiors of the British weakness in artillery and manpower. Colonel Cobbold wrote to his wife that the General had sent him to Paris on a special mission, " a kind way of giving me a few days' rest.")

November 2. A letter from Mr Cullen, written from hospital. I went off at once. He was shot in the jaw, nearly all right again. He goes home tomorrow and back at the end of the month.

Letter from Frank, November 2:

We have moved back about four miles and I am now in a very mild line of trenches where nothing much happens. We have had a lot of shells over us lately—'Black Marias' and 'Coal Boxes' and 'Jack Johnsons'—two burst within ten yards of my dugout. Their effect is extraordinarily local but to see and hear them you would think that everyone for yards around must be annihilated. Bailey and his company had a post in about half an acre of ground. The enemy put about fifty shells on it but not a single man was touched.

Please thank Mama for her delightful parcel. I should very much like to find in the next parcel you send me a tin of unsweetened condensed milk. It is very comforting in the night with a little rum in it, and sardines are rather nice things too. If Father chooses to send me a pipe I shouldn't mind. I have only got one now. I'm afraid this letter is all about things I want, rather like boys at school. It is very hard to be at school when you are 45, but I hope this is really positively my last go of it.

November 7. A letter from Alice Neville who had seen Captain Jackson looking very delicate but his arm getting on, he said Frank was well when he left but wished I could tell him not to expose himself so much, he seemed very fearless of danger.

. .

Tell Mama how much I enjoyed James's 'Bundle of Letters' which she so kindly sent me. There is such a delightful refinement about them which one particularly appreciates out here. I offered my literary corporal a book yesterday and gave him that detective book you sent. I thought he looked very disappointed and saw that he had fixed his eye on the Hibbert Journal, rather a dull theological magazine which Henry sent. So I offered him that and he was delighted, said he always read it at home. I don't know if he was pulling my leg or not!

We had another draft yesterday, funny homely elderly old things, they spend their time cooking and making their family arrangements in the most peaceful style. However I think they are really more reliable in the long run than the very young ones.

November 9. The Russians are in Germany at two points and the Allies still hold their own. The Strand crowded for the Lord Mayor's Show, a purely military one this year. The Lord Mayor's gorgeous coach the one bright object, troops all in khaki.

Letter from Frank, November 9:

It is curious how little these horrors affect me. I don't seem to realize them—and in any case we haven't had any of the very awful scenes of carnage which one reads about in the papers. I am sure some of the men write as if we were in a regular inferno and we haven't been in anything of the sort.

I am indeed, as Henry says, lucky in the big things of life, but I think if *you* are, it is entirely owing to yourself, for I am conscious of very often being extremely tiresome and wanting in what Henry grandly calls 'reciprocity'. However I'm glad to feel that the two boys and our circumstances generally are 'fairly' successful, and although I am afraid you don't like soldiering generally, yet it has given us some good times—? I am sorry Richard is peevish and disagreeable. Tell him from me that soldiers (and their sons) are never like that and ready to put up with any disagreeables. He is quite old enough to be impressed by that, and not old enough to know how untrue it is!!

Letter from Frank, November 11:

I am glad Henry saw Westby, he really is a splendid chap, so full of go and his first thought was always for 'his' officers. Why he thought I was so delicate I don't know, the little internal trouble that I had arose entirely from over-eating.

The farm behind us is a brewery and there were large stores of spirits in it, and as the men were constantly getting off there and getting the stuff, the Colonel said it must be burned, which we did. It burned merrily all night but in the morning when I looked the only thing left were the five barrels of spirits which were quite untouched, so the Colour Sergeant and I went and smashed them up—you can't think what a delightful sensation it is!

November 11. After breakfast to the War Office to see if I could find out about Bell and if he was a prisoner or in hospital, but though we know he was wounded his name has not come through.

November 12. Took Richard out. We walked up and down on Hungerford Bridge to watch the trains and signals which are simply an endless delight and he sits for half an hour together at the dining-room window quite absorbed!

Letter from Frank, November 12:

We had a very wet cold night last night and today there is a cold high wind and the trenches are a mass of mud and very miserable. Some people seem to think the Germans will collapse suddenly but je m'en doute. The Saturday Review is very pessimistic and I am afraid I share their views.

November 15. [At Hindhead.] Christopher and I round by Witley Camp, one of the many where huts are being built for the Kitchener's men. They say they are to be heated and all ready after Christmas. Meantime, now that the weather is getting winterly, the men and officers will be billeted out. News that Lord Roberts had died at the Front where he had gone to visit the Indian Troops of whom he is nominally in command. He caught a chill and died peacefully and suddenly, serving his country to the last, at the age of 82. C back to tea and I to evening chapel, after which we said goodbye. St Edmunds is to have 40 men and 3 officers billeted on them, of the Rifle Brigade.

Letter from Frank, November 15:

We have been taken out of the trenches to have a few days' rest; we arrived here at dead of night and were put into a farm already full of B Company. It snowed a little this morning and one can't think what it will be like when the winter really sets in in earnest. I think it is about the time you were going down to Hindhead. I hope Christopher will come to the scratch and show 'reciprocity'.

Letter from Frank, November 16:

We are having what I really think is *the* worst time we have had—seven officers sleep in a little room. Altogether I shall be thankful to get back to the trenches. However of course one's dry here and eight miles from the nearest German. Oh, how I do long for a little orderliness and peace and quiet!

I hope you met Henry. Really he and Muriel have been perfect bricks, and so has Moey.

November 17. Jack Isherwood to dinner. He is very busy with drilling and rifle practice for home defence.

Letter from Frank, November 18 (?):

I am glad to tell you we have moved to another farm in the village and are now by ourselves. The people at the last farm parted with me with tears, and without any reason at all they looked upon me as their saviour and thought I had arranged for them to stop in their farm. It was rather embarrassing as very voluble people kept arriving to ask all sorts of conundrums and wouldn't believe I had no power to do anything for them. However I did save an old couple of 76 from moving and in return she washed my shirts and warm underclothes.

Letter from Frank, November 19:

It is rather terrible here, all the unfortunate people are being turned out of their farms. It means absolute ruin to them, as they have to leave their stock and household goods which of course they will never see again.

I can't think that Jackson had the impudence to tell you that I exposed myself unnecessarily. It was an absolute lie. I am most cautious. Of course one has to lead the men forward and to take risks in doing so, but I never do anything unnecessary or foolish, I can promise you that, and I have got at the back of my mind the determination to get back to see you again.

Letter from Frank, November 20:

I am afraid I am not a christian, at least perhaps I am. I don't find it at all difficult to love my enemy—but one's friends! Sometimes one feels one can't bear the sight of them. It is so difficult to get away from anyone here and nothing to take one away. There are none of those dear little amazing moments which one has to oneself and when one realizes how beautiful everything is—as a matter of fact things are not beautiful here, so I suppose that is why one misses the moments!

November 22. To see Maud Greenway in afternoon. She looked so nice in black with her hair tightly done and a little straight fringe like in old-fashioned photographs. Cleveland had arrived back with his nerves broken down, so trying just when he was doing good work commanding one of the new battalions of the Rifle Brigade, and she was very much the patient but much tried wife. She had two wounded and four more arriving that afternoon and it keeps her very busy doing the housekeeping and sending in reports. She has voluntary helpers of course, nurses and a sister in charge and her own doctor attends.

November 23. In afternoon Richard and Nurse and I went up the Strand, then to the National Gallery, which he said was a very nice station but there were no puff-puffs. At 6.45 a wire from Frank to say he was arriving at 8.15, on ten days leave. I could hardly believe such wonderful news! Went to Charing Cross but found that Folkestone trains arrive at Victoria, so went there and found him looking so well. It was delightful. He slept in the dining-room.

November 24. Frank and I went to Nathan's for him to get some repairs done and new tunic made, his things are in a pretty bad state. Then to the Old Watercolour Society in Pall Mall. The most interesting things were by Clausen, Mildred Butler and Charles Sims. In afternoon F and I took Richard by underground railway to South Kensington to Porter's toyshop to buy a signal, and back the same way, which he loved, and then we visited Charing Cross station to look at the puff-puffs there. F and I to see 'Mr Wu' in evening, a rather gruesome piece.

November 25. To Nathan and then to the National Gallery where Mr Kaine Smith was lecturing on Goya, very interestingly, speaking of the great reserve force one always felt in Spanish painting and how they never painted unless they had something to say. F and I by the 2.30 to Marple. When we got to the house we found quite a party assembled on the lawn to cheer him, and a large 'welcome home' over the front door and flags flying and the warmest and kindest of welcomes back from all there, all so glad to see him looking so well.

.   .

November 26. Henry and Muriel motored over to lunch. Had a slight chill, I think, and during dinner turned so faint I had to get up and leave the table, fortunately Frank came with me, I collapsed in the hall and knew no more till I found myself on my bed, after which I was very sick. Most unpleasant!

November 27. Reached London about 2. F and I to the Hippodrome to see the 'Revue', a series of scenes to do with the War, the recruiting, the sewing parties, the charge of the cavalry, and with patriotic songs all through, in which Violet Lorraine was very good. The whole thing was well done in its own particular line and a skit on the questions of the moment, the German spies and the Germans and their proposed invasion.

November 28. F and I left for Hindhead by the 11.10. Christopher very excited and pleased to see Frank and in the afternoon we motored to Aldershot for tea. After dinner F played, the first time he had touched a piano for many weeks.

November 29. To school chapel at 11. C came back with us after and stayed to lunch. We got to London a little before 6.30, travelling up with various degrees of Kitchener's new army, most of them soldiers of four to seven weeks' standing. Their conversation most amusing!

November 30. Saw Richard and Nurse off at St Pancras and joined F and Mama at the Club. To see 'The Outcast' in the evening. Gerald du Maurier, Grace Lane and Hilda Moore. Very interesting and well acted. Enjoyed it much.

December 1. Toothache and seedy. Frank and I to the National Gallery and heard delightful lecture on the Tuscan School, the Florentine and Sienese, their methods and characteristics. In afternoon he, Mama and I to the Coliseum to see a variety entertainment including many patriotic songs, a war play and the Follies etc, rather depressing as a whole. Frank's last evening before leave is up.

December 2. Cold. Frank and I to Victoria. Though we got there before 8 there were a good many before us—officers returning and Red Cross people, nuns and Belgians and we think the Queen of the Belgians too, and the train steamed off and another goodbye. . . . . the ten days went like a dream. Again toothache.

Letter from Frank, December 3:

My dear, we had rather a rough crossing yesterday but thanks to Mothersill I didn't feel a qualm. At Boulogne we had time for dejeuner, in the company of the Queen of the Belgians (she is very worn and sad and no wonder, poor thing) and at 1.30 pm we started off sixty miles in a motor bus. We stopped at Army Headquarters en route and I tried to buy some candles. There wasn't one to be had in the town! However I eventually secured two Christmas tree sort of things of blue wax! At our Army Corps Headquarters we transferred into a motor lorry which took us to Divisional Headquarters. There a kind staff officer lent me a motor, so I was driven to Battalion Headquarters, at least to a farm where the reserve is. I had dinner with Clemson and then went down an interminable communicating trench. The trenches are a labyrinth, I have already lost myself repeatedly, and are quite the worst I have seen. (I hope posterity when they read this won't think I am grumbling but you can't get out of them and walk about the country or see anything at all but two muddy walls on each side of you.) I found Cowley rather ill. The doctor thinks he has an internal abcess. I slept in a dugout with him and this morning he has gone off to go home and I have got the dugout. It is not bad, the sides are covered with straw and it is quite warm, not to say stuffy, but unless one sits in the doorway it is pitch dark.

I did so hate saying goodbye to you again yesterday morning. Everyone else seems such dull company after you and Mama, who share my real feelings in so many ways although we don't always agree! Things are very safe here. There is hardly any firing or shell fire going on at all.

Letter from Frank, December 4:

I am delighted with the waterproof Jaeger helmet and the pipe lighter is a most successful toy. Leecroft has got one not nearly such a good pattern, which won't light at once. But, as I told him, anything that I got from my Wife was sure to be the best obtainable. I am sinking back perforce into my original state of dirt. It is impossible to wash as there is no water. I did insist on a cupful to clean my teeth with yesterday, but my servant looked at me very reproachfully, horrified at such extravagance. He is dirty beyond words himself and getting rather bloated-looking. Everyone is getting very fat out here. No exercise and lots of food I suppose. Bayley came back from Paris. He says it is very quiet there and everything shut up at ten o'clock. London is apparently gay in comparison.

Letter from Frank, December 5:

It rained a bit yesterday and all the dugouts proceeded to fall in, one man was buried but luckily not hurt. It was like a horrid dream, one was busy bolstering up one, with a bit of wood and sandbags, and turned round and saw the mud walls cracking and another gave way. My home leaks to a certain extent but not badly and I sit up in the straw reading 'Dr Thorne' with a frog watching me with great interest from the shelf at my head. It thinks itself in unusual luxury with a little lamp to warm itself at. It all depends on the point of view!

December 5. Took parcel of woollies to send off to Frank, then fetched Mama and we went to the National Gallery. A delightful lecture on the Barbizon School and how they have given us all they saw in nature, its kindness, its strength and its peace.

Letter from Frank, December 8:

I must say we are having a perfectly awful time, much the worst since we came out. It is not the Germans, who are quiescent, but the weather and the mud. D Company have already got a stream running through their trenches. I only hope the Germans are in the same boat, or rather out of it and in the water. I wish I was at home again and reading this letter retrospectively. It *will* be a time to look back upon.

Letter from Frank, December 11:

I am now second in command, although I am still commanding my company as there aren't enough officers to go round. The only difference it makes is that I see more of dear old Clemson and hear all the battalion secrets, some of which would rather surprise you I think. I suppose this will find you bracing yourself for your visit to Marple. I hope that having the children will make you enjoy it to some extent. Christopher is certainly a very pleasant companion. I think Mama would be unwise to invite the lecturer to tea. There was something about his tie and his boots which made me suspect that he wouldn't quite fit into her atmosphere. Besides I feel sure that he is married.

December 12. To lunch with Mrs R, hardly altered at all and as well-dressed and worldly as ever, though she must be nearly 80. She told me two war stories. One of the General who, receiving a parcel of comforts from the Queen, with *Mary R.* and *The Empire* on it, remarked he couldn't remember any girl at The Empire called Mary R, and he thought he knew them all! The second, a would-be recruit at the office of the London and Scottish, who on hearing that neither his father or mother were Scotch said he was not eligible to join them. To which he replied he had some property in Perthshire. They replied that in that case his name could be entered. On his friend who was with him remarking he had no idea he had any property in Scotland he replied, I have a pair of trousers being cleaned at Pullers in Perth.

December 14. Heard from Mrs Cobbold the Colonel is back on sick leave, concussion of the nerves of the head and eyes. He feels as if the ground was heaving up and no feeling in the top of his head, since being in a house over which seventy German shells burst.

December 15. To Briggs to order walking stick for Frank's Father for his golden wedding.

Letter from Frank, December 15:

I have now moved back to the farm in rear. I was very sorry to give up my company and to become second in command which I think is a dull job. The trenches however are not much fun in this weather. I expect I shall get a cold now I have come into a house. I have been sleeping in wet straw, in wet blankets and wet socks for ten days and haven't had a vestige of a cold or rheumatism. The cough I had at home disappeared instantly when I got back into the trenches. Isn't it extraordinary! I suppose we shall all have to live in future in the garden and leave the houses to our wives and children.

I do hope you will have a pretty tolerable time at Christmas. It is a dreadful period and I am not in the least sorry to miss it. We are bombarded with plum puddings. Edge who is here with me has an enormous one which is brought in at each meal and we nibble at it—the smell of it makes me quite sick.

December 16. At midday came out the news that the Germans had shelled three east coast towns, Scarborough, Whitby and Hartlepool this morning with a certain amount of damage.

• •

Letter from Frank, December 16:

The York and Lancaster man at Brabyns is named Russell. He was in the Mess at Blackdown, Father says, so I expect I know him well. I had a letter from Father and Mother today. It seems somehow so pathetic that Father minds my being out here. I never thought he cared particularly about me one way or another.

(*In her book of Frank's letters, Kathleen has copied out a paragraph from* The North Cheshire Herald, *December 12, 1914:*

> *There are now twenty soldiers in the Brabyns Military Hospital. One of the men, Corporal Russell of the York and Lancasters, who came in on Monday last, suffering from a wound in the shoulder, is in the same regiment as Major Isherwood. Mr J. Bradshaw-Isherwood saw Corporal Russell on Tuesday and the man said he was delighted to meet the father of so splendid an officer. He was a fine man and a brave one and a soldier who inspired confidence in his men.*

Frank was often mentioned in this paper and was much amused by its grandiose style.)

Letter from Frank, December 17:

We are in billets—Clemson, the Doctor, Philby (the new Adjutant), Monsieur Pensevero the interpreter and myself live in a wretched little house in a row. Upstairs there is one small room where Clemson and I sleep and another for Philby and the Doctor. I will say that Clemson does *not* snore as I expected *but* we had his views on the war last night, louder and louder, and all the time orderlies and people rushing in with messages and the servants stumping up and down stairs. The noise was deafening and, when they all went, the silence was quite stunning. We hear very exciting rumours of Scarborough and Whitby having been shelled. Scarborough is now such a mess of asphalt that I don't mind if

430

they smashed it to bits, and as none of you are there I can't help thinking it is a very good thing and will awaken people up to the situation. Please don't send any more knitted things. There is a room here full from floor to ceiling with presents.

December 18. Interviewed Mr Baker, the keeper of the National Gallery, and got a new student's card to copy. Many questions asked, among others if I were a suffragette!!!

Letter from Frank, December 19:

Please do NOT send any more woollen things, we really don't know what to do with them. There was a bit of a fight last night. It was rather a fine sight to see the shells bursting and the search-lights playing and shifting about in the sky. With much love to you all and every good wish for a Merry Christmas. I never wish to see another if it's going to be like this.

Letter from Frank, December 20:

PLEASE DO NOT SEND ANY MORE KNITTED THINGS. We cannot get rid of them. Jarrett and the Doctor and I went to church at ——, I suppose I mustn't mention names. Coming out, a young lady offered me her hand which I shook warmly, but Jarrett said she wished to give me holy water. I am delighted with 'The New Macchiavelli'. I think Wells does understand the relation between males awfully well, though his women aren't so good. But I don't feel at all literary now—or indeed anything.

December 21. Met Christopher at Waterloo. Left St Pancras 2.30, arrived in time to dress for dinner to which Fanny Hudson came to keep the Golden Wedding! Henry gave a silver gilt caddy, Moey a spoon, Jack and Esther's present was to follow, Mrs Hardcastle a very handsome ivory and gold-mounted paper knife, Fanny Hudson a little gold filigree box, Ann a Staffordshire willow soup tureen and ladle over a hundred years old, the Children gold patterned ash tray and vases, F and I walking stick and silver gilt prayerbook markers.

(The walking stick qualified as a golden-wedding present by having a gold band around it with an engraved inscription.)

Letter from Frank, December 21:

Presents and parcels keep arriving. I hope to get them all thanked, but even with my rapid style it takes time. Clemson is really awfully kind. He has been second in command so lately himself that he realizes how dull it is and constantly gives me odd jobs to do. However I cannot like it so well as having my own company where one reigned supreme. Since writing the above I have been into the town to order beer and have managed to buy twenty pairs of boots. Clemson has just told me that the Regiment has to go into the trenches on the 23rd. This will be a dreadful blow for the men as they were so looking forward to that sacred function, the Christmas Dinner, outside.

Letter from Frank, December 24:

I am quite tired out today as we find that the Shropshires, who had been in here, had done nothing to the communication trench which is my special care, so we had to work all night. My position as a Marple Hero takes a lot of living up to! I am sorry to say that my brother officers, who are all by way of being heroes too, were tremendously amused at the North Cheshire Herald paragraphs!

December 25. We had crackers and a great Christmas dinner, Richard coming in for dessert. He thoroughly enjoyed the crackers.

.   .

432

Letter from Frank, December 25:

All the men seem to be pining for their Christmas dinner, a thing I do not mind missing at all. We are having a rest today from bullets, none have come over today and the guns have not fired. Last night the Germans were singing loudly in their trenches 'while shepherds watched their flocks by night' and threw up lights and all was peace and goodwill, but unfortunately some evilly disposed person (on their side) began to throw bombs in a very uncalled for way. I haven't heard that they hit anybody, though. I hope you will take Christopher to 'The Three Musketeers' which I see is in Manchester, and have lunch at Parker's etc, and also take him for a good visit to London.

Letter from Frank, December 26:

Hazler (of the Buffs) told me that on Christmas Day two of his men went out on patrol and met a German patrol to whom they began to talk and the Germans asked them to bring them an English paper, so they went back to get one, and then they took the Germans on, to our 'wire' where a lieutenant and a captain appeared and there was a great deal of talk. They tried to induce the Germans to come into our trenches, which however they refused. When they wanted to return, the lieutenant wanted to let them go but the captain didn't—however they appealed to the major and he said they could go if they were unarmed, which they were, so they returned. In the next trenches, the Regiment called out to the Germans in the trench in front of them that they wouldn't shoot if they didn't. Eventually they both came out into the middle and all talked to one another. They were Saxons and they said they were all tired to death of the war, but that they were quite well fed and clothed. I think eventually a general came along and said that they might talk in the middle but neither side was to go near the other's trenches. I believe a photograph was taken, so you will probably see a lot of gush about it in the papers.

.   .

Letter from Frank, December 27:

Bayley's trenches are really most elaborate and he has notices up, this way to the drying room, bathroom, ammunition store, etc. The Doctor declares it's all eyewash and there is nothing at all there, but when Winston Churchill came round he was very much impressed and the Brigadier of another Brigade went back to his unfortunate people and said, where is your drying room, where is your bath, etc etc. I found Clemson sitting up with the Doctor and Jarrett and Philby. They seemed to be having most dreary jokes, calling up Bayley and telling him to mobilize all his cooks, and that sort of thing. Mr Pensevero the interpreter is a most amusing person. He is dreadfully annoyed with the head interpreter, M. Dreyfus. 'He is horrid fellow, I do not wish to know him,' he says, and has an awful grievance as he is not allowed to go to Paris, 'to give one kiss to my fiancée! The war will not stand still because I go to Paris.'

Letter from Frank, December 29–31:

Mr H came to see us yesterday. He was very manly and breezy and talked the slang of the year before last, as parsons always do. It is incredible that we began this year so peacefully. I do hope that by this time next year all this will seem like a dream. We are living in an awful state of mud and wretchedness—at least, I personally am quite clean and comfortable but it is dreadful to see the men in such a state. They are absolutely wonderful. Arrangements were made for fifty of A Company to be relieved out of the trenches by men down here—but they refused to come out when the time came and said they would stick it out. The General was delighted. People absolutely stick up to the waist in mud. Poor old Clemson had to be dug out the other day!

December 31. In the carriage with Mr Isherwood to the village, back late and did not get out from lunch till after three, after which a party of the wounded from Brabyns arrived to see the house and have tea. After tea Christopher and I and his Granny played Old Maid and I read out *Ivanhoe*, so no New Year's letters got written. In the evening the carol singers sang in the hall.

1915. January 1. Letter from Frank, saying over fifty new men had come out, *all* wanting scarves and socks and mittens, so the 'drug on the market' is at an end. Mr Isherwood, C and I by taxi to Manchester to see Lewis Waller in The Three Musketeers. It was very well put on.

January 2. C's leg started acting again. The best cure seems bed and to wrap it tightly in a woollen scarf, whether it is a sort of rheumatism subject to change of weather, or cramp, or growing pain, I cannot *think*. He has had it everywhere and used to have it at Frimley too, as well as Limerick.

Letter from Frank, January 5:

While I think of it, can you get me a little primer of knitting which would describe to me how you turn the heel of a sock. I am just getting to the critical point and don't quite know (to put it mildly) what to do next.

Letter from Frank, January 8:

A dam or something has burst and all the headquarters and the communication trenches are under water. The Leicesters, who are on our right, only eighty yards from the enemy, were flooded out and had to vacate their trenches. They went back at dawn and began to mend their parapets and when dawn broke there were the enemy doing the same thing. Neither side could do anything, and really about here it seems to be a deadlock. I am so sorry you all have colds, I know what Marple's like when that sort of thing starts.

. .

435

Letter from Frank, to Henry:

You seem to be rather pessimistic for 1915, and Hardy, who has just come back from England, says he noticed the same thing with everyone over there. To us who are in the thick of it, things don't seem very dreadful, and one sees one's dearest friend lying dead on the ground with complete composure, in fact I was quite shocked with myself the first time for feeling so callous. I suppose all this 'season of trial' is a perfectly natural result from some cause which we overlook. I cannot think myself that the God whom modern religion visualizes has anything whatever to do with it.

Letter from Frank, January 10, in Armentières:

We didn't go into the trenches after all. We are now in a very handsome house and have a great dining-room, painted white, with a Fragonard over the fireplace. I slept last night under a violet canopy. The master and mistress are in the house, but they all slept in the cellars! They are nice old people, very distinguished looking as the Interpreter says. It is a perfectly lovely day today and we feel rather shut in in the town. This house is heated by hot water pipes and is rather stuffy. One is never content!

Letter from Frank, January 15, Armentières:

We are leaving today and going into the trenches. We are very sorry to leave our nice quarters here and poor Monsieur and Madame. She says it is most trying having relays of officers in the house. We try to be as pleasant as possible, but really the Shropshires who are coming in after us behaved exactly as if the place belonged to them. I had to tell their second in command he was talking to a lady, the mistress of the house.

You are the only person who doesn't write the most depressing letters. Henry seems to have lost his faith in his country and God and everything else. Even the Pope is in disgrace!! It is just these people who have suffered nothing who make the most fuss.

. .

January 19. [In London.] To Comedy Restaurant, after which we found a delightful conjuring shop in Green St out of Leicester Square and then we went into the Portrait Gallery, after which Christopher went back to Buckingham St to practice his conjuring and I went to have my hair washed and dressed at the Army and Navy. C and I dined with Henry at Sussex Mansions, C wearing a white piqué waistcoat with his etons and looked so sweet and so smart. We went to see 'David Copperfield', well put on and interesting though not convincing as a whole. Tree duplicated Wilkins Micawber and Daniel Peggotty and of course occupied the stage entirely!

January 20. There has been the first raid of zeppelins, to Yarmouth and Sandringham, not much damage. C and I to St Paul's and visited the conjuring shop again. Then to Maskelyne and Devant. Jack Isherwood turned up and took C out to dine and the theatre.

Letter from Frank, January 20:

We move in and out of the trenches now every four days, too often I think, as one is no sooner settled anywhere than one is off again. I expect you feel frightfully unsettled too and I dare say in some ways that the war is worse for you people in England than it is here. The King I believe said that the only cheerful faces he had seen for the last six months were in France.

Letter from Frank, January 21:

Nothing particular happens and, looking back on this, it will seem a time of appalling dullness. We hang about all the morning doing little odd jobs and in the afternoon wander vaguely about the town over the most awful cobbles. Yesterday we spent the afternoon looking for the Sanitary Inspector, not particularly because we wanted to find him but for something to do.

Letter from Frank, January 22:

The Parson came to tea last night, not H but another creature whom I particularly dislike. He can't talk the King's English. To begin with, he has a dreadful accent and he uses most horrible slang, talks of people being off their rockers etc and says damn, a thing I disapprove of extremely in one of his cloth.

January 27. It felt very flat and sad to think it was the last day of the holidays. We went to say goodbye to Mama and found letters from Frank delighted with Christopher's parcel which he had just received. Left at 3 for Waterloo where we joined the other boys and Cyril. Such a cold afternoon, do hope St Edmund's will be warmed!

Letter from Frank, February 3:

I am again sitting down to write to you wondering what on earth I am going to write about. Yesterday it rained all day and we sat in the farm and waded out in the evening. We were out again this morning when it had become fine and we saw a sea of mud with two very much battered trees sticking up against a morning sky, Clemson said it reminded him of an Indian scene to which I am afraid I replied rather snappily that in that case I never wished to go to India.

February 11. The fashions have now appeared and are a complete change from the old; wide umbrella skirts or at any rate overskirts, in contrast to the very tight and clinging.

Letter from Frank, February 11:

You mustn't think I am having a dreadful time at all, I have all sorts of little secret joys which I manage to keep to myself in spite of the crowd in which I live. We went yesterday to see the

Fourth Division Follies, they are a party of pierrots got up by the motor ambulance people. The first part of the performance, consisting of songs in the 'Folly' manner, was quite good but afterwards they had a sort of revue which was more deadly than anything I have ever seen. In the interval, one of them came in front of the curtain and told stories. One of them was about the Bishop whose wife wrote a book and also had a child, and when a gushing lady complimented him about the child he thought she meant the book and said, 'wasn't it clever of her—she did it almost entirely by herself; she got no help from me and very little from the Archdeacon!' This shocked Clemson most dreadfully and he murmured about it all the way home and all the evening.

I had an impassioned letter from the lady whose house we are in now. She wrote that her late husband's piano was sacred and that she begged we would respect it as we would her and her children, it must not leave the house even for a few minutes. It doesn't seem quite the thing one would be likely to take out for a walk with one, and in any case it is locked and muffled beyond anything that I have ever done with *my* sacred instrument.

Letter from Frank, February 14:

There is just a chance that I may get home on the 22nd, I am afraid I shan't know till quite the last minute. The idea of Henry out here is really very amusing. I don't think he would last five days. I certainly don't want to change with him and his dreadful life of tea-parties. It is an extraordinary taste on his part.

February 18. *Frank's name mentioned in Dispatches today*, for 'gallant and distinguished service in the field'. He and Major Bayley the only two of the officers selected out of the names the Colonel sent up for consideration of the Brigadier. So pleased. All seven of the searchlights out tonight, the first time for several weeks. Today begins the threatened German blockade of our merchant ships. Placards announce that channel steamers have stopped running but do not know if this is true.

439

February 19. In the King's list of honours Frank is made a brevet lieutenant-colonel, Colonel Cobbold gets a C.B. and Major Bayley and Captain Blunt D.S.O. No one else anything. Very proud and pleased, especially that *other* people should see that Frank is properly appreciated.

Letter from Frank, February 19:

You have probably seen in the gazette that I have got a brevet and am now a lieutenant-colonel. I feel so awfully sorry that poor old Clemson has got nothing up to date. He has taken it so well and was really delighted at our getting these things, but at the same time it is rather sickening, I think, as it is he and he alone who has kept the Regiment together. It will be a bit more pay for me and it is what I always secretly hoped I should get out of the War but I never expected to get it so soon.

February 20. Cook came in soon after 6.30 with a wire which was from Frank to say, alas, 'cannot come'. So disappointing. Many letters of congratulation. To see Graham Greene to ask if it is true boats not running, as if so I shall *wire* congratulations. He says they run differently now and, now that blockade is on, officers *not* encouraged to go backwards and forwards on leave.

February 22. Wire came at 8 am to say Frank was arriving at Victoria 8.30 am! I hadn't time to go to the station but he got here soon after 8.30, looking very well. A very rainy day. Frank and I to the tailor where he ordered a new tunic and great coat. To the Victoria and Albert Museum and tea at Harrods. Back here after. Zeppelin over Colchester and Braintree but little damage.

February 23. Frank to see Henry at Sussex Mansions. He and I walked to the Tate Gallery and back along the other side of the river, looking into St Mary Lambeth to look at the Pedlar window. It is *so* happy to have him back. We had a quiet evening at home and it snowed.

February 24. From St Pancras at 2.30 to Marple. All well there.

February 25. Frank up the village with his Father. Lunched early and motored to Buxton. Interesting lecture from the British ex-Consul of Antwerp on its fall. Richard very lively and very goodlooking in scarlet coat and black beaver hat.

February 26. Left for London. Jack Isherwood to dine.

February 27. To lunch with Henry at Sussex Mansions. Found when we got there Esther Toogood had telephoned to say she was staying on and could she come to lunch to meet Frank. Hadn't seen her for three or four years and certainly should not have known her. She looked very pretty with her hair grown grey and a bright colour, dressed in black velvet and less like a parson's wife than anything one could imagine! Frank and I to the Queen's Hall to a concert. Enjoyed very much though F thought Henry Wood's conducting ruined it. Grand Symphony number 5, New World. An infant prodigy played on the piano a Grieg concerto, child's name Solomon.

February 28. F and I left by the 9.20 for Hazlemere. Found chapel going on. C came out with the others about 12 and we took him off to lunch at Thurlstane, going by way of Grayshott and through woods. His legs seem to have been bad and his ankle bound up and he walked quite lame and seemed much less bright than usual. There are four or five cases of measles. Taxi to the 4.30 to London.

March 1. To see Mama off for Southsea en route to Isle of Wight. F and I back to lunch at Buckingham St. We did not go far in the afternoon and returned for high tea. Then we drove in a taxi to Victoria and he left at 6 pm. Such a crowd of officers and men and two trains full for the boat train which runs to Folkestone for Boulogne. The boat waiting to start till a given signal to make its dash across. Packed all the evening and felt very wretched.

March 2. To Southsea, Queen's Hotel. Big gorgeous drawing-rooms full of expensive people and soldiers and smart young women in and out. Mama in small room on second floor, seven shillings a night, very dear. Rosa wrote to say C had gone to bed yesterday with measles but not very seedy yet. Had *so* hoped he would have escaped the measles, very worried. Boats not running regularly to the island and it is difficult to know what to do or where to go.

Letter from Frank, March 2:

It was very rough and in spite of the Mothersill I was sick! We journeyed all night and reached our destination about 5 a.m. There wasn't a sign of anything to meet me but I managed to play the idiot boy and got into a car belonging to the Tenth Brigade which brought me very nearly into the town. I was so dreadfully sorry to leave you last night.

March 3. Out after breakfast about rooms. Decided on drawing-room and two bedrooms, two pounds fifteen a week. A dreary lookout across a muddy common to low forts, over which we see the sea and the Isle of Wight. Wind whistles and the bugles sound and Kitchener's men drill on common. Rosa writes that darling Christopher is going on very well and cheerfully.

Letter from Frank, March 3:

We all went out and round the trenches this morning. Purden was very much annoyed with me as he said I saluted the colonels on the staff and called them 'Sir'. I simply cannot remember that I am one myself.

·   ·

March 4. In afternoon walked across the Common to Portsmouth which seems to have so many quaint old houses and corners left. George Villiers Duke of Buckingham buried here, he was murdered at a house in the High Street, still to be seen. Darling Christopher's temperature on night of March 2nd was 105, which seems dreadfully high, but last night 102. Dr is satisfied however, all measles cases seem to have had temperatures of 104 to 105.

Letter from Frank, March 4:

We are still going on in just the same old way. Clemson is singing loudly The Bullfighter's Song, the servants are indulging in a dreadful sort of drone in the kitchen, the telegraphists are cursing and swearing 'something awful' and the Doctor is repeating poetry, and such poetry! (The Ingoldsby Legends, I think.) However he has now got out his box of drawing materials and his first lesson from Mr Percy Bradshaw which he is reading aloud. I believe all leave is stopped now and that the great crowd on Monday was the last lot returning. I am glad I got mine in in time.

March 6. Rosa wrote C was doing very well, temp yesterday morning normal. Soldiers drill in front of windows all the morning, one might be living in a barrack square.

Letter from Frank, March 7:

Our Padre put his foot into it by saying he knew that we were all longing for the war to be at an end and to get home. I saw Bayley swelling visibly, and after the service he flew at the Padre and said that he for one had no wish to get home or for the war to end.

Letter from Frank, March 8:

Kitty the little mare is in great form and full of her funny little ways and tricks but she looks better than any horse out here and

443

everyone admires her tremendously. I am as stiff as ten pokers, riding just catches muscles which you never use otherwise, and as we generally gallop hell for leather along the canal bank and neither Purden or Houston have very much control over their horses, one has to grip very tight!

Letter from Frank, March 10:

Isn't it twelve years ago today since we were married? We have had some ups and downs, haven't we, but I hope on the whole that you will be able to feel that it has been a happy time. I think you enjoyed the actual day itself a great deal more than I did, but I can never feel thankful enough now nor grateful enough to you for what you have been and are being. I don't think we have spent the day apart before and I hope it will be the last time that we do so. Anyhow I am with you in spirit, but that is nothing unusual. I am afraid I never realized quite what an easy person you were to live with until I had to live so closely with other people, and I shall be thankful when we can sit down together over the fire again in a home of our own. It is not that these people are particularly difficult or anything, but they are not you.

I do hope you haven't got the measles and I beg you not to go and see Christopher. It is much more serious when grown up people get it.

March 12. The twelfth anniversary of our wedding day, such a sad and different day, no sun and one's mind full of dread and anxiety over this terrible war. Rosa thinks by the 22nd Christopher will be quite free of infection and if he is fit enough and the weather appropriate it would be a good thing for him to get a change to the sea. Mama and I for an hour's drive in closed carriage into Portsmouth.

Letter from Frank, March 12:

It is misty and very airless. The country is beginning to smell 'something fearful' as the water goes down. Our moat is full of dead cows. However I believe the country and towns up north are much worse, which makes me realize we are very lucky to be here.

March 13. I feel so full of dread and anxiety every time the bell rings. I hope it is only the place that makes me so nervous, and certainly the air is very depressing.

March 14. Wire from Rosa to ring up Grayshott. Felt very alarmed and went off to the Queen's Hotel to get on to the trunk there. C's temp has gone up to 103 again.

March 15. Mama and I left by the 1.46 boat, luggage and all, arrived Ventnor 3.8. Found all preparations made for us at Alto House and it seemed so homelike and comfortable and soothing after Southsea!

Letter from Frank, March 15:

I am sorry about C's temperature but hope he will be better and get a change soon. I do hope it won't be long now before we are able to be together again. We must go on wishing for Kneller Hall though I am afraid it is a full colonel's appointment and I don't know if they would give it to a brevet lieutenant-colonel. Still, after the war, things will be jumbled up rather, I expect, and one never knows.

I think with you that the Browns are most irritating. What can they mean by saying that Christopher is 'not very communicative' about Divinity? I don't think it matters very much what Christopher learns as long as he remains himself and keeps his individuality and develops on his own lines, though of course I am afraid you ought to sit on him for being lazy—that is our big weakness, I can see it in us all and it just makes our cleverness come to nothing—I mean by this my side of the family, for except his sweet disposition I can't see your character in Christopher.

(Kneller Hall, at Twickenham, is the headquarters of the Royal Military School of Music. For some years Frank had cherished

the hope that he might end his career by becoming its comman-
dant. The remark about Divinity quoted above must refer to
Christopher's half-term report.)

March 16. The *Dresden* caught at last and sunk off the west
coast of South America. Heard C is nearly normal again.

(*The light cruiser* Glasgow, *which was chiefly responsible for
the* Dresden's *sinking, was commanded by Captain John Luce.
Captain Luce was Elizabeth Isherwood's nephew, hence this almost idolatrous tribute from one of the Cheshire papers:*

> *We have again the pleasurable opportunity of offering
> congratulations to the revered family at Marple Hall.
> . . . Captain Luce has earned immortal fame. . . . [He]
> and his men will go down to history as great British sea-
> men. They proved themselves true Englishmen, for they
> . . . saved almost all the crew of the German battleship
> . . . and held aloft the British standard which stands for
> humanity and justice. Marple people will rejoice with the
> Isherwood family in this new glory. . . .*)

March 17. Very worrying disturbing news. They had had a
specialist and bacteriologist down to St Edmund's to overhaul the
boys and find darling C has a touch of pneumonia just developing.
Fear it will be a long business, no one knows how long.

Letter from Frank, March 17:

When we do have a home again you will find that I have become the tidiest person in the world, indeed I spend my time now
in picking other people's (principally Purden's) cigarette ends up
and straightening the papers and hiding brown paper and string
thrown about by Clemson. I think the fact that I have no definite
work to do makes it worse, for really, for all the good I am, I
might just as well not be here at all.

. .

March 18. Went to Post Office at 6 but it was nearly an hour before I could get on to Grayshott. C has his temp lower today, breathing fairly good. He sent a message of love and he was better and looking forward to my coming.

March 20. Reached Haslemere 1.30. C was a little low though very pleased to see me. Sat by his bed. There are ten ill, he and Llewellyn Smith and Tudor are together in one room, a big airy one with fire all the time and windows open day and night. They are all on liquid food and all thin and weak. They have night nurse.

Letter from Frank, March 20:

It is dreadfully upsetting about Christopher and I hate to think he has been more or less seriously ill for three days without my knowing it. However Purden says that it is not at all an unusual thing after measles, and I hope it may be more a threat of pneumonia than anything else. The Germans shelled the village behind us all yesterday and eventually the spire came down with a crash. I am sorry to say I didn't actually see the spire come down, though if you ever hear me say I did you mustn't contradict me!

March 21. C had a fairly good day but seems quiet and depressed and his arms are like *sticks*. An old boy, Sparks, came out with measles in evening, we thought him very queer all day. Do trust I shan't fall a victim next. So tiresome for everyone and I do so want to get C away the moment he is fit.

March 22. Saw the Doctor who said C was going on well. Wire from Nurse, her Father very ill, could she go. Felt *very disturbed*, wired to her to make the best arrangement she could. Cyril read out loud in evening, *The Brushwood Boy*, quite charming.

March 31. [Ventnor.] Madgie arrived with Christopher in motor. He all wrapped up with bankets but very bright and pleased. The chauffeur carried him to the boat and there Nurse and Richard joined us from London. We arrived safely Ventnor, C to bed and the Dr to see him, thought he had stood the journey well. So thankful to have got the children here.

Letter from Frank, March 31:

I am sorry to tell you that Francis died this morning. He was so badly wounded that if he had lived I think he would have been a cripple. I feel sure that both he and Sandys were such innately good sweet-tempered fellows that they have a happy time, if you call it time, before them. I am wondering so much if Christopher is moving today. I am sorry to think that you and Mama are wrestling with Russian literature. That 'Brothers Karamazov' is a most dismal book.

April 1. C went in the donkey chair down to the beach, then it went back and fetched Mama. It was very hot in the sun. Richard and Nurse also came down. Mama and I read out loud *The Brothers Karamazov*, which gives a dreadful idea of Russian Man, the women apparently go in for hysteria and the men simply low beasts.

Letter from Frank, April 1:

I did rather a good sketch last night of the ruined church tower with the sunset behind it. People are living all round it, and ploughing is going on just as if nothing was happening. Shells scream over their heads but unless they are actually dropping into the village they take no notice.

April 2. C walked down to the beach as the Dr advised using his legs a little more each day.

April 3. Heard from Frank that Mr Francis died from his wounds. He was so very patient when ill so long with his broken leg at Limerick and his career has been sadly short. When he arrived there to join he was such a very robust and athletic young man. Richard came down after tea and behaved like the little angel he always looks but is very far from being.

April 4. C down directly after breakfast and had his easter egg hunt in the sitting room with all his usual enjoyment of the search and the clues. Baby's were hidden in C's and my bedroom. In afternoon we all walked down to the pier and back, the farthest either Mama or C had walked.

Letter from Frank, April 5:

I couldn't make out from A's letter whether Richard had killed Mrs D or only threatened to do so, I suppose the latter as he is still at large. I can quite imagine how dreadfully irritating that sort of hushabye baby attitude of hers would be to a person of his violent temperament. I am afraid he wants a father's attention. Tell Christopher he must take my place! The Brigade called for the names of people who could speak German and I sent mine in. I am now rather frightened as my German is distinctly limited. I am trying to find someone who will talk it with me for practice but people are rather shy of owning that they can, for fear of being taken for spies. We are all feeling very hopeful. The Russians seem to be simply walking it in the Carpathians, and one has the impression that Joffre has something up his sleeve and is only waiting for the psychological moment.

April 6. Nurse, poor thing, had a wire to say her Father passed away this afternoon.

April 9. [*This entry is in Christopher's handwriting.*] C discovered rash on my face when we woke! So wrote a note for the doctor to come. He at once pronounced it to be measles, my arms, neck and chest covered with rash. C is allowed to see me.

449

My eyes ached intolerably, also my back and side. No cough or cold yet.

Letter from Frank, April 9:

I am glad C is going on well. I don't much agree with the Dr about boarding schools, as I think that most boys, Richard for instance, are much better at them, but in Christopher's case I shouldn't object at all to sending him as a day boy if it were possible. The whole point of sending him to school was to flatten him out, so to speak, and to make him like other boys and, when all is said and done, I don't know that it is at all desirable or necessary, and I for one would much rather have him as he is. He has tried the experiment and we know that he can hold his own and he could retire with all the honours of war to a day school, if we ever had the chance of sending him to one. But at present it seems rather impossible.

I don't think, in view of the difficult financial time which is before us that I should be justified in giving up the Army. Indeed, if I were offered a command, which I should think is on the cards, I should have to take it for the sake of the extra pay and pension, and that might lead to what is our sole ambition, Kneller Hall!

I am so afraid that Mama will suffer from the fall in dividends and that brewery property will not be very valuable, owing to the (very proper) agitation for temperance. Clemson says very grandly that one mustn't think of one's own pocket at all, but it's all very well—we cannot see our Mama starve.

April 10. My rash well out all over and pricked a good deal. All my joints feel tender and achey and my eyes like boiled gooseberries and very painful. Had green venetian blinds down. Doctor came and said my temperature was normal and I wasn't at all ill! Christopher enveloped in a white petticoat comes and visits me.

April 11. Rash died away off arms and nearly altogether. C read me the collect, epistle and gospel, he reads so well. Mama came and had a conversation outside my door, but no one but C, the Doctor and Mrs B. allowed inside.

Letter from Frank to Christopher, April 11:

My dear Boy, I was delighted to get your letter. We had great excitement yesterday afternoon. There were lots of aeroplanes flying about over the town and the Germans opened fire on ours and you could see little white puffs of smoke all round it where the shells were bursting. Then a German aeroplane began to hover about, hoping to drop a bomb, I expect, then our guns opened fire on it and it wobbled a good deal and was I think hit in the tail but it managed to plane down into their lines. I can't think what happens to all the bullets out of the shells that are fired at the aeroplanes, they don't seem to come down into the town. We are back in the trenches again now. Everything is very quiet in front of us. I am writing on the paper that my pal Princess Mary sent me at Christmas. I don't think much of it and if I had subscribed to the fund I should want my money back. With much love, ever your affectionate Father.

April 14. Really, now that I have no aches and my eyes are so much better, it is most annoying not to be up and about. However I am lucky to have had it so lightly and I am glad it is English and not German measles!!

Letter from Frank, April 15:

I was so glad to hear from Mama that you were going on so well. It is an awful nuisance though for you to be shut up, especially if the weather is as fine as it is here. I have been sitting out under a safe bank sketching the farm but the glare was almost too great to see what one was doing. It does seem so ridiculous to carry on a war in this beautiful weather! The Germans threw a letter into one of our trenches in which they said 'I am sure you are all as sick of this war as we are—do let us finish the war before the cherry blossom comes out'. This seems to me rather nice. I am sure none of our men would ever dream of dating anything by blossom or even noticing that it was there.

April 16. Got up and dressed.

Letter from Frank, April 16:

I hope today you are able to sit up a bit. Yesterday I went to sleep over a book of Benson's all about the very best society. It was very disconcerting to wake up from a dream of duchesses with the guns firing over my head, indeed it is always a shock to me when I wake and find where I am. I can never get used to this state of things. I think next time I shall be a Spaniard, they seem to be the only people in Europe quite unmoved by all this fighting and row.

April 17. 139,347 casualties since the beginning of the war. It seems simply appalling, and this along a line of thirty-one and a quarter miles in length, whereas the French front extends 543 miles. One wonders what *theirs* can be?

April 18. A most lovely day and my time of leisure ended! Had a hot bath with sanitas and all clean clothes after. Then the room fumigated, chimney stopped up and windows shut and clothes hung out, books and drawers open for four hours. Came down and lay on verandah in sun—and then *Nurse took to her bed!* She seemed so chilly and to have sore throat and headache, so sent for Doctor. Said her temperature was 101 and that it was tonsilitis. So lucky I was up.

Letter from Frank, April 20:

I am hoping that I may hear from you yourself today or to-morrow. I shall be so glad to see your handwriting again. I have been reading *The Small House at Allington* which I think is much

the best of the Trollope books. I saw some wallflowers out yesterday which made me feel very homesick. Clemson proclaims night
and day that the war is to be over in June but he doesn't seem to
have any reason for saying so. Ada Lance's astrologer says the
same, and if not in June, August to October, as Jupiter the peace
planet is then in the ascendant, but we have got to jolly well beat
the Germans first and that thoroughly.

April 21. Perfectly lovely day, everything seemed leisured and
peaceful and even the War to weigh less on one's mind on a day
like this. Dr to see Nurse, she is to get up for three hours or so,
but though giddy *would* remain up longer!

April 22. Nurse up for lunch but still seemed shaky and chilly
though she *would* bath Baby and do things she needn't.

April 26. It looks as if the second battle for the coast was starting in Flanders, indeed started last Thursday, but so far the worst
fighting appears to be round Ypres.

Letter from Frank, April 26:

We are all feeling very anxious to hear the result of the battle
which we can hear going on up north. The Germans seem to be
making a big push and I cannot see what they could gain by it
even if they got through, which seems very unlikely, nor how
they can afford to chuck away more men at this juncture. It really
looks like a last despairing effort. The men are digging up the
garden and everything here is most peaceful. I am going down
into the town to see the Mayor about paying for billets, which
will be a nice walk.

(Later) The last wires are encouraging and we seem to be pushing the foe back. I think if we hadn't had the good luck or good
management to seize Hill 60 just before the German attack north
of it, it might have been a more serious thing and we might have

lost the Ypres salient. I fancy poor old Ypres has caught it pretty badly.

Letter from Frank, April 27:

A line in great haste to tell you that I have been suddenly ordered off to command the first Battalion. I don't know where they are but it is somewhere vaguely to the north. You mustn't be anxious as the fighting up there seems virtually over. It is however very tiresome as I was settled here and I hate going off at a moment's notice in the dark.

April 28. Very hot bright sun. C out with his friend the donkey-man in chair and we went after to the beach. Saw an illuminated hospital ship go by at night, all fairy green lights and a big one in red. It is so unusual nowadays to see anything illuminated at night-time.

Letter from Major Clemson, April 28:

Dear Mrs Isherwood, I am a sad man today. We have just got a wire that the Colonel (Bunny) has to proceed at once to take temporary command of the first Battalion and so we lose him and if I were to write to you for a week I couldn't tell you how sorry I am he is going for he has been of enormous help to me, but I'm afraid I'm selfish as he will probably now get promotion and be covered with honour, anyway he is going strong and wherever he is he will, I'm convinced, do well. He will be too late to be in the present scuffle I think, still that won't prevent his returning a General. I was so glad when I heard you had all got over your measles. I have asked Bunny to return to us if ever he gets a chance and he has promised he will, but I think he will probably get a permanent command very soon and be a big man, then I shall ask him to give me a billet!!! With my very best salaams, hoping soon to see you again, yours sincerely, W. F. Clemson.

.   .

("Bunny" had always been Frank's regimental nickname; origin unknown.)

April 29. C is sleeping in my room again but gets up for breakfast. Richard comes and draws in my bed after, always trains and signals! Heard yesterday that Colonel Cobbold is put on home defence.

Letter from Frank, April 29:

My dear, I have arrived with the first Battalion who are in huts near a very famous town [Ypres] not so peaceful or comfortable as our old quarters. However I think the worst of the fighting is over and the Battalion isn't likely to be put in again as they lost very heavily and there are hardly any of them left. However the General says that their action saved the situation. The colonel and the major were killed and the adjutant and several others, and a lot wounded, and there are only seven officers left. I think things are going all right and that the German rush is checked for this time. I hope you won't feel anxious at my being up here. I am always thinking of you and my peaceful home and longing to hear from you again.

(In The York and Lancaster Regiment, 1758–1919, *Colonel H. C. Wylly, C.B., quotes, from what he calls 'The Official History,' an appalling comment on the fighting done by the First Battalion just before Frank joined it: "It certainly had the effect of stopping the enemy's advance in this quarter, but the price paid had been very heavy, and actually no ground was gained that could not have been secured, probably without any casualties, by a simple advance after dark, to which the openness of the country lent itself.")*

April 30. Richard much enjoyed making a castle with Violet Biddlecombe in the afternoon and distinguished himself greatly by knocking over two hostile babies who dared attack it, one flew before his avenging arm and the other was swept to the ground screaming! Christopher to bed very tired. It seems as if he couldn't get beyond a certain point or quite lose his cough which is disappointing. Zeppelins dropped bombs on Bury and several other places in Suffolk but no loss of life though damage to property.

Letter from Frank, April 30:

We are beginning to evolve a little order out of rather chaotic conditions, but the remains of three regiments are crowded into a little camp of huts designed to hold one battalion, so as you may suppose it is rather difficult to do anything. Lousada seems a capital little chap and will I think make a good adjutant. The battle rages round us. Last night I lay in bed or rather on the floor and it sounded exactly as if we were in the very middle of it all. However no one seemed to be at all excited or disturbed and after a time it fizzled out, but there has been another burst this morning. I am very well and it is very nice having a show of my own and something definite to do, so I don't really regret my comfortable quarters as much as you might suppose. I suppose there is something horrid in my nature as I much enjoy having the chance of jumping on people and telling off the wicked. I began by falling on the Quartermaster who was very much surprised and hurt.

I suppose tomorrow or the next day you are all going back, Christopher to school and you to London and Marple.

May 1. Very upset to hear from Frank that he has been given temporary command of the first Battalion which is where the violent fighting is going on. Clemson wrote me a very nice letter. Poor Christopher very elderly all day with lumbago in his back, and did not go out.

Letter from Frank, May 1:

It is again a lovely day here and we are I hope getting things a bit more shipshape. We live on the fat of the land and have every

456

imaginable form of tinned thing. They seem to have made great arrangements with Fortnum and Mason to send things out. Mrs East wrote and said that Mrs Bamford had heard that her husband was killed but couldn't believe it so has started for France. It seems a hopeless thing to do, for even if he was alive, which he isn't, it would be hopeless to try and find him as she wouldn't get farther than Boulogne.

May 2. Rather damp. C's legs both stiff and aching and he hardly seemed able to move. If he sat long he got stiff and going up and downstairs a great effort. Fear he got a chill on beach on Friday when I wasn't with him. Frank reached his destination to find half the Regiment cut up. My heart sinks at the thought of him in command and just in the fighting area of the road to Paris.

Letter from Frank, May 2:

I have had no letter from you yet. The weather has turned much colder with a high wind and I am afraid it is inclined to rain which will make it very unpleasant. I rather expect we are going into the trenches tomorrow, as the battalions which are there now have been in for fourteen days. I am wondering so much where you all are and whether C goes back to school tomorrow. We seem to be so cut off here from all news. It is very quiet today and there are no sounds of battle and less shelling going on.

I am writing to you sitting on the orderly room floor. I have my straw in it and sleep there. The other officers are crowded into two huts. I am addressing this to Marple as I expect you are sure to be there by the time this arrives. I hope you will find it pleasant, it is quite at its best in the spring, I think. With much love to you all.

May 3. This morning the pain seemed concentrated in C's big toe which was apparently horribly painful. Richard on the beach morning and afternoon, the only one of the party in the fullest health and spirits and for that I am truly thankful. Heard from Frank by last post. They are in huts, the remains of three regiments. The fighting must have been awful.

May 4. Doctor to see Christopher, said he must stay in bed for some days at least. It does seem so hard on him, poor little boy. He lay there reading and drawing and the tears coming when the pain was very bad. Drove with Mama in afternoon. Heard again from Frank, dated the 1st, working hard to get things shipshape.

Letter from Frank, May 4:

My dear, I haven't been able to write to you as I have been so busy. Yesterday we moved up to support the Rifle Brigade but when we got there we weren't wanted. We got shelled a bit going up but very little damage was done. Wedgewood got hit in the thumb I am sorry to say, so my only senior officer is gone. It is very tiresome. Today we are in the trenches. The enemy is shelling a good bit, horrible stinking gas. The companies are holding their own all right but it is an anxious time and I shall be glad when night comes. My headquarters are back, *so I am quite safe myself.* We can't get letters out or a post in and I haven't heard from you since I came round this way. No time for more.

May 5. Lovely day but Dr thinks C must stay in bed another day or two. This strong rheumatic tendency, specially the symptom of swollen joints, pointing to the possibility of rheumatic fever unless carefully watched and at once treated. Doubted advisability of boarding school through winter, doesn't think him a strong child like Richard, all of which is like a nail through me! C amused himself with poker patience and reading, his legs nearly normal, though toe still slightly swollen.

Letter from Frank, May 5:

My dear, we are still in the thick of it. Our trenches were very heavily shelled this morning but the artillery have now I hope stopped them and we have got the situation in hand. It is a wearing time but nice to feel that one is really doing something and I like it much better than hanging about as second in command and writing letters to thank people for sending us socks. I am very well, living in a funny little hovel with Lousada. It is a queer life, one is going all night and only gets a little sleep in the early morning. However I don't feel at all tired. No time for more. I haven't had any letters from you since I came to these parts.

May 6. A most heavenly day. Sun from morning till night, the trees flooded with fresh spring green and the wallflowers and forgetmenots a blaze of colour in the gardens. Richard left at 8.5, Mama left at 1.8. C to have another day in bed. The Germans have partly retaken Hill 60 and advanced nearer Ypres. Felt very heavy hearted.

Letter from Frank, May 6:

My dear, I got 5 letters from you last night. I was so glad to get them, though it is rather trying to think of you and your atmosphere from this one. We are however having quite a quiet day today. They gave us a bad time yesterday and the day before. One could see shells of every description bursting along the line of the trenches. Beastly gassy ones which made everyone feel ill and suffocated and it really looked as if they were all wiped out. However it appeared afterwards that there were comparatively few casualties but it made me feel very anxious.

Of course I am out of it, behind. I am rather hoping we shall get relieved tonight as there are so few officers that they get very little rest and the men are all pretty tired and done. However they are marvellously cheerful and I hope the worst is over. The enemy's infantry seem to be no good. They mass in a half-hearted way behind the farms and hedges in front but don't come on. It really looks as if they were simply chucking away their gun ammunition too.

The amount of lead they have poured into this unhappy bit of country in the last few weeks is astounding and the amount of damage of any military value that they have done is very small. It is rather a nice country, ridges and small woods with the poor old ruined town in the middle. I am feeling quite well but shall be glad of a little sleep. The nights are not nearly long enough now to get all one wants done.

The Browns' bill does seem enormous, if C had been ill at home it wouldn't have cost half the money. I don't feel very pleased with them altogether, do you? But I suppose any other school would be just as bad. With very much love to you all, ever your affectionate husband.

May 8. The big Cunard liner the Lusitania torpedoed and sunk. But still more awful is the account of the poor soldiers killed by the foul gasses of those fiendish Germans. Fine day and very pleasant, though the very beauty of the spring seems sad. C in donkey chair in afternoon. Nothing from Frank since Thursday evening.

May 9. Lovely day. Doctor said Christopher might go for a drive in afternoon. It looked lovely all along by the Undercliffe with the lilacs out, the mass of fresh green and the apple blossom. One chestnut tree all in flower and laburnums budding. Nothing from Frank again, feel so anxious to know how he is getting on.

From Colonel Wylly's The York and Lancaster Regiment:

> *On the night of the 7th–8th, the Battalion was relieved and went back to the huts at Ypres. . . .*
> *There was, however, no prolonged rest for the Battalion; at 11.45 a.m. on the 8th it was ordered to retake some trenches which had been lost during the night and, moving by Zonnebeke, it had reached and occupied by 5 p.m. a line of support trenches southeast of Frezenberg, the march thither having been under shell fire practically throughout. Here the full force of the enemy shelling was met and casualties at once began to mount up.*

None the less, the Battalion was ordered to attack, and at 8 p.m., with little or no preliminary bombardment or covering artillery fire, the German position was assaulted. The enemy position was reached and some few gallant men even entered it, but were there immediately bayonetted.

In this attack practically every officer present was put out of action, Captain East being killed, while Lieut-Colonel Isherwood, Lieutenants Lousada and Wylie and 2nd Lieutenant Dodwell were missing, and Lieutenant Gauntlett and 2nd Lieutenants Taylor and Morgan were wounded.

Sergeant South managed to collect some thirty men and dug in on the support line, where he was later joined by Sergeant Taylor with another fortyfive men. At midnight, the Battalion was ordered to reform and attack again, but before Sergeant South could obey the order it was countermanded, the Brigadier having learnt that there were only eighty-three men under Sergeant South's command. The Sergeant was then directed to take what was left of the Battalion back to the support line and join the Middlesex Regiment, which he did.

17

May 10. Lovely day. C out in donkey chair. I packed. We sat in the verandah, the sun glorious. Got a card and letters of 4th, 5th and 6th from Frank. They had been badly shelled for two days, beastly gassy ones which made everyone feel ill and suffocated. Comparatively few casualties but it made him very anxious and he has no one to help or support him.

May 11. We left Ventnor at 8.5, the place looking the *very ideal* of spring. We reached London at 11.50. Drove by Buckingham St to fetch Mama and she, C and I lunched together at St Pancras, C and I leaving there 2.30 for Marple. He felt a little sickly from the shaking of the train but better when we arrived. It was raining, which his leg gave warning of before we got there. Everything beautifully green and fresh.

May 12. A telegram redirected on from Ventnor of last night: Lt Col F. E. B. Isherwood York Lancaster Regt reported wounded 9th May nature and degree not stated Secy War Office. And this is Wednesday and nothing from him or any hospital. Wired to War Office but no further news forthcoming. Miss Hudson came down kindly before lunch and offered to stay, she was a great help. A sad long day of no news and horrible anxiety. Very cold and rainy though the trees and country are very green and forward. My passport came from Coxes, they say it is well to have one as they cannot be got at a moment's notice and photographs are required, etc.

May 13. Left Marple 8.47. Reached St Pancras 1.15. Cold and wet. No news. A Mr Robertson came to see me (friend of Jack Isherwood's) more than kind, went to War Office twice, promising to come again in morning. (Jack laid up at Shere, bicycle accident.) Wrote to Graham Greene to see if he could suggest any further steps to take, there seemed to be *none*. Went to see Col Lousada in case he should have had news, his young cousin being also with the 1st Battalion. He was in Wales. Madgie Reid has also had enquiries made through Coxes Enquiry Bureau for Officers.

(*Madgie Reid, like Elizabeth Isherwood, was a Luce by birth. Elizabeth was her aunt and Frank her first cousin. Jack Reid, her son, had joined the Regiment at Limerick and had been with Frank in the Armentières sector. Thus Madgie and Kathleen were drawn together by shared anxiety. Madgie now became Kathleen's most devoted friend and helper in her time of trouble.*

Jack Reid was badly wounded in 1916, losing one of his legs. After the war he had a distinguished legal career and became a judge.)

May 14. Out before 10 to War Office. I thought possibly I might hear of other wounded 1st Y & L officers already in hospital in London, but Capt Wedgewood is at Oxford. Then to the Horse Guards where Capt Brand has lists of the officers in all the London Hospitals, but no 1st Y & L among them. Mr Robertson came later in day and went again to War Office. They talk of Frank possibly and probably being in a detention hospital and unable to send wires, and were quite sure he *could not possibly be missing*. The suspense is awful. Then Mr Robertson wired through to an address at Boulogne they gave him, to the Commandant No 7 Stationary Hospital, but no answer came, nor from Coxes.

May 15. Lovely morning. Madgie to see me soon after breakfast. She had heard from Jack, dated 11th, nothing much going on then near Armentières, apparently. Jack Isherwood came in en route to Marple. He sent wires to Mumby the Brigade Major and the Brigadier for me, but it all seems useless. Mr Robertson came too, he had been again to the War Office and went also to the Horse Guards. Many wounded officers came home last night but neither Frank nor Mr Lousada among them. Colonel Bridgeford, who was wounded the same day, is back in Limerick by now. A wire, very late, to say Frank not at Boulogne, from Commandant.

May 16. Mr Robertson came up from Wimbledon on his motor bike and went to the War Office and the Horse Guards. From the latter he heard of a Lieutenant Gauntlett, 1st Y & L, in the Free Hospital, Greys Inn Rd, so went on there and heard from him and Mr Cowley that, though wounded before Frank, they had crossed from France only a night or two ago with the Brigadier [Boyle] who told them that Frank had been wounded in the arm, and he and Mr Lousada had been hit by the same shell. It was very cheering to even hear that something was known of him and he wasn't missing. Went myself to see Capt Cowley and Capt Gauntlett, both just promoted, and was able to hear of the whereabouts of Regiment when they were there.

May 17. Rained all day. Wire from Henry to say Lily Belgrave had seen a Corporal Parry in hospital who said he had helped to bind up Frank when he was wounded. There seems to be another Red Cross enquiry bureau, 20 Arlington St. Madgie Reid went to enquire for me there. Wire from Lily Belgrave to talk to her on the telephone. Went up to Charing Cross P.O. and arranged to go to hospital with her tomorrow.

May 18. Pouring with rain. To meet Lily Belgrave at Portland Rd station and together to the Eye Hospital where she visits and had discovered Corporal Parry. His story not *very* clear but it appears that they went back for a rest late on Friday the 7th and had not got into huts till nearly 4 a.m. Saturday, when by 9 a.m. they were sent for to go into action. His idea is it was Saturday Frank was wounded. He says he met him going to the dressing-station to have his wound dressed and gave him something to apply to it. (In yesterday's story he bound it up.) After that, he imag-ined, Frank had been taken to hospital at Bailleul. (But, if so, he could have easily wired. It looks more as if he had never gone away to hospital and gone on fighting.)

May 19. Many letters. Mr Robertson came and arranged to go round to War Office to get any further suggestions as to pos-sibilities of wiring. Mrs B took me to see a Red Cross lady who meets wounded officers and promised to enquire for Y & L ones wounded since Frank.

May 20. It seems Miss Marker, Mr Lousada's half sister, had just the same wire as mine and has heard nothing since—and it was a comfort to her hearing the little I could tell her, what the Brigadier had said.

May 21. *No news of Frank.* Papers full of a coalition govern-ment to be formed and The Daily Mail screaming over Lord Kitchener, saying he is responsible for our shortage of high ex-plosive shells—if so, he deserves anything, for the shortness of am-munition has wasted endless lives. Our artillery unable to properly support the troops, the other day at Ypres. Mama and I to see Mr Pennell's exhibition of London in War Time, clever charcoal drawings, effects of searchlights at night, etc. Mr Robertson called in afternoon but alas no news and the awful silence con-tinues.

May 22. No news. It seems an everlasting silence. By train from Victoria to Denmark Hill to the 4th London Hospital there, only to find that Private Lawton, 1st Y & L, had gone to convalescent home at Morden Hall, Mitcham. Tried to get there but owing to partial train strike got to standstill on Clapham Common and came back as it was already five.

May 23. Met Miss Marker, Mr Lousada's half sister, at Waterloo. To Wimbledon where we changed for Morden. Found it quite countrified and a few minutes brought us to a beautiful park with deer and a river running through and the chestnuts in full glory. I hardly remember such a lovely spring. Morden Hall is in the park and Mr Hatfield has given it over as a convalescent home for soldiers. The men looked as if they had reached paradise. Poor Private Lawton quite a boy, could only beam content with his present surroundings and kept on saying in reference to France it was 'orrible, orrible'. He was wounded before Frank so could give no news.

May 24. King Victor signed the decree declaring war on Austria at 2 p.m. yesterday, so now Italy too is at war. Two men had wired in reply to telegram to Rouen and Versailles. The first said several people who had been asked said Frank had been brought in. The second that Frank was wounded in a charge at Zillebeke, near Hill 60. Madgie came round just before dinner with a letter from Captain Salmond who said he could not find out much about Frank except that a shrapnel bullet got him in the leg and that it is rumoured that he is going on well. Jack Reid writes that Major Bayley went to take over the command of the 1st Battalion on the 17th. I wonder so if the leg wound was a second and later one to that in the arm mentioned by the Brigadier.

May 27. Wrote letters as usual. Jack Isherwood came. His idea of comfort seems to be to catalogue and label the different degrees of dreadfulness of things that might have happened, then argue from the different hearsay reports that these things *haven't happened* and therefore why be anxious? Just as if the mere fact of not knowing isn't quite enough in itself for anxiety.

• •

May 28. Wrote letters as usual most of the morning and yet it always seems as if I was six behind. Another day and no news. Now they have been telegraphing through to the clearing hospitals, but Mr Lousada had been through none of those applied to, and of course that means Frank hasn't either.

May 29. The sun shone and Mama sat out in the Embankment Gardens. It is three weeks tomorrow and it seems incredible that we can hear nothing. I feel very very downhearted. Mama and I to see 'A Bit 'o Love' by John Galsworthy, touching and very fine in parts, laid in Devonshire village, and the tragedy of a young clergyman and his faithless wife.

May 31. Heard from 5 of the 6 clearing and casualty stations near Ypres. All wrote most kindly but Frank and Mr Lousada hadn't passed through. I simply feel in utter despair. Wrote to Lord Kitchener.

June 1. Zeppelins over London last night, the papers told not to say where but it was somewhere in the East End. To Arlington St to suggest to Mrs Buckler that Frank and Mr Lousada might be prisoners, since they do not appear to have passed through any hospital. She said she had thought so for some time. If so, all we can do is to wait for the lists to come through from Geneva.

June 2. Jack Reid is on his way up towards Ypres with the 2nd Battalion. Poor Madgie. Mr Robertson in before lunch. He had been to the War Office and seen Kitchener's secretary. They had had my letter and enquiries are at last being put on foot.

June 3. To Coxes. Saw Mr Street. He said he heard there *had* been a temporary retreat, though the ground had been regained later. I do not know if that may have been after Frank was wounded, and so he was taken prisoner. It would be so terrible for him to be taken prisoner, and yet what *else* is there to hope for. All that the special War Office enquiry resulted in was a

467

wire to say Lt Col F. E. B. Isherwood, York and Lancaster Regiment, now reported missing—a fact which has been obvious for some time.

June 6. Aggravating note from E, saying what a fearful and glorious fight they must have had on the 9th for so few to be left to account for the remainder. Further raids of zeppelins reported from the East End but details are now kept dark. Everyone is buying respirators to wear against the poisonous gases which it is expected the Germans will explode when the big raid comes, and many sleep with jewellery and money packed close to hand.

June 7. Muriel and Henry both say that Mr Isherwood and Esther appeared quite hopeful when they went to Marple and as if there was nothing to worry about.

June 8. The children seem quite happy at Marple. A letter from Mr Isherwood in which Frank's being a prisoner (which alas we do not even *know*) he seems to think is quite a blessing in disguise. It all *makes me feel so lonely*, though of course I have dearest Mama. Mrs Buckler promised to get her husband to enquire of the American Ambassador in Berlin, making a personal matter of it. Heard that the Brigade Major Mumby says the lost ground was *never* retaken. It had been such a comfort to think it had, and that Frank must have been taken prisoner or he would have been found. Even that hope is gone and I feel more miserable than I can say.

June 10. To Coxes to ask Mr Street if I ought to see about Frank's kit being sent home. He seemed to think it would come.

June 11. A letter Henry sent me from George W. to his father, saying he had been in Sunderland and had heard how terribly Frank had been wounded and condoling over his loss. I wrote to Colonel Lousada to ask him to enquire what foundation there was for this report, it is all so *dreadful*.

June 13. Mr Robertson went down to Woolwich to hospital, as a soldier wounded in France was sure Frank was there. Of course he wasn't. There were two Y & L men but one was wounded before Frank and the other too ill to speak, though he said he knew him.

June 14. Mama and I went on a tram to New Cross, got off there and had tea at an Italian cafe and then walked up quite a steep street to Telegraph Hill. A most marvellous view. An old man up there told me the landmarks and said there were seven currents of air and it was finer than Brighton itself. A line from Col Lousada to say Col Howe in Sunderland had heard none of the reports mentioned by George W.

June 15. A letter from George W. saying he had heard about 'poor Frank' from Col Howe, which seems utterly *extraordinary* when Col Howe had heard none of the reports mentioned.

June 16. Miss Marker came, just back from seeing Von Bourg, a clairvoyant, who had given her most reassuring and circumstantial accounts of her Brother, who, he said, was in hospital near Lille, in German hands but doing well. Frank was not with him but he described him going down the same road. V.B. says the hospital where Lousada is will be retaken by us in August. How splendid if so!

June 19. Henry sent me on a letter from Pt Webster in the Irvine Hospital, Ayrshire (who Mrs Buckler said was not a witness she thought much reliance should be placed on) most *terribly* upsetting, stating that Frank met his death when leading them in an attack at Ypres on German trenches, that he was by his side when he fell, he did not move, blood was coming from his head and chest. Henry said he was miserable to send in such a letter, only I wanted all news however hard, and he feels that the statement cannot be dismissed as rumour or invention, although it is uncorroborated evidence—and Godley the groom said he had left Frank in a ditch for safety after binding up his wound. If this were true he surely could not have led the men as stated, and yet what is one to believe. It seems to me that God is very cruel. If it is all for some big wise end, why can't we see it—why all this agony—why, when one is happy, is it snatched from us?

June 20. Turned out the shelves in wardrobe and refolded Frank's things. Moth in his wedding trousers.

June 21. Madgie called for me and we went together to King George's Hospital, where Lady Wynn is working. Her Son has been a prisoner in Westphalia since Mons, he was reported killed and she and her Husband went to hospitals all over England to get news of his end. Three different soldiers, one a man of his own company, told them in detail how he died. Six weeks later he wrote to them from Germany and said he had never even been wounded. Could not help feeling cheered, it seemed another ray of hope that there is no truth in Webster's statement.

June 22. Mrs Buckler sent two more reports from privates, one regarding the position of the ambulance, the other saying he was sure he had seen Frank wounded in a train at Boulogne. A letter from Miss Scott Moncrieff saying a Y & L man in hospital at York was sure Frank was a prisoner.

(*Among the various conflicting statements about Frank's wounding or death—all of them equally unconfirmed, to this day —is one that he was killed by the direct hit of a shell on the ambulance which was taking him to hospital. This may explain Kathleen's reference to the ambulance, above.*)

June 24. Drove with Mama to the Club and on to the bank and to see Miss Robins. I fetched Mama and we dined at the Comedy on our way home. In the evening came a terrible letter from Arlington St, The British Red Cross and Order of St John: 'We much regret to say that according to the Geneva list of June 12th received here on the 23rd inst., it is intimated that a disc was found on a dead soldier close to Frezenberg early in May with the following inscription on it:—Isherwood. F. E. B. Y & L Regiment, Siche 5. C of E. We greatly fear this disc may have belonged to Col. Isherwood. Yours faithfully, Louis Mallet.' . . . . . and so passes hope and life.

June 25. Mama wired to Uncle Charlie Fry and I to Henry and wrote to Marple to Jack. As he and Esther, or at any rate the latter, continue to think it strange Henry can see anything to be so worried about, they may still see hope. Graham Greene came round at lunch time to see Mama, did not see him. I don't know how the rest of the day passed, except that time seemed to have stood still and there appeared a vista of endless hopeless days of loneliness ahead . . . . . everything reminds me of him, the places we used to go together, our outings and the way he had of making everything nice and all his thousand kind and thoughtful ways . . . . . one could bear the parting when one had the future but now there seems nothing but the stabs of pain from each happy memory. Uncle Charlie arrived about 9 p.m.

June 26. A lovely morning. Breakfasted with Uncle Charlie who went out directly after to Arlington St. He found them talking the case over but there seemed little hope. He went on to the War Office, they hadn't yet had the Geneva intimation but should not close the thing as final unless they received still more conclusive proof or, as time went on, *we* wished it. Not, I think, that Major Doonagh either had much hope but I suppose everything is a matter of form there. Uncle C was very kind and we talked of the future, the sad hopeless future and the boys. Thank God I still have them and Mama. But all the happy days are gone when we felt so young together and had such happy travelling days and days at home together. Mama and I by steamer to Putney. Back by train.

June 27. To early service. Seven weeks ago today. I pray the days and weeks may not all be as long as these have been.

471

June 28. I had many letters. Col Lousada's pleased me. He said, 'ever since I first met your Husband I have had the greatest affection and respect for him. He was the truest straightest gentleman I ever met and the most gallant. I always remember his absolute fearlessness in South Africa. I know nothing can lesson your grief but you must always remember how beautiful his life was and how splendidly he gave it up'.

Mrs Buckler too wrote so kindly, 'it makes my heart ache in a way you may think absurd, even intrusive in a stranger. But I had been so much touched and moved to admiration by your courage and the heroic way in which you bore the ghastly suspense and haunting fear that I ended by taking a tremendous personal interest in it, so you mustn't mind if I cry a few tears for your sake and hold out a sympathizing hand. . . .' I am glad I seemed brave, it would please Frank and seems to make me a little worthy of him.

June 29. By the 11.15 to Corwen. Aggie Trevor and her Raymond and my two and Nurse to meet me. Christopher and Richard arrived there yesterday. Maesmor looked so green and cool and peaceful, and darling C very sweet and dear. It seems so dreadful that such a loss should have fallen on him so young. But I am *very* thankful for all I still have.

July 1. Frank's birthday. Heaps of dreadful letters.

July 2. Henry wants to put notices in the papers now, but I am against doing so at present.

July 3. They want me to go to Marple but I don't feel I *could* face it just yet.

July 7. Had letter from War Office stating that they had heard that Col Isherwood was killed near Frezenberg in May and that a disc bearing his name had been found. In view of these facts, the Military Secretary would be obliged if I would say whether I am prepared to accept this information and begs to express on behalf of Lord Kitchener his sincere sympathy.

(Kathleen does not refer in her diary to a letter which she must have received, on July 9 probably, from Mr Robertson:

Dear Mrs Isherwood, your letter made me feel very sad for you. It has been a terribly sad time while it grew gradually darker, with all the signs less and less hopeful. Yet the finding of the disc may mean really nothing at all, it is a little thing easily lost, and the stories of Wood and Webster must remain unacceptable in the absence of that official confirmation which the War Office is unable to give. I gathered from what Jack said that the family had decided to accept the evidence, yet I would like to try to persuade you at least to postpone acceptance, to remember too that many a man officially reported dead turns up whole.

You say, could you but know the end was swift, that he had no sense of loneliness, no drawn out suffering. Comfort yourself in the knowledge that mortal wounds do not hurt severely, and that to a man of your Husband's keen sense of duty a passing wave of loneliness would make way for that peace and content which would surely settle upon him in that he had done his all. The bullet which kills kills quickly, it is when it continues cleaving through the defenceless lives behind the life which it has taken that the torture comes.

His life taken, No! I rather see that it is given. And if he is, as I earnestly, so confidently hope, a close prisoner, though properly tended, take comfort in the realization that a man hit hard could no more reproach himself in that, than he could feel humiliated in being rendered helpless by unloving hands from the debris of some street accident. It is your sense of loneliness, your drawn out suffering that I dread.

Do please keep in mind what a privilege it would be to me to do anything in my power to try to alleviate these—if there is anything I can do, anything at all, don't hesitate to use me. Though all my sympathies are with you I still have high hopes. Yours very sincerely, R. B. Robertson.

However kindly meant, this seems to belong to Kathleen's category of "dreadful letters"; its writer is so moved by his own emotions that he sets himself, no doubt quite unconsciously, to play on those of his reader, first offering her painful and useless hopes, then wordy consolations. Surely it is a model of how not *to write to a widow? But, however Kathleen may have felt when she read it, she remembered only her gratitude when she met Mr Robertson again, at Jack's house at Shere, in 1936: "I hadn't seen him since 1915, when he and Jack were working at Somerset House and he helped me in the vain and hopeless search for news of my dear Frank. I shall never forget his kindness and sympathy, no trouble seemed too great and he was so understanding. Mama and I both felt that his initials R.B. might well stand for Real Brother during all that terrible time."*)

July 11. Nine weeks today. Now and then I have such hope and peace. I think it *must* be well, and if he has gone beyond think he must have found the things he loved, and peace, and it may be the beyond is near if one could *only know* and see.

July 12. Sent blue serge coat and skirt to be dyed at Puller's. C and I bicycled along the road to Corwen, am not even yet at home on a free wheel or like it so well as the old way. A letter from Cope saying how well Frank's little mare looked, and that he had his sword safe.

July 16. I had a letter from Major Bayley yesterday, it said it made them all the more determined to wage this war to the end, 'bitter to the Germans as we mean it to be; it is due to the memory of your Husband and others like him that we out here should do all we can to avenge them; rest assured we shall all do our best'. Which makes me feel the lives that have been given have not been

474

given in vain, but serve to stimulate by their example—and that does so gladden one's heart.

July 22. Henry sent me a letter from Dorothy B. who had seen a letter from Doctor Purden to his Aunt, saying he had helped to bury Col Isherwood, 'whose body we identified'. It seems so incredible that Purden never wrote to me, and quite unforgivable. I wrote to him and to Col Clemson.

July 27. [In London.] A woman from Barker, the mourning warehouse, arrived between 10 and 11, laden with boxes of hats, bonnets, blouses and costumes and coats—all the latter designed for the very ample matron, and I was quite swamped! However we chose designs to have dresses made. Mama and I each a dull black silk and she a serge too, hats etc. Took till lunch.

July 29. Letter from Col Clemson, quite *sure it is all a mistake* about Dr Purden having identified Frank, as he had promised all he heard to let him know at once.

July 30. Was fitted at Barker's for my black silk coat and skirt—feeling all the time so hopeful—and yet there are alas no grounds for it. Mama and I reached Oxford soon after three.

July 31. To Christ Church to see about Extension Lectures, they are all held there this year instead of in the Examination Schools which are given over to military purposes. Indeed it is a military Oxford, with soldiers billeted in houses on either side of us and all over the town, public buildings turned into hospitals. So different to the peaceful atmosphere of old and I feel glad to have it different. Letter from Dr Purden, not a word of truth in Miss Dorothy B's report. He wrote a very nice letter.

August 1. Wore my new black things. Very depressing. Have only worn ordinary black till now. It is twelve weeks ago today since the 9th of May.

Letter from Emily in London to Kathleen at Marple Hall, August 5:

Ownest and Most Precious, I do hope you had a peaceful journey and were properly met. I trust you found all well. Darling, I can't tell you how much I admire your courage and bravery. I trust the children will be a help and support. So far as anything can be nice just now, it was nice being together. Don't overtax your strength and nerves. If feeling hard to keep up, take Ignatia, as for the time it *deadens one's feelings*. Goodbye, Sweetest and Best. Thine for ever and ever. You are ever in my thoughts and prayers. It cuts me to the heart to see my bright Darling in her sad garb, looking so sweet and touching, and it seems impossible to say Thy Will Be Done.

September 7. A year since Frank went from Cambridge with the Regiment. Mr Isherwood offered me Wyberslegh again as Mrs Humphreys is dead and it is vacant, but there are so many things to consider and dearly as I loved it with my dear Frank I can't imagine it without *him*.

September 8. In the paper today under 'previously officially reported missing now unofficially reported killed' is Frank's name. I think I miss him more every day and life seems harder and harder.

September 9. Telegram of condolence from the King and Queen.

September 11. Heard from Graham Greene he had replied for me to the Keeper of the Privy Purse: 'Please convey to Their Majesties with humble duty our grateful appreciation of their gracious sympathy'. I should never have dreamt of putting 'humble duty'!

• •

September 15. Christopher and I to London to stay with Mama at the Ladies Park Club as flat not ready. There seems to have been a fairly bad zeppelin raid last Wednesday, they did a good deal of damage and the noise was *terrific* with our guns firing at it, it passed right over London, quite a scare in Club but it only lasted about 15 minutes.

September 16. C and I to Maskelyne and Devant's, very good juggling and mystery tricks.

September 17. To Waterloo, where C joined the rest of the boys. Do pray he will keep well this term.

September 23. To Colchester, where Moey met me. We talked of Frank and Moey still can't believe it's true.

September 26. Unpacked My Dear's things, unspeakably sad to see the dear familiar things and the green valise Bell and I made at Limerick, nearly everything has come back except his watch and a luminous torch. His sword Cope still has.

September 27. In the evening I received from the War Office the disc bearing my Husband's name—very polished up and torn from its string. It didn't seem real somehow.

September 29. Met Mr Robertson at the entrance to Somerset House and he took me into various bewildering departments in connection with presenting the will and valuing the property, which but for him would have been very tedious and distressing. Felt so proud to say there were *no* debts—few can say that. On to War Office to ask for an application for exemption from tax— more departments and finally to huts in St James Park, where a Mr Norman had the whole correspondence and made no difficulty, promising to send in the necessary recommendation at once. To tea at the Stanhope Hotel to meet Jack Reid and when I got there

I found Colonel (or more properly Brigadier General) Clemson, very glad to see him as a link with My Dear.

(Elsewhere Kathleen writes: "Col Clemson has come home and is going to be given a brigade—how hard it all seems, he who has no one to come home to. . . .")

October 5. A Mr Robertson (not Jack's friend) from the Probate, about my going to reswear a statement. They cavil at the dates being given as the 8th or 9th and have inserted instead 'between the 8th and 11th', though *what* difference it can make I can't imagine, but this is the Registrar's wish and what he is prepared to accept.

(According to the account of the battle which is quoted from Colonel Wylly's book at the end of the last chapter, it would seem that Frank was probably killed between 8 P.M. and midnight on May 8. However, by next spring Kathleen had made up her mind the ninth was the day of his death. Her reason for doing this may have been based on some piece of evidence which isn't recorded in her diary.)

October 14. [At Marple.] Nurse went off for her holiday to Cambridge. Richard is fretful and exacting and I am afraid very spoilt. Very much disturbed to see that there had been an air raid again in the London area last night. They never give the whereabouts. However wire came from Mama to say all well though she had heard the guns.

October 22. Fanny Hudson had seen the last of her convalescents off this morning and was going to shut up and have a good clean out and a rest before reopening with her new ward (the dining-room) and its eight additional beds. The papers today full of the particulars about Miss Edith Cavell's death. Indignation is intense.

• •

October 28. Nurse returned from her holiday, gave a dreadful account of the darkness of Cambridge for fear of raids and at her home at Chevington zeppelins appear to frequently pass over, making an alarming noise and throwing down searchlights which illuminate all the village.

October 30. A most lovely day, more like spring than autumn. Richard and I went for a walk along the Priest's walk and on to the canal and round by the acqueduct and viaduct. He appreciated all the signals and trains enormously. In afternoon he looked ceaselessly at his different books of trains in the sitting-room. No others have *any* interest for him! The Home Defence Corps of Marple, Romilly and Compstall drilled in the Park.

November 2. To Stockport to catch the 12 o'clock. Nurse and Richard came to the station too, the latter very firm about not leaving the carriage for fear he should be taken away from his beloved Marple. As for my departure, he took that with the utmost philosophy, saying 'but I like Nanny best'!

November 20. [At Nether Hall.] We have quite War dinners. Fish today, for a treat three herrings!!!

November 21. Uncle Walter and I motored to St Peter's, Thurston. Do not think, though I have stayed at Nether, that I have been to service there since that happy 12th of March 1903 when Frank and I were married there. The scene all came *so* vividly and the contrast of what was and what is.

November 22. Bright but very cold. Poor Mama terribly afraid she would not be well enough to leave and would be laid up at Nether, she has had *such* indigestion and has so felt the cold and not been out once. Home about 4. Mama straight to bed.

November 23. To the Alliance Insurance Company. They registered the probate with a view to paying out money. On to intercession service at Westminster Abbey. Met Madgie Reid. Jack Reid is now a captain after little more than eighteen months service..

November 29. Had to write a 'heavy' letter to Christopher, whose half-term report spoke of inattention and not taking enough interest in some of the subjects, also a complacence on his part!

December 5. Venus to tea and a talk about books and writers. Liked seeing her.

December 12. Very cold. To the service at St John's Westminster to hear Canon Wilberforce. The church very full and very still and many there who were in mourning and sorrow. The hereafter is very real to him.

December 21. Went to meet Christopher at Waterloo.

December 24. [At Marple.] Went out in afternoon to get things for Richard's stocking, which, after the latter was asleep, Christopher and Nurse filled and distributed his presents round him. After dinner the Marple boys came with two concertinas and sat round the fire in the hall, about eight or nine of them, and sang Christmas carols and were refreshed with coffee and mince pies.

December 25. Christopher woke up soon after five and the presents were looked at soon after, but I went to sleep again. Nurse made me a beautiful tea cloth, all drawn thread work and lace. I think the children enjoyed it all but to me seemed additionally sad and lonely, and so cruel to feel all the children are missing, which made one's own loss the harder to face. No one can ever make up to them for Frank.

December 30. Drove with Mr Isherwood up the village and then on over the Ridge past Wyberslegh which seems to belong now to another existence—so long ago as to be a thing apart.

Letter from Emily to Kathleen, New Year's Day, 1916:

Darling Own, my heart and thoughts are near you. God grant strength and courage may be given you and that life may still hold *much* of happiness for you. Sometimes I feel dear dear Frank is, and ever will be, near us all, almost living with us and interested in everything and understanding everything. . . .

May 9, 1916. The longest saddest year of all my life.

May 8, 1917. Two years ago this morning the Regiment left their billets after but a few hours rest (so few were the men and so great the need) and the devastating second battle for Ypres continued, all Saturday and Sunday they were in it with the shortage of men and particularly of guns to support them. A nightmare to think of. By the evening of the 9th only 120 men of the 1st York and Lancaster Regt answered the roll call and one subaltern (the only officer left) and he was killed next day.

May 9, 1917. Two years ago today . . . . . only two years!

May 8, 1918. Today and tomorrow are the third anniversary days of the second battle of Ypres, and this morning I dreamt so vividly that he came in at the Marple gates.

May 9, 1919. It is four years today since my dear Frank was missing. It seems a lifetime and yet only like yesterday.

18

As long as the War went on, Kathleen must have had some lingering hope that Frank might after all be in a German prison camp. And even when it was over, one couldn't say with absolute certainty that a missing man was dead. Throughout the nineteen-twenties, tales were told of shell-shocked men who had lost their memory and were identified years later, living in England under other names. The tales may have been mostly untrue, but at least they were based on a possibility. This was what made Kathleen's predicament so cruel. Nobody could tell her when to stop hoping. She had to decide that for herself.

In her early fifties, Kathleen remained an attractive woman; indeed, she could now be described as beautiful. Her eyes had a depth and a sadness which became her, as did the simple black clothes she wore. Grief hadn't stricken her with ugly lines; she looked touchingly young for her age. When she talked and laughed and showed an interest in the present moment, one was often aware that she was grieving. But she never gave way in public to self-indulgent sulky melancholy; she had far too much pride and character for that.

She spent most of her time at 14 Buckingham Street with Emily. From there she could visit Richard at weekends. In the autumn of 1919 he had begun going to school at Berkhamsted, which is only twenty-eight miles from London; he and Nanny lived in lodgings in the town. Kathleen seldom saw Christopher except during the holidays, for he had left St. Edmund's at the end of *1918* and started life as a public-school boy at Repton, near Derby. Repton had also been Jack Isherwood's school.

Emily was now entering her eighties. Advancing age showed itself chiefly in her increased capriciousness. She had the positions of the furniture in the flat changed several times a month and would make sudden moves, with a great deal of luggage, to some London hotel or country resort she temporarily fancied, often returning home disenchanted after twenty-four hours. She was as eager as ever for pleasure and excitement. During the War, when the Germans made occasional daylight raids, Emily had insisted on enjoying the spectacle from the roof. Reclining in a deck chair, she had watched the planes through a pair of opera glasses with a long handle like a lorgnette. Kathleen deplored such recklessness and sighed over the amount of unnecessary work Emily caused. Yet Kathleen lived vicariously on Emily's appetite for pleasures which her own puritanism would have prevented her from enjoying alone.

Nevertheless, Emily's physical strength was failing, and the flat had one serious disadvantage for an old lady: it could be reached only by a tall circular stone staircase, there was no lift. Emily's doctor began to warn her that this was a strain on her heart and she should consider living elsewhere.

It was obvious that Kathleen too would soon have to find a home for herself and her children. She had put off doing this, for she knew that getting her furniture out of storage and arranging it in new rooms would remind her cruelly of the old days with Frank. At the same time, she realized that Marple Hall was unlikely to be open to them much longer.

In March *1921*, Elizabeth Isherwood died. Kathleen wrote in her diary: "It is indeed a comfort to feel that her poor patient self is now free and that life is hers again. I love to think how Frank will welcome her."

That autumn Kathleen rented a house in London—*36 St. Mary*

*Abbot's Terrace, which was at the western end of Kensington
High Street, near Olympia. And Emily moved into it with them.*

*In 1924, John Isherwood died—on May the ninth. Kathleen was
powerfully impressed by the coincidence of the two death-dates.
Henceforward, she would often refer to this as "the Double
Anniversary."*

*When John died, Henry had been living at Marple Hall for
some time already. He had turned the library into his private
sitting room and filled it with miniatures, snuffboxes, statuettes,
signed photographs of society ladies, antique coins, Venetian-
glass paperweights and other personal treasures. Its atmosphere
was now enriched with the incense which he burned in the fireplace. Henry had moved out of Oakes because he and Muriel had
agreed to separate. Thus their marriage ended, without scandal or
recrimination, and fortunately without children.*

*Kathleen's comment on John's death is realistic rather than emo-
tional: "Felt very grieved, he has been such a kind friend to us
and it means an end to Marple as a home where one always received a welcome." Henry had evidently made it clear to Kathleen that he wasn't going to offer her the same hospitality. She
didn't take offense at this. In any event, she would never have
felt at ease as Henry's guest. And before long, Henry left Marple
Hall for good and took a flat in London. He and Kathleen continued to see each other there from time to time.*

*After settling down with Kathleen at St. Mary Abbot's Ter-
race, Emily became less eager to roam. By October 1924 she
seemed even to have lost her appetite for theatergoing. Then, unexpectedly, she announced that she would take Kathleen to the
theater as a birthday treat, on October 7. They saw* The Mask
and the Face, *with Athene Seyler and Frank Cellier, and* The
Letter of the Law *a few days later. These two plays quite restored Emily's appetite. By the first of November she had seen
three more: Violet Vanburgh in* In the Next Room, *Mrs. Patrick
Campbell in* The Thirteenth Chair, *and* Fata Morgana, *in which
Jeanne de Casalis played the lead with Tom Douglas, a young*

American actor who was making many English hearts beat faster, including Christopher's.

Having enjoyed her little fling, Emily became suddenly very ill with bronchitis and more than usually cantankerous. She refused to eat any kind of food which had a yellow color and rapped fiercely on the ceiling with her cane whenever she heard the slightest sound. Pneumonia set in. On November 10, at 10:45 P.M., she died.

According to her often-expressed wishes, Emily was cremated and her ashes were scattered. Kathleen felt obliged to consent to this although she would have much preferred to keep them in an urn, so that they could be mingled with her own, one day. The funeral was held at Golders Green. Christopher came down for it from Corpus Christi College, Cambridge, where he was now an undergraduate. He remembers the dismally untheatrical ending of the ceremony. "Scatter me to the winds!" Emily had told them. But there was no wind. The clergyman scooped the ashes out of their container with a sort of trowel; they fell on the ground and lay there and that was that.

Afterward, Kathleen and Christopher went to visit Frederick's grave at Brompton Cemetery. Kathleen's comment was, "The first attention he has received for some time, poor darling!"

Next day she wrote: "I feel how little she realized how deeply my life is bound up in hers. I might have been so much more loving to her and now it is too late. If one only felt sure she could understand and forgive." This seems an excess of scruple; few mothers have had a more devoted daughter. Perhaps Kathleen was feeling obscurely guilty that she had ever left Emily in the first place and got married. Oughtn't an only daughter to devote her life to a widowed (or about-to-be-widowed) mother? Kathleen could still think in such Victorian terms. Perhaps she even wondered sometimes if Frank's death might have been a punishment. . . .

And yet, as Kathleen made the transition from youth to age, a change came over her. Her earlier fears and scruples, her vulnerability and even her grief were modified by a saving tough-

*ness: the toughness of an organism which has decided to survive.
One aspect of Kathleen's toughness was that she had grown
relatively unshockable. (Christopher may have helped in this, by
dosing her ruthlessly with the writings of his contemporaries and
quoting their pub-talk.) Jack Reid, in a letter to Christopher
written many years later, describes going to have tea, sometime
in the mid-twenties, with his mother, Madgie, and with Kathleen,
who had just been serving on a grand jury:*

When asked about her experiences, your Mother said they had
had an absurd case about a man in a bus who had put his hand up
a woman's skirt. What enormity he had then perpetrated I don't
recollect, but it was plain that both ladies thought it rather a good
joke. On being asked what the jury did, your Mother said, 'Oh of
course we threw it out, it was a most ridiculous case'. At that time
there used to be much talk of 'Victorian hypocrisy' and I was
rather shaken and amused by such down to earth views.

*On July 25, 1927, the newly-built Menin Gate was dedicated at
Ypres, as a memorial to British troops killed on the Salient whose
bodies had remained unfound and unburied—it is almost incredible
that these numbered more than fifty-six thousand. Frank's name
was not amongst them.*

*Kathleen therefore protested to the Imperial War Graves Com-
mission, starting a correspondence which dragged on into 1928.
They told her that another memorial was to be erected at
Ploegsteert, near Armentières, which would include Frank's name
among eleven thousand of the missing dead from that area. They
had put Frank on the Ploegsteert list because he had belonged
officially to the Second Battalion of the regiment. The fact that
he had commanded the First Battalion and died on its battleground
was seemingly of no significance to these bureaucrats! (And besides, the Menin Gate was the memorial to be on; who cared about
unpronounceable Ploegsteert—these Flemish names were almost as
hideous as German ones!) Kathleen's indignation had now become
passionate. This was the kind of injustice which she described as*

486

"*monstrous, too monstrously unfair.*" *At long last she prevailed. The authorities agreed that Frank's name should be added to the list on the Menin Gate and also allowed to remain on the Ploegsteert memorial, remarking grumpily that "the duplication is annoying as a precedent but it cannot be helped."*

In the summer of 1929, Kathleen decided that they should leave St. Mary Abbot's Terrace. She hadn't cared much for the house since Emily's death, and now it was getting noisy and shook continually as the traffic along Kensington High Street grew heavier, year by year. (In 1934–35, the Terrace was demolished and a big block of flats was built on its site.)

They moved into 19 Pembroke Gardens. Pembroke Gardens were only a few minutes' walk away, on the south side of the High Street, leading out of Edwardes Square. Number 19 was a smaller but much pleasanter house than the other, and the street was very quiet.

Toward the end of 1929, Christopher settled down in Berlin and only returned to London on fairly short visits. From then on, Kathleen and he saw little of each other. When Hitler came into power in 1933, Christopher left Germany, but he still spent most of his time abroad, living in Greece, the Canary Islands, Spain, France, Denmark, Portugal, Holland, Belgium. Kathleen must have suffered a great deal of anxiety and embarrassment on his account. His behavior must often have seemed inexplicable to her and sometimes self-destructive. How could she have been expected to understand why he got himself requested to leave Cambridge in 1925, why he then took a job as secretary to a string quartet which had no prospects and paid only a pound a week, why he decided to become a medical student in 1928 but stopped studying after two terms? And how was she to explain to her friends why he had gone to Berlin?

Christopher himself answered these questions a few years later, in a book called Lions and Shadows. *It was really an indirect apology to Kathleen for his unkindness to her. But Christopher*

487

*was then unwilling to admit this to himself, so he keeps her name
out of the book altogether. On the few occasions when he is
forced to refer to her, he does so as "my female relative," or in
the plural as "my relatives" or "my family"!*

*Kathleen certainly didn't expect an apology or even an explana-
tion. She had long since given up attempting to understand Christopher's doings. Now she accepted them as she had accepted
Emily's, and tried not to worry too much. She counted her bless-
ings. She had Richard still with her, and several faithful and loving
friends. She had her books and her lectures and her art galleries.
She had many beautiful old churches to choose from, for her
Sunday services. Above all, she had her sustaining daily routine.
She planned meals with the cook, listened to Nanny's complaints
and tales about the neighbors, brought the household accounts up
to date, shopped. You run a house because it has to be kept going.
Life has to be kept going. You have had twelve years of happiness;
now you are paying for them. The price is simply outrageous, but
you were warned about that in advance.*

*In 1930, Kathleen revisited Wyberslegh. She had heard that the
front part of the house was temporarily unoccupied and being put
in order for a new tenant. On an impulse she wrote to the Coopers
and asked if she might stay a night with them at the farm.*

December 13. The years and worries seemed to slip away as I
passed the old familiar scenes and walked down the little Wyberslegh drive. How wonderful those days were. . . . Signs of work-
men but none about. It was already getting dark and the place was
mine again. Mrs Cooper gave me a kind welcome and the little
parlour was warm and snug. I remember so well when I was first
engaged, coming to the farm with Frank and his Mother and
visiting old Mrs Cooper.

December 14. I was awakened so cheerfully by sounds of the
farm, and there were the white chickens fluttering in the misty
morning. After breakfast in the spotless little farm parlour, look-

ing out on to the beloved garden, I went across to the kitchen
entrance of our Wyberslegh and spent more than half an hour
alone with it. The future tenants came to see me there at 11.30.
It was all so quiet and full of memories, memories which after
twenty years cheered and helped me. At one time I couldn't bear
even to pass the house I had so loved, but it is different now and
seeing it today, while it is temporarily empty and unoccupied, I
could 'furnish' it as it used to be. Electric light is to be put in for
the future tenants and washing basins and a new kitchen stove, etc.

*Oddly enough, says Richard, Kathleen had never talked to him
about Wyberslegh before the time of this visit; he had scarcely
been aware that it existed. He doesn't believe that the 1930 visit
made her want to go back and live there; she still felt this would
be too painful without Frank. However, she did tell him then that
she would like to have her ashes scattered in the Wyberslegh
garden, but that she didn't suppose this would be possible, as the
tenants would probably object.*

*Richard thinks that it wasn't until the early nineteen-thirties that
Kathleen became really able to enjoy herself again. Her description of the lying-in-state of George V does indeed show all her
old relish for such events:*

January 24, 1936. Went with Katie to see the Lying in State at
Westminster Hall. It was an orderly crowd, hardly a word spoken
and everybody wearing some emblem of mourning. When we
reached the high steps leading down into the great hall, everyone
paused before descending. It was one of the most impressive sights
I have ever seen—the huge bare spaciousness, the beautiful angel
roof faintly lighted by reversed lights and a soft bare greyness
everywhere. But there in the centre was a blaze of colour which
almost took one's breath away. Mounted on the steps stood the
great catafalque, bearing the coffin. The whole of the coffin
draped with the royal standard. Four great candlesticks at each
corner; four guardsmen in dazzling scarlet guarded the coffin and

at the bottom of the steps four yeomen of the guard in their gorgeous livery. All absolutely rigid and still. I never saw anything so utterly gorgeous in the midst of the encircling gloom, with a soft radiance over the coffin.

On January 28, Kathleen tried to watch the funeral procession, but the crowds were too much for her and she returned home, remembering "the big guns booming in the most sad way." She had also noted with pleasure that there was a poster in the lift of the Tube announcing the public opening of The Dog Beneath the Skin, *by W. H. Auden and Christopher Isherwood, at the Westminster Theatre.*

Christopher's career as a writer was now going quite well, and Kathleen followed it enthusiastically. She can't have cared much for his Mr. Norris—*its humor was too sour, it was too preoccupied with drinking and dirty rooms and low-life types to suit her taste—but her own opinion meant little to her. What mattered was that the outside world should appreciate Christopher.*

This mattered to Christopher too. He and Kathleen came together again over his press notices. He was gracious to her now and on his best behavior when he stayed at Pembroke Gardens. In 1936 he invited her to come out to Portugal and stay with him at Sintra, where he was then living. Kathleen traveled all the way to Lisbon by boat. The voyage was an alarming experience for her, by far the longest she had ever made. But she felt pleased with herself for having made it, and she reveled in a tour of serious sight-seeing: the Hieronymite monastery at Belem, the Bom Jesus at Braga, the library at Coimbra, Our Lady of Victory at Batalha, the Palace of Pena and the monastery-palace of Mafra. A young Frenchman who was being introduced to Kathleen at a party bowed over her hand and kissed it. Christopher remembers the expression on her face—embarrassed, pleased, girlish.

In January 1938, Christopher went off with Auden to report on the war in China. Newspapers published photographs of them about to board the boat-train. The press approved, and Kathleen was proud. Exactly one year later they left England again, for the

United States. *And before another year had passed, the press dis-approved, strongly; they were being denounced as war-dodgers. Kathleen must have found these ups and downs in Christopher's stock sadly disconcerting. But at least she could be wholeheartedly loyal to him as long as his name was mud.*

On August 30, 1939, Kathleen left London—believing, like many other people, that Nazi air raids would begin as soon as war was declared. Richard accompanied her. They went to stay with some cousins at Penmaenmawr—a rather depressing place in winter, but safe. Kathleen was there for nearly two years, with only occasional return trips to Pembroke Gardens.

In the spring of 1940, Henry Isherwood became seriously ill. As May the ninth approached, he expressed a fear that he would share the Double Anniversary. Kathleen was kept informed of his condition by his housekeeper.

May 9. The anniversary of my dear Frank's death and nine years later of Mr Isherwood. The report of Henry slightly better. The Doctor thought that if Muriel came she might see him. H. was surprised to hear that she knew of his being ill and was pleased that she should come. She was out as soon as she got the letter and bicycled over to the station, fifteen miles away, to catch the train—just as she was, in her muddy boots, from working on the land—buying a pair of gloves on the way. Mrs L took her to the nursing home and Henry put his arms out and said 'can I kiss you?' and was very pleased with some lovely flowers she brought. She said she would put up opposite to the nursing home, at a hotel.

Henry's fear seemed to have been unfounded, but it wasn't altogether. For he did die on the ninth—the ninth of July, that same year. And the Double Anniversary did eventually become a triple one: Muriel herself died on May 9, 1966.

Soon after Christopher came of age, Henry had started giving him an allowance; a very small one, but enough to make him independent when it was added to his own earnings and what he got from Kathleen. Henry referred to Christopher as "my favorite nephew" and recommended his books to his friends. Their bond wasn't literature, however, but the discovery that they had similar sexual tastes.

When they dined together at Henry's flat, they giggled like age-mates over Henry's adventures with guardsmen and Christopher's encounters in the boy-bars of Berlin. "I find it so extwardinawily soothin', don't you know," Henry would say, referring to his acts of lust. These he confessed conscientiously, though without much pretense of contrition, to an understanding priest—for, in his own way, he had remained sincerely devout.

Henry lost touch with Christopher as soon as he got off this topic and began talking of Italy, where he spent all his winters, and of his admiration for Mussolini, who had made the trains run on time. Or when he rambled on about county families and their property and inheritance taxes. "He's as poor as a church mouse," Henry would say, twisting his mouth in a grimace of contemptuous satisfaction, "he isn't worth a penny piece, don't you know." By now Christopher would have stopped listening and begun drinking, lest he should get angry and say something aggressive and offend Henry and perhaps lose his allowance. His glass would be diligently filled by Henry's smiling Italian valet. At the end of the evening he would be drunk and so would Henry—with the result that Christopher would get a good-night kiss which was too warm and searching for any nephew, even one's favorite.

When the news of Henry's death reached Christopher in California, he wrote in his diary:

I was fond of him and he of me. He always thought of me as being after his money—as indeed I was. But this seemed to him perfectly natural and proper. He had the eighteenth-century conception of the relation between uncle and heir.

I often used to wonder just when this would happen—and I always half-knew that when it did, when Marple and all the money became mine, it would be too late. It is too late now—not merely because of the War but because the absurd boyhood dream of riches is over forever. It is too late to invite my friends to a banquet, to burn the Flemish tapestry and the Elizabethan beds, to turn the house into a brothel. I no longer want to be revenged on the Past. Several weeks ago, I wrote that Richard is to have everything, house and money. It's his, not mine, by right, because he loves the place and is prepared to live there. I confirmed this by cable today.

When Christopher writes about Richard going to live at Marple, he obviously has no idea of the condition it is in. Richard had been spending weekends there with the caretakers from time to time, but the house could never again be fully reopened. Henry's death did mean, however, that Richard could now offer Wyberslegh to Kathleen.

Richard had meanwhile begun doing his wartime national service as a farmworker on the Wyberslegh farm. Later he transferred to a farm called Dan Bank, which adjoined the Marple Hall park. He couldn't bring Kathleen to live at Wyberslegh until the present tenant, who was an elderly lady, had found another home. It was just as well that there was this delay, for on January 9, 1941, Wyberslegh was hit by some small incendiary bombs which must have been dumped haphazard by a German plane returning from a raid over the Manchester-Liverpool area. Richard describes what happened:

It was a very still peaceful warm (for January) moonlight night. The fire bombs seemed suddenly to spring out of the ground instead of coming down from the sky—in the Wyberslegh garden and all over the farmyard. Of course we all rushed out. Luckily the Farmer and the farm hands were all there and there was a stirrup-pump and buckets of sand and water handy. The funny thing was that the bombs all bounced off the roof of the house but one or two went through the outbuildings and started a fire in the hayloft and a lot of the hay was ruined. It was all too sudden and pleasurably exciting to think about any possible danger. I suppose they might have dropped high explosive bombs on us, as the farm was lit up as if it had been Guy Fawkes Night. I think the raiders must have travelled along the Ridge; no bombs were dropped in High Lane, then or ever, or in Marple.

On July 15, 1941, Kathleen, who had been staying for a few days previously in Marple village, came back to live at Wyberslegh after thirty-three years:

We had a very pleasant busy day. My bedroom was thoroughly cleaned, windows washed and the drawing-room swept ready for putting down the carpet, and the dining-room too had a good clean and really things began to look wonderful! It seemed almost unbelievable that it could have been so *far* accomplished. I picked roses and syringa and delphinium and had a lovely nosegay from our own garden! And it was all so cosy and peaceful. Mrs Cooper brought in cold meat and salad and custard with rhubarb from our garden for our supper, when Richard arrived about 7.30. We could hardly believe that we were half way to being settled again into Wyberslegh at last! And it seemed as if it must all be a dream.

July 16. It was a weird, almost uncanny night, our first at Wyberslegh! There was no electric light on, and, as we had no blackout curtains up yet, the windows, except those with shutters, were exposed and we could only creep about with a torch.

After this, Kathleen and Richard went down to London, to arrange for the removal of more of their furniture from Pembroke Gardens. They returned to Wyberslegh on August 1. Kathleen writes: "We sat over the Stone Parlour fire until quite late, enjoying it all."
Nanny had been in Cambridge meanwhile, visiting her sister. She came back on September 12 and proceeded to criticize all the arrangements which Kathleen and Richard had made in the house,

implying that they were a pair of unpractical amateurs. From then on, Kathleen and Richard were to become the workers and Nanny their overseer and professional critic.

When Christopher paid them his first visit after the war, in January 1947, Nanny was already very frail. She did only the lightest housework and spent most of her day sitting by the fire in the kitchen, being waited on by Kathleen and Richard. To Christopher she seemed to have turned into a Beatrix Potter character, a tiny bright-eyed animal-person, smiling and full of mischief. He found her adorable—as he could well afford to, not having to live with her. But Nanny's smile could exasperate Kathleen as much as ever, especially when it was directed mockingly at the meals Kathleen had prepared.

Kathleen was now cooking regularly for the first time in her life, and doing it under conditions which Christopher regarded as primitive, even slumlike. Eight years in middle-class America, with its gleaming, hygienic kitchens, had made him dainty-minded, no doubt. He had almost forgotten ranges that burn coal, and how coal-dust can work its way deeply into carpets. At Wyberslegh there was no vacuum-cleaner to suck it out again. There was no refrigerator either. Kathleen assured him that they didn't need one, the food stayed quite cold enough in the stone larder. But the larder was part of the cellar where they kept the coal! Christopher reproved himself for his fussiness and tried to be of help. He looked in vain for a detergent, to get the hard ridges of old fat out of the frying pans. Instead of the throwaway paper towels he was accustomed to, there were some foully ancient black rags he dared not even sniff at; they made him think of the workhouse in Oliver Twist. When he offered to buy Kathleen a vacuum-cleaner, she became almost indignant—partly, perhaps, because she suspected Nanny of having slyly put the idea into his head (which she had), but chiefly because Kathleen's hatred of the Present, about which she often spoke with intense aversion, made her unwilling to use any of its products if she could possibly do without them.

And then it began to snow. This was a long-remembered winter of blizzards. The national reserve of fuel was insufficient, so gas had to be rationed; during the daylight hours it was reduced to a minute blue ghost of a flame in the gas-fire. Christopher felt the cold more than the rest of them. Richard sweetly sympathized with his numbness and tried to warm him with cups of tea. Kathleen sympathized, too, but you could see that she delighted in the weather and the discomfort; it actually gave her strength.

Her strength amazed Christopher. The local doctor told him, "There's really nothing wrong with your Mother, nothing at all; she may go on for a long long time." Christopher could see little, if any, physical or mental change in her. You didn't have to talk loudly to her; she wasn't in the least deaf. You didn't have to talk slowly; her attention didn't wander. You didn't have to explain references you made to people or happenings in the past; her memory was excellent. Much as she disapproved of the world, she was well aware of what was going on in it. She even knew quite a lot of American slang.

In the autumn of 1948, Nanny was taken ill while visiting her niece at Cambridge. It will be noticed that Kathleen, in writing about this, has at last stopped using the official "Nurse":

November 12. A letter with the distressing news that poor Nanny had had 'another form of stroke' and since then has become rather weaker. Less than a quarter of an hour later, her niece Gwen rang up to tell us that dear Nanny had passed away. It just seemed unbelievable! She who had been one of us for forty-four years, always faithful and true, considering our interests, ready to speed us on our way and there to welcome us back, a prop in the background, our interests hers too, so fond and proud of Christopher and Richard, so full of pride in our possessions, so careful of them. I just can't imagine going on here without her and we just broke down and wept hopelessly. Personally I feel filled with remorse to think that I have not been and done all that I might, but I realize now how much I valued her services underneath, even when I was sometimes irritated by her little ways. But all the time we fundamentally respected each other. We felt so dazed and unhappy.

November 14. Gwen telegraphed to say that the cremation would be at Cambridge on Tuesday, but as much as I would wish to pay her the last tribute of our deep appreciation and gratitude for her loyal and faithful devotion, we felt we couldn't go to see her poor little frail body put away, and this I know she will understand.

Christopher was with Kathleen and Richard in London in the winter of 1951–52. He and Kathleen went to plays together, and once, at her suggestion, they walked back from a West End theater halfway to Kensington. On Christmas Day, he offered to go to church with her. (This was a peace gesture, for church had been a sore subject between them in the past; it was also a gentle reminder that a Vedantist respects all religions—unlike some Christians.) As it turned out, he enjoyed the service much more than Kathleen did; the church, which they had chosen simply because it was near their hotel, proved too ritualistic for her taste. Christopher was fascinated by the genuflections, changing of vestments, chanting and censing, and his Christmas was really made when someone handed him the offertory plate and he looked up and it was T. S. Eliot!

In January 1956, Christopher was at Wyberslegh again. Kathleen was now eighty-seven. A friend had recently spoken of her as being "pretty and feminine," and this description seemed apt. Her cheeks were pink, her hair was thick and she still looked womanly, not androgynous as many old women do. Her body had grown rather bulky and her knees were stiff, sometimes she had to be helped out of her chair. But she went on cooking the meals. Richard did most of the other work, for the cleaning-woman who came in could stay only an hour or two; he was busy all day long, engaged in an endless losing struggle against damp and dirt. It seemed to Christopher that Richard and Kathleen were no longer the owners of Wyberslegh, they had become its servants.

While he was there, a young woman came over to be interviewed as a maid. She wasn't ideal, but she was possible, and it was hard enough to find anybody who would take domestic service under the conditions that Wyberslegh imposed. Nevertheless, it was obvious that Kathleen didn't really want to employ her; she didn't want any stranger living in the house. She cross-examined the girl quite sternly, raised difficulties, held out no inducements. Looking at Kathleen from the girl's point of view, Christopher realized that she appeared much too young and self-reliant to arouse any sympathy for herself, she was incapable of playing the poor old lady who desperately needed a helping hand. And, sure enough, the girl phoned later saying she had decided not to take the job.

In March, when Christopher was about to leave England, Kathleen and Richard traveled down to London to be with him for a few days. Kathleen at once became her metropolitan social self, charmingly ready to be interested in Christopher's friends and appreciate whatever they did to entertain her. She astonished them all by her vitality. It was so reassuring to see someone of her age really enjoying herself, they said.

This was to be her last visit to London.

In April 1958, Kathleen had a stroke and lost the use of her right hand for some time. From then on, she dictated her diary to Richard. She began to do this already in the nursing-home to which she had been taken after her stroke. Richard felt bound to object to some of the remarks she wanted him to write down about the sister in charge, they were so savage.

When Christopher saw Kathleen in August 1959, she had largely recovered the use of her hand; the strength of its grasp surprised him. Her speech was still sometimes a little indistinct. And she was blind in one eye, because she refused to have a cataract removed, although the surgeon assured her he could restore her sight almost completely. She had always hated surgery, *she said, and she could manage perfectly with the other eye. It seemed that she could. If Christopher hadn't been told, he would never have noticed that the area of her vision was reduced.*

Within this damaged but still workable human vehicle, Kathleen the driver remained at all times very much present and in control. Christopher was conscious of her powerful, directing will; there was no hint of hesitation or weakness. It wasn't a will to survive for survival's sake. It was a will to endure as long as endurance was called for. Never for one moment did he feel that she was afraid to die.

Once she asked him if Vedanta philosophy included a belief in an afterlife. He answered yes; it would have been pedantic and cruel to qualify his yes with doubts about the degree to which the individual personality survives. Kathleen then told him she believed that she and Frank would be together again. She said this with conviction; yet she was keeping her indignation in reserve, to be turned against God Himself if necessary—for she added, "That must be true, otherwise everything would really be too monstrously unfair!"

When Christopher kissed her goodbye, he said to himself, I shan't see you again. But he remembered thinking the same thing at the end of his first postwar visit to England—and that was now twelve years ago.

In May 1960 Kathleen had several more strokes. Then she got a chill which turned into bronchitis and pneumonia. On June 15 she died.

Richard wrote to Christopher:

She didn't do any more dictating to me after her final illness, as she had more or less lost her speech, except in snatches. Not long before she died, she did say to me, 'try and not mind too much'. I did feel she was most definitely glad to go, that she was escaping from the modern world which had become more than she could cope with, and I tried hard to feel glad about it.

The morning of the day she died, she kept on saying, 'oh for peace, for peace', which wrung one's heart. I was alone with her when she passed away, holding her hand, but she had fallen asleep and did not wake up again. Just before this, I told her how much you and I loved her and she pressed my hand with hers and I knew she understood, although she had got beyond articulating.

Kathleen's funeral was at the church at High Lane. Then Richard brought back her ashes and buried them, as she had wished, in the Wyberslegh garden. They are in a grass-covered bank near the house, lying close beside the remains of Pandy and Perkie, her two much-loved black and white cats.

Afterword

When Christopher came back to St. Edmund's in September *1915*, after his summer of convalescence, he wore a black crape band around his sleeve. He had now acquired a social status which was respected by everybody in wartime England, including the Crown, the Church and the Press: he was an Orphan of a Dead Hero. At St. Edmund's there were only two or three others who shared this distinction, and at first he was vain of it; it made you, or rather your mourning-armband, slightly sacred. The band mustn't on any account be torn or even rumpled, and therefore you yourself couldn't be attacked as long as you were wearing your jacket with the band on it. This taboo had been established by the boys, not the staff. They had done it without any discussion, instinctively, for they had the psychology of primitive tribesmen and could recognize a numen when they saw one. What they couldn't understand was the grownup concept of grief as a continuing state of mind which had to be maintained, inwardly and outwardly, over a long period; to this they merely paid lip-service. When Christopher reappeared amongst them he was greeted with "Bad luck, Isherwood!," which was their formula of condolence and excused them from further sympathy. If Christopher, or any other bereaved boy, happened to remember his loss and was moved to shed a few tears over it, that was something he had to cope with by himself, like an attack of hiccups. If, on the other hand, he felt like ragging, all he needed to do was strip off *his jacket and join in the fun; none of his schoolfellows would think this improper.*

However, Christopher soon found that being a Sacred Orphan had grave disadvantages—that it was indeed a kind of curse which was going to be upon him, seemingly, for the rest of his life. Henceforward, he was under an obligation to be worthy of Frank, his Hero-Father, at all times and in all ways. Cyril and Rosa were the first to make him aware of this obligation. Later there were many more who tried to do so: people he actually met, and disembodied voices from pulpits, newspapers, books. He began to think of them collectively as The Others.

It was easy for these impressive adults to make a suggestible little boy feel guilty. Yet he soon started to react against his guilt. Timidly and secretly at first, but with passion, with a rage against The Others which possessed him to the marrow of his bones, he rejected their Hero-Father. Such a rejection leads to a much larger one. By denying your duty toward the Hero-Father, you deny the authority of the Flag, the Old School Tie, the Unknown Soldier, The Land That Bore You and the God of Battles. Christopher's realization that he had done this—and that he must tell The Others he had done it—came to him only by degrees and not until he was nearly grown up. The rejection caused him much anxiety at first and some moments of panic; later it gave him immense relief and even a little courage.

Richard too rejected the nursery version of the Hero-Father:

I did so hate being everlastingly reminded of him, when I was young. Everybody kept saying how perfect he was, such a hero and so good at everything. He was always held up as someone you could never hope to be worthy of, and whenever I did anything wrong I was told I was a disgrace to him. You know, I used to have a recurring nightmare that he wasn't dead after all and that he was coming back to live with us! And then I was horrified, and I wanted to run away from home and hide somewhere before he arrived. I used to simply loathe him.

.   .   .

*In 1968 Richard read some of Frank's letters which Christopher
had just copied. They astonished him, he said; they made Frank
seem like somebody quite different—a human being, in fact. Richard was glad to have Frank and the Hero-Father finally disen-
tangled from each other in his mind; but he couldn't be expected
to feel strongly about him as a person. He had been less than four
years old when Frank was killed, and hardly remembered him
at all.*

*With Christopher it was a different matter. He hadn't grieved
much for Frank in 1915, but that was because he had then regarded Frank's death chiefly as an injury done to Kathleen. He
had also been jealous of Frank when he came between him and
Kathleen by dying and thus monopolizing her emotions. And
then the Hero-Father had come between him and Frank. Nevertheless, the Frank he had known was still in his memory: the
Frank who had told stories and drawn drawings for him and
taught him the magic of make-believe. He wasn't going to surrender his Frank to The Others. They could keep their Hero-
Father. He would create a father-figure of his own, the anti-
heroic hero he now needed—and therefore declared Frank to have
been.*

*This wasn't difficult. Nothing had to be invented. Christopher
had only to select certain of Frank's characteristics, doings and
sayings (which meant censoring the rest) and make a person out
of them, giving it Frank's body and voice.*

*The Anti-Heroic Hero always appears in uniform, because this
is his disguise; he isn't really a soldier. He is an artist who has re-
nounced his painting, music and writing in order to dedicate his
life to an antimilitary masquerade. He lives this masquerade right
through, day by day to the end, and crowns his performance by
actually getting himself killed in battle. By thus fooling everybody (except Christopher) into believing he is the Hero-Father,
he demonstrates the absurdity of the military mystique and its
solemn cult of War and Death.*

*When one understands this, one sees that all his behavior is
intentionally subversive. He shows his contempt for Army docu-*

ments by doing comic sketches on them, and for his dignity as an officer by knitting in the midst of a bombardment. He tells Christopher that his sword is useless except for toasting bread and that he never fires his revolver because he can't hit anything with it and hates the bang it makes. There was a report, which Christopher accepted because he wanted to believe it, that Frank had last been seen signaling directions to his men with a short swagger cane as he led them into action. Christopher made this symbolic: The Anti-Heroic Hero mocks the loud Wagnerian Hero-Death by flourishing a stick like a baton at it, as if conducting an opera.

In November 1935, while he was staying in Brussels, Christopher decided, on a sudden impulse, to visit Ypres. Kathleen had occasionally hinted that it would be "nice" if he did. And he himself had always felt a curiosity, slightly mixed with fear, about Frank's deathplace. Afterward he wrote in his diary:

Roeslare is a sordid little cobbled town; it is here that you begin to smell the War. The girl at the café said she hoped there'd be another war soon, as then they'd earn some money. We drove in a bus over the plain to Ypres. Almost all the houses are new and bright pink—here and there the darker bricks mark the outlines of a former ruin. There are no trenches to be seen, only fragments of concrete gun-emplacements and pillboxes, among the fields.

The towers of Ypres, which looked grand in the distance against the sunset, in the cup of the plain, are new and quite meaningless, like London County Council architecture, when you see them close. The Menin Gate—ugly enough, in any case, to be an entrance for the Wembley Exhibition—is made merely absurd by being piled up against the end of the street, on to which it doesn't fit. We searched for Daddy's name and finally found it, high up in a corner, heading a list of Addenda. The town is certainly "forever England"—the England of sordid little teashops, faked souvenirs and touts.

Christopher's visit to Ypres had been on November 11; he can't now remember if this was by accident or design, but the violence

504

of his reactions may have been partly due to the date, for he always hated Armistice Day and thought of it as being preeminently The Day of The Others.

So this was the vulgar sarcophagus in which they imagined they held Frank enshrined! Christopher declared that it was empty. No Hero-Ghost could ever come forth from it to delight them by disowning his unworthy son. The real Frank was beyond their reach. And, far from disowning his son, he gave him his blessing. Christopher had proof of this, in Frank's own handwriting.

Kathleen probably showed Christopher Frank's letters of March 15 and April 9 soon after she received them, at Ventnor in 1915. If she did, it isn't surprising that they made no great impression on him at that time. Frank was still alive then, and Christopher had yet to be confronted with the Hero-Father. It was only much later that he began to see their enormous value to himself, as a statement of Frank's last wishes and a speech for his defense: "I don't think it matters very much what Christopher learns as long as he remains himself and keeps his individuality and develops on his own lines . . ." (Christopher censored the rest of the sentence, about his laziness.) "The whole point of sending him to school was . . . to make him like other boys . . . I for one would much rather have him as he is."

Christopher interpreted this freely as "Don't follow in my footsteps! Be all the things I never was. Do all the things I never did and would have liked to do—including the things I was afraid of doing, if you can guess what they were! Be anything except the son The Others tell you you ought to be. I should be ashamed of that kind of son. I want an Anti-Son. I want him to horrify The Others and disgrace my name in their eyes. I shall look on and applaud!"

A Hero-Father leaves behind him a Holy Widow-Mother, who shames her children by her sacred grief. Like Charles the First, she teaches them to "remember!," which actually means "avenge!" Kathleen was sometimes pressured by The Others into playing this role, for she too was intimidated by them. It was therefore the duty of the Anti-Son to rescue Kathleen from them, by pouring scorn on the Holy Widow role whenever she tried to assume it.

As Holy Widow, Kathleen had to believe that Frank's death had been an irreparable loss to Christopher and Richard. As Anti-Son, Christopher had to challenge this. He did so quite sincerely, for he was convinced that Richard and he had both been better off without Frank as they grew up. Speaking for himself, he could say that all he really required was his idea of a father—the Anti-Heroic Hero. If you are in temporary need of an adviser, an inspirer or a backer, a willing substitute-father can usually be found; it is a mutually agreeable relationship, easily terminated. No, to be honest, he hadn't needed Frank.

And what kind of a father would Frank have been in his fifties and sixties, if he had survived to become a brigadier general and the commandant of Kneller Hall? He might have tried hard to understand Christopher as a young man of the Freudian twenties, but how could he possibly have succeeded, with all his prejudices, his snobbery, his "Early English" attitudes? At best they might have agreed to differ like gentlemen, after Christopher had wasted years of precious youth-time breaking the dreadful news slowly to Frank about boy-love—then later about marxism, and finally pacifism. It was more likely that Frank would have forgotten he had ever wanted Christopher to "develop on his own lines"; that he would have ended by disowning this Anti-Son.

But Christopher did need Kathleen. Frank had been right about him in saying that his danger was laziness; he had to have an opponent to prod him continually into revolt. The Others were no good for this, because they lacked conviction. Their religion and their moral indignation were fundamentally hypocritical. As opponents, they were hopelessly unserious. And the contempt you finally learned to feel for them didn't strengthen you, it merely made you cynical and therefore weaker.

Kathleen's opposition, on the other hand, was serious. It sprang from the depths of her nature—even when her cause was absurd and indefensible. For example, one morning in January 1928 she had looked up from reading the newspaper and remarked, "I can't think why they want to bury that ridiculous Thomas Hardy in the Abbey." *Christopher was so furious with her that he got up and left the room, to her genuine dismay. In general she deferred to Christopher's opinions about writers, and she knew that he admired this one greatly. Also, she would have been the first to agree that one shouldn't insult the newly dead. Yet some ancient prejudice against Hardy—maybe dating back to the public attacks on* Jude the Obscure *in 1895—had suddenly asserted itself, sweeping all other considerations aside!*

It was wonderful how naturally they disagreed. Christopher used to say that if Kathleen and he had landed on an alien planet where there were two political parties about which they knew nothing, the Uggs and the Oggs, she would have instantly chosen one of them and he the other, simply by reacting to the sound of their names.

Kathleen's opposition was rooted in obstinacy; as she grew older, obstinacy became the form in which her astonishing vitality most often expressed itself. Her skepticism was obstinate; she could never quite take anything for a fact, and this she showed by the almost daily use of "it seems" and "it appears" in her diary. Her sense of duty was obstinate. Her patriotism was obstinate. Her religious belief was obstinate. Even her mourning for Frank was obstinate—and much admired by everybody, except Christopher. He wanted her either to remarry, so that he would feel no more responsibility for her, or else to forget Frank and submit to him, Christopher, in all things, so that they might be friends. What Christopher didn't realize until many years later was that, in either of these events, the loss would have been his: he would have lost the counterforce which gave him strength.

It was Kathleen, more than anybody else, who saved him from becoming a mother's boy, a churchgoer, an academic, a conservative, a patriot and a respectable citizen. His friends were all rebels in their different ways, they set him an example and gave him plenty of encouragement; but without Kathleen's counterpressure and the rage it inspired in him, he might still have wavered and lapsed. It was she who made the snug home-womb uninhabitable, despite his desire to hide in it. It was she who thrust the Church upon him as an intolerable loyalty-test, thus making sure he wouldn't betray his own beliefs by accepting its security. It was she who stopped him from pretending to himself that he could be happy in the academic world, by confronting him with her dream-portrait of Christopher as a delightful dead-alive don. Her talk about the necessity of choosing a career which "led somewhere" drove him to venture into the studios of Chelsea and the slums of Berlin, despite his timid misgivings. Her peculiarly feminine patriotism disgusted him with England, the Motherland, thus causing him to be attracted to Germany, the Fatherland which had killed the Hero-Father. When he defiantly told her he was homosexual, she didn't seem at all upset. But this, he suspected, was because she simply didn't believe that a relationship without a woman in it could be serious, or indeed anything more than an infantile game. He sensed her assurance that he would one day have children, her grandchildren—never mind what became of the wretched cheated wife! This arrogant demand of hers would have been enough to deter Christopher from the cowardly crime of an unnatural respectable-mock marriage, if he had ever felt tempted to commit it.

Kathleen, he knew, felt their quarrels deeply and grieved over them in private. Yet he didn't feel guilty. He could see that they gave her strength as well as himself. And she and he remained intimate in their opposition. He continued to tell her in detail about every book he was planning or had begun to work on. She was always a member of his private audience. One of the aims of his writing—never quite achieved—was to seduce her into liking it in spite of herself.

His final ritual act of breaking free from her was to become a citizen of the United States, thus separating himself from Mother and Motherland at one stroke. But this was equally a recognition of the fact that the days of his opposition to Kathleen were over. Ironically, his life in the States had involved him more and more in activities which she would be able to approve of, at least partially. By teaching in colleges he had become an academic, even if he had also become a clown. By embracing Vedanta he had joined the ranks of the religious, even while remaining anti-

church. By opposing those fellow-citizens whom he regarded as a menace to his adopted country he had turned into a patriot, even though his enemies did all the flag-waving. So, when he later came back to England on visits, Kathleen and he had more common ground to meet on than ever before. When they were about to part for the last time, in 1959, she told him she was glad he had settled in America, because he had evidently found happiness there. This was a tremendous concession on her part, and it moved him very much. He took it as her blessing.

About 1960, Christopher began to consider a project which he called The Autobiography of My Books; it was to be a discussion, as objective as possible, of the relation between his own life and the subject-matter of his books. The questions asked would be: To what extent do these books describe their writer's life? In what ways and for what reasons do they distort or hide facts about it? How far do the writer's father- and mother-characters resemble his own parents? What are the main themes of these books and how do they relate to the writer's personal problems? And so on.

Before starting to write this Autobiography, Christopher tried thinking out loud about it by giving a series of lectures. But the lectures showed him he didn't know his subject sufficiently well. He needed to study his Family and his own childhood in depth. So he began by questioning Richard and later borrowed from him Kathleen's diaries and Frank's letters, which Richard had kept at Wyberslegh.

While reading through these, Christopher saw how heredity and kinship create a woven fabric; its patterns vary, but its strands are the same throughout. Impossible to say exactly where Kathleen and Frank end and Richard and Christopher begin; they merge into each other. It is easy to dismiss this as a commonplace literary metaphor; hard to accept it as literal truth in relation to oneself. Christopher has found that he is far more closely interwoven with Kathleen and Frank than he had supposed, or liked to believe.

And as he went on reading he made another discovery. If these *diaries and letters were part of his project, he was part of theirs—for they in themselves were a project, too. Its nature was revealed by those coy but broad hints dropped by Kathleen and by Frank: "Perhaps someone will be glad of it, some day," "What a pity your husband's life is never likely to be written!," "I hope posterity when they read this won't think I am grumbling."*

So now Christopher's project has become theirs; their demand to be recorded is met by his eagerness to record. For once the Anti-Son is in perfect harmony with his Parents, for he can say, "Our will be done!" Kathleen and Frank *will seem at first to be their story rather than his. But the reader should remember* The Adventures of Mummy and Daddy, *that lost childhood work, and Kathleen's ironical comment on it (November 6, 1909). Perhaps, on closer examination, this book too may prove to be chiefly about Christopher.*